THE VOICE OF THE PAST

Paul Thompson is Professor in Social History at the
University of Essex, Founder of the National Life Story
Collection at the British Library National Sound Archive
and founder-editor of *Oral History*.

'Paul Thompson is a passionate and convincing crusader in the cause of oral history.' *The Times Educational Supplement*

'It must be rare in modern academic life to replace your own unrivalled book after 10 years with an even better one, but he has done so. His new material on memory and the self, and on drama as therapy, should be read by literary critics in their infancy.' *The Independent*

'. . . the first book to combine a theory of oral history, the technical processes involved, and a road map of where oral evidence fits into the landscape of western historiography.' *American Historical Review*

'Certainly any teacher contemplating oral History either in or outwith the classroom should have a copy of this book.' B. B. J. Elliot, *Scottish Association of Teachers of History*

'This is a fully revised edition of a pioneering work which is both scholarly and practical. This is an invaluable work for the student with a project to complete, and above all it raises deeper questions about the nature of history for the rest of us to ponder.' B. D. Bates, *Lore and Language, Vol. 10 No. 2*

'. . . a handbook which has become a treasury of the work of his own circle and of, by now, thousands of others.' *New Society*

The Voice of the Past

Oral History
Third edition

Paul Thompson

OXFORD
UNIVERSITY PRESS

OXFORD

UNIVERSITY PRESS

Great Clarendon Street, Oxford OX2 6DP

Oxford University Press is a department of the University of Oxford.
It furthers the University's objective of excellence in research, scholarship,
and education by publishing worldwide in

Oxford New York

Auckland Bangkok Buenos Aires Cape Town Chennai
Dar es Salaam Delhi Hong Kong Istanbul Karachi Kolkata
Kuala Lumpur Madrid Melbourne Mexico City Mumbai Nairobi
São Paulo Shanghai Taipei Tokyo Toronto

Oxford is a registered trade mark of Oxford University Press
in the UK and in certain other countries

Published in the United States
by Oxford University Press Inc., New York

First published 1978 as an Oxford University Press paperback and
simultaneously in a hardback edition
Second edition 1988

British Library Cataloguing in Publication Data

Data available

Library of Congress Cataloging in Publication Data

Thompson, Paul Richard 1935–
The voice of the past. (OPUS)
Bibliography p. Includes index.
1. Oral history. 2. History—Methodology.

ISBN 0–19–289317–3

5

Typeset by J&L Composition Ltd, Filey, North Yorkshire
Printed in Great Britain by
Clays Ltd, St Ives plc

Preface to the First Edition

This is a book about both the method, and the meaning, of history. It is, first of all, an introduction to the use of oral sources by the historian. But the very use of these sources raises fundamental issues, and I have decided to take these at the beginning, moving step by step towards the more practical later chapters. At the same time, I have tried to write with many different types of reader in mind. Some may be more immediately concerned with how to write with many different types of reader in mind. Some may be more immediately concerned with how to design a project, and to collect and evaluate interview material. They will find practical advice in Chapters 6 (Projects), 7 (The Interview), and 8 (Storing and Sifting). There would be, indeed, good sense in starting from field-work. The practical experience of oral history will itself lead on to deeper questions about the nature of history.

These concern, first, the character of evidence. How reliable is oral evidence? How does it compare with the modern historian's more familiar documentary sources? These critical and immediate questions are confronted in Chapter 4 (Evidence). But they are better understood when placed within the wider context of the development of historical writing. Chapter 3 (The Achievement of Oral History) provides an assessment of recent writing and contribution which oral evidence has made in providing new perspectives and opening up fresh fields of inquiry. Chapter 2 (Historians and Oral History) pursues the question back into the past of history itself, exploring the changing approach of historians to evidence, from the original primacy of oral tradition to the eras of the written document and the tape recorder.

But inevitably this leads to a second set of questions concering the social function of history. Indeed, it became clear in writing Chapter 2 that the evolution of scholarly techniques could only be convincingly explained in such a social context. And the problems in selecting and evaluating oral evidence had already pointed in the same direction. How do we choose who to listen to? History survives as social activity only because it has a meaning for people today. The voice of the past matters to the present. But whose voice – or voices – are to be heard?

Thus, while method and meaning can be treated as independent themes, they are at bottom inseparable. The choice of evidence must reflect the role of history in the community. This is in part a political question, on which historians can only reach their own position independently. Consequently, although even here most of the argument is straightforwardly human rather than political, Chapter 1 (History and the Community) is written from a socialist perspective. And I myself believe that the richest possibilities for oral history lie within the development of a more socially conscious and democratic history. Of course, a telling case could equally be made, from a conservative position, for the use of oral history in perserving the full richness and value of tradition. The merit of oral history is not that it entails this or that political stance, but that it leads historians to an awareness that their activity is inevitably pursued within a social context and with political implications. This, then, is a practical book about how oral sources can be collected and used by historians. But it is equally intended to provoke historians to ask themselves what they are doing, and why. On whose authority is their reconstruction of the past based? For whom is it intended? In short, *whose* is *The Voice of the Past*?

I have been fortunate when writing this book in being able to depend on the help of many friends and colleagues, especially in the Oral History Society and at the University of Essex. It is impossible to acknowledge more than a very few separately but

I should like to thank them all. In ten years of research activity and student projects, and a widening circle of discussions and conferences, experiments, mistakes, and successes, I have built up a widely shared collective experience. It is on this that the book rests. Above all, it draws on the joint work, in research and then in graduate teaching, through which Thea Vigne and I came upon and ourselves explored the possibilities of oral evidence in social history. I owe an immeasurable debt to her. I should also like to thank again those others who are mentioned in the preface to the first-fruit of that research, *The Edwardians*, and particularly George Ewart Evans and Mary Girling. And for this present text, for specific contributions to it and for comments on earlier drafts, I am especially grateful to Keith Thomas, Geoffrey Hawthorn, Bill Williams, Colin Bundy, Trevor Lummis, Roy Hay, Michael Winstanley, Gina Harkell, Joanna Bornat, Alun Howkins, Eve Hostettler, Natasha Burchardt, and Raphael Samuel.

Preface to the Second Edition

In the ten years since I first wrote this book much has happened. The work which was then starting has resulted in some outstanding published history. We have moved forward in our understanding of the complexity of the memory process and the interpretation of oral sources. We have watched a vigorous spread of local community projects, and the rise of new movements in adult literacy, drama, and reminiscence therapy. We have learnt more about the past of oral history. We have developed firmer links with life-story sociology, and we have joined together to form an international community of oral historians.

All these developments are reflected in this new edition. In particular, I have expanded the first three chapters on history and the community, historians and oral history, and the achievement of oral history; I have introduced a new discussion of 'subjectivity', psychoanalysis, and memory as therapy in a rewritten chapter on evidence (4) and a new chapter on memory and the self (5); and I have rewritten and expanded the final chapter on interpretation (9).

I wish I could thank all those who have helped me over the years with the rethinking and experience which is reflected in this revised edition; but more than ever, they are too many to mention individually. To those British friends and colleagues to whom I continue to owe so much I would now want to add many from other countries, and especially many generous hosts on journeys in Scandinavia, Poland, France and Italy, Belgium and Spain, North America, and China. Let me simply salute Ron Grele for his crucial role in creating an international forum for oral history; and indicate the very special personal debt which I owe to Daniel Bertaux, Isabelle Bertaux-Wiame, Luisa Passerini, and our other friends of Turin, with whom we have worked on common research projects over these years.

Preface to the Third Edition

Ten years on again since the Second Edition, oral history continues to strengthen and develop, and in this Third Edition I have taken full account of the changes and new publications of the 1990s. In particular, I have substantially revised the text and the references of my review of oral history publications in Chapter 3. I have also updated my comments on archiving and copyright issues, and on the technology of recording, on video and on multimedia, and also on the international and interdisciplinary aspects of the movement; and I have expanded my discussion of narrative approaches to oral history, especially in Chapter 9.

No doubt if I were writing *The Voice of the Past* again as a fresh book I would have changed its shape in important ways. For example, the book included no definition of oral history, or of life-stories; and it took for granted the merits of interdisciplinary work: neither had then been problematic issues. By the 1990s the *New Shorter Oxford English Dictionary* has provided us with a definition of oral history: 'tape-recorded historical information drawn from the speaker's personal knowledge; the use or interpretation of this as an academic subject'. But I also feel that the interdisciplinary character of the movement, which gives it so much of its vitality and interest, and has inspired, for example, the move towards a more narrative perspective, now needs to be more explicitly vindicated. For while relations between different groups using life-story evidence are generally amicable, one can see in the basic differences in terminology used—oral histories, life (hi)stories, documents of life, personal documents, life documents, life narratives, auto/biographies—and in the differing techniques of analysis, the potential seeds for sectarian fragmentations from which all would be the losers. This is a debate, however, which would fit awkwardly here.

I have in fact deliberately kept the Second Edition text intact as far as possible. This is above all because its basic argument holds strongly, and I believe it is still very much needed. Certainly it was written in a social and political context which was more hopeful than today's. But as historians we have learnt that change goes in spirals; and also that human hope of positive change is crucial to social progress. I know that the message of this book has inspired numerous oral historians, internationally; and I hope that message will continue to ring out with the Third Edition.

For their suggestions in this revision I would particularly like to thank William Beinart, Joanna Bornat, Natasha Burchardt, Leonore Davidoff, Ron Grele, Janet Hart, Rob Perks, Ken Plummer, Michael Roper, Richard Candida Smith, Elizabeth Tonkin, and Bill Williams.

Contents

History and the Community

All history depends ultimately upon its social purpose. This is why in the past it has been handed down by oral tradition and written chronicle, and why today professional historians are supported from public funds, children are taught history in schools, amateur history societies blossom, and popular history books rank among the strongest bestsellers. Sometimes the social purpose of history is obscure. There are academics who pursue fact-finding research on remote problems, avoiding any entanglement with wider interpretations or contemporary issues, insisting only on the pursuit of knowledge for its own sake. They have one thing in common with the bland contemporary tourism which exploits the past as if it were another foreign country to escape to: a heritage of buildings and landscape so lovingly cared for that it is almost inhumanly comfortable, purged of social suffering, cruelty, and conflict to the point that a slavery plantation becomes a positive pleasure. Both look to their incomes free from interference, and in return stir no challenge to the social system. At the other extreme the social purpose of history can be quite blatant: used to provide justification for war and conquest, territorial seizure, revolution and counter-revolution, the rule of one class or race over another. Where no history is readily at hand, it will be created. South Africa's white rulers divided their urban blacks between tribes and 'homelands'; Welsh nationalists gather at bardic eisteddfods; the Chinese of the cultural revolution were urged to construct the new 'four histories' of grass-roots struggle; radical feminists looked to the history of wet-nursing in their search for mothers without maternal instinct. Between these two extremes are many other purposes, more or less obvious. For politicians the past is a quarry for supportive symbols: imperial victories, martyrs, Victorian values, hunger marches. And almost equally telling are the gaps in the public presentation of history: the long silences in Russia on Trotsky, in West Germany on the Nazi era, in France on the Algerian war.[1]

These multifaceted possibilities are even evident in the potential of oral history for use in development work, one of the new directions of oral history work in the 1990s, which Hugo Slim and I advocated in *Listening for a Change* (1990). In this case historical work only takes place with an explicit social purpose. Nevertheless it can vary fundamentally in perspective. Among refugee peoples such as the Palestinians or the Guatemalans the aim of projects has been to help people hold onto and sustain their culture through recording it. The documenting of American Indian traditional hunting and land rights through oral evidence, which has been increasingly used in legal battles, is typically intended to be more actively restorative of a lost past; and likewise the collecting of information on traditional land management techniques in desert regions like the sub-Saharan Sahel. By contrast the oral history projects which have helped to give Brazilian shanty-town dwellers the confidence to mobilize and demand recognition of their landholding and basic services such as water and electricity, because they are concerned with the needs of new settlements, have focused much more on the moral dynamic of change through migration and on mythologized justifications of their present tenure.[2]

In such diverse ways, through history ordinary people seek to understand the upheavals and changes which they experience in their own lives: wars, social transformations like the changing position of youth, technological changes like the end of steam power, or personal migration to a new community. Family history especially can give an individual a strong sense of a much longer personal lifespan, which will even survive their own death. Through local history a village or town seeks meaning for its own changing character and newcomers can gain a sense of roots in personal historical knowledge. Through political and social history taught in schools children are helped to understand, and accept, how the political and social system under which they live came about, and how force and conflict have played, and continue to play, their part in that evolution.

The challenge of oral history lies partly in relation to this essential social purpose of history. This is a major reason why it has so excited some historians, and so frightened others. In fact, fear of oral history as such is groundless. We shall see later that the use of interviews as a source by professional historians is long-standing and perfectly compatible with scholarly standards. American experience shows clearly enough that the oral history method can be regularly used in a socially and politically conservative manner; or indeed pushed as far as sympathy with Fascism in John Toland's portrait of *Adolf Hitler* (New York, 1976).

Oral history is not necessarily an instrument for change; it depends upon the spirit in which it is used. Nevertheless, oral history certainly can be a means for transforming both the content and the purpose of history. It can be used to change the focus of history itself, and open up new areas of inquiry; it can break down barriers between teachers and students, between generations, between educational institutions and the world outside; and in the writing of history—whether in books, or museums, or radio and film—it can give back to the people who made and experienced history, through their own words, a central place.

Until the present century, the focus of history was essentially political: a documentation of the struggle for power, in which the lives of ordinary people, or the workings of the economy or religion, were given little attention except in times of crisis such as the Reformation, the English Civil War, or the French Revolution. Historical time was divided up by reigns and dynasties. Even local history was concerned with the administration of the hundred and parish rather than the day-to-day life of the community and the street. This was partly because historians, who themselves then belonged to the administering and governing classes, thought that this was what mattered most. They had developed no interest in the point of view of the labourer, unless he was specifically troublesome; nor—being men—would they have wished to inquire into the changing life experiences of women. But even if they had wished to write a different kind of history, it would have been far from easy, for the raw material from which history was written, the documents, had been kept or destroyed by people with the same priorities. The more personal, local, and unofficial a document, the less likely it was to survive. The very power structure worked as a great recording machine shaping the past in its own image.

This has remained true even after the establishment of local record offices. Registers of births and marriages, minutes of councils and the administration of poor relief and welfare, national and local newspapers, schoolteachers' log books— legal records of all kinds are kept in quantity; very often there are also church archives and accounts and other books from large private firms and landed estates, and even private correspondence from the ruling landowner class. But of the innumerable postcards, letters, diaries, and ephemera of working-class men and women, or the papers of small businesses like corner shops or hill farmers, for example, very little has been preserved anywhere.

Consequently, even as the scope of history has widened, the original political and administrative focus has remained. Where ordinary people have been brought in, it has been generally as statistical aggregates derived from some earlier administrative investigation. Thus economic history is constructed around three types of source: aggregate rates of wages, prices, and unemployment; national and international political interventions into the economy and the information which arises from these; and studies of particular trades and industries, depending on the bigger and more successful firms for records of individual enterprises. Similarly, labour history for long consisted of studies on the one hand of the relationship between the working classes and the state in general, and on the other of particular but essentially institutional accounts of trade unions and working-class political organizations; and, inevitably, it is the larger and more successful organizations which normally leave records or commission their own histories. Social history has remained especially concerned with legislative and administrative developments like the rise of the welfare state; or with aggregate data such as population size, birth rates, age at marriage, household and family structure. And among more recent historical specialisms, demography has been almost exclusively concerned with aggregates; the history of the family, despite some ambitious but mostly ill-judged attempts to break through to a history of emotion and feeling, has tended to follow the lines of conventional social history; while for many years even women's history to a remarkable extent focused on the political struggle for civil equality, and above all for the vote.

There are, of course, important exceptions in each of these fields, which show that different approaches are possible even with the existing sources. And there is a remarkable amount of unexploited personal and ordinary information even in official records—such as court documents—which can be used in new ways. The continuing pattern of historical writing probably reflects the priorities of the majority of the profession—even if no longer of the ruling class itself—in an age of bureaucracy, state power, science, and statistics. Nevertheless, it remains true that to write any other kind of history from documentary sources remains a very difficult task, requiring special ingenuity. It is indicative of the situation that E. P. Thompson's *The Making of the English Working Class* (1963) and James Hinton's *The First Shop Stewards' Movement* (1973) each depended to a large extent on reports by paid government informers, in the early nineteenth-century and First World War respectively. When socialist historians are reduced to writing history from the records of government spies, the constraints imposed are clearly extreme. We cannot, alas, interview tombstones, but at least for the First World War period and back into the late nineteenth-century, the use of oral history immediately provides a rich and varied source for the creative historian.

In the most general sense, once the life experience of people of all kinds can be used as its raw material, a new dimension is given to history. Oral history provides a source quite similar in character to published autobiography, but much wider in scope. The overwhelming majority of published autobiographies are from a restricted group of political, social, and intellectual leaders, and even when the historian is lucky enough to find an autobiography from the particular place, time, and social group which he happens to need, it may well give little or no attention to the point at issue. Oral historians, by contrast, may choose precisely whom to interview and what to ask about. The interview will provide, too, a means of discovering written documents and photographs which would not have otherwise been traced. The confines of the scholar's world are no longer the well-thumbed volumes of the old catalogue. Oral historians can think now as if they themselves were publishers: imagine what evidence is needed, seek it out and capture it.

For most existing kinds of history, probably the critical effect of this new approach is to allow evidence from a new direction. The historian of working-class politics can juxtapose the statements of the government or the trade union headquarters with the voice of the rank and file—both apathetic and militant. There can be no doubt that this should make for a more realistic reconstruction of the past. Reality is complex and many-sided; and it is a primary merit of oral history that, to a much greater extent than most sources, it allows the original multiplicity of standpoints to be recreated. But this advantage is important not just for the writing of history. Most historians make implicit or explicit judgements—quite properly, since the social purpose of history demands an understanding of the past which relates directly or indirectly to the present. Modern professional historians are less open with their social message than Macaulay or Marx, since scholarly standards are seen to conflict with declared bias. But the social message is usually present, however obscured. It is quite easy for a historian to give most of his attention and quotations to those social leaders whom he admires, without giving any direct opinion of his own. Since the nature of most existing records is to reflect the standpoint of authority, it is not surprising that the judgement of history has more often than not vindicated the wisdom of the powers that be. Oral history by contrast makes a much fairer trial possible: witnesses can now also be called from the under-classes, the unprivileged, and the defeated. It provides a more realistic and fair reconstruction of the past, a challenge to the established account. In so doing, oral history has radical implication for the social message of history as a whole.

At the same time oral history implies for most kinds of history some shift of focus. Thus the educational historian becomes concerned with the experiences of children and students as well as the problems of teachers and administrators. The military and naval historian can look beyond command-level strategy and equipment to the conditions, recreations, and morale of other ranks and the lower deck. The social historian can turn from bureaucrats and politicians to poverty itself, and learn how the poor saw the relieving officer and how they survived his refusals. The political historian can approach the voter at home and at work; and can hope to understand even the working-class conservative, who produced no newspapers or organizations for investigation. The economist can watch both employer and worker as social beings and at their ordinary work, and so come closer to understanding the typical economic process, and its successes and contradictions.

In some fields, oral history can result not merely in a shift in focus, but also in the opening up of important new areas of inquiry. Labour historians, for example, are enabled for the first time to undertake effective studies of the ill-unionized majority of male workers, of women workers, and of the normal experience of work and its impact on the family and the community. They are no longer confined to those trades which were unionized, or those which gained contemporary publicity and investigation because of strikes or extreme poverty. Urban historians similarly can turn from well-explored problem areas like the slums to look at other typical forms of urban social life: the small industrial or market town, for example, or the middle-class suburb, constructing the local patterns of social distinctions, mutual help between neighbours and kin, leisure and work. They can even approach from the inside the history of immigrant groups—a kind of history which is certain to become more important in Britain, and is mainly documented only from outside as a social problem. These opportunities—and many—others are shared by social historians: the study of working-class leisure and culture, for example; or of crime from the point of view of the ordinary, often undetected and socially semi-tolerated poacher, shoplifter, or work-pilferer.

Perhaps the most striking feature of all, however, is the transforming impact of oral history upon the history of the family. Without its evidence, the historian can discover very little indeed about either the ordinary family's contacts with neighbours and kin, or its internal relationships. The roles of husband and wife, the upbringing of girls and boys, emotional and material conflicts and dependence, the struggle of youth for independence, courtship, sexual behaviour within and outside marriage, contraception and abortion—all these were effectively secret areas. The only clues were to be gleaned from aggregate statistics, and from a few (usually partial) observers. The historical paucity which results is well summed up in Michael Anderson's brilliant, speculative, but abstract study of *Family Structure in Nineteenth-Century Lancashire* (1971): a lop-sided, empty frame. With the use of interviewing, it is now possible to develop a much fuller history of the family over the last ninety years, and to establish its main patterns and changes over time, and from place to place, during the life cycle and between the sexes. The history of childhood as a whole becomes practicable for the first time. And given the dominance of the family through housework, domestic service, and motherhood in the lives of most women, an almost equivalent broadening of scope is brought to the history of women.

In all these fields of history, by introducing new evidence from the underside, by shifting the focus and opening new areas of inquiry, by challenging some of the assumptions and accepted judgements of historians, by bringing recognition to substantial groups of people who had been ignored, a cumulative process of transformation is set in motion. The scope of historical writing itself is enlarged and enriched; and at the same time its social message changes. History becomes, to put it simply, more democratic. The chronicle of kings has taken into its concern the life experience of ordinary people. But there is another dimension to this change, of equal importance. The process of writing history changes along with the content. The use of oral evidence breaks through the barriers between the chroniclers and their audience; between the educational institution and the outside world.[3]

This change springs from the essentially creative and co-operative nature of the oral history method. Of course oral evidence once recorded can and indeed should be used by lone scholars in libraries just like any other type of documentary source. But to be content with this is to lose a key advantage of the method: its flexibility, the ability to pin down evidence just where it is needed. Once historians start to interview they find themselves inevitably working with others—at the least, with their informants. And to be a successful interviewer a new set of skills is needed, including an understanding of human relationships. Some people can find these skills almost immediately, others need to learn them; but in contrast to the cumulative process of learning and amassing information which gives such advantage in documentary analysis and interpretation to the professional historian well on in life, it is possible to learn quite quickly to become an effective interviewer. Hence historians as field-workers, while in important respects retaining the advantages of professional knowledge, also find themselves off their desks, sharing experience on a human level.

Because of these characteristics, oral history is peculiarly suited to project work, both for groups and for individual student enterprises: in schools, universities, colleges, adult education, or community centres. It can be carried out anywhere. In any part of the country there is an abundance of topics which can be studied locally; the history of a local industry or craft, social relationships in a particular community, culture and dialect, change in the gender roles at work or in the family, the impact of wars and strikes, and so on. An oral history project will be certainly feasible. It will also demonstrate very well, especially if the project focuses on the historical roots of some contemporary concern, the relevance of historical study to the immediate environment.

In schools, projects on children's own family history have been developed which provide an effective way of linking their own environment with a wider past. Family history has two other special educational merits. It assists a child-centred approach, for it uses as the project's basis the child's own knowledge of its family and kin and access to photographs, old letters and documents, newspaper cuttings, and memories. Equally, family history encourages the involvement of parents in school activity.

A child's own family history represents perhaps the simplest type of project subject. It is more suited to suggesting than to solving a historical problem. Older groups are likely to choose some issue of more collective interest. At Corpus Christi College, Oxford, for example, Brian Harrison led a group of his students in a small research study on the history of college servants, a group of workers whose old-fashioned deferential respect for their employers, loyalty, meticulousness in their craft, and formality of dress and manner, were understandably perplexing to most students today. Through the project they came to a better understanding of the college servants (and vice versa) and at the same time of the significance of history itself. As one commented: 'I found equally important and interesting . . . seeing the impact of social change in really close detail . . . how changes in the general social environment changed the style of life, values, and relationships within a traditional community.'[4] The immediate environment also gains, through the sense of discovery in interviews, a vivid historical dimension: an awareness of the past which is not just known, but personally felt. This is especially true for a newcomer to a community or district. It is one thing to know that streets or fields around a home had a past before one's own arrival; quite different to have received from the remembered past, still alive in the minds of the older people of the place, personal intimacies of love across those particular fields, neighbours and homes in that particular street, work in that particular shop.

Such fragmentary facts are not merely evocative in themselves, but can be used as the raw material for worthwhile history. It is possible for even a single student in a summer vacation project, with interviews, to make a useful extension of historical knowledge—and also to create new resources which others may be able to use later. With a group project the opportunities naturally enlarge. The number of interviews can be greater, the archival searches more extensive, the subject more ambitious.

The group project has some special characteristics of its own. Instead of the atmosphere of competition common in education, it requires a spirit of intellectual co-operation. Isolated reading, examinations, and lecture sessions give way to collaborative historical research. The joint inquiry will also bring teachers and students into a much closer, less hierarchical relationship, giving far more chance of informal contact between them. Their dependence will become mutual. The teacher may bring special experience in interpretation and in knowledge of existing sources, but will rely on the support of the students as organizers and field-workers. In these ways some of the students are likely to show unexpected skills. The best essay-writer is not necessarily the best interviewer—nor is the teacher. A much more equal situation is created. But, paradoxically, at the same time, by resolving—or at least suspending—the conflict between research and teaching, it enables the teacher to be a better professional. The group project is both research and teaching, inextricably mixed, and as a result each is done more effectively.

The essential value of both group and single projects is, however, similar. Students can share in the excitements and satisfactions of creative historical research of intrinsic worth. At the same time they gain personal experience of the difficulties of such work. They formulate an interpretation or theory and then find exceptional facts which are difficult to explain away. They find that the people whom they interview do not fit easily into the social types presented by the preliminary reading. They need facts, or people, or records which prove tantalizingly elusive. They encounter the problems of bias, contradiction, and interpretation in evidence. Above all, they are brought back from the grand patterns of written history to the awkwardly individual human lives which are its basis.

Both kinds of project also have the important consequence of taking education out of its institutional retreats into the world. Both sides gain from this. Interviewing can bring together people from different social classes and age groups who would otherwise rarely meet, let alone get to know each other closely. Much of the widespread hostility to students is based on little knowledge of what they are actually like or do, and these meetings can bring an appreciation of the serious-mindedness and idealism which is widespread among them. They can also show ordinary people that history need not be irrelevant to their own lives. Conversely, teachers and students can become more directly aware of the image which they present to the wider public. And through entering into the lives of their informants, they gain more understanding of values which they do not share, and often respect for the courage shown in lives much less privileged than their own.

Yet the nature of the interview implies a breaking of the boundary between the educational institution and the world, between the professional and the ordinary public, more fundamental than this. For the historian comes to the interview to learn: to sit at the feet of others who, because they come from a different social class, or are less educated, or older, know more about something. The reconstruction of history itself becomes a much more widely collaborative process, in which non-professionals must play a critical part. By giving a central place in its writing and presentation to people of all kinds, history gains immensely. And old people especially benefit too. An oral history project can not only bring them new social contacts and sometimes lead to lasting friendships; it can render them an inestimable service. Too often ignored, and economically emasculated, they can be given a dignity, a sense of purpose, in going back over their lives and handing on valuable information to a younger generation.

These changes made possible through oral history are not confined to the writing of books or projects. They also affect the presentation of history in museums, record offices, and libraries. These all now have a means of infusing life into their collections, and through this, of bringing themselves into a more active relationship with their community. They can set up their own research projects, like Birmingham's on the city's baths and washhouses and Southampton's on its West Indian port community, or the Imperial War Museum programmes on early aviation and on conscientious objectors. In the 1970s and 1980s many British museums were among sponsors of oral history projects giving short-term work to the young unemployed through the Manpower Services Commission, in a way which recalls the Federal Writers Projects of the New Deal era in the United States. A particularly remarkable approach was the 'ecomusée' programme begun in Belgium by Étienne Bernard, with the ideal of a museum without a building, working through communities with recording projects and temporary exhibitions of photographs and objects from the neighbourhood, which are then returned to their owners. Interestingly, the Jewish Museum at Manchester was an outcome of the Manchester Studies oral history programme launched by Bill Williams from the Polytechnic, which stimulated the city's Jewish community to save a closed Victorian synagogue. It has been opened as a permanent museum where you can lift a phone as you look at a display of the objects given and listen to memories relating to them. At Erddig, a National Trust house in Cheshire, you can now enter through the servants' quarters to the sound of the voices of the last generation of servants and their masters.

Oral history research can also help bring the display itself closer to the historical original. The 'period setting' for objects is replaced by the reconstruction of a real room, with, for example, tools and shavings and half-made baskets left about as if the craftsman was still using it. Indeed, in some museums it will still be used from time to time; and there are a few, like the working farm museum at Acton Scott in Shropshire, where recording work and daily use of the old processes are the linked objective of the whole enterprise. When older local people see this kind of museum, they are likely to have comments, and may even help with improvements by offering articles of their own. In one lively East London museum, attendants who heard this kind of conversation would alert a curator, and the old people would immediately be offered a cup of tea and a chance to record some of their impressions on the spot. As in most community projects, some of the recordings will be used to make educational tapes for use in local schools; and weekends have been arranged for the schoolchildren—normally Sixth Formers—to meet the old people. Thus an active dialogue develops between old people, their own local history, and a museum which has become a social centre. Here is a model of a social role for history with great potential, which needs to be taken up elsewhere.

The use of interviewing for historical presentation in broadcasting is of course long-standing. Here indeed is a fine tradition of oral history techniques which goes back many years—in fact well before the term 'oral history' was introduced. Professional historians are also given their own chance for brief lectures in the intervals between programmes on Radio Three. But most of those I know show much more interest in those radio and television programmes which re-evoke history through the use of raw material, some of it dating from the original period, some recorded retrospectively. For the historian of the future the preservation of many of these programmes, along with others in the BBC Sound Archives, will provide a rich source. Undoubtedly the most ambitious of all these radio initiatives is the nationally co-ordinated millennial local radio series 'Speaking the Century', which is intended to bring together an unprecedentedly large set of some 6,000 interviews right across the country, which will all be available to researchers in the British Library. It is by contrast very unfortunate that at present only a very small proportion of what is being broadcast on television is being preserved, and historians have shown curiously little interest in this systematic destruction of records.

In historical broadcasting it is the introduction of people, the original actors, which brings the programmes alive. Some local radio stations have deliberately used this type of programme to encourage links and exchanges with their local community, through programmes of voices stimulating listeners to send in their own comments and offer to be interviewed in turn. A weekly series of this kind by Radio Stoke-on-Trent lasted for two years. The 'Making of Modern London' series on London Weekend Television was linked with a competition for projects by viewers themselves, for which local schools and old people's centres as well as individuals entered. For their 'Making Cars' series, Television History Workshop opened a shop near the factory to gather materials, and also reactions to the programmes as broadcast. But perhaps the most impressive broadcasting experiment has been in Sweden. Here Bengt Jansson was able to organize through Swedish educational television a series on social change ('Bygd i förvardling'), concentrating on two regions of the country, where 700 local discussion circles were set up in association with the programmes, bringing together in all 80,000 people to join in exchanging their own experience of history in a lifetime.

Although television seems a much more remote medium than local radio, perhaps partly because it is daunting for an older person to be interviewed for it, I have been repeatedly impressed by how much care the best producers take in the human relationship with those whom they film. This was especially true in the BBC's series 'The Nineties', for which all the participants were aged ninety or over.[5] Television can also evoke a direct and especially powerful response from its audience. Thus for a recent BBC oral history documentary by Testimony Films on experiences of sexual abuse in the Catholic Magdalen homes, which had until then been an unspoken matter in Ireland, a telephone helpline was provided which was overwhelmed by hundreds of calls from the Republic.

Television and film can bring history to far greater audiences than any other medium: internationally, millions have watched films like *Roots* or *Shoah*, or in Britain alone oral history television documentary series such as 'The Secret World of Sex'. But they both differ from radio artistically in that they have to hold an audience with a speaker's physical presence as well as voice, and this makes them much more selective mediums in terms of whom they can present as witnesses. They also suffer from the recurrent problem that a series of interwoven interviews easily becomes visually repetitive, and—despite vivid moments—lacks dramatic action. When available, old film is most often used to provide an effective contrast. A strikingly different approach was used for the filming of Ronald Blythe's *Akenfield*, with local people re-enacting some of the scenes, their words unscripted. They gave their services to the film freely at weekends, and brought to each session clothes, props, and food. They would simply be warned in advance what the scene was to be about, so that they could meet in the appropriate dress and frame of mind. The result was certainly a remarkable, if somewhat puzzling film. It has moments which are deeply moving just because they are so ordinary: like the funeral sequence, with its awkward silences, the inadequacy of words when they come, the too slowly sung hymn, and afterwards the bad jokes and stories told again and again. But some who saw the film found it simply boring, ordinary, and without any obvious point. Above all it lacked a strong story.

This is one reason why some of the parallel experiments in drama have proved more successful. Angela Hewins's *The Dillen* movingly records the life of George Hewins, a man who wrote with difficulty yet had a rare gift for words in telling his story, brought up as an orphan by his grandmother in a Stratford-on-Avon common lodging-house, struggling for a living as a casual labourer, cruelly maimed in the trenches in the First World War. It was produced as a play by the Royal Shakespeare Company, with a core of professional actors supported by 150 local volunteers, who made their own costumes, and included a band; and the actual performance left the theatre itself to move round the town, stopping for scenes in a park, a building site, by the river, and on a disused rail track. Each night a crowd who soon outnumbered the original audience would gather and follow, and in the fairground atmosphere of the interval out in the meadows you could listen to groups of them exchanging their own memories of just these same places. After the shattering First World War scenes, huddled into a military tent, the performance would culminate in a torchlit peace procession of actors, audience, and bystanders, by now 700-strong, back into the town. This was an entirely new, and powerfully moving, form of community theatre. Several other companies, such as Age Exchange, have in a more modest way developed work based on oral history material for performances in village halls and community centres. In most work of this kind, however, although the words and even the acting have come from local people, the essential direction has remained in other hands. If there was a common purpose, it was one imposed from without.

An alternative approach to reminiscence theatre can be found in participatory drama like that developed by Elyse Dodgson in work for London schools, which was based on the Royal Court Young People's Theatre. In this children have gathered material from their own families and then worked together in producing a joint performance of impressively high quality. There are no doubt special difficulties in theatre and film because of the technical requirements and costs of the medium and its domination by an international professionalism. A similar problem applies in national broadcasting. Nevertheless, a choice, often difficult, has to be made in most other types of project, especially in education. For the co-operative nature of the oral history approach has led to a radical questioning of the fundamental relationship between history and the community. Historical information need not be taken away from the community for interpretation and presentation by the professional historian. Through oral history the community can, and should, be given the confidence to write its own history.

Some of the most interesting ventures in this direction have again come from Sweden, particularly through the role of the Swedish state exhibition-organization in encouraging local self-help exhibitions, and Sven Lindqvist's book *Grav där du står* (1978) (*Dig Where You Stand*) which has provided a practical manual for workers to write the histories of their own work-places—from their own standpoint, rather than that of employ-ers and shareholders—combining both documentary and oral sources.

The full possibilities of the approach were, however, still more strikingly revealed in Poland. It is true that the tape recorder has been slower to make its impact there, so that the life-history movement, which dates back to a 'humanistic' tradition in Polish sociology established between the wars, still works through the encouragement of written autobiographical mem-oirs rather than oral testimony. No doubt this limits who can participate in it. Nevertheless, after 1945 memoir-writing became an important form of popular self-expression in Poland, allowing discussion not only of pre-war society and the experience of Nazi occupation, but also of the radical social reconstruction which took place under subsequent Communist rule. The key to this success was the use of memoir competi-tions, organized by the national newspapers and radio, and by local newspapers in every big city. Broad themes were set, and quite substantial prizes offered, two or three times a year. Each competition normally attracted a thousand or more entries. The best results were serialized in newspapers, and published as collections in book form. By now several hundred thousand Poles have entered for competitions, and a special national archive has been developed for the material collected. Popular memoir-writing, in short, became a recognized part of the new national way of life, to an extent which had few parallels either in other Communist countries or in the West. The closest is the use of life-story competitions, which has been an impress-ively systematic aspect of the Swedish national museums and educational service. The emphasis in Scandinavian life-story work—which is partly written, partly oral—is as much on the resourcefulness with which people cope with the complexities of the present as of the past. Marianne Gullestad nicely summed up the approach in her book on a competition which she recently organized in Norway, *Everyday Philosophers* (1996).

The Polish success in generating a form for democratic enthusiasm for history also led on to the forming of collective memoir-writing groups at some of the big factories, mines, and steelworks. A sociologist might launch the initial meeting, and help with suggesting themes and later with the publication of books produced by the group, but the essential dynamic was provided by the commitment of the group members. Where else could you have found co-operative groups of industrial workers, up to 200 in number, helping to correct and enlarge their own life-history drafts through coming together regularly, after work, for two-hour discussion meetings?

A similar hope has inspired some of the relatively small British co-operative local oral history groups which have issued cheap cyclostyled broadsheets of transcribed extracts from recordings, adult education local history projects, and joint projects between oral historians and trade unionists. The springing up of such groups in every major city was indeed one of the most striking early features of the oral history movement: in London alone, the 1985 Exploring Living Memory exhibition held in the Festival Hall attracted 100,000 visitors in a fortnight, infusing it with a constant hubbub of talking as they saw and discussed the work of ninety projects from local history and publishing groups, hospitals and old people's centres, schools and so on. Among them, perhaps the most radical model was provided by the People's Autobiography of Hackney. This arose from a group, originally connected with the WEA (Workers' Educational Association), which met in a local book and community centre called Centreprise. Members of the group varied in age from their teens to their seventies, but all lived in or near Hackney in East London. Their occupations were very mixed. The group was an open one, brought together by notices in the local papers, libraries, and other places. Any member could record anyone else. At the group meetings they played and discussed their tapes—sometimes also recording these discussions—and planned ways of sharing what was collected with a Hackney audience. For this reason they especially emphasized publishing and issued a series of cheap pamphlets, assisted by a local library subsidy, based on transcriptions and written accounts of people's lives, which have had a large local circulation. These pamphlets in turn stimulated reactions from other people and led to more discussion and recordings. The group also collected photographs, and combined this material as tapes and slides for historical presentations to audiences in the community such as hospital patients and pensioners' associations—another way of giving back to people their own history, showing them it was valued, and stimulating their own contributions. The People's Autobiography thus aimed, on the one hand, to build up through a series of individual accounts a composite history of life and work in Hackney, and, on the other, to give people confidence in their own memories and interpretations of the past, their ability to contribute to the writing of history—confidence, too, in their own words: in short, in themselves.

This is not only true of old people who are still active and interested in life. Another very striking development of oral history has been reminiscence therapy. It has been increasingly recognized by specialists on ageing that reminiscing may be one important way in which old people keep their sense of self in a changing world. More remarkably, it can be used to rekindle the spirit of the acutely withdrawn and depressed, and even as a form of treatment for psychotic and dementing old people. The 'Recall' reminiscence tape and slide kit created by the oral historian Joanna Bornat at Help the Aged has sparked a growing movement, which we discuss in detail in Chapter 5, among professionals caring for the old.

The possibility of using history for such a constructive social and personal purpose comes from the intrinsic nature of the oral approach. It is about individual lives—and any life is of interest. And it depends upon speech, not upon the much more demanding and restricted skill of writing. Moreover, the tape recorder not only allows history to be taken down in spoken words but also to be presented through them. In a 'Recall' tape and slide show, or a museum demonstration of craft techniques, or a historical talk, the use of a human voice, fresh, personal, particular, always brings the past into the present with extraordinary immediacy. The words may be idiosyncratically phrased, but all the more expressive for that. They breathe life into history.

Something more is to be learnt from them than mere content. Recordings demonstrate the rich ability of people of all walks of life to express themselves. George Ewart Evans has shown in his many books how the dialect of the East Anglian farm labourer, long scorned by the county landowning class for its notable inarticulacy, carries a Chaucerian grammatical and expressive strength which is hard to equal in conventional English. And this kind of discovery has been shared by oral historians wherever they have worked. The tape recorder has allowed the speech of ordinary people—their narrative skill for example— to be seriously understood for the first time. Educationists a few years ago, under the influence of Basil Bernstein, were assuming that working-class speech was a fatal handicap, a constraint which imprisoned all but the simplest types of thought. But with the help of tape recorders, the magazine *Language and Class Workshop* was able to challenge Bernstein's theories with its published transcripts; and in America 'urban folklore' has become an accepted literary genre. However, it may well be a long time before such revaluations reach general acceptance. Meanwhile, one of the key social contributions which can be made by the oral historian, whether in projects or through bringing direct quotation into written history, is to help give ordinary people confidence in their own speech.

In discovering such a purpose, oral historians have travelled a long way from their original aim—and there is, undoubtedly, some danger of conflict between the two. On the level of the interview itself, for example, there have been telling criticisms of a relationship with informants in which a middle-class professional determines who is to be interviewed and what is to be discussed and then disappears with a tape of somebody's life which they never hear about again—and if they did, might be indignant at the unintended meanings imposed on their words. There are clear social advantages in the contrasting ideal of a self-selected group, or an open public meeting, which focuses on equal discussion and encourages local publication of its results; and of individual recording sessions which are conversations rather than directed interviews. But there are also drawbacks in the alternative.

The self-selected group will rarely be fully representative of a community. It is much more likely to be composed from its central groups—people from a skilled working-class or lower middle-class background. The local upper class will rarely be there, nor will the very poor, the less confident especially among women, or the immigrant from its racial minority. A truer and socially more valuable form of local oral history will be created when these other groups are drawn in. Its publications will be much more telling if they can juxtapose, for example, the mistress with the domestic servant, or a millowner with the mill-workers. It will then reveal the variety of social experience in the community, the groups which had the better or the worse of it—and perhaps lead to a consideration of what might be done about it. Local history drawn from a more restricted social stratum tends to be more complacent, a re-enactment of community myth. This certainly needs to be recorded, and a self-sufficient local group which can do this is undoubtedly helping many others besides itself. But for the radical historian it is hardly sufficient. History should not merely comfort; it should provide a challenge, and understanding which helps towards change. For this the myth needs to become dynamic. It has to encompass the complexities of conflict. And for the historian who wishes to work and write as a socialist, the task must be not simply to celebrate the working class as it is, but to raise its consciousness. There is no point in replacing a conservative myth of upper-class wisdom with a lower-class one. A history is required which leads to action: not to confirm, but to change the world.

In principle there is no reason why local projects should not have such an object, while at the same time continuing to encourage self-confidence and the writing of history from within the community. Most groups will normally contain some members with more historical experience. They certainly need to use tact; to undervalue rather than emphasize their advantage. But it is everybody's loss in the long run if they disown it: their contribution should be to help the group towards a wider perspective. Similar observations apply in the recording session where the essential need is mutual respect. A superior, dominating attitude does not make for a good interview anyway. The oral historian has to be a good listener, the informant an active helper. As George Ewart Evans puts it, 'although the old survivors were walking books, I could not just leaf them over. They were persons.'[6] And so are historians. They have come for a purpose, to get information, and if ultimately ashamed of this they should not have come at all. A historian who just engages in collecting haphazard reminiscence will collect interesting pieces of information, but will throw away the chance of winning the critical evidence for the structure of historical argument and interpretation.

The relationship between history and the community should not be one-sided in either direction, but rather a series of exchanges, a dialectic, between information and interpretation, between educationists and their localities, between classes and generations. There will be room for many kinds of oral history and it will have many different social consequences. But at bottom they are all related.

Oral history is a history built around people. It thrusts life into history itself and it widens its scope. It allows heroes not just from the leaders, but from the unknown majority of the people. It encourages teachers and students to become fellow-workers. It brings history into, and out of, the community. It helps the less privileged, and especially the old, towards dignity and self-confidence. It makes for contact—and thence understanding—between social classes, and between generations. And to individual historians and others, with shared meanings, it can give a sense of belonging to a place or in time. In short, it makes for fuller human beings. Equally, oral history offers a challenge to the accepted myths of history, to the authoritarian judgement inherent in its tradition. It provides a means for a radical transformation of the social meaning of history.

2

Historians and Oral History

The extensive modern use of the term 'oral history' is new, like the tape recorder; and it has radical implications for the future. But this does not mean that it has no past. In fact, oral history is as old as history itself. It was the *first* kind of history. And it is only quite recently that skill in handling oral evidence has ceased to be one of the marks of the great historian. When the leading professional historian of mid-nineteenth-century France, Jules Michelet, professor of the École Normale, the Sorbonne, and the Collège de France, and chief historical curator of the National Archives, came to write his *History of the French Revolution* (1847–53), he assumed that written documents should be but one source among many. He could draw on his own memory: he had been born in Paris in 1798, within a decade of the fall of the Bastille. But for ten years he had also been systematically collecting oral evidence outside Paris. His intention was to counterbalance the evidence of official documents with the political judgement of popular oral tradition:

When I say *oral* tradition, I mean *national* tradition, which remained generally scattered in the mouths of the people, which everybody said and repeated, peasants, townsfolk, old men, women, even children; which you can hear if you enter of an evening into a village tavern; which you may gather if, finding on the road a passer-by at rest, you begin to converse with him about the rain, the season, then the high price of victuals, then the times of the Emperor, then the times of the Revolution.

Michelet was clearly skilled at listening, and drawing an informant out. He also had distinct ideas about the areas in which oral evidence was more, or less, reliable. As a scholar in his own time he was exceptional; but he was certainly not peculiar. Yet within a century the historical profession had so far turned its back on its own traditional skills, that Professor James Westfall Thompson commented on Michelet's passage, in his monumental *History of Historical Writing*, 'this may seem like a strange way of collecting historical data'.[1] How did this reversal come about? What were the stages by which oral history lost its original eminence?

One of the underlying reasons becomes clear as soon as we look at the scope of oral tradition in pre-literate societies. At this stage all history was oral history. But everything else had to be remembered too: crafts and skills, the time and season, the sky, territory, law, speeches, transactions, bargains. And oral tradition itself was very varied. Jan Vansina in his classic *Oral Tradition: A Study in Historical Methodology* (1965),[2] divided African oral tradition into five categories. First there are formulas—learning formulas, rituals, slogans and titles. Next there are lists of place-names and personal names. Then come official and private poetry—historical, religious, or personal. Fourthly there are stories—historical, didactic, artistic, or personal. Lastly there are legal and other commentaries. Not all of these can be found in all African societies. Official poetry and historical stories, for example, arise only with a relatively high degree of political organization. Nevertheless, in most societies there is normally a considerable range of oral evidence. The social importance of some of these oral traditions also resulted in reliable systems for handing them down from generation to generation with a minimum of distortion. Practices such as group testimony on ritual occasions, disputations, schools for teaching traditional lore, and recitations on taking office, could preserve exact texts through the centuries, including archaisms even after they had ceased to be understood. Traditions of this type resemble legal documents, or sacred books, and their bearers become in many African courts highly specialized officials. In Rwanda, for example, genealogists, memorialists, rhapsodists, and *abiiru* were each responsible for the preservation of different types of tradition. The genealogists, *abacurah-wenge*, had to remember the lists of kings and queen mothers; the memoralists, *abateekerezi*, the most important events of the various reigns; the rhapsodists, *abasizi*, preserved the pan-egyrics on the kings; and the *abiiru* the secrets of the dynasty. 'Without us the names of kings would vanish into oblivion, we are the memory of mankind', the praise singers justly claimed: 'I teach kings the history of their ancestors so that the lives of the ancients might serve them as an example, for the world is old, but the future springs from the past.'[3]

There were also village tradition-bearers, who, more often than the court specialists, have continued to hand down tradi-tions into the present. They had their equivalents in many other cultures, as in the Scandinavian *skald* or the Indian *rajput*. A dramatic encounter with one such West African *griot* has been described by Alex Haley in his account of the rediscovery of his own ancestry subsequently given great publicity in the semi-fictionalized form of *Roots* (1976). His family had a tradition rare among black Americans—of how their first ancestor came to the colonies as a slave, including a few details: how he had been captured when chopping wood, his African name had been Kintay, he called a guitar a 'ko' and a river 'Kamby Bolongo'; how he had landed at 'Naplis' and worked with the English name Toby for Mas' William Waller. For this black family descent in America itself, Haley was able to provide proof from archival researches, down to an advertisement in the *Maryland Gazette* of October 1767 for 'fresh slaves for sale' of the *Lord Ligonier* and a transfer deed between the brothers John and William Wailer of 'one Negro man slave called Toby'. But all this followed the high moment of his search, back across the Atlantic—a moment in which it now seems enthusiasm may have gone further than the evidence warranted. His ancestor's language had been identified as Mandinka and 'Kamby Bolongo' as the Gambia River; and then, in Gambia, he found that there was an old family clan called Kinte. So far so good. Then after a search, a tradition-bearer of the clan, or *griot*, was located in a tiny, distant hamlet in the interior. Accompanied by interpreters and musicians, Alex Haley eventually reached him: 'And from a distance I could see this small man with a pillbox hat and an off-white robe, and even from a distance there was an air of "somebodiness" about him.' The people gathered around Alex Haley in a horseshoe to stare at the first black American they had seen. And then they turned to the old man:

The old man, the griot, the oral historian, Kebba Kanga Fofana, 73 rains of age, began now to tell me the ancestral history of the Kinte clan as it had been told down across the centuries, from the times of the forefathers. It was as if a scroll was being read. It wasn't just talk as we talk. It was a very formal occasion. The people became mouse quiet, rigid. The old man sat in a chair and when he would speak he would come up forward, his body would grow rigid, the cords in his neck stood out and he spoke words as though they were physical objects coming out of his mouth. He'd speak a sentence or so, he would go limp, relax, and the translation would come. Out of this man's head came spilling lineage details incredible to behold. Two, three centuries back. Who married whom, who had what children, what children married whom and their children, and so forth, just unbelievable. I was struck not only by the profusion of details, but also by the biblical pattern of the way they expressed it. It would be something like: 'and so and so took as a wife so and so and begat and begat and begat', and he'd name their mates and their children, and so forth. When they would date things it was not with calendar dates, but they would date things with physical events, such as . . . a flood.

So step by step the old man recounted the history of the Kinte clan: how they had come out of Old Mali, had been blacksmiths, potters, and weavers, had settled in the present village, until, roughly between 1750 and 1760, a younger son of the family, Omoro Kinte, took a wife, Binta Kebba, by whom he had four sons, whose names were Kunta, Lamin, Suwadu, and Madi.

By the time he got down to that level of the family, the griot had talked for probably five hours. He had stopped maybe fifty times in the course of that narrative . . . And then a translation came as all the others had come, calmly, and it began, 'About the time the king's soldiers came'. That was one of those time-fixing references. Later in England, in

British Parliamentary records, I went feverishly searching to find out what he was talking about, because I had to have the calendar date. But now in back country Africa, the *griot* Kebba Kanga Fofana, the oral historian, was telling the story as it had come down for centuries from the time of the forefathers of the Kinte clan. 'About the time the king's soldiers came, the eldest of these four sons, Kunta, went away from this village to chop wood and was seen never again.' And he went on with his story. I sat there as if I was carved of rock . . .

Alex Haley did, after a few moments, pull out his own notebook, and show the interpreters that this was the same story that he had himself heard as a child from his grand-mother on the front porch of her house in Tennessee; and there then followed a spontaneous ceremony of reconciliation with his own people, in which he laid hands on their infants, and they took him into their mosque and prayed in Arabic, 'Praise be to Allah for one long lost from us whom Allah has returned.'[4]

For a number of reasons, the identification of Kinte is much more doubtful than Alex Haley believed in that moment. His *griot*, who lacked the full traditional training, was not an ideal tradition-bearer, but like a good *griot* was searching the genea-logical store in his mind for the evidence needed for an audi-ence, and he may have had an idea in advance of what Haley wanted. Subsequently, there have been variations in minor detail when he has repeated his testimony. More importantly, the African and American generations fit awkwardly—although this could be due to a telescoping not uncommon in oral tradition—and the time-fixing reference is very weak for an area in which European soldiers had been present for a long time. But we can easily find other instances of accuracy of oral tradition in non-literate societies if we look elsewhere; for example, to ancient Greece, where the accuracy of description of details of obsolete armour and name-lists of abandoned cities, preserved orally for 600 years before the first written versions of the *Iliad* were circulated, has been vindicated by classical scholarship and archaeology.

Nevertheless, Haley's story does bring home with rare power

the *standing* of the oral historian before the spread of documentation in literate societies made redundant such public moments of historical revelation. We can no longer distinguish, like the Swahili, between the 'living dead', whose names are still recalled in oral tradition, and the absolutely forgotten. The modern genealogist works in private silence in a record office. Memory is demoted from the status of public authority to that of a private aid. People still remember rituals, names, songs, stories, skills; but it is now the document which stands as the final authority, and the guarantee of transmission to the future. Consequently, it is just those public and long-term oral traditions which were once the most prestigious which have proved most vulnerable. By contrast, personal reminiscence and private family traditions, which are rarely committed to paper just because most people do not think them of much importance to others, have become the standard type of oral evidence. And it is normally only among social groups of low prestige, such as children, the urban poor, or isolated country people, that other oral traditions such as games, songs, ballads, and historical stories are now collected. And the strongest communal memories are those of beleaguered out-groups. The Gaelic-speaking crofting communities of north-west Britain remember the eighteenth-century Highland sheep clearances which drove them out of their old townships to the sea's edge, as if they had been yesterday. In France the royalist families of the Vendée handed down their story of resistance to the republic for 150 years. Still more remarkably, in the Protestant mountain valleys of the Cévennes today, family traditions still yield a more accurate interpretation than contemporary documents of the unprecedented, and hence misreported, guerrilla war of the Camisards ('whiteshirts') in 1702–4, in which their peasant ancestors successfully held at bay the royal army of Louis XIV and secured the survival of their faith. The changing social standing of the bearers of oral tradition is thus clearly related to its long-term decline in prestige and, conversely, to its current radicality.[5]

In Western Europe this came about very slowly. The first

written histories probably go back 3,000 years. They set down existing oral tradition about the distant past and gradually also began to chronicle the present. Just because it began so early in Europe, this stage is more easily observed where it happened more recently: in the systematic collecting of historical traditions from commoners by the third-century Chinese royal historian Sima Qian and from noble families ordered by the Japanese emperor in the eighth century, the assembling of memories of the prophets in the ninth-century Muslim world, or the precious documentation of pre-conquest Aztec history and culture from the memory of old men by Sahagun and the Spanish Franciscan friars in mid-sixteenth-century Mexico. But we know that from quite an early stage there were a few outstanding European historical writers who tried to evaluate their evidence. The method of Herodotus, for example, in the fifth century BC was to seek out eyewitnesses and cross-question them. By the third century AD we can find Lucian advising the would-be historian to look for his informant's motives; while Herodian cites enough of his sources to suggest the order in which he rates them: antiquarian authorities, palace information, letters, senate proceedings, and other witnesses. And in the early eighth century Bede, in the preface to his *History of the English Church and People*, carefully distinguished his sources. For most of the English provinces he had to rely on oral traditions sent to him by other clergy, but he was able to draw on the records at Canterbury, and he even secured copies of letters from the papal archives through a London priest who visited Rome. But he was surest of the evidence for his own Northumbria, where 'I am not dependent on any one author, but on countless faithful *witnesses* who either know or remember the facts, apart from what I know myself.'[6]

Bede's attitude to evidence, and his assumption that he could be most trusted where he had been able to collect oral evidence from eyewitnesses himself, would have been shared by all the most critical historians into the eighteenth-century—not to mention the many less meticulous chroniclers and hagiographers who stood between them. Neither the spread of printing, nor the secular rationality of the Renaissance, brought any changes in this way. This is perhaps less surprising when it is realized that the typical scholar *heard*, rather than himself *read*, the printed books which became available. And when the truth mattered most, it had to be spoken. The popes pronounced their final words on Catholic doctrine *ex cathedra*: and in both the Christian and Muslim worlds the courts—which had quickly enough discovered how easy it was to forge a written charter—continued to insist that witnesses must be heard, because only then could they be cross-examined. Even accounts had to be checked aloud, or 'audited', each year. And in practice the best-known historians remained rather less careful than Bede. Guiccardini in sixteenth-century Italy, for example, avoids the direct quotation of documents, and assumes his own participation in the times he describes is a sufficient guarantee of truth. *Clarendon's History of the Rebellion and Civil Wars in England* (1704) carries a similar tone, although he does occasionally refer to reminiscence, and he did trouble to look at the journals of the House of Commons for the ten years when he was not a Member. Bishop Burnet's *History of His Own Time* (1724) is less magisterial, but again assumes the prime value of oral evidence, which he handles with a notable care. He cites the authors of his stories regularly, and when his witnesses disagree he sets them against each other. Printed authorities, by contrast, he assumes to be inferior: 'I leave all common transactions to ordinary books. If at any time I say things that occur in any books, it is partly to keep the thread of the narration in an unentangled method.'[7]

It is perhaps more surprising to find little immediate change, at least in the attitude to evidence for recent history, amongst the historians of the eighteenth-century Enlightenment. Voltaire was certainly cynical enough about the 'absurd' myths of oral tradition from the remote past, recited from generation to generation, which had been the original 'foundations of history': indeed, the remoter their origin, the less their value, for 'they lose a degree of probability at every successive transmission'. He rejoiced that 'omens, prodigies, and apparitions are now being sent back to the regions of fable. History stood in need of being enlightened by philosophy.' From modern historians he demanded 'more details, better ascertained facts'. But although for his own works he collected both oral and documentary evidence, he rarely cited his sources and his general comments suggest a lack of distinction between them. He boasted in his *History of Charles XII* (1731), for example, that he had 'not ventured to advance a single fact, without consulting eyewitnesses of undoubted veracity'. After its publication, he cited as an indication of his reliability a letter of approval from the king of Poland, who 'himself had been an eyewitness' of some of the events described. He also defended his failure to cite authorities in *The Age of Louis XIV* (1751) on the ground that 'the events of the first years, being known to every one, wanted only to be placed in their proper light; and as to those of a later date, the author speaks of them as eyewitness'. By contrast he did feel a need in his *History of the Russian Empire under Peter the Great* (1759–63) to name, at least at the start, 'his vouchers, the principal of which is Peter the Great himself'.[8] For this work he had the assistance of documents selected and copied by the Russian officials and sent to his home in Geneva. Voltaire, while retaining a special regard for personal witness, reveals curiously little awareness of the possible bias either in a monarch's own judgement of his reign, or in a set of documents preserved and even selected by the royal officials themselves.

Voltaire was, moreover, a historian with many distinguished admirers. James Boswell recorded a breakfast discussion in 1773 between Samuel Johnson, who had left the codifying of the English language and the delights of London to seek the direct experience of a primitive society in the Scottish islands, and two leaders of the Edinburgh Enlightenment, the lawyer Lord Elibank, and the philosopher-historian William Robertson, Principal of the university. Johnson, it should be noted, had earlier championed the significance of ordinary people for biography, asserting that 'more knowledge may be gained of a man's real character, by a short conversation with one of his servants, than from a formal and studied narrative, begun with his pedigree, and ended with his funeral'. But at the breakfast the conversation turned to the last great revolt of the Scottish Highlands against English rule, the 1745 rebellion. Johnson agreed that this 'would make a fine piece of history', but countered Elibank's doubt 'whether any man of this age could give it impartially' by citing Voltaire's method in his *Louis XIV*: 'A man, by talking with those of different sides, who were actors in it, and putting down all that he hears, may in time collect the materials of a good narrative. You are to consider, all history was at first oral.' And he was firmly backed by the Scots historian, who also knew Voltaire: 'It was now full time to make such a collection as Dr Johnson suggested; for many of the people who were then in arms, were dropping off; and both Whigs and Jacobites were now come to talk with moderation.'[9]

It is no accident that this remarkable early call for an 'oral history' project came at this moment. They stood at the edge of a period of great change in the nature of historical scholarship. Behind it lay the cumulative effects of two centuries of printing: an explosion in historical resources which was both quantitative and qualitative. We may take, for an example, *A New Method of Studying History: recommending more easy and complete instructions for improvements in that science*, published by Langlet du Fresnoy, librarian to the prince of Savoy, in 1713, and subsequently translated into Dutch, German, and English. As it happens there is nothing very new in the method itself which Fresnoy puts forward—he even asserts that those historians who combine 'hard study, and a great experience of affairs' are considerably superior to those 'that shut themselves in their closets to examine there, upon the credit of others, the facts which themselves were not able to be informed of'.[10] Much more remarkable is his second volume, for it consists entirely of bibliography, listing altogether some 10,000 titles of historical works in the major European languages. The production of such a list indicates a substantial community of scholars. It also shows the development of basic professional resources.

An English historian, for example, could now make use of a series of county and local histories, biographies and biographical collections, and travellers' accounts. Printed sets of church inscriptions, manuscript chronicles, and medieval public rolls were being published. In Bishop William Nicolson's *English Historical Library* he had available a critical bibliography. The apparatus for writing history from the closet was being assembled: it was becoming possible for some historians at least to dispense with their own field-work, and rely on documents and oral evidence published by others.

Nevertheless, the immediate effect of the immense expansion of printed sources which continued through the eighteenth-century was a positive enrichment of historical writing. Voltaire could reasonably insist that a good modern historian pay 'more attention to customs, laws, mores, commerce, finance, agriculture, population. It is with history as it is with mathematics and physics. The scope has increased prodigiously.'[11] One can see the long-term impact of change particularly well in Macaulay, whose *History of England* (1848–55) was in terms of sales probably the most popular nineteenth-century history book in the English language. As a practising politician, and a master of style, Macaulay might be seen as an heir to Guiccardini and Clarendon. But perhaps the most brilliant passages of his book are those in which he gives the social background, from the way of life of the country squire to the condition of the urban and rural poor. He uses as his raw materials contemporary surveys, poetry and novels, diaries, and published reminiscences. He also makes particularly interesting use of oral tradition. In stories of the highwaymen who 'held an aristocratical position in the community of thieves', anecdotes

of their ferocity and audacity, of their occasional acts of generosity and good nature, of their amours, of their miraculous escapes . . . there is doubtless a large mixture of fable; but they are not on that account unworthy of being recorded; for it is both an authentic and an important fact that such tales, whether false or true, were heard by our ancestors with eagerness and faith.

He quotes at length a broadside street ballad which he calls 'the vehement and bitter cry of labour against capital', and argues that evidence of this kind must be used for social history. 'The common people of that age were not in the habit of meeting for public discussion, or haranguing, or of petitioning parliament. No newspaper pleaded their cause . . . A great part of their history is to be learned only from ballads.'[12]

As a general historian, Macaulay drew not simply on a wider range of published sources, but also on the development of a whole series of other modes of historical writing. One of the authorities he cited in using oral tradition was Sir Walter Scott. As a young man, before he began writing novels, Scott was a Border Country lawyer, and one of his first publications was a *Minstrelsy of the Scottish Border* (1802), a set of popular ballads which he had collected from country people with his friend Robert Shortreed. His own interest had in turn been partly awakened by a still earlier collection, Bishop Percy's *Reliques of Ancient English Poetry* (1765). But he could have chanced on others. Perhaps best known was William Camden's *Britannia* (1586), which includes chapters on the development of the English language, proverbs, and names as well as poetry. It is one of the founding works of the historical study of language and folklore. There was also the contrastingly radical work of the Newcastle populists, John Brand and Joseph Ritson, who saw the study of popular culture as a duty of 'the friends of man', and combined the collecting of oral tradition with schemes for encouraging popular self-expression in a simplified spelling of English based on the spoken vernacular language.[13]

Scott went on to make a still more important contribution to a second new form of historical writing, the historical novel. Here again he collected much of the oral evidence which he needed himself. He visited the Highlands, 'talking to Jacobites who had taken part in the '45 Rebellion'. Scott recognized through conversing with these old men what had really happened as a result of the '45. Culloden saw the end of a culture; the dispersal or the destruction of the Highland clans, a tribal society, and an older, fundamentally different way of life. 'The old men he talked to were truly historical documents; and contact with them helped to give his writing that veracity which informs earlier novels like *Waverley, The Antiquary, Rob Roy,* and *Guy Mannering.*' It was to honour his sources as much as to chaff himself that he prefaced some of his novels with Robert Burns's warning lines:

A chiel's amang you takin' notes
An' faith he'll prent it.[14]

Both as a note-taker, and in the form of the historical novel itself, Scott set the pattern for some of the major imaginative works of the nineteenth-century. Dickens, for example, deliberately set many of his novels in the London world which he could remember from childhood, and when he could not draw easily on oral memory, as for *Hard Times*, set out for special fieldwork. Charlotte Brontë's *Shirley* draws much of its drama from her knowledge of local memories of the Luddite rising. George Moore's life-story of a domestic servant, *Esther Waters*, owes its realism to his habitual chatting below stairs in country houses and elsewhere. George Borrow came to understand the East Anglian gypsies in a similar way. In France, the work of Émile Zola sought the material for *Germinal* from his talks with the miners of Mons. Later on in Britain, Arnold Bennett was another great note-taker, and his *Clayhanger* was again a reconstruction of a remembered world. Closer still to Scott was Thomas Hardy, with his shrewd observation of traditional country customs, and ability to use them as illustrations of conflict and change within the whole social structure. But this is looking ahead and to a stage when, to their own loss, historians were less prepared to learn from novelists.

A third type of historical work which had expanded especially fast from the end of the seventeenth century was the biographical memoir. In this the use of oral evidence remained, of course, an assumed method. The growing popularity of memoirs brought interesting extensions in scope. First, there were a number of projects for collections of biographies which aimed to represent whole social groups, rather than simply exceptional individuals. The most famous of these projects, John Aubrey's *Brief Lives*, although known in his lifetime, was not in fact published until two centuries later, in 1898. Aubrey, who wrote that from boyhood 'he did ever love to converse with old men, as Living Histories', was an impoverished country gentleman, forced to turn his hobby into a living as an antiquarian research assistant working for others.[15] In the course of this he found time to put together stories and information from innumerable sources to compose a biographical portrait of his social circle, the seventeenth-century intelligentsia, as a whole. A more obscure example on a local level was Richard Gough's *Human Nature Displayed in the History of Myddle* (1833), in Shropshire, which had been written in 1706, and has recently attracted the interest of historians. In his preface to its republication W. G. Hoskins calls it 'a unique book. It gives us a picture of seventeenth-century England in all its wonderful and varied detail such as no other book that I know even remotely approaches.' Gough started by discussing the buildings of the parish; but once he reached the parish church he used its pews as the framework for a social survey, taking each pew-holding family in turn, discussing their origins and their occupations, and relating with relish either their successes, or their failings— drink, bribery, and whoring. This information, moreover, is not merely illustrative; for its value has also emerged, in a modern historical study, in establishing basic demographic facts, and correcting the misinterpretations which would otherwise have been made from more conventional sources such as wills and registers.[16] In the frankness with which he documented scandal, Gough is perhaps unique; but his focus on people rather than institutions provides one of the first instances of a valuable minority form of local history. A later example is the *History and Traditions of Darwen and its People* which J. G. Shaw, the editor of a local newspaper, recorded in shorthand from an old man in the town and published in 1889.

Still more striking, and undoubtedly a reflection of the early social and political emergence of the working class in Britain, was the remarkable nineteenth-century flowering of a very varied individual working-class autobiography: intellectual, political, or personal. It had several sources. One was the life published as a moral example. The religious autobiographies of mid-seventeenth-century Puritan sectarians were the first from the lower classes; and the groups of *Spirituall Experiences* published included, still more rarely, some testimonies by women. Stories of conversion and rescue were again collected in the eighteenth century from the Protestant Camisards in France and from old dissenters and Methodist pioneers in Britain: and in the 1820s one local historian of northern Wesleyanism not only secured a resolution by Conference that it should be a duty of every superintendent to collect testimonies of zeal and sufferings from early Methodists, but chose as the frontispiece to his own book a sketch (by himself) of ninety-year-old Richard Bradley who had been one of his own 'living oracles'.[17] Other mid-nineteenth-century lives were edited by religious pamphleteers, introduced by parsons, or given titles like *The Working Man's Way in the World*. Morality was secularized by Samuel Smiles, who published biographical collections of engineers, ironworkers, and toolmakers as well as his classic, *Self-Help: with Illustrations of Character and Conduct* (1859).[18] The notably full, early autobiography of the self-improving tailor Thomas Carter was published by the moral and educational popularizer Charles Knight in 1845 in much the same spirit. Quite a different vein was represented by the memoir of picaresque adventure. In the eighteenth century this normally implied gambling or sexual intrigue, but it could be extended into other forms of 'low life', and circusmen's or poachers' autobiographies later carried some of the same flavour.

.There was a convergence of these two autobiographical approaches in the mid-nineteenth-century, as the working classes made their political presence felt, and came to be seen as a problem. The semi-autobiographical works of the journeyman engineer, Thomas Wright—*Some Habits and Customs of the Working Classes* (1867), *The Great Unwashed* (1868), and *Our New Masters* (1873)—provided information for the middle

class which was comforting as well as colourful. There are signs
too of a concern in some authors to retain something of the
liveliness of working speech forms in print. And at the same
time the working-class movement itself began to produce autobiography, with the early *Memoir of Thomas Hardy* (1832), on
the French revolutionary years, followed before long by classics
such as Samuel Bamford's *Early Days* (1848) and Chartist autobiographies like *The Life and Times of William Lovett* (1876);
although the labour political biography eventually settled into a
rather narrow form. The early emergence of a masculine working-
class autobiography in Britain can therefore be linked closely
to working-class activity, first in religion and then in politics.
The same is true rather later on in France. It is striking that
by contrast in Germany no tradition either of the social novel
or of working-class autobiography was established in the
nineteenth-century. Only in 1904 did the socialist deputy in
the Reichstag, Paul Göhre, launch the first series of autobiographies with the deliberate intention of revealing to middle-
class readers both the conditions of ordinary life, and that
working-class people shared 'human thoughts and feelings,
and reacted to joy and suffering in the same way they did'.[19]

Lastly, among the new forms of historical writing can be seen,
towards the end of the eighteenth century, the beginnings of an
independent social history. At this stage there was no professional separation between the processes of creating information,
constructing social theory and historical analysis, so that they
proceed sometimes together, sometimes apart. One cannot, as a
result, separate the origins of an 'oral history' method from
general developments in the collection and use of oral evidence.
Two of the earliest achievements, for example, came from
Scotland. In 1781 John Millar published his *Origin of the
Distinctions of Ranks*, which puts forward a historical and
comparative theory of inequality. He did not merely anticipate
Marx by linking the stages in master–servant relationships
with changes in economic organization, but produced in his
discussion 'of the rank and condition of women in different
ages' one of the first historical explanations of sexual inequality.

This pioneering exercise in historical sociology depended on a wide variety of published sources from ancient histories to the recent descriptions of local social customs by European travellers in other continents. Then years later came a major step in the creation of source material, the first *Statistical Account of Scotland* (1791–9), a national collection of contemporary and historical social information carried out through the parish clergy and edited by Sir John Sinclair. There had been no investigation on a comparable scale in the British Isles since Domesday. Meanwhile, in England, one important model of social investigation was provided by the 'field-work' travels of Arthur Young, bringing together both his own observations and interviews with others in his influential reports on the state of British agriculture. William Cobbett's later travels, documenting the often devastating social consequences of economic progress in agriculture, used the same method in reply to Young. Others, less energetic, devised short-cuts which were to prove key methodological devices for the future. The first questionnaire has been attributed to David Davies, a Berkshire rector, who was investigating farm labourers' budgets, and sent out printed abstracts to potential collaborators, whom he hoped might collect similar information in other places. And it was for another investigation of *The State of the Poor*, again in the 1790s, that Sir Frederick Eden sent out one of the first modern interviewers: 'a remarkably faithful and intelligent person; who had spent more than a year in travelling from place to place, for the express purpose of obtaining exact information, agreeably to a set of queries with which I furnished him'.[20]

The nineteenth-century was to see this process of development in field-work method, historical analysis, and social theory carried rapidly forward but in a context of increasing separation and specialization. This was even true within field-work methodology itself. The travelling investigation, for example, became a field-work specialism of the colonial anthropologist, and the survey of the sociologist of 'modern' societies. And sharp differences emerged even between the form of survey method used in different European countries. In France,

Belgium, and Germany, as well as in Britain, the survey was first used by independent philanthropists, medical reformers, and sometimes newspapers, and then taken up for official government investigations. But when the French began their first large-scale 'enquête ouvrière' under fear of the revolutionary uprisings of 1848, they did not seek evidence directly, but through their well-organized local bureaucracy. And the German social surveys which were begun in the 1870s were invariably sent out to local officials, clergy, teachers, or landowners, for return in essay form, following the model of the French and Belgian 'enquêtes'.

In Britain, by contrast, techniques for the direct collection of evidence were adopted. This began regularly with the launching in 1801 of the decennial census, carried out under central instructions by investigators dispersed throughout the country —thus establishing the national interview survey. Only the sum findings of the census were published. But the parliamentary social inquiries and Royal Commissions which increasingly came to be published as Blue Books were also commonly conducted through interviewing, although of a different kind. Sometimes an on-the-spot investigation was made, but normally witnesses were summoned before the inquiring committee and questioned by them. The exchanges and arguments between the committee and witnesses were often reproduced along with the publication of the official report. They constitute a rich repository of autobiographical and other oral evidence. And their potential as source material was quickly realized. The Blue Books were the basis of Disraeli's descriptions of working-class life in *Coningsby* and *Sybil*. And they proved equally useful to Karl Marx.

Marx and Engels, in their more immediate political writings, normally drew substantially both on direct experience of their own, and on reports, written and oral, from their innumerable correspondents and visitors. Equally, Engels's *Condition of the Working Class in England in 1844* combines material from newspapers, Blue Books, and other contemporary comment with his own eyewitness accounts of working-class life. Engels had come to Manchester in 1842 to work in the English branch of his father's firm, and in his spare hours from the cotton mill was able to explore the industrial conditions of the city and to meet, with the help of a working-class girl, Mary Burns, some of the Chartist leaders. For his culminating theoretical analysis, however, Marx relied on published source material. *Capital* is heavily documented with both bibliography and footnotes. Apart from occasional quotations from classical literature, Marx cites two types of source: contemporary economic and political theory and comment; and contemporary description, often including vivid anecdotes, from newspapers and from the parliamentary Blue Books. No doubt this decision of Marx to use only already published oral material, rather than carry out any new field-work, was partly due to personal taste, and partly to enable him to buttress his arguments with unassailable authorities. But given the influence which *Capital* was to have on the future of social history, it set a key precedent.

It is equally significant of the changing situation that such a choice was open to Marx. For we have still not exhausted the major new steps in the creation of oral source material for social history. In addition to the investigations of the government, social survey work was undertaken by voluntary bodies. By the late 1830s there were Statistical Societies in London, Manchester, and other cities, composed mainly of doctors, prosperous businessmen, and other professionals, which made important contributions to the techniques of collecting and analysing social information. They carried out local inquiries into working-class conditions, making pioneer use of the door-to-door questionnaire survey by paid interviewers, and publishing their findings in statistical tables prefaced by a brief report. In this form most of the original interview evidence was suppressed.

On the other hand, an alternative model was created by the newspaper investigation, which was developed in the 1840s, and culminated in the *Morning Chronicle* survey under Henry Mayhew. This inquiry, conceived in the wake of the great cholera epidemic of 1849, has been called 'the first empirical survey into

poverty *as such*'.[21] Mayhew's aim was to demonstrate the relationship between industrial wage levels and social conditions.
Instead of a door-to-door survey he therefore analysed a series
of trades through a strategic sample. In each trade he looked for
representative workers at each job level, and then took supplementary information from unusually well-paid workers at one
extreme and distressed casual workers at the other. He obtained
his information both from correspondence and by direct interview, and for both he gradually developed a detailed schedule of
questions. Most striking was his actual interview technique. He
seems to have felt a respect for his informants which was very
rare among investigators of his time. His comments show both
emotional sympathy and a willingness to listen to their views.
Indeed, his changing standpoint shows that he was genuinely
prepared to be influenced by them. No doubt this attitude
helped him to be accepted into working-class family homes
and receive their life-stories and feelings. And, significantly, it
was linked to an unusual concern with their exact words. He
normally went to interviews accompanied by a stenographer, so
that everything said could be directly recorded in shorthand.
And in his reports he gave very substantial space to direct
quotation. In Mayhew's pages, as nowhere else, one can hear
the ordinary people of mid-Victorian England speaking. It is
because of this that they continue to be read.

Despite his popularity, Mayhew had no direct successors. But
with the rise of the socialist movement in the late nineteenth-
century, a new concern to understand both the conditions and
the spirit of the working classes was felt both in Britain and in
Germany. One result was the 'settlement' movement, which
encouraged idealistic middle-class men and women to live
among the poor, sometimes in groups as voluntary workers,
but also alone, and even in disguise. In England, for example,
a number of 'glimpses into the abyss' inside common lodging-
houses and workhouses were written besides the famous
accounts of Jack London and, later, George Orwell. In Germany
in 1890 Paul Göhre, as a young theology student, worked
incognito in a Chemnitz machine-tool factory to produce *Three*

Months in a Workshop (1895): a study of factory culture which marked a turning-point in German social inquiry, as well as setting Göhre on the path which later led him, as we have seen, to launch the first German working-class autobiographies. Robert Sherard also used clandestine techniques for his vivid accounts of industrial conditions in *The White Slaves of England* (1897): 'the factories I visited were visited by me as a trespasser, and at a trespasser's risk'. He generally avoided contact with employers, finding that they just laughed at his 'stories of grievances' in their 'luxurious smoking-rooms'. A similar direct understanding of working-class culture was openly sought by Alexander Paterson, whose *Across the Bridges* (1911) is based on his years living in South London. In rural studies it is expressed in the respect for country people of George Sturt's *Change in the Village* (1912), and still more in Stephen Reynolds's books on the Devon fisher-people with whom he shared a house, *A Poor Man's House* (1909) and *Seems So!* (1913). Reynolds's sympathy was carried to an explicit 'repudiation of middle-class life' in the belief that the simpler lives of the poor were fundamentally 'better than the lives of the sort of people I was brought up among'.[22] Few, of course, would have gone this far. But something of the new sympathy and understanding can be found even in the most formidable and influential of late nineteenth-century English social investigations, Charles Booth's *Life and Labour of the People in London* (1889–1903). Booth used a variety of methods, including participant observation, taking lodgings incognito in a working-class household, although for his main survey of poverty he did not use direct interviews, but relied on reports from school visitors. He took a great deal of oral evidence for his religious inquiry, but this was chiefly from clergy. For all its richness, his seventeen-volume masterpiece thus lacks the immediacy of working-class speech. Seebohm Rowntree, in developing Booth's method for his own study of York, *Poverty* (1901), did undertake direct interviewing, although his report was in the statistical tradition, avoiding quotation. But his later *Unemployment* (1911) uses direct quotations from interviewers' notes very effectively, and although this remains well short of Mayhew's standard, it provided an important early instance of the twentieth-century sociological survey, with its combination of tables and interview quotations. Another less well-known pioneering work is the cultural study of *The Equipment of the Workers* (1919), carried out by a high-minded adult education group at the St Philip's Settlement in Sheffield, using both a quantitative sample frame and a selected number of deeper qualitative interviews incorporating life histories. It is an odd book, but again an example of a method which might have been, although in the event was not taken up at this time by historians.

A second line of influence from Booth's social survey leads more directly into history. One of his team of investigators was the young Beatrice Webb. Her contributions on dock labour and the sweated tailoring trade are the best industrial analyses in Booth's whole series. She also had early experience in door-to-door interrogation as a rent collector for Octavia Hill. Thus when she came to write her first independent historical study, *The Co-operative Movement in Britain* (1891), and later, with Sidney Webb, in their classic *History of Trade Unionism* (1894), she undertook the collection of oral, along with documentary, evidence in a highly systematic way. From the start, Beatrice combined searches through records with visits to Co-operative Societies and interviews with leading Co-operative personalities. Later she evolved with Sidney a method of occasional intensive field-work forays, setting up headquarters in lodgings in a provincial town for two or three weeks, and 'working hard; looking through minute books, interviewing and attending business meetings of trade unions'. Although at first Sidney preferred documentary work, being 'shy in cross-examining officials, who generally begin by being unwilling witnesses and need gentle but firm handling', they apparently hit upon a devastating technique of joint interview, in which they battered from either side the object of their attentions—sometimes a political opponent, sometimes an official who had not devoted much thought to the underlying implications of his official

actions—with a steady left–right of question, argument, assertion, and contradiction, and left him converted, bewildered, or
indignant, as the case might be.[23]

Later on Beatrice put these and other less dubious interviewing skills to effect in deliberately creating the evidence
she wanted before the 1905 Poor Law Commission, both
through procuring and briefing witnesses, and through her
own cross-examining.

In their published histories, the Webbs cited only documentary sources. But they depended heavily on their interviewing
both for their overall interpretation and for their treatment of
facts. Each field-work visit resulted in an overall assessment of a
particular organization, and a set of penetrating portraits of its
personalities. The Webbs were careful to pass on their method
to the school of British labour history of which they were the
founders. Page Arnot, for example, followed it for his histories
of the miners' trade unions. The notes on interviewing which
Beatrice Webb published in *My Apprenticeship* (1926) still command respect. And it must surely be her example which inspired
the leading economic historian, J. H. Clapham, in 1906, to call
for the training of interviewers to collect 'the memories of
business-men' which were, in his view, 'the best original authorities' for recent economic history: and 'with them often die
some of the most valuable records of nineteenth-century history'.[24] But nothing came of this; and, indeed, the Webbs
themselves were to have few immediate followers, even in labour
history.

It is no accident, however, that this innovative historical work
by the Webbs was part of a lifetime dedicated to social change
and practical politics. Where other notable experiments in the
use of oral material by historians can be found in this period,
the context is typically exceptional, and often literally at the
frontiers. Thus as the British expanded their imperial control in
Africa, missionaries and colonial civil servants would begin
recording local native traditions; and by the 1900s especially
in Uganda and among the Nigerian Yoruba, historical writing
extensively drawn from their own oral tradition flourished

among the conquered people themselves. In the Pacific the American missionary Sheldon Dibble organized his seminary class into a student research group, sending them out to 'the oldest and most knowing of the chiefs and people' armed with questions to elicit 'the main facts of Hawaiian history', for his *History of the Sandwich Islands* (1843). And more ambitiously, in the 1860s H. H. Bancroft, whose family firm were the largest booksellers, stationers, and publishers in the American Far West, decided to collect material on a very large scale for his historical studies of the recently colonized Pacific coast of California. Over a period of fifty years he employed altogether 600 assistants, who built up, indexed, and abstracted his library. In addition to buying all the documents he could find and sending his agents to harass financially embarrassed families and corporations, he mobilized a whole army of reporters to extract conversations from surviving witnesses. Perhaps the most skilled of these was the Spanish-speaking Enrique Cerruti. Bancroft himself claimed that his library included

two hundred volumes of original narratives from memory by as many early Californians, native and pioneer, written by themselves or taken down from their lips . . . There were a thousand, five thousand witnesses to the early history of this coast yet living, whom, as before intimated, Mr Bancroft resolved to see and question, all of them possible; and a thousand he did see, and a thousand his assistants saw, and wrote down from their own mouths the vivid narratives of their experiences.[25]

Bancroft's methods clearly had many weaknesses, and he proved unable to write up the material he collected in a convincing enough form. But in his willingness to use oral evidence, he set a precedent which was subsequently followed both in serious scholarship and in popular local journalism. Frederick Jackson Turner partly reached his famous thesis on the significance of the open frontier in this way. Similarly, from the 1920s it was a regular policy of the Arizona *Republican* to collect stories for publication from 'old-timers' at annually organized pioneers' reunions. And certainly Bancroft himself had been able, through his own private wealth, to organize one of the most elaborate purely historical research enterprises of the nineteenth-century, anticipating some of the giant public and privately funded projects of a hundred years later.

It may perhaps be a salutary warning that, although his library now forms the centre of the great Berkeley university campus, as a historian Bancroft is now largely forgotten. In this he stands in sharp contrast to another pioneer of oral history, the French historian Jules Michelet. Michelet is rightly remembered; and more needs to be said at this point about his use of oral evidence. He is a remarkable figure: both the leading professional of his age, and a great popular historian; and as imaginative in seeing the possibilities of documentary archives, as of oral tradition. Besides this he was one of the first historians to bring an understanding of the land and landscape into his writing. His influence was diffuse. One can see it in W. G. Hoskins, following *The Making of the English Landscape* (1955) along the hedgerows; or in France, the great medievalist Marc Bloch combining his searches in archives with the study of field patterns, place-names, and folklore, tramping round the French countryside talking with a peasantry who in the early twentieth century still worked the land with some of the means and spirit of their medieval predecessors. Michelet himself used oral evidence, especially in his *History of the French Revolution*, where he realized that the official documents preserved only one side of the political story. In 1846 he had also published *Le Peuple*, a remarkable essay on the impact of mechanization on the social classes of France. Its preface contains a striking—indeed passionate—statement of how he came to his method, and gained from it. He had been collecting information outside Paris for ten years, starting with Lyons, and then moving to other provincial towns, and into the countryside. 'My inquiry among *living* documents', he wrote, 'taught me many things that are not in our statistics . . . The mass of new information I have thus acquired, and which is not in any book, would scarcely be credited.' This was how he had first noticed the immense increase in the use of linen articles by poor families, and from this deduced an important shift within the structure of the family itself:

This fact, important in itself as an advance in cleanliness . . . proves an increasing stability in households and families—above all the influence of woman, who, gaining little by her own means, can only make this outlay by appropriating part of the wages of the husband. Woman, in these households, is economy, order, and providence . . . This was a useful indication of the insufficiency of the documents gathered from statistics and other works of political economy, for comprehending the people; such documents offer partial, artificial results, views taken at a sharp angle, which may be wrongly interpreted.

Michelet felt exceptionally at ease with this kind of research. This was partly because of his early life in a Parisian printer's family. Interviewing brought him back close to his own social origins, from which he had been separated through his education. 'I have made this book of *myself*, of my life, and of my heart. It is the fruit of my experience . . . I have derived it from my own observation, and my intercourse with friends and neighbours; I have gleaned it from the highway.' He seems to have been considerably happier talking to poor people than he was with the social class into which he had risen:

Next to the conversation of men of genius and profound erudition, that of the people is certainly the most instructive. If one be not able to converse with Beranger, Lamennais, or Lamartine, we must go into the fields and chat with a peasant. What is to be learnt from the middle class? As to the *salons*, I never left them without finding my heart shrunk and chilled . . .

Even so, it had been far from easy for Michelet to reach an open recognition of such feeling. As a young man, competitive, moving upwards through education, he had become intensely withdrawn. 'The fierce trial at college had altered my character— had made me reserved and close, shy and distrustful . . . I desired less and less the society of men.' His rediscovery of others and of himself came through his teaching at the École Normale:

Those young people, amiable and confiding, who believed in me, reconciled me to mankind . . . The lonely writer plunged again into the crowd, listened to their noise, and noted their words. They were perfectly the same people . . . (My pupils) had done me, without knowing it, an immense service. If I had, as a historian, any special merit to sustain me on a level with my illustrious predecessors, I should owe it to teaching, which for me was friendship. Those great historians have been brilliant, judicious, and profound; as for me, I have loved more.

Nineteenth-century historians were not given to self-analysis. Michelet therefore provides, in the few, vivid paragraphs of this preface, a powerful indication of an increasing barrier to the practice of oral history: class. The nineteenth-century was everywhere an age of increasing class and status consciousness. Historians were themselves evolving into a close profession, recruited through education. The very few who made their way into it from relatively humble backgrounds were much more likely to remain, because of the difficult experience of social mobility, withdrawn, like Michelet in his early adulthood. Among these Michelet was exceptional: few shared either the political commitment or the personality which enabled him to break back into easy contact with the people. As we shall see, the exclusive professionalism exemplified in Germany proved more compelling. And the very fecundity of production of secondary oral sources made it more possible, by the mid-nineteenth-century, for a great historian to write without the use of any 'living documents'.

Michelet himself knew this as well as any man of his time. In 1831 he had been appointed chief of the historical section of the National Archives of France, an immense collection which had been brought together when the French Revolution 'emptied the contents of monasteries, castles, and other receptacles on one common floor'. He used it for his own *History of France* (1833–67), and his afterword to its second volume provides an equally telling psychological insight, this time into the personality of the archival historian. It is a species of fantasy-hymn:

The day will be ours, for we are death. All gravitates to us, and every revolution turns to our profit. Sooner or later, conquering or con-quered come to us. We have the monarchy, safe and sound, from its alpha to its omega . . . the keys of the Bastille, the minute of the declaration of the rights of man.

As for me, when I first entered these catacombs of manuscripts, this wonderful necropolis of national monuments, I would willingly have exclaimed . . . 'This is my rest for ever; here will I dwell, for I have desired it!'

However, I was not slow to discern in the midst of the apparent silence of these galleries, a movement and a murmur which were not those of death. These papers and parchments, so long deserted, desired no better than to be restored to the light of day: yet they are not papers, but lives of men, of provinces, and of nations . . . All lived and spoke, and surrounded the author with an army speaking a hundred tongues.

As I breathed on their dust, I saw them rise up. They raised from the sepulchre, one the head, the other the hand, as in the Last Judgement of Michelangelo, or in the Dance of Death. This galvanic dance, which they performed around me, I have essayed to reproduce in this work.

The notion that the document is not mere paper, but reality, is here converted into a macabre gothic delusion, a romantic nightmare. But it is nevertheless one of the psychological assumptions which underpin the documentary empirical tradition in history generally, and not in France alone. In a much more careful, veiled form, for example, one may find the same dream in that early masterpiece of English professional scholarship, F. W. Maitland's *Domesday Book and Beyond* (1897). 'If English history is to be understood, the law of Domesday Book must be mastered.' Maitland looks forward to a future in which the documents have all been reorganized, edited, analysed. Only then, he writes, 'by slow degrees the thoughts of our forefathers, their common thoughts about common things, will have become thinkable once more . . .'. And the dream is there in the title itself. 'Domesday Book appears to me, not indeed as the known, but as the knowable. Beyond is still very dark: but the way to it lies through the Norman record.'[26]

It was this documentary tradition which emerged during the nineteenth-century as the central discipline of a new professional history. Its roots go back to the negative scepticism of the Enlightenment as well as to the archival dreams of the Romantics. We have already met the Scottish historian William Robertson at breakfast with Dr Johnson. Robertson, in his *History of the Reign of Charles V* (1769), publicly reprimanded Voltaire for his failure to cite sources. He had himself gone to unusual lengths to base his *History of Scotland* (1759) on original documents, and was able to cite seven major archives, including the British Museum, although 'that Noble Collection' was

not yet open to the public. . . . Publick archives, as well as the repositories of private men, have been ransacked . . . But many important papers have escaped the notice of (others) . . . It was my duty to search for these, and I found this unpleasant task attended with considerable utility . . . By consulting them, I have been enabled, in many instances, to correct the inaccuracies of former Historians.

Archival research at this stage is thus seen essentially as a distasteful corrective duty, rather than a creative skill. And it is the same negative scepticism which leads Robertson to reject out of hand the entire oral tradition of early Scottish history, dismissing it as 'the fabulous tales of . . . ignorant Chroniclers'. The history of Scotland before the tenth century was not even worth study. 'Everything beyond that short period to which well attested annals reach, is obscure . . . the region of pure fable and conjecture, and ought to be totally neglected.'[27]

It is less easy to see why this sceptical approach should have triumphed in the nineteenth-century. Paradoxically, the same romanticism which breathed life into the documentary method also set going folklore-collecting all over Europe, and recovered for the great epics and sagas of oral traditions the respect which they deserved. In Britain the folklore movement developed independently of professional history, on a local antiquarian or literary basis, largely amateur, and adopted its own special evolutionary theory of 'survivals' from Darwin. In France and Italy—where interest could be traced back at least to the eighteenth-century philosopher-historian Vico—folklore became a much more respected branch of scholarship. But it gained its greatest hold in Scandinavia and in Germany. Here, as in Britain, there had been earlier instances of collecting and publishing, but this initial antiquarianism was succeeded by the sophisticated methodology of ethnology, using a historical-geographical framework for systematic documentation and comparison. In this form it has, as we shall see, made a direct contribution to the modern oral history movement. At the same time it came to be seen as an important way of recovering a lost national spirit and culture, not only in Scandinavia, but also in Germany.

Equally important, the Romantic Movement led in the philosophy of history to a widespread acceptance of the importance of cultural history and the need to understand the different standards of judgement of earlier epochs and, eventually, other societies. This was again especially true of Germany where the narrowly confident universalistic rationalism of the Enlightenment had been resisted almost from the start, most notably by Herder, with his belief that the very essence of history was in its plenitude and variety. Here already were the first steps towards a cultural relativism. And it was from Vienna that, at the end of the nineteenth-century, the modern understanding of individual personality through psychology originated, carrying with it the implications of a less judgemental, more relativist attitude towards individuals in history. German philosophers of history unfortunately took little consistent interest in psychology. But the possibility of a new understanding of the historical value of individual life-stories was certainly there, and at least one German philosopher, Wilhelm Dilthey, came at times very close to it, as is demonstrated in some of his reflections on the meaning of History:

Autobiography is the highest and most instructive form in which the understanding of life confronts us. Here is the outward, phenomenal course of a life which forms the basis for understanding what has produced it within a certain environment . . . The person who seeks the connecting threads in the history of his life has already, from different points of view, created a coherence in that life which he is now putting into words . . . He has, in his memory, singled out and accentuated the moments which he experienced as significant; others he has allowed to sink into forgetfulness . . . Thus, the first problem of grasping and presenting historical connections is already half solved by life.[28]

How was this opportunity lost? What led the documentary method to its narrowing, scarcely mitigated by triumph in the very same decades through German example? This is a question which needs to be more fully explored. But part of the explanation undoubtedly lies in the changing social position of the historian. The development of an academic, historical profession in the nineteenth-century brought with it a more precise and conscious social standing. It also required that historians, like other professionals, should have some form of distinctive training. And both the research doctorate, and the systematic teaching of historical methodology, are derived from Germany. Research training was begun by Leopold von Ranke after his appointment in 1825 as professor at Berlin. Ranke was already 30, but he was to live to the age of 90, and during the succeeding decades his research seminar became the most influential historical training-ground in Europe. He was in some ways an old-fashioned figure, a sceptic as much as a romantic despite his fascination with medieval Germany. It was a rejection of Scott's novels as factually unreliable which first led him to resolve that in his own work he would avoid all fabrication and fiction, and stick severely to the facts. But in his first great masterpiece, the *Histories of the Latin and Germanic Nations* (1824), despite his famous destruction of Guiccardini's credibility and his dictum that history should be written *wie es eigentlich gewesen ist* (as it really was), he also declared himself opposed to research for its own sake; it was only in the final stage of his work that he had resorted to archives for confirmation. And although the *History of the Popes* (1837) was based on a more active approach, he certainly never shared the positive fascination with archives of his contemporary Michelet. Indeed, later in life he evolved a routine which avoided any direct contact with archives. Documents were brought to him in his own home by his own research assistants, who would read them aloud. If he so instructed, the assistant would make a copy of the document. Ranke would work each day from 9.30 a.m. until 2 p.m. with his first assistant, and from 7 p.m. with his second, in between taking a walk with a servant in the park, dinner, and a brief sleep. What mattered most was the relentlessness of his systematic, critical spirit. He directly trained more than a hundred eminent German university historians. In his research seminar, although they were allowed to choose their own topic, he set them on to medieval documentary work simply because that was the most difficult to master. And when professional training began to spread, first to France in the 1860s and later elsewhere in Europe and in America, it was founded on Ranke's assumptions. C.-V. Langlois and Charles Seignobos of the Sorbonne opened their classic manual, *Introduction to the Study of History* (1898), with the unqualified statement: 'The historian works with documents. . . . There is no substitute for documents: no documents, no history.'[29]

The documentary method not only provided an ideal training-ground, but it offered three other key advantages to the professional historian. First, the test of a young scholar's ability could become the writing of a monograph, the exploration of a corner of the past, perhaps minute, but based on original documents, and therefore, in that sense at least, original. Secondly, it gave to the discipline a distinct method of its own, which—unlike the use of oral evidence—could be claimed as an expert specialism, not shared by others. This self-identification around a distinct method like the archaeological dig, the sociological survey, the anthropologist's field-trip, is typical of nineteenth-century professionalism and had the added function of making the evaluation of expertise an internal matter, not subject to the judgement of outsiders. Thirdly, for the increasing number of historians who preferred being shut up in their studies to mixing with either the society of the rich and powerful or with ordinary people, documentary research was an invaluable social protection. By cutting themselves off they could also pretend to an objective neutrality, and thence even come to believe that insulation from the social world was a positive professional virtue. Nor is it accidental that the cradle of this academic professionalism should have been nineteenth-century Germany, where university professors constituted a narrow patrician middle-class group, particularly sharply cut off through their isolation in small provincial towns, political impotence, and the acute hierarchical status-consciousness of Germany, from the realities of political and social life.

In Britain the full development of these tendencies came relatively late. Although the documents of the Constitution had been firmly enough enshrined by Bishop Stubbs, eminent late nineteenth-century scholars like Thorold Rogers and J. R. Green did not trouble to footnote their main works, and even the *Cambridge Modern History*, launched by Lord Acton in 1902 as 'the final stage in the conditions of historical learning', was intended to be without footnotes.[30] The academic establishment was still widely linked both through kin and personal careers with London society and the political world. Thus Beatrice and Sidney Webb, in the midst of their political work for the Poor Law Commission, were also writing the chapter on social movements for the *Cambridge Modern History*; while R. C. K. Ensor, who wrote the highly successful Oxford volume on *England 1870–1914* (1936), had spent most of his life in journalism, politics, and social work. Lewis Namier's famous puncturing of the old Whig school of history, *The Structure of Politics at the Accession of George III*, only came out in 1929. It was not until the post-Second World War expansion of the universities that the research doctorate became the standard method of entry into the historical profession. Its full advantages, and disadvantages, are therefore a comparative novelty to British historians.

By this stage the ideal moment of the documentary method had already passed. It always had its critics. Even Langlois and Seignobos warned against the 'mental deformations' which critical scholarship had led to in Germany: a textual criticism lost in insignificant minutiae, separated by a chasm from not just general culture, but the larger questions of history itself.

'Some of the most accomplished critics merely make a trade of their skill, and have never reflected on the ends to which their art is a means.' They also commented on the ease with which a 'spontaneous credulity' of anything documented can develop (rather characteristically instancing memoirs as a type of document deserving 'special distrust') and argued for both analytic criticism and comparative evidence for establishing facts: 'It is by combining observations that every science is built up: a scientific fact is a centre on which several different observations converge.' Their first point is repeated by R. G. Collingwood in *The Idea of History* (1946), who condemns a training that 'led to the corollary that nothing was a legitimate problem for history unless it was either a microscopic problem, or else capable of being treated as a group of microscopic problems'; he instances Mommsen, who 'was able to compile a corpus of inscriptions or a handbook of Roman Constitutional law with almost incredible accuracy . . . but his attempt to write a history of Rome broke down exactly at the point where his own contributions to Roman history began to be important'.[31] If such comments had force then they have still more today in a rapidly changing world which demands explanations for its own instability. An escape from major problems of historical interpretation into microscopic investigation is increasingly difficult to justify. The documentary tradition has thus found itself increasingly on the defensive in the face of the growth of the social sciences, with their claims to superior powers of interpretation and theory.

Still more critically, the documentary school faces a shifting of its very foundation, for the document itself has changed its social function in two ways. First, the most important communications between people are no longer made through documents (if they ever were) but orally, by meeting or telephone. Secondly, the record has lost its innocence (if it ever had one); it is now understood to have potential value as future propaganda.

The stages of this change have been shrewdly discussed by A. J. P. Taylor, the prime master of the modern English documentary school. They first presented themselves in the documentation of diplomatic history:

The historian of the Middle Ages, who looks down on the 'contemporary' historian, is inclined to forget that his prized sources are an accidental collection, which have survived the ravages of time and which the archivist allows him to see. All sources are suspect; and there is no reason why the diplomatic historian should be less critical than his colleagues. Our sources are primarily the records which foreign offices keep of their main dealings with each other; and the writer who bases himself solely on the archives is likely to claim scholarly virtue. But foreign policy has to be defined as well as executed . . . Public opinion had to be considered; the public had to be educated . . . Foreign policy had to be justified both before and after it was made. The historian will never forget that the material thus provided was devised for purposes of advocacy, not as a contribution to pure scholarship; but he would be foolish if he rejected it as worthless . . . The same is true of the volumes of memoirs, in which statesmen seek to justify themselves in the eyes of their fellow countrymen or of posterity. All politicians have selective memories; and this is most true of politicians who originally practised as historians. The diplomatic record is itself drawn on as an engine of publicity. Here Great Britain led the way . . .

in the parliamentary Blue Books; followed in the 1860s by France and Austria, and later by Germany and Russia. Specially favoured historians were also allowed access to the archives to write their histories. Next came the fuller publications from archives by governments, normally either to justify or to discredit their predecessors. The first of these great collections was the French series on the origins of the 1870 war, published from 1910 onwards; but 'the real battle of diplomatic documents' opened at the end of the First World War with the Russian publication of the secret treaties, and then successive series issued from Germany, France, Britain, and Italy.[32]

From the 1920s, therefore, no diplomat could possibly forget that any document which he eventually retained might later be used against him. The original record must therefore be as judicious as possible; and periodic weeding of the files was always desirable. Meanwhile a similar process of change had started with home documents. Confidential Cabinet papers were being kept by politicians and some were able to use them in their memoirs. For a long time this tendency was fought, but effective recognition that no document could be regarded as permanently confidential (except perhaps by the police or secret services) came with the reduction of the waiting period for normal access to scholars to a mere thirty years. The consequence can be seen in the comment made to A. J. P. Taylor by Richard Crossman, former Cabinet minister:

I've discovered, having read all the Cabinet papers about the meetings I attended, that the documents often bear virtually no relation to what actually happened. I know now that the Cabinet Minutes are written by Burke Trend (secretary to the Cabinet), not to say what *did* happen in the Cabinet, but what the Civil Service wishes it to be believed happened, so that a clear directive can be given.

In the decades before the First World War, however, such tampering was only beginning. Equally important was the fact that this was the golden era of the personal letter. When dealing with the post-First World War period, Taylor himself has argued for the use of 'non-literary sources . . . The more evidence we have, the more questioning we often become. Now we have recording instruments for both sight and sound.' But he saw such needs in contrast to an earlier period:

The seventy years covered by this book are an ideal field for the diplomatic historian. Full records were kept, without thought that they would ever be published, except for the occasional dispatch which a British statesman composed 'for the Blue Book'. It was the great age of writing. Even close colleagues wrote to each other, sometimes two or three times a day. Bismarck did all his thinking on paper, and he was not alone. Only Napoleon III kept his secrets to himself and thwarted posterity. Now the telephone and the personal meeting leave gaps in our knowledge which can never be filled. While diplomacy has become more formal, the real process of decision escapes us.[33]

We have arrived, in short, at the age of the telephone and the tape recorder: a change in methods of communication which will in time bring about as important an alteration to the character of history as the manuscript, the printing press, and the archive have in the past.

It looks, too, as if it may be a swifter change. The technological basis has certainly evolved with great rapidity. The first recording machine, the phonograph, was invented in 1877, and the steel wire recorder just before 1900. By the 1930s a considerably improved version was good enough for use in broadcasting. A decade later magnetic tape was available and the first tape recorders of the reel-to-reel type sold on the market. The much cheaper cassette recorders came in the early 1960s. Today it is practicable for any historian to consider using a recorder in collecting evidence. This transformation of technology provides one reason why the modern oral history movement has its origins in most countries in substantially and quite often nationally funded enterprises, yet has more recently been growing equally fast as a form of diffused local and popular history.

Let us turn then to the pattern of the revival, bearing in mind the constraints imposed by resources. Where has oral history grown most strongly? How have the intellectual contributions to the reviving use of oral evidence, and the patterns of sponsorship, varied from place to place? We can start most conveniently with North America, which has seen the most explosive growth of all.

The antecedents of the movement there go back many years. H. H. Bancroft's interviewing of the 1860s was succeeded by other intermittent work on the frontier settlements; and the American Folklore Society dates back to 1888. More important was the great breaking away of American urban sociology from its English-influenced origins to the Chicago studies of the 1920s, like Harvey Zorbaugh's *Gold Coast and Slum* (1929), vibrant with direct observation and interpretation of city life, and centrally concerned with documenting and explaining it. In these early years the Chicago sociologists were remarkably inventive in their methods, making use of direct interviewing, participant observation, documentary research, mapping, and statistics. They developed a special interest in the life-history method for studying two aspects of urban social problems.

The first was a practical contribution to criminology. Clifford Shaw's masterpieces, such as *The Jack Roller: A Delinquent Boy's Own Story* (1930) or *Brothers in Crime* (1938), used a mere few of many hundreds of life-stories which he collected from the youth of Chicago's inner-city slums. Shaw's technique can be traced back not only to Henry Mayhew's lives of London criminals, but also to the traditional seeking of confessions from convicts on the scaffold or—as the reformers renamed the prison—in the penitentiary. In Britain John Clay, the prison chaplain at Preston, encouraged inmates to write or dictate 'short narratives of their lives, their delinquencies, their self-convictions, and their penitence', believing such stories to illustrate 'a history of which we are yet too ignorant, the actual social and moral state of our poor fellow-subjects'. Clay published some of the stories he gathered in his prison reports from the 1840s, using them to argue in support of the separate cell system. Similarly in America in the 1900s Judge Ben Lindsay of Denver used 'life speech' confessions as a means of treating youths in his model juvenile court, and Dr William Healey, founder of the Institute for Juvenile Research, which Shaw later led, and originator of the psychiatric case conference, used a parallel 'own story' technique both for therapy and for seeking understanding of delinquents' own attitudes. The crucial influence of this life-story approach in social casework and therapy today is so fundamental that it is taken for granted, but was then new. Equally Shaw's books, setting life-stories with great care in their family and social context, showed so convincingly that delinquency was not just the outcome of pathological character but a response to social deprivation, that eventually they seemed redundant: the point was taken.[34]

The second focus, long-term social change, overlaps more obviously with oral history, drawing on older informants: but as much by persuading them to write autobiographies or diaries, or lend letters, as by life-story interviewing. Thus W. I. Thomas and F. Znaniecki in their massive pioneering account of immigration, *The Polish Peasant in Europe and America* (1918–20), gave an entire volume to the *Life Record of an Immigrant*, a specially solicited written autobiography which provides a link between studies on social disorganization in Poland and the origins of emigration, and on the Polish community in Chicago. Znaniecki continued to work in both Poland and America. He founded the distinctive 'humanistic tradition' in Polish sociology, which systematically uses public competitions to collect written 'memoirs' on particular themes. It was developed by radical social commentators who used it to demonstrate the plight of the Polish peasantry and unemployed in the 1930s (and inspired a similar British volume of *Memoirs of the Unemployed* collected through a radio appeal in 1933).[35] In post-war Poland memoir competitions became an astonishingly lively form of popular culture. A continuation of interest can be seen in John Dollard's early study, *Criteria for Life History* (1935). But direct links with more recent life-story sociology are surprisingly rare. Polish work is little known in the West; while the Chicago school, despite such a promising beginning, before long became a victim of professionalization among sociologists, and retreated from the immediacy of the city around it to the security of research doctorates based on statistical analysis and abstract general theory.

Its legacy was not forgotten. It is still alive in the work of the Chicago broadcaster and oral historian, Studs Terkel. He has moulded his conversations with ordinary citizens to form a series of best-selling books, each confronting big issues: war or work, unemployment or race, people's hopes and dreams. In academic research Shaw's own Institute launched a fertile revival of life-stories in the sociology of deviance with the publication of *The Fantastic Lodge: The Autobiography of a Girl Drug Addict* (1961) from recordings made with Howard Becker. Another link with the present is through American anthropology. The inter-war years were a period in which the general tendency in anthropology was strongly influenced by Malinowski's argument that oral traditions, just because their key function was to justify and explain the present, had virtually no value as history: myth was 'neither a fictitious story, nor an account of a dead past; it is a statement of a bigger reality still partially alive'. Although his views applied more to oral tradition than to direct personal life-story evidence, they undoubtedly inhibited any move in this direction too. The European anthropologists who had scattered for their field-work to the remotest corners of the colonial empires rarely showed concern for the actual words of their informants. In America, however, anthropologists working among North American Indians and in Mexico were also in contact with the development of psychology and sociology, and took up the life-history method. Thus the work of Oscar Lewis and Sidney Mintz from the 1950s can be traced back, through Leo Simmons's *Sun Chief* (1942), an oral history project jointly sponsored by the anthropologists, psychiatrists, and sociologists at Yale, to Paul Radin's *Crashing Thunder* (1926), an American-Indian life-story inspired by the need 'of obtaining an inside view of their culture from their own lips and by their own initiative'. These antecedents include Ruth Landes's brilliant portrayal of nomadic Canadian Indian hunting people in *The Ojibwa Woman* (1938), which includes a rare early collection of women's life-stories.[36]

Most striking of all was an experiment launched under government sponsorship to fight unemployment in the New Deal: the Federal Writers Project of the 1930s. An astonishing series of life-story interviews was collected right across the country with former black slaves, workers, and homesteaders, the richness of which only more recently came to be fully appreciated. Much of this material remained long unpublished, but one contemporary selection, published in North Carolina and edited by W. T. Couch under the title *These Are Our Lives* (1939), shows a remarkable understanding of the radical potential of oral history. Sociology, Couch argued, had been 'content in the main to treat human beings as abstractions', or when case histories were used, to dissect them as 'segments of experience' in the analysis of particular problems such as social maladjustment. But it would be possible, 'through life histories selected to represent the different types present among the people', in appropriate proportions, to portray an entire community. His own collection of life histories was intended to represent for their region 'a fair picture of the structure and working of society. So far as I know, this method of portraying the quality of life of a people, of revealing the real workings of institutions, customs, habits, has never before been used for the people of any region or country.'[37]

Despite such anticipations, it was from another direction that the key step in the modern movement came: political history. 'Oral history', the (American) Oral History Association declared, 'was established in 1948 as a modern technique for historical documentation when Columbia University historian Allan Nevins began recording the memoirs of persons signifi- cant in American life.' The Columbia approach, the privately financed 'great man' recording project, proved immensely attractive to both national foundations and local fund-givers, and especially to retiring politicians. With a much broader scope, at its fiftieth anniversary in 1998, celebrated with the issue of a CD of excerpts, the Columbia archive with now 7,000 testimonies running to 700,000 pages of transcript remains probably the world's largest oral history collection. Indeed, for at least two decades it was 'oral history' in America. It was only from the 1970s that the oral history method was vigorously revived for Indian history, black history, and folk- lore, and in the 1980s extended into new fields like women's history. An interesting new parallel development of the 1990s is the initiation by linguists and psychologists of journals such as the *Journal of Narrative and Life History* and *The Narrative Study of Lives*. The North American scene is now one of both variety and vitality. It includes the Canadian Oral History Association formed in 1974, with its own journal. The Oral History Association itself has some 1,200 members. As early as 1971 in the two countries together there were reported to be 100,000 recorded hours of interviews collected, and over a million pages of transcript. More recently, a survey of Canada alone revealed some 1,800 collections in 350 repositories. These figures reflect the sheer resources which have made such a scale of field-work possible. One consequence is that an exceptionally high proportion of American oral historians are still archivists. But alongside community work especially from the 1980s onwards there was also a growing academic current, clearly reflected in the papers and bibliographies of the Association's *Oral History Review;* and notably through the influence of Ron Grele, who now heads the Columbia programme, founder of the *International Journal of Oral History* in 1980, in introducing perspectives from anthropology and from European oral history, it became a more reflective and outward-looking movement.

The second great concentration is in Western Europe. It was here, beginning in Bologna in 1976 and Colchester in 1979, that the biennial international oral history conferences were held, up until the founding of the International Oral History Association which resulted in the holding of the first transatlantic conference in the series at Rio de Janeiro in 1998. But as these conferences show, there is now oral history activity right round the world.

In Latin America, the lively and varied scene draws on several influences:[38] the life-story school in American anthropology; Mexico's impressive national oral history programme, recording social movements, politics, and culture, developed since 1959; the continuing achievements of social science researchers such as the Brazilian psychologist Eclea Bosi and the Argentinian sociologist Elizabeth Jelin; and contemporary political history programmes as at Rio, which have an added urgency in a continent where repeated political upheavals regularly destroy written documentation. A particularly striking innovation of the mid-1990s was the exceptionally elegant use of multimedia for oral history developed by the Museu da Pessoa in São Paulo. National oral history associations were founded in both Brazil (with its own journal) and Mexico in the 1990s. In the continent as a whole the Brazilian scene is the most turbulently varied and dynamic.

In Australia oral history has had its own association and journal since the late 1970s, bringing local and social historians together with anthropologists of the Aboriginal peoples. In south-east Asia, a cluster of nations led by Singapore have official oral history archives. Very surprisingly, in India, despite the special richness of its oral cultures, most work still depends on scholars or broadcasters from Britain. Again in Japan, although there have been studies in women's history and labour history and of war victims, there has been little enthusiasm for oral history, either academic or popular: perhaps more understandably in a hierarchical society which has been very reluctant to face the darker sides of its recent past.[39] China is yet another story. Here activity has primarily depended on the fluctuating interest of the Communist government. The national collecting of revolutionary memories began in the 1950s, quite soon after the Communist victory; in 1958, with the first wave of the Cultural Revolution, the emphasis shifted to grass-roots factory, brigade, and village history groups, including illiterate older workers, investigating the 'tortuous and complex', 'hard and glorious struggle of the working classes'; but both campaigns disappeared in the anti-intellectualism and ultimate chaos of the Cultural Revolution years.[40] In their aftermath it was left to an American, William Hinton, to return and make sense of them in a masterpiece of oral history, *Shenfan: The Continuing Revolution in a Chinese Village* (1983).

In the Communist world in general there was very little tape-recorded oral history. Poland's development of popular written autobiographical competitions and the Cuban encouragement of the literature of 'testimonios' were exceptional. So was the oral history work in Hungary, before and after 1990. Russia under Communism fostered a propagandizing genre of optimistic heroic worker booklets which now seem travesties of oral history. The fall of Communism, by contrast, unleashed a tide of memories which for a brief period washed through television, as well as the more painstaking work at documenting the abuses of Stalinism, focusing on political oppressions, killings, and the Gulag begun by the Memorial movement. There has also been an important growth of academic work, both by insiders and outsiders, building up a social history of everyday life under Communism. In these countries it has not been so much the destruction of written documentation as the extent to which it is fundamentally untrustworthy and distorting which has created a problem for any historical work. And while this makes remembered evidence all the more vital, the very instabilities of public perceptions of the past leave their marks on many individual memories too.[41] At an individual level there have been particularly dramatic confrontations between memory and written documentation through the opening of secret service files. In *The File* (1997), Timothy Garton Ash provides a sensitive exploration of his own experience of opening his own STASI file on his visits to East Germany and then seeking explanations from those, whom he had often believed to be friends, who had reported on him.

In Africa, and in Israel too, political changes and past sufferings have again shaped the form of oral history work. For Israel, after the systematic destruction of Jewish communities under Fascism, oral evidence from witnesses of every variety became a vital part of a national and cultural struggle for survival. The Yad Vashem archive in Jerusalem was the first monument to this. Subsequently this Jewish effort has internationalized, generating much worthwhile research as well as spectacular manifestations like the national Holocaust Memorial Museum in Washington and the massive Spielberg video recording programme. In Africa, by contrast, although resurgent nationalism did result in official recording programmes in some countries, the main change has been in the perspective of historical research. In the post-colonial era the history of Africa, which had been that of the imperial powers, abruptly shifted its focus to the largely undocumented African nations. But ironically the new school which arose, making increasingly subtle use of oral tradition as a source, has been predominantly Anglo-American; and it was also surprisingly slow to include social history recording the experience of ordinary African people. South Africa is again different, for here academic oral history has grown since the 1980s as an important method of documenting the experiences and oppressions of living under apartheid. And as after the fall of Communism in Europe, the transition from white rule led to a tremendous public outpouring of memories, but in this case focused on the horrifying confessions and tense personal confrontations in the state Truth Commission of 1997–8, which was made fully available both as text on the Internet and continuously throughout the nation on television.

Within Europe the political context of historical work has also been an important influence, more remotely in the link between nineteenth-century nationalism and folklore collecting, but also directly on oral history. In Italy one of the origins of contemporary oral history was the network of local centres for studying the anti-Fascist wartime Partisans. Subsequently the perplexing political and social results of the post-war boom, with peasant immigration into the cities and changing working-class consciousness, created an interdisciplinary oral history fashion in the 1970s, as well as stimulating sustained research: notably by the sociologist Franco Ferrarotti on the slums and shanty towns of Rome; by Sandro Portelli's cultural interpretations of the steelmakers of Terni, insights which he was soon to parallel across the Atlantic with the Kentucky miners; and the cluster of social history studies of peasants, workers, and women in Piedmont and Turin. It was from this last circle that Italy's oral history journal of the 1980s, *Fonti orali*, was edited by Luisa Passerini; and it included both Primo Levi, classic autobiographer of the Holocaust, and Nuto Revelli, most widely read of Italian oral historians, whose powerful books of testimonies have moved, indicatively, from war and resistance to peasant poverty and, finally, to the memories of mountain peasant women.[42] Documenting Fascism was also a principal object in the Netherlands where since 1962 oral history has grown from a well-organized co-operation between contemporary political historians, the International Institute for Social History, and Dutch radio, subsequently broadening into social history.

Conversely, the development of oral history in Spain had to wait for the ending of Franco's long regime, with the path first led by the English oral historian Ronald Fraser. From the 1980s there were clusters of research activity especially in Madrid and in Barcelona, from where *Historia y Fuente Oral* was edited from 1989 by Mercedes Vilanova, with its strong links with Latin America and regular translations of papers in other European languages building an important new southern channel of transatlantic influence. The late start of an oral history movement in Germany is again explained by the impact of Nazism, which had discredited the folklore movement by espousing it, and at the same time destroyed the germs of a more fruitful approach to survey research which by the early 1930s had been shown in a study like *Marienthal*. More importantly, Nazism left a generation ashamed of its own experience, and a nation more anxious to bury its past than to investigate it. Nevertheless, by the 1980s the social history research on the Ruhr working class led by Lutz Niethammer[43] stood between, on the one hand, a growing range of local history projects, and on the other, an organized network of theoretically and methodologically innovative life-story sociologists, who, especially through the influence of Gabriele Rosenthal, have developed an intensive 'hermeneutical' method of analysing interviews— of which more later. It is important to note here, however, how this new approach was generated out of the difficulties of interviewing in a society in which most of the older generation now wanted to understate or obscure the extent to which when younger they had participated in aspects of Nazism.

It is much less clear why France, with a widespread interest in war and resistance history, and with the example not only of Michelet but of the sociological school of Durkheim (which drew together anthropological and folklore material), and even a remarkable pioneering work by Maurice Halbwachs on the social nature of memory to build upon, was not only also late but also less sustained in developing activity in oral history.[44] The extreme concentration of French academic research in specialized institutes in Paris, lacking links with local communities, may be one reason. Although oral history has had its influence on French schools, community work developed more notably in Belgium. There have been two important poles of research influence. One is from Philippe Joutard and his interdisciplinary

group of linguists, ethnologists, and historians in the south at
Aix-en-Provence. The other is the 'reconstructive' school of life-
story research in sociology, pioneered by Daniel Bertaux, and
for two decades sustained by him not only in France but also in
the international sociological community.[45]

It is, however, in Scandinavia, and in the British Isles, that the
most strongly established European developments can be
found. In Scandinavia the roots lie in the systematic folklore
collecting of the nineteenth-century. The first archives for direct
field-work were set up in Finland as early as the 1830s. The
Finnish example was followed especially in Sweden. Students at
the University of Uppsala formed dialect societies in the 1870s
to collect provincial words and expressions which they feared
were threatened with extinction. Already by the 1890s this collecting had been systematized into a national questionnaire
interview survey, answered in a thousand different locations
over the whole country, and by 1914 the Institute for Dialect
and Folklore Research was founded with financial support from
the Swedish Parliament. The scope of its collecting gradually
widened into a national study of rural society, culture, and
economy. And from 1935 the Institute made regular use of
recording machines in its field-work—probably the first organization to do so for the purposes of historical research. Closely
linked to this field-work was the special development of ethnology in Scandinavia as a central academic discipline in the social
sciences, fusing social history and sociology. In Stockholm the
'Memory' section of the Nordic Museum Archive now provides
a computerized national information service, including material
from their regular essay competitions which go back to the 1920s
and oral history interviews with essayists. The notable Scandinavian use of written life-story competitions was especially
encouraged by ethnologists. In the 1950s, led by the Norwegian
historian Edvard Bull, ethnological field-work collection was
extended to the urban and industrial populations; and by the
1970s ethnologists such as Orvar Löfgren and Sven Ek were
using this earlier work to study long-term social change. There
have also been important experiments in popular history,

through the imaginative museum and broadcasting services, and also the workers' factory history campaign launched by the Swedish writer Sven Lindqvist in his challenging book, *Grav där du står* (1978) and the tented travelling exhibition under the same title: 'Dig Where You Stand'.

This early Swedish example proved of particular importance to the development of oral history in some parts of Britain. Here again a strong interest had developed in folklore, mainly on an amateur basis; but in England folklore studies have never escaped from the stigma of amateurism. The most important centres have been from the 1950s to the 1970s the Dialect Survey based at Leeds University and the subsequent Centre for English Cultural Tradition and Language at Sheffield. But in Ireland and Wales, and to a lesser extent in Scotland, folklore was reinforced through association with nationalist movements. The Irish government began to assist collecting in 1930, and in 1935 set up the Irish Folklore Institute. From the start this had direct links with Swedish scholars and also made use of recording machines. In Wales, the main centre became the Welsh Folk Museum at St Fagans; in Scotland systematic collecting was led from the Edinburgh University School of Scottish Studies, whose archive was started in 1951, originally with a Gaelic and literary focus but before long also drawing in social and English-language material.

It was post-war political change, however, which in Britain too lay behind the revival of oral history. One current came from the dismantling of empire. As colonial Africa moved to independence its new nations needed a history of their own. From the 1950s, led by the Belgian scholar Jan Vansina—later from Wisconsin—and John Fage and Roland Oliver from Britain, historians began to collect their own oral material in the field, alongside anthropologists, exchanging experience of methods and interpretation with them.

The coming to power of the working-class movement in the 1945 Labour government and the popular confidence from the long post-war boom years brought, more slowly, a parallel change at home: a quickening interest in labour history, by the 1960s broadening into social history, paralleled by a new enthusiasm for working-class autobiography and later for television series using ordinary people's memories like 'Yesterday's Witness'. Some historians also became aware through their own radio activities of the remarkable resources of the BBC Sound Archives, which had been founded in the 1930s. The crucial influence came, however, through a new sociology of the 1950s concerned, not just with poverty, but with working-class culture and community in its own right. Some of these classic studies, such as Peter Townsend's *The Family Life of Old People* (1957) and Brian Jackson's and Dennis Marsden's *Education and the Working Class* (1962), made an effective use of individual working-class memories, while Richard Hoggart's semi-autobiographical *The Uses of Literacy* (1957) sought to interpret working-class forms of thought in speech and oral tradition. With Edward Thompson's *The Making of the English Working Class* (1963) this new sympathy was matched with a history which sought 'to rescue the poor stockinger, the Luddite cropper, the "obsolete" hand-loom weaver, the "utopian" artisan, and even the deluded follower of Joanna Southcott, from the enormous condescension of posterity', seeing their ideas instead as 'valid in terms of their own experience'.[45]

This convergence of sociology and history was encouraged through the founding of the new universities of the 1960s with their interdisciplinary experiments, and the rapid expansion of a sociology which was showing an increasing concern with the historical dimension in social analysis. The potential of oral history was brought home through the popular success of Ronald Blythe's *Akenfield: Portrait of an English Village* (1969), a blend of literature, history, and sociology based on tape recordings from Suffolk country people. Nor is it an accident that one of the most significant later books using oral evidence is a historical study of the relationship between religion, economics, and class-consciousness by a sociologist, Robert Moore's *Pit-Men, Preachers and Politics* (1974). Thea Vigne and I started our own national interview survey of family life, work, and community before 1918 from the sociology department of Essex University in 1968. We drew on the sociological experience of colleagues such as Peter Townsend and were given the financial support of the newly established Social Science Research Council.

Since then oral history has grown fast in Britain. The Oral History Society was formed in 1973, and within six years had some 600 members, rising to 1,000 in the 1990s, its journal *Oral History* circulating internationally. From the start the larger new projects have tended to be in social history, funded by the government Research Council and strongly shaped by sociological influence. The link with sociology has remained strong, although, as the current journal *Auto/biography* demonstrates, sociological interest has radically shifted from the empirical to the subjective and introspective, and even to fiction—a parallel with the recent tendency to self-biography among anthropologists; a reorientation even sharper than the parallel changes in oral history itself.[46]

Earlier, one particularly important step was in military history, for the Imperial War Museum set up its own generously funded Department of Sound Archives, providing an important model for museum work. The growth of the oral history movement also brought renewed activity in those branches of history which, for different reasons, had retained at least a minority tradition of oral field-work: recent political history, labour history, and local history.

In recent political history the change has been least obvious, because although often not cited, there has been continuous use of the interview as a method of exploration, discovering documents, and checking interpretation. A modern political biographer would always seek to learn from conversation with a subject, just as, for example, John Morley did from the ageing Gladstone. David Butler could even write that his *Electoral System in Britain* 1918–51 (1953) 'owes more to the personal recollections of the surviving protagonists than to any published lives or historians'.[47] But the advent of the tape recorder provided a more systematic method of collecting interview evidence.

With labour history the line of development from the Webbs is clearer. There has been a great deal of activity in this field, including substantial projects; and oral evidence has from the start been one of the distinctive marks of the History Workshop movement, which began out of working-class labour and social history at Ruskin College, Oxford, and has widened its range to address itself, in its journal's words, 'to the fundamental elements of social life—work and material culture, class relations and politics, sex divisions and marriage, family, school, and home'. Its workshops in the 1970s especially encouraged the spread of oral history into family history and women's history.

There has also been a great growth in local history, although the pattern of development is much less easy to trace. The roots go back especially far in rural work. Gough has been mentioned as one type; folklore collecting provided another; and a remarkable example was also set by the Women's Institute histories from the 1920s. These were village surveys, based partly on the example of the Scottish Statistical Accounts, but equally— through the influence of C. V. Butler—on Rowntree's social surveys. Joan Wake's *How to Compile a History and Present Day Record of Village Life* (1925) was written for the Women's Institute surveys, and gives excellent advice both on documentary research and the use of interviews to collect information from old people: on farming methods, tenancies, wages, trades and industry, transport, emigrants, schools, clubs, friendly societies, trade unions, health, food, religion, and crime; old stories, folklore, songs, and games; and personal reminiscences. 'Why not have "reminiscence parties" when each in turn would recall and relate his or her experiences, while someone took them down in shorthand?' she suggested. After the Second World War Women's Institutes or Old People's Welfare Councils in many counties sponsored essay competitions; extracts have been published as Pat Barr's *I Remember* (1970) as well as in local booklets. It is partly from this strong tradition of local history, as well as from his understanding of folklore and of work experience, that the work of George Ewart Evans springs, especially in his first book, *Ask the Fellows who Cut the Hay* (1956). In its title and introduction this village study in fact constitutes the first appeal for the present English oral history movement. Since the 1970s, however, there has been a still stronger flowering of local community-history projects in the cities. Many of these projects have proved short-lived, but others, such as Bradford Heritage Recording Unit or Southampton City Heritage, have flourished over many years; and while some have been self-supporting, many others have been funded through urban aid or, during the mounting unemployment of the 1980s, through the Manpower Services Commission; and increasingly, yet others museum-based.

British oral history in the 1990s remains a strong current despite having suffered, along with so much other local cultural activity, from the continual paring down of funding. It has continuingly fertile research currents based in sociology, social geography, and cultural studies as much as in history; a lively documentary tradition on television; a key position in history teaching for young children in schools; and over the last ten years a strong archival base through the National Sound Archive and the National Life Story Collection at the British Library. One may note two important shifts of the decade. One is the increasing concern by social science funders that significant interviews from both earlier and current projects should be archived as a resource for future researchers, a national policy for which Qualidata at the University of Essex has become the action unit. The other is the cross-disciplinary interest in all the forms of autobiographical memory which is symbolized by the launching of the new Routledge series 'Memory and Narrative'.

Oral history, in short, has grown where there was a surviving tradition of field-work within history itself, as with political history, labour, and local history, or where historians have been brought into contact with other field-work disciplines such as sociology, anthropology, or dialect and folklore research. Its geographical distribution also reflects the availability of money for field-work: hence the high concentration in North America and north-west Europe. For the same reason government sponsorship, especially of folklore collection, but also through unemployment schemes, radio archives, and social science research councils, have been key influences in most countries. In the United States, by contrast, some major government projects exist, but they chiefly concern the military forces and the experience of war. As a result, private funding has been dominant, much of it supporting admirable work, but overall risking too great an emphasis on the recording of just those people who are most likely to leave written records, the national and local élites. There are even oral history projects on the fund-giving foundations themselves. Thus the patterns of sponsorship—and, it could be argued, the political assumptions which lie behind them—have also been key factors in shaping different national developments.

There is, however, one more factor: the nature of opposition. The system of private funding in America has had, in this respect, the happy consequence of allowing oral historians to go their own way, loosely attached to local universities, colleges, and libraries; although less fortunately it led for many years to the typical American oral historian being primarily an archivist and collector rather than a historian as such. In Britain, by contrast, a sharper struggle for resources and recognition was inevitable. With the onset of economic recessions and public spending cuts from the mid-1970s, any new claimant for scarce public funds was bound to meet opposition. Even the Social Science Research Council from cautious support had by 1976 switched to an openly hostile policy of 'containment'.[48] In the research world fortunately this proved a very temporary setback. On the other hand, there can be no doubt that in the subsequent university cuts from the 1980s, the newest developments proved most vulnerable, and the well-established political and economic history of the safely remote past best able to protect itself. And there are also other countries, notably including Italy, Japan, and India, in which the wind of oral history, even at its strongest, never seems to have even rattled the bulwarks of academic conservatism.

Where such opposition succeeds, the main damage is to

professional historians themselves. They leave oral history to be developed principally within institutions by sociologists and researchers on culture, and in the community by either lay historians or aid workers. Professional historians thus miss the stimulation both of inter-disciplinary work, and also of contact with their own basic constituency; and they will allow oral history to evolve in ways which disregard their own needs and standards. For example, the widespread inadequacy of archival facilities for sound materials, and the consequent destruction of a high proportion of the oral evidence which is actually being collected, is likely to continue until the historical profession accepts that oral records are of as much value as written documentation. Thus while in advanced countries such as Sweden, Canada, Australia, and the United States, federal and state archives have been collecting oral history material as part of their regular programmes since the 1950s, few European countries have followed such examples, and in Britain it was only in the 1990s that the British Library became a national focus for oral history collecting and archiving.

Nevertheless, in the long run it seems most likely that the current forms of hostility to oral history will dissolve, and professional historians will return to their earlier view of the acceptability of oral evidence as one of many kinds of historical source. The change in methods of communication which has ousted the paper document from its central role make this ultimately difficult to avoid. And the opposition turns out on closer examination to be united by feeling rather than principle. Principles are cited, but they are contradictory, and derive from two extremes of the profession.

There are, first, schools of researchers in both social science and in history which rest on the belief that truth can only be sought through quantification. In social research the lion's share of funding goes to survey research units which in practice inter-act minimally with the lone craft researchers who typically carry out in-depth research. Survey researchers do well enough on their own not to need to look beyond their quantitative frame-works, except when speculating for explanations for their figures;

and in a world in which the computer is the prime symbol of technical progress, it is indeed probably easiest for them to ignore the sometimes awkward questions which are raised by qualitative life-story research—let alone by post-modernism— which could challenge confidence in their practice. Although less well-endowed, there are also historians, chiefly in economic history and demography, who wish to disregard any qualitative evidence which is not open to statistical analysis. As a school, they can be traced back to the 1920s when economic history was establishing its autonomy, and social history was moving from the impressionist elegance of G. M. Trevelyan towards the more severe standards of Georges Lefebvre, with his slogan, *Il faut compter*. More recent quantitative history has presented itself, under the new banner of 'cliometrics', as the path to a truly scientific history.

But such high claims have themselves brought disillusion-ment. Statistical history can no more unravel the past unaided than sociology can provide answers to all current social problems. The best economic historians and demographers have of course always recognized this: like the *Annales* school in France, or in Britain K. H. Connell, who in his influential discussion of the post famine demographic transformation of the Irish family used oral tradition collected by the Irish Folklore Commission as one key source of evidence. Since the 1970s there has been a reaction within sociology itself against a predominantly statistical methodology in survey analysis, and a return to life-story interviewing in the field which has brought sociology closer to oral history. Thus the earlier extravagant hopes of the neo-positivist statistical school now look increasingly dated. One can see more clearly how far Michael Anderson's analysis of *Family Structure in Nineteenth Century Lancashire* is distorted by sticking to a rigid economistic model of the family which allows, for a half-Catholic town in the decade of Chartist unrest, neither political, nor religious, nor psychological factors to be considered. And the daring acrobatics of an economic historian like R.W. Fogel, who will construct data when he cannot find it, and aspire to re-evaluate the entire experience of slavery with sets of tables, now seem sorties which reveal more of the pitfalls of the method than its strengths. It is difficult to believe that economic history and demography, which through their closeness to the social sciences are naturally more familiar with the interviewing method than most branches of history, and have indeed already produced some notable supporters of oral history, will remain long-term obstacles to its advance.[49]

The worldwide professional old guard looks at first sight more formidable. But the situation is in practice less fixed than it may appear. The traditional historian, partly because he is suspicious of theories and prefers to construct his interpretation from individual pieces of evidence gathered wherever he can locate them, is at heart an eclectic, a jackdaw. If he is suspicious of oral evidence, it is chiefly just because until very recently it was, to an extent which now seems difficult to recall, either hidden or unrecognized by him. Arthur Marwick in his *The Nature of History*, published in 1970, included a very catholic discussion of historical sources in his chapter on 'The Historian at Work', ranging from the accepted hierarchy of primary and secondary written sources to statistics, maps, buildings, landscape, imaginative literature, art, customs, and 'the folkways of the period'. He even argued that 'a history based exclusively on non-documentary sources, as say the history of an African community, may be a sketchier, less satisfactory history than one drawn from documents; but it is history all the same'. Yet he included no reference whatsoever to oral evidence as such. It seems unlikely that he would write a similar passage today without discussing both the interview method and oral tradition.[50] The awareness of these potential sources is now widespread, and awareness itself brings a degree of acceptance. In addition, oral history projects have created increasing numbers of archives, which are being used by research students and cited in their theses, frequently with the encouragement of their supervisors. For this new generation then, oral evidence is again counted among acceptable sources. And since it can be cited in their theses, they have become generally willing, when this seemed potentially worthwhile, to consider collecting such evidence themselves in direct field-work.

The fact is that the opposition to oral evidence is as much founded on feeling as on principle. The older generation of historians who hold the chairs and the purse-strings are instinctively apprehensive about the advent of a new method. It implies that they no longer command all the techniques of their profession. Hence the disparaging comments about young men tramping the streets with tape recorders, and the grasping of straws to justify their scepticism: usually a reminiscence (it should be noted) about the inaccuracy of either their own or some other person's memory. Beyond this there is—and not only among older scholars—a fear of the social experience of interviewing, of the need to come out of the closet and talk with ordinary people. But time will temper most of these feelings: the old will be succeeded; and an increasing number will themselves know the positive social and intellectual experience of oral history.

The discovery of 'oral history' by historians which is now under way is, then, unlikely to be obscured. And it is not only a discovery but a recovery. It gives history a future no longer tied to the cultural significance of the paper document. It also gives back to historians the oldest skill of their own craft.

3

The Achievement of Oral History

How do we measure the achievement of oral history? Against a roll-call of its long past: Herodotus, Bede, Clarendon, Scott, Michelet, Mayhew . . .? Or its present ambitions and diversity? It is not possible to mark any clear boundary around the work of a movement which brings together so many different kinds of specialists. The method of oral history is also used by many scholars, especially sociologists and anthropologists, who do not think of themselves as oral historians. The same is true of journalists. Yet all may be writing history; and they are certainly providing for it. And for different reasons professional historians are also unlikely to conceive of their work as 'oral history'. Quite properly, their focus is on a chosen historical problem rather than the methods used in solving it; and will normally choose to use oral evidence along with the other sources, rather than alone. The term 'oral history' is itself a contribution to this confusion:

. . . it implies a misleading analogy with already differentiated aspects of history—economic, agricultural, medical, legal, and so on. Whereas oral history can never be a 'compartment' of history in its own right, it is a technique that could conceivably be used in any branch of the discipline. The title also suggests, indeed invites, another hiving off when in fact it is clear to anyone who has taken oral evidence in the field over any length of time that compiling oral sources is an activity that points to the connectedness of all aspects of history and not to their divisions from each other.[1]

If the full potential of oral history is realized, it will result not so much in a specific list of titles in a section of historical bibliographies, as in an underlying change in the way in which history is written and learnt, in its questions and its judgements, and in its texture. What follows is a discussion of simply one dimension of oral history—the impact of new oral evidence in existing fields of historical study—and the examples cited are deliberately limited to modern works. Even so, it is difficult to make any satisfactory balanced choice between, on the one hand, the considerable number of often brief articles, especially on research in progress, which are known through direct publication in journals and bibliographies of the formal oral history movement, and on the other, the infinite but often substantial publications in sociology, anthropology, folklore, contemporary history, politics, and biography which lie to its fringes. A full survey of each field in turn would indeed be impossibly lengthy, and this will be simply an illustrative discussion.

Let us begin with economic history. Few will need to match the boldness—in more than one sense—of historians of pre-colonial central Africa like Robert Harms, exploring the tributaries of the inner Congo in his own canoe, who pieced together the emerging patterns of production, trade, and markets in their regions principally from communal and family oral traditions. The role of oral evidence in economic history has normally been relatively modest: first, as a corrective and supplement to existing sources, and secondly in opening up new problems for consideration. For some aspects of economic history, such as government policy, foreign trade, or banking and insurance, the existing documentation is abundant even if sometimes narrow in focus. But some of the major aggregate historical statistical indices, for example of real wages, of hours, and of productivity, are compilations resting to a quite considerable extent on either inadequate documentation or on absolute guesswork, despite the confidence with which they are normally presented. They are the basis, for example, of the great debates on the standard of living in industrial Britain: but Elizabeth Roberts has demonstrated from interviews with working-class families in two Lancashire towns how many factors have been misconceived or completely left out of calculations for statistical indices of the standard of living. And the sources prove equally defective for studying the history of many major industries. Take mining, for example: Christopher Storm-Clark has shown how existing documentary records are both insufficient and misleading. The mining industry before the late nineteenth-century consisted chiefly of small, shallow, and often short-lived local pits; yet the evidence which survives is not merely scarce and fragmentary, but heavily biased towards the atypical large-scale capital-intensive pits and their associated settlements. The closure of pits and consequent destruction of their records from the inter-war depression years onwards, the unwillingness of owners to allow their examination, and the subsequently similar fears of the National Coal Board, have improved neither their availability nor their informative content. For his own research, Storm-Clark therefore used interviewing partly to collect basic information about the technology and work organization of the type of pit whose records are missing. Interviews also supply much fuller evidence of the processes of recruitment into the pits and migration into mining districts than any colliery records. Perhaps most striking, however, has been their value in elucidating and correcting the very information which, at least for certain pits, Colliery Wage Books do supply on working hours and wages. Interviews indicate that for the individual miner hours remained very flexible; while the system of piecework payments divided between workgroups of miners was so complex and variable that the concept of a wage *rate* for the period before 1914 is 'almost entirely meaningless'.[2]

The same kinds of arguments for the value of oral evidence in relation to documents apply to other industries. Thus Allan Nevins's massive social and industrial biography of Henry Ford, his company, and the automobile industry, shows how oral evidence can bring out more clearly than documents the working methods of a great innovator. And for our own *Living the Fishing*—on an industry dominated by small firms and seasonal labour—interviewing proved the quickest way of constructing an outline local economic history of each community and each family enterprise, and also helped us to see some of the errors in the abundant government documentation and statistics, which had reflected local pride or evasion or guesswork in supplying information for the official records; but still more importantly, it gave us the vital information on the contrasts in entrepreneurial culture between communities, which helped to explain why some had died while others continued to thrive. Indeed, more generally, it is as important to understand, in contrast to the big success story, the small firm like a country town iron foundry which did not grow into a great company; and, a step further back, the rural craftsmen—wheelwrights, smiths, thatchers, and so on—for whom written documentation is still sparser, but for whom now exists abundant literature drawing considerably on oral sources. Again, it is often only oral evidence which allows adequate study of a transient economic activity which may be a vital part of the wider picture. Thus there are virtually no written records of itinerant trades— hawking, credit-drapery, market-trading, and so on—and even for the highly organized brewing industry, there was only the barest documentation of the regular organized seasonal migration of farm labourers from East Anglia to Burton-on-Trent.[3]

The most sustained oral history work, of critical significance for economic history, has, however, concerned agriculture. Here again accounts, wage books, and diaries can normally only be found for the larger and more technologically advanced farms. The very existence of such records denotes an unusual degree of efficiency. Even where records exist, the information provided on, for example, wage rates or work techniques is normally inadequate, and frequently either incomprehensible or misleading. To secure any reliable indication of the normal labour patterns or the variations in technological level within a particular district, oral evidence is essential. The collecting of such source material has been most systematically carried out in Wales and Scotland, but as sociology, anthropology, or folklore rather than as economic history. The demonstration of the relevance of oral field-work to agricultural economic history was led by George Ewart Evans, in his studies of East Anglian agriculture, *The Horse in the Furrow, The Farm and the Village*, and especially *Where Beards Wag All*: its methods, from the large steam-powered farm to the smallholding; cattle and corn economies; dealers, farmers, and farm labourers.[4]

Several of these studies hint at another form in which oral evidence is beginning to contribute to economic history: the study of the entrepreneur. Although there is abundant autobiographical material on the upper- and middle-class intelligentsia, such information on the manufacturing and business classes has been extraordinarily sparse. Without it, questions such as the role of the family firm and the socialization and attitudes of entrepreneurs in British economic decline cannot be answered. But economic historians have been surprisingly slow in following the example of sociologists in collecting life histories from industrial managers and from petty entrepreneurs. These sociological studies brought important new findings: the lack of ambition of English small businessmen in contrast to managers, for instance, and the absolutely crucial economic role played by their wives. More recent oral history studies of industrial managers and London City financiers have highlighted the importance of masculinity in business culture, of initial rituals, bonding, and schoolboyish games at work, and how such attitudes prolonged an unsystematic amateurishness at the top of the British economy. It remains a paradox that still probably the most revealing single life-story we have of a businessman is of an Italian-American fence dealing in stolen goods, recorded for a study of deviance. Clearly there is a major opportunity to do much more here.[5]

There is also a potential link between economic history and the history of technological and scientific discovery, although at present those oral history studies which do exist in the history of science are more concerned with its socially prestigious forms. David Edge has provided in his *Astronomy Transformed: The Emergence of Radio Astronomy in Britain*, a penetrating analysis of the post-war growth of the most spectacular, expensive, and perhaps least socially relevant 'big science', radio astronomy. Partly through his own previous experience in the same science, he understood that the paucity of records left by scientists was no accident; they did not regard their own earlier gropings and mistakes as relevant to the history of science, which they believed proceeded in a rational sequence of discoveries. Through interview evidence he has been able to show that the true picture is very different: a story of dead ends, of misunderstandings, and of discoveries by accident, within a social setting of acute rivalries, partly handled by group specialization, but sometimes leading to the deliberate concealment of information. This constitutes therefore an important contribution to the historical study of scientific method; in which the scientist himself, from cool, rational superman, becomes a more human and more political animal.[6]

In the history of medicine there has been long-standing American activity, and more recently there have been many British projects in this field. They range from studies of scientific innovation and the development of new medical specialties to the role of women in medicine, the life-stories of general practitioners, and histories of particular institutions—and hence also from intellectual to social history. Thus Diana Gittins in *Madness in its Place*, the history of a large mental hospital, on the one hand explores its working as a community, and how whole families became encapsulated in it as staff; but she also demonstrates the struggles over innovation, especially the pulling down of the walls between inmates and the outside world, and still more remarkably, how some of the hospital doctors continued to be so focused on research that for years they were willing to carry out operations on patients illegally.[7]

The history of science is of course but one branch of intellectual history. Another particularly interesting area is the history of religion, for oral sources can here be used to distinguish the beliefs and practices of ordinary adherents from those of their leaders. It is possible also to examine the 'common religion', superstitions, and rituals at birth, marriage, or death of the non-religious—by their nature areas mostly out of the reach of recent institutional religious documentation. There have been studies, for example, on the conflicts between radical popular Christianity and traditional elite values in Botswana; or on how

different generations of a Moroccan family use Islam in interpreting their experiences of change. And in Britain, since the
relationship between economic development and the religious
ideologies of entrepreneurs and their workforces has long
been a key subject of historical debate, this provides another
point where oral evidence can continue economic history. A
re-evaluation of the arguments of Weber, Halévy, and E. P.
Thompson on this issue is the focus of Robert Moore's *Pit-men,
Preachers and Politics*. This study of a Durham mining valley
shows the role which Primitive Methodism, with its emphasis
on individual self-improvement, backed by the paternalism of
local pit-owners, played in inhibiting the growth of militant
class-consciousness among the miners, until its influence, along
with the paternalism of the owners, collapsed in the face of the
twentieth-century economic crisis of the industry. The account
of religion, including the identification of those who were local
adherents but not members of the chapels, depends heavily on
oral evidence, and the combination of a painstaking local
reconstruction with a general theoretical argument makes this
book a significant landmark.[8]

It also brings us to an area contingent on economic history,
but of especially early significance for oral history, that of labour
history. The range of work here has been considerable, running
from local booklets, and articles in journals such as the *Bulletin
of the Society for the Study of Labour History* or *Radical
America*, to substantial books and archive collections.

The contribution of oral evidence can be seen in several
different forms. The simplest is biographical. Even labour
leaders do not normally leave substantial private records, so
that oral evidence has proved of regular value in an undertaking
such as John Saville and Joyce Bellamy's *Dictionary of Labour
Biography*, as well as in individual studies. But it has also
transformed the character of labour autobiography. Despite
some exceptions, the typical labour autobiography was until
quite recently written by a trade-union secretary or parliamen-
tarian about his public life, at best prefaced by a few brief pages
on his childhood and first job. Through the combined influence

of oral historians, especially in community history projects, and also of broadcasting, we now have life-stories from a much wider range of authors: from local as well as national leaders, from the ordinary rank and file, and also from non-unionized workers; from women as well as from men; from labourers, domestic servants, sweated and casual workers, as well as from miners and labour aristocrats. Equally important, the content and language have shifted from the public life to the ordinary experience of work and family. A more intimate and anecdotal type of autobiography has emerged, leaving its mark on the published life-story. Its influence can be clearly seen in the extracts from recent manuscript autobiographies included by John Burnett in his fine collection, *Useful Toil*. A very considerable number of similar oral autobiographies are now available in record offices and archives. A selection have been published, most often as small local booklets, but also as collections like Alice and Staughton Lynd's *Rank and File: Personal Histories by Working Class Organisers from America*. There are also a growing number of remarkable printed auto-biographies of the new kind, which started as oral recollections, like Margaret Powell's *Below Stairs*, a domestic servant's life. But still more powerful is Angela Hewins's *The Dillen*, an auto-biographical masterpiece recorded direct from a man who could never have written it, but had a rare gift for the spoken word. An orphan brought up in a Stratford-on-Avon common lodging-house among down-and-outs and prostitutes, he was appren-ticed to a local builder through his great-aunt's determination, but fell for an early marriage and failed to serve his full time. His life became a relentless struggle to feed his growing family as a casual labourer, turned to bitterness through his savage mutilation as a First World War soldier: an unknown life of labour, yet unforgettable, which could have come to us in no other way.[9]

Oral evidence can also be used to amplify information on specific events in labour history, such as the evolution of an organization, or the course of a strike. An exceptional example to which we shall return is Peter Friedlander's study of *The*

Emergence of a UAW Local 1936–1939—the unionization of a Detroit car factory—which he built up almost entirely from a very searching form of interview. More usually, the oral evidence has been combined with documentary sources, and the advantage gained by the historian has been both in the spread of informants and the broadening of information to cover more of ordinary experience. There are many instances of this type of work, such as the analysis of a series of strikes like the harvest strikes of Norfolk farmworkers; of the early unionization of women in woollen mills; of how devices such as profit-sharing were used by employers to suppress militancy; or of a sustained campaign like the Welsh miners' response to the Spanish Civil War. The particular strength which oral evidence can bring to such themes is to get beyond the formalities and heroics of contending leaderships, as represented in newspapers and records, to the more humdrum, confused reality and different standpoints within the rank and file, including even that of the blacklegs.[10]

A third form of oral labour history, which runs in close parallel to sociological research, is the community study, focusing on towns largely dependent on a single industry. The impact of oral history here can be suggested by contrasting the earlier sociological classic, Norman Dennis, F. Henriques, and C. Slaughter's *Coal is our Life* (1956), based on interviews, but largely dismissive of the historical material which they collected, with the more recently historical and sociological work of Robert Moore and Robert Waller, or of Jacquelyn Dowd Hall's work on a North Carolina textile town, in which the retrospective reconstruction of class relationships and sense of community from oral evidence becomes a major concern. Mining and fishing communities are the classic subjects of this type of work, but the use of oral evidence has also allowed the extension of historical community study to much more sparsely documented occupations, such as the casual labourers, carters, quarrymen, and laundrywomen of Raphael Samuel's 'Quarry Roughs'.[11]

Deindustrialization since the 1970s has brought a sharply

different phase, with weakened and less militant trade unions, few strikes to record, but on the contrary, many industrial communities left economically bereft through the closing of their mine or mill. We can expect more studies like Thomas Dublin's *When the Mines Closed* which describe the struggles for survival which followed. The same issues are taken up in *Portraits in Steel*, which combines striking photographs with life-stories of Buffalo steelworkers. From earlier periods there are also national accounts of workers who were unemployed: both of their organizations, and of their experience of life out of work—the long, fruitless search for a job, the pinching of food, the humiliation of welfare—an experience depressingly similar whether in North America, Australia, or Britain. The widest collections of such evidence are in Studs Terkel's *Hard Times* and Barry Broadfoot's *Ten Lost Years*. Nevertheless, two contemporary sociological studies give a more reflective analysis, showing the use of the life-story at its best. Dennis Marsden and E. Duff's *Workless* combines photographs with testimonies; while Elliot Liebow worked as a volunteer in a night shelter for the homeless, recording the women's lives, their accounts of rejection by their families and husbands, their search for solace and talk about God, in *Tell Them Who I Am*.[12]

Finally, oral evidence has a special value to the labour historian concerned with the work process itself—not merely its technology, which we have discussed earlier, but the experience of work, and the social relationships and culture which follow from it. The experience of work is the concern of Studs Terkel's classic masterpiece, *Working*. As with all his books, the effect is made not by explicit argument, but from cumulative interview extracts. It is a thick book: 600 pages in which 130 Americans pour out their work stories; old and young; real-estate woman, priest, factory owner, industrial spy, airline stewardess, hair stylist, bar pianist, strip-miner, car-welder, truck-driver, policeman, garbage man, washroom attendant . . . I know no other book which conveys so vividly the feeling of so many different kinds of job: the incessant, relentless tensions of the telephone receptionist; the loneliness of a top consultant struggling to survive in the jungle of management; the steel-millworker who would like the names of the workmen to be inscribed on what they make ('Somebody built the pyramids . . .') and short of this leaves here and there 'a little dent . . . a mistake, mine . . . my signature on 'em, too'. One constructs one's own interpretations, although Studs Terkel no doubt has a shrewd idea of how they are likely to shape.[13]

Much more clearly articulated studies of this type of history have now been published: on Fiat car workers and Terni steelworkers in Italy, on textile workers in Manchester, New England, on French and Spanish telephone operators and Carrara marble quarrymen, on London male craft coopers and female assembly workers, on Paris bakers, on white and black domestic servants, and much else. In Italy the search to understand working-class consciousness through the direct feelings of workers themselves led on the one hand to outstandingly perceptive historical studies such as Luisa Passerini's *Fascism in Popular Memory*, and on the other hand, especially in the 1970s and 1980s, to the collection and publication of factory interviews, songs, and poetry, by workers' groups, journals like *I giorni cantati* and archives such as the Istituto Ernesto di Martino in Milan. In researching on car workers myself in Turin and Coventry I was especially struck by how the interviews revealed the importance of the culture of the workplace. It seemed that skilled men who now worked on assembly lines sustained their self-image not only by elaborate systems of work rotation and self-pacing, but equally by play at work, including socializing, cooking rabbits, studying, and constructing giant festival lights out of car parts.[14]

Again one of the best studies concerns mining. George Ewart Evans sets out the system of the anthracite district of the South Wales coalfield, where the coal was near the surface, so that it was relatively easy for a small man to start his own drift mine; while its irregular geology gave special importance to the miner's skill. Owners and men lived and worked closely together. He then shows the impact of mechanization on the whole local social system, not merely destroying the status of the craftsmen, but also the close bond—sometimes paternal, sometimes exploitative—with the boys who formerly worked with them in their stalls, but now became a separate group beyond the control of the older generation. We have here an excellent example of how the exploration of a particular technical reorganization can illuminate its connections with other major processes of social change.[15]

We have already touched, in considering the basis of changing class-relationships, upon a key aspect of political history; and the biography of labour leaders can be taken as another. Biography is one of the forms in which historians most often use interviews, whether explicitly or not, usually in an informal and exploratory manner to supplement written sources. Sometimes such biographers may find the need to go further in the use of oral sources. Thus Bernard Donoughue and George Jones interviewed over 300 people for their *Herbert Morrison: Portrait of a Politician.*

We were forced from the beginning to resort to interviews because of the lack of certain other documentary sources. Morrison himself left very few papers, having burned the majority of them when moving house late in his life. The official papers for the 1945–51 government, in which he played a dominant role, are also not available because of the thirty-year rule.

Turning to interviews 'in some desperation . . . we were rapidly converted to appreciating their enormous value. They proved to be not just a stop-gap substitute for better sources, but a quite distinctly valuable source in themselves.' In particular, it proved possible to build up a much fuller range 'of perspectives and insights to the man . . . his virtues and his vices, and the extent to which the one was so often the reverse side of the coin to the other'. An early political life, so often skipped over by a biographer, could be reconstructed in remarkable detail. And throughout his career, Morrison could be revealed at work, as a minister or in local government, through 'the various groups of people on whom he made an impact: his political associates, his political opponents, the civil servants working with him, the people at the grass roots who were supporting him or on the receiving end of his policies'. The result, it can be added, is a biography which is not merely unusually rounded in itself, but has also created significant new historical source material for the future.[16]

There are also political biographies intentionally based from the start on interviews. The most striking instances are from the Americas, such as T. Harry Williams's *Huey Long*, or Valentina da Rocha Lima's collage portrait of the Brazilian political leader *Getulio*, each built from over 200 interviews. Still more remarkable, however, have been two individual oral history autobiographies. Jung Chang's *Wild Swans* charts political and social change through three Chinese generations, especially vividly conveying the agonies and humiliations suffered by her committed Communist parents during the Cultural Revolution. *I, Rigoberta Mench* is the autobiography, recorded in Paris by Elizabeth Burgos, of a radical young Guatemalan Indian peasant, probably incorporating as her own some experiences of other Indians, but a genuine and notably powerful account of the persecution of her people. It was deliberately intended to raise support for their cause, and with its multiple translations has indeed succeeded in giving them worldwide publicity.[17]

Oral sources have an equal potential for exploring the political attitudes and personal lives of the more typical unknown activists, and equally of the unorganized, quiescent majority of the population. Neglect of this has meant, for example, that we still have only the sketchiest understanding of working-class Conservatism in Britain, despite its key role in political history. Kathleen Blee's account of *Women of the Klan*, and the everyday normality and even pride with which they recall their active membership of an extremist organization, is a notable instance of what a study of right-wing populism can reveal. Other historians have recorded life-stories with radical activists, ranging from British socialists to African *Peasant Intellectuals*. And in general, oral evidence can provide much missing information on the activities and attitudes of the rank and file of the parties:

their reading, their social backgrounds and occupations and relationships.[18]

Another form is the political oral documentary, of which William Manchester's *The Death of a President*, drawing on over 250 interviews, was a classic American instance. Such investigative journalism can provide crucial material for future historians. More impressive, however, is the demonstration that reconstructions of political organizations at the grassroots level are possible, even where documentation is by definition largely non-existent, in William Hinton's *Shenfan*. Hinton had returned to the same village which he had documented in the earliest years of the revolution, and now, through the retrospective testimony of the villagers of Long Bow, he was able to unravel, uniquely illuminatingly, the complex feuds and devastating chaos of the Chinese Cultural Revolution. There are a variety of studies of other political struggles: narratives of the civil rights movement in the American South, of Mexico's long and confusing revolution, of men and women in Spanish anarchism, and also of European resistance to Fascism and underground political movements during the Second World War.[19]

For the Second World War period in Europe the outstanding examples have been the local studies of the Partisans in north Italy, and the impressively extensive international research on the Nazi extermination of the Jews and the Holocaust. These enterprises have however been responses to rare and scarcely documented national disasters, which have transformed the whole meaning of world political history. The story of the concentration camps, whether told by survivors, or collaborators, or the children of victims, still proves exceptionally harrowing, both for those who tell and for those who hear. Unfortunately such memories are not altogether unique: there are parallels in the memories of survivors of the earlier Armenian genocide, and also of the Hiroshima atomic bombing, not to mention in the contemporary resurgence of genocide. And only a little less painful is the history of Spain under Fascism, the fear which drove men to live the best part of their lives in hiding, and the manifold, confusing, ambivalent experience of civil war for ordinary townspeople and peasants, men and women, winners and losers, which has been so brilliantly conveyed through oral history in Ronald Fraser's *Blood of Spain*.[20]

More broadly, there have been several large-scale American and British projects collecting oral evidence in the field of military history. Again, they have been particularly important in illuminating ordinary experience, like 'life on the lower deck' of the navy, in the barrack-room, the wives of prisoners-of-war who felt marginalized and lonely 'like an unwed mother', or of the black soldier on the Second World War battlefields. Similarly, they offer otherwise unobtainable information on anti-war activities by conscientious objectors, passive resistance, sabotage, or outright mutiny within the forces. Portelli has also studied the wartime refugees behind the battlefronts, living off the little they could steal. He suggests that war especially highlights the essence of oral historical work, contrasting the public history of wars, of victorious nations, with private tragedies, above all in the deaths of husbands, wives, and children:

they are the price paid for this victory they do not share, and they are its meaning. [Recognizing] the indissoluble bond between 'history' and personal experience, between the private unique and solitary spores of sorrow in houses, kitchens, and anguished memories, and the historian's perception and reconstruction of broad, public historical events . . . the task and theme of oral history, an art dealing with the individual in social and historical context, is to explore this distance and this bond.

In this spirit in *Anzac Memories* Alastair Thomson subtly shows the relationship between celebratory Australian public memories and the sometimes bitterly painful recollections of battle veterans. And Portelli himself in *The Battle of Valle Giulia* includes an exploration of the 'divided memory' of Civitella, a hill village in Tuscany, where in June 1944 the retreating German army massacred all of its men in reprisal for three Germans shot by the Partisans. Yet in the midst of this pro-Partisan and Communist-voting countryside the surviving women and children of the village have always blamed the

Partisans for their losses, rather than the German army, and over time have added stories of their heroic (anti-Communist) priest offering his life for those of the village men, and of an anonymous former German soldier returning to express his repentance, in contrast to the continuing public triumphalism of the ex-Partisans.[21]

The implications of European wars and politics of course extend far beyond domestic events, especially obviously in the case of Britain, which in the early twentieth century was an imperial power controlling a quarter of the world's surface and a colonial population of some 400 million people. One type of oral history work responding to this imperial context has focused on the colonial administration or the white settler population. Thus the Cambridge South Asian Archive focused on imperial rule in India, the Oxford Colonial Records Project on Africa. The fascination of a broader type of colonial social history was strikingly shown through Michael Mason's radio programmes on the British in India, and their printed sequel, Charles Allen's *Plain Tales from the Raj*. Through them, as in no other way, one may enter the strange, caste- and class-ridden world of the imperial white elite: the messes and homes of the officers and soldiers of the Indian army, the pilots of the Calcutta river, the 'heavenborn' of the Indian Civil Service, their brothels, mistresses, and 'Memsahib: the Wives and Daughters of the Raj'.[22]

The other side of the story concerns the people who were themselves colonized. We have seen how in the Americas there has been a long tradition of life-story work with indigenous peoples by anthropologists, as well as more political oral auto-biographical *testimonios*; a notable recent example is the story of Gregorio, a Quecha Indian. There is continuing oral history work with American and Canadian Indians, and also with Australian Aborigines. In Africa and Asia, by contrast, individual voices from among the colonized have been much rarer, no doubt in part because the European anthropologists who followed the colonizers lacked the American interest in life-stories. Thus early oral autobiographies such as James Freeman's

Untouchable, Indian outcaste, labourer, and pimp, or *Kiki*, child in a New Guinea village of cannibals, or Mary Smith's *Baba of Karo*, the personal story of a Muslim Hausa woman in purdah and her marriages, divorces, and co-wives, remained as unusual as they were outstanding. Hence recent work such as Tim Keegan's *Facing the Storm* on sharecropping families in the South African highveld, or Pat Caplan's *African Voices* on a Tanzanian smallholder and Islam, are both innovative in giving full voice to their subjects.[23]

In Africa especially, however, both for political and social history, oral sources play a crucial role. Documentation, although certainly present, is much less prolific than that of societies which became literate earlier, while oral source material is abundant. It has been systematically used by historians of Africa since the 1950s, with an increasingly sophisticated methodology, including the development of special techniques for the establishing of chronologies of oral traditions which quite often reach back to the sixteenth century, and in some cases still further. At first these traditions were understood essentially as orally transmitted documents, most valuable when they had survived intact from the remote past, so that the method required formal historical traditions and was more effectively used for the political history of relatively strongly organized African kingdoms, particularly in the period preceding their nineteenth-century colonization. Increasingly interest has shifted to the process by which oral traditions are varied and reassembled over time, and therefore to more diffused local political systems, where the very contradictions in the oral traditions of different communities or families provide the clues from which past political struggles and migration movements can be worked out. David Cohen's *Womunafu's Bonafu* and John Lamphear's *The Traditional History of the Jie* are remarkable histories of small forest and hill peoples in Uganda reconstructed in this way, while Paul Irwin's *Liptako Speaks* equally deftly exploits the contradictions in what he learnt among a savannah people on the upper Niger. The symbolic and social interpretation of origin myths has brought new meanings from them too, not only from an anthropologist like Steven Feierman in his *The Shambaa Kingdom*, but also from historians like Roy Willis, who in his *A State in the Making* pins the Fipa myth to the moment when these mountain Tanzanians shifted from slash and burn to compost agriculture. Perhaps the sheer ingenuity required to establish the elementary patterns of settlement and political power in pre-colonial Africa from oral sources diverted energies from exploiting their equal potential for the development of recent African social history, but the balance is now shifting, with oral history interviewing used by historians studying environmental, religious, and family history. An important influence has been the work of Terence Ranger in his research on nationalism and social change in Zimbabwe.[24]

This slowness in listening to what local people really had to say also left its mark on environmental understanding. Given the strong influence of environmental movements in North America and Europe in the last thirty years, the growth of oral history projects concerned with local issues has been perhaps surprisingly slow. One early exception is Kai Erikson's account of a mountain community's reaction to a flood disaster caused by a burst dam. There are also now a growing number of studies of Western activists, ranging from Canadian Greens, Englishmen in the Amazon, and animal rights militants, to the loose anarchistical nomadic American group who celebrate provocatively in the forests, known as the Rainbow Family of Living Light. Equally striking, however, has been the growth of environmental oral history work in the Third World. Sometimes this is linked to development and aid work, like *At the Desert's Edge* which brings together local memory and traditional expertise of farming in the challenging semi-arid Sahel; sometimes to history, and sometimes to ecological research. A particularly striking conclusion was reached by Melissa Leach and James Fairhead in their ecological work in Guinea, where, by combining participant observation with aerial photographic and oral history evidence, they were able to show that the colonizers had completely misinterpreted the jungle landscape. They had assumed that areas of partial forests were relics of full forest

cover resulting from slash and burn agriculture, and with this
conviction they set out to protect the local environment by
taking control from the locals, whom they blamed for declining
rainfall, and they even imposed the death penalty for bush fires.
Yet as Leach and Fairhead convincingly demonstrate, the locals
were far better environmentalists than the colonizers had
imagined, for they had been settling outside the full forest
rather than within it, and they had been extending rather
than diminishing it by planting trees round their settlements.
The villagers saw their landscape 'as half-filled and filling with
forest, not half-emptied and emptying of it'; in short, the colonizers, imposing their presumptions without listening, had been
'reading forest history backwards'.[25]

Yet it is above all in social history, to which we now turn, that
the relevance of oral evidence is most inescapable. My own *The
Edwardians: The Remaking of British Society* was originally
conceived as an overall reassessment of the social history of
the period, rather than a field-work venture. But I fairly soon
discovered that although there was a wealth of printed publications from the early twentieth century, including numerous
government papers, and some pioneering sociological studies,
much of what I wished to know was either treated from a single,
unsatisfactory perspective, or altogether ignored. Manuscript
material could not fill these gaps because where normally accessible it simply enlarged on the bureaucratic perspectives already
available in the printed sources. It was too recent a period for a
satisfactory range of more personal documents to have reached
the county record offices. I wanted to know what it was like to
be a child or a parent at that time; how young people met and
courted; how they lived together as husbands and wives; how
they found jobs, moved between them; how they felt about work;
how they saw their employers and fellow-workers; how they
survived and felt when out of work; how class-consciousness
varied between city, country, and occupations. None of these
questions seemed answerable from conventional historical
sources, but when Thea Vigne and I began to collect the evidence
of, eventually, some 500 interviews, the richness of information

available through this method was at once apparent. Indeed, much more was collected than could be exploited in a single book, so that in the end *The Edwardians* became as much a beginning as a conclusion, and the interviews collected for it have already provided an archival resource for many other historical studies. Nevertheless the book does indicate something of the overall scope of oral sources for social history. Interviews provided a pervasive background to the interpretations; they were cited in all but two of twenty-two chapters; and some sections, particularly on the family, rely heavily on direct quotation. Equally important, as an antidote to the simplifications of an overall outline of social structure, I was able to present fourteen accounts of real Edwardian families, drawn from a range of classes and places over Britain, but obstinately individual—'the untidy reality upon which . . . both theoretical sociology and historical myth rest'.[26]

The field-work for *The Edwardians* was on a scale so far unusual, and in one respect for the moment unique: the choice of informants was guided by a 'quota sample', so that the men and women recorded broadly represent the regions, city and country, and occupational social classes of early twentieth-century Britain as a whole. Such a research plan is clearly not within the means of an individual scholar. The characteristic contribution of oral evidence has thus been not the essay in general social history, but the monograph, in various distinctive areas.

Let us take first rural social history. We have already seen how the way here was led by George Ewart Evans. His books are in their special way unsurpassable: direct yet subtle intertwinings of agricultural and economic history with cultural and community studies, portraits of individuals, and stories. In one work he may explore the social structure of an 'open' Suffolk village like Blaxhall of *Ask the Fellows Who Cut the Hay*, or contrast it with the paternalistic Helmingham of *Where Beards Wag All*. In another, with the eye of an anthropologist, he will suggest the significance of some superstition or tale concerning animals, or an odd dress custom like the 'breeching' of boys on leaving behind the long hair and petticoats of infancy. Perhaps best of all is his feeling for the life and the speech of the East Anglian farm labourer. Now and then he will point to the very particular quality of popular language: its syntax, its humour, its directness; and there is always the same care shown in his transcripts. In all these ways he set an exacting standard for what has become one of the best-known areas for oral history. It is perhaps hardly surprising that when Ronald Blythe's *Akenfield: Portrait of an English Village* made an international literary success of Suffolk oral history, it was with less careful scholarship. Despite its title, *Akenfield* consists of life-stories from several villages rather than a portrait of a single community; while in detail not only the language of the transcripts, but even its attachment to particular informants, cannot be trusted. But if as a model for sociology or history *Akenfield* cut too many corners, it proved indisputably successful in popularizing a new form of rural literature, a cross between the interview documentary and the novel. Nor can there be any doubt that oral evidence constitutes its real strength. Thus although the book opens with an idyll of cottages around the parish church, the hard reality of a village labourer's life at once breaks through with the first section of recollections by the older farm workers. It also becomes possible to see the community from conflicting standpoints, both of generation and of class, as one hears in turn farm labourer and farmer, vicar and gravedigger, Tory magistrate and Labour agent. Above all, it succeeds through the immediacy with which the spoken word confronts a reader with the presence of the people themselves.[27]

Akenfield has therefore, despite particular—and avoidable—defects, proved a stimulus to oral history for essentially the right reasons. Subsequently, through offering authentic voices from the Italian and the French peasantry, Nuto Revelli in *Il mondo dei vinti (The World of the Defeated)* and Pierre Jakez Hélias in *Le Cheval d'orgueil (The Horse of Pride)* have likewise fired the imagination in their own countries. And *Akenfield* has been followed by other community studies, often pushing rural history well beyond the concerns which were possible when only documentary evidence was employed. Raphael Samuel's fine study of Headington Quarry concerns a squireless hamlet of migrant farm workers, diggers, builders, pedlars, poachers, and washerwomen which is largely undocumented just because it was so egalitarian and ill-controlled, but, he argues, an essential and far from uncommon element in the nineteenth-century rural social economy. Oral evidence also allows a much fuller treatment of women in rural history. Mary Chamberlain's *Fenwomen* is a village study, influenced by *Akenfield*, but drawn entirely from the evidence of women, and again revealing an often harsh reality in a community in which 'men were the masters': in family and school, courtship and childbirth, chapel and village society, in service, whether in the kitchens, or out weeding on the windswept black-earth fields. Here again, the use of oral sources brings at once a new dimension to history.[28]

All these examples come from the southern and eastern countryside of England: the region of arable farming and hired labourers. The family-farm regions of the north and west attracted scholars concerned for oral evidence much earlier: collectors of literature and folklore, especially in Wales, Scotland, and Ireland, but also sociologists and anthropologists. The result was a series of outstanding community studies from C. M. Arensberg and S. T. Kimball's *Family and Community in Ireland* (1940) onwards, all based on oral field-work. Two of the most stimulating are W. M. Williams's successive books on *The Sociology of an English Village: Gosforth* in Cumbria and the Devon village of *Ashworthy*. In the first, his emphasis is on the recent erosion of a traditional, stable social system; but in the second he argues that rural society was always in flux, readjusting from external pressures, economic, technological, or political, as well as from the rise and fall of individuals and their families. James Littlejohn's *Westrigg* is also particularly relevant, because it provides a successful model for a community oral history as an alternative to *Akenfield*: a very effective analysis of the changes in local class-structure during the past sixty years, as farmers have bought their own holdings from the old landowning class, and the former dominance of the sheep-farming economy of the Scottish borders has given way before the advance of forestry. And in another study, Ian Carter seeks to explain why farm workers in north-east Scotland, in contrast to their English equivalents, were not deferential in their social attitudes—yet failed to unionize. Subsequently social historians of these regions took up oral sources too. In the Scottish Highlands, for a social history of the island of Tiree, Eric Cregeen used oral sources not only as his major evidence for the beliefs and customs of the people, and for their accounts of the conflicts between the landowner and his factor and the community of crofters, and to balance the documents of an agriculturally 'improving' landlord with the continuing working system on the land; but more astonishingly to build up a picture of personalities, family relationships, occupations, and migrations from the *mid*-nineteenth-century, with the result that the bare listings of the 1851 census are not merely enriched and interconnected, but given a time dimension, so overcoming one of their most serious limitations as historical evidence. David Jenkins was also able to draw on some remarkably detailed oral information for his *The Agricultural Community in South West Wales at the turn of the Twentieth Century*, allowing him to construct a meticulous and stimulating account of a local system of the division of labour and status which included, besides the wage-relations normal between farmers and servants, a type of 'work-debt' or labour service at the corn harvest taken in return for the provision of cottage potato-land.[29]

The potential impact of oral evidence is equally strong if we turn from rural to urban history. Here, however, at first it generally produced new source material, rather than new forms of analysis. An exception was Richard Hoggart's classic study of the impact of magazines, films, and the other mass media on the culture and moral relationships of the working-class city community. *The Uses of Literacy* draws heavily on Hoggart's own recollections over forty years of a childhood in northern England. It is more explicitly oral history—one chapter is headed 'An Oral Tradition: Resistance and Adaptation: A

Formal Way of Life'—in its attempt to examine working-class speech conventions in relation to social change. Hoggart's influence here, however, through his emphasis on the limitations of working-class speech, proved as much a handicap as a help, and still has its ramifications in oral history. It provided an explanatory theme for Jeremy Seabrook's depressing studies of the prejudice and narrowness of the urban working classes, *The Unprivileged* and *City Close-Up*. Both of these were partly historical, the first an autobiographical family view from Northampton, the second from the northern mill-town of Blackburn; and if a useful counter to cosy romanticism, they seem too much shaped by bitter comment and tendentious interviewing by the author. Hoggart's negative interpretation of working-class speech was also taken up by educationists such as Basil Bernstein. But much more typical of urban oral history work was the local community history, often combining photographs with testimonies, which have proved successful local publications in cities as diverse as Brighton and Manchester, Boston and Buenos Aires.[30]

There have, however, been special difficulties in moving from 'voices from within' to a successful interpretation of urban oral history. This is partly because urban history has concentrated on the big cities, and here the community study makes least sense, because even when a neighbourhood can be identified with distinctive boundaries, its people will almost invariably look beyond it for work, services, and definitions of their place in the city's social structure. One solution, to take a single block or street and follow the movements of all its people inwards and outwards, has been followed by Jerry White with notable success in two books, *Rothschild Buildings* and *The Worst Street in North London*, one on an East London Jewish tenement court and the other on a street of casual labourers and petty thieves, deprived families, and common lodging-houses. He has a sense of physical and social space rare among historians, which provides a firm foundation for each book; and through the framework of local economy, policing, welfare, and culture, he deftly weaves the individual and family lives of each of these tiny corners of the great city. The result is a microcosm of the metropolis: a compelling new model for urban history. An alternative, but more illustrative, approach is the portrait of a neighbourhood, of which the most convincing example is Studs Terkel's classic in the Chicago sociological tradition, *Division Street: America*. This was conceived around his own boyhood in Chicago's Near North Side, where his mother ran a rooming house for single men. But he found that his search for 'a cross-section of urban thought' could no longer be confined to a single neighbourhood, and it grew into a hunt across the entire city: 'with the scattering of the species, it had to be in the nature of guerrilla journalism'. His people talk about both their past and the present; family, ambitions, work, politics; and they are men and women of all ages: black and white homeowners and home-makers from the window-washer to the aristocrat; archi-tects and ad-men, craftsmen, the hot-dog man, the men's mag girl; the Republican precinct captain cab-driver, bar landladies and the police; and the migrants—Appalachians, the Puerto Rican nightwatchman, the Greek pastry-shop owner, Jesus Lopez the steelman. *Division Street*, vibrant with the class, racial, and cultural variety of that struggling city, is undoubt-edly one of the masterpieces of oral history.[31]

The great cities have drawn the attention, if only because their social problems have been the most acute: but the majority of people continue to live in the smaller towns. Although much more manageable subjects for community studies, sociologists and oral historians have so far taken little interest in them. The most brilliant insights have come as chance by-products: a factory portrait such as *Amoskeag* also gives us an American company town, a single life like *The Dillen* the underworld of Stratford-on-Avon. Most recently, in *Tales of the City* Ruth Finnegan focuses on different kinds of narratives about a New Town of the 1960s, contrasting the heroic stories of town planners, and the media disaster tales of its artificiality and soullessness, with local residents' accounts of its humanity and ordinariness. But the pioneering series of sociological studies from the 1920s by the Lynds of America's *Middletown* and Margaret Stacey's much later *Tradition and Change: A Study of Banbury* have had few followers; and while local small town histories exist drawing on interview evidence, there have been few of distinction. This alone made Melvyn Bragg's oral history of Wigton in Cumbria, *Speak for England*, an important landmark. The social change in this part-agricultural and part-industrial town is set out through the voices of a cross-section of its people: miners and farmers, dog breeders and pigeon fanciers, councillors, schoolteachers, housewives, and shop-keepers. There are patchwork sections on particular periods: the Edwardian days dominated by the Big House on the hill with its peacocks; the young men who went to the First World War to fight under colonels who called them 'rubbish' and returned to the bewildered disillusionment and unemployment of the 1920s; the beginning of better times for many ordinary people at the end of the 1930s, and the subsequent post-Second World War move towards much greater comfort, security, and leisure. Another section focuses on Wigton's chief factory, from its first keen pioneers to a present in which the labour organizer has become personnel manager, and a disillusioned shop-floor worker can harangue the 'rat-race' of 'snakes', while a pro-moted apprentice finds his way round the problems of eating his first managerial lobster. There is also a set of eight much fuller individual lives. They include such characters as Dickie Lowther, semi-crippled ex-valet to the aristocracy, griffon-breeder, Scoutmaster, and ritualist. But in significant contrast to the city oral history, the tones of Wigton are generally less spectacular. The quiet push of working-class people towards improvement which they document is perhaps thus all the more significant for the urban historian.[32]

Some of the most telling sections of *Speak for England* con-cern the social history of culture—religion, education, language and folklore, music and leisure. This is another area in which the use of oral evidence has made a considerable impact. I have referred earlier to work on the social history of religion. In the history of education the major contribution has been made by sociologists, such as Brian Jackson and Dennis Marsden in their classic *Education and the Working Class*, based on life-story interviews from their own town of Huddersfield. Equally important, and very much on its own, is Iona and Peter Opie's *The Lore and Language of School Children*, which revealed an astonishing historical depth of oral tradition surviving in the contemporary school playground. Oral traditions and stories are a common element in dialect studies, which have gradually shifted from their earlier concentration on rural communities, most notably in the United States, where there has been a strong interest in urban language and oral modes since the 1970s. As a result, studies of urban folktales and folklore and even folk preaching have been added to the already numerous publications concerning rural superstitions, storytelling, and crafts. Of these rural studies, two classics are Henry Glassie's *Passing the Time in Ballymenone*, and the imaginative blend of social history, folklore, and anthropology offered by George Ewart Evans and George Thomson's *The Leaping Hare*.[33]

There is also a well-developed scholarship in the study of music and folk-song. Here, thanks especially to the work of Edward Ives in New England, we now have not only studies of traditional song and its general historical context, but also social and musical biographies of individual singers. At the same time, researchers have turned their interests to relatively new elements in popular culture, such as the northern industrial bands portrayed by Brian Jackson and Dennis Marsden in *Working Class Community*. Since such leisure activities rarely leave many records, they cannot be seriously examined without oral evidence. There have been oral history studies of many particular leisure forms and activities, including fairs, bands, and baseball, and also of the role of the public house. And Andrew Davies has provided a notable overview of inner-city urban culture in his *Leisure, Gender and Poverty*, in which he emphasizes how much more restricted women's leisure was than men's. Women had less time and less money to spend, and their presence in the pubs was only ambivalently accepted. This was why the advent of the cinema as a new acceptable recreation for women with or without friends and family offered such a crucial new freedom.[34]

Leisure almost inevitably, whether as a means of courting to the unmarried, or of escape from home to public house of the married man, points towards family history. Here the impact of oral evidence has been especially important, enabling the historian to consider critical questions which were previously closed. The potential was first demonstrated by anthropologists and sociologists. Oscar Lewis's deeply moving portraits of Mexican families, such as *The Children of Sanchez*, became rightly famous. Many of the most notable community studies have been as much concerned with family, as titles such as *Family and Community in Ireland, Family and Kinship in East London* or *The Family and Social Change* demonstrate; and these, like the family sociology of Lee Rainwater's accounts of American working-class marriage in *And the Poor Get Children*, also depend on rich life-story evidence.[35]

It was the almost complete absence of earlier testimony of this kind from ordinary people which allowed leading family historians to propagate the very condescending notion that love between parents and children or between married couples was a novel, 'modern' development of the last two centuries. This view has collapsed with the more recent cumulation of evidence. One rare early glimpse of the intimacies of everyday family life in the Middle Ages, was reconstructed by Le Roy Ladurie from the testimonies of shepherd families in the Pyrenean hamlet of *Montaillou* who were being investigated for heresy; while Martine Segalen, drawing on the rich French archives of folk traditions, has powerfully argued against misreadings of proverbs and customs and reasserted the crucial importance of love in French peasant family relationships. The lack of similar archival evidence in Britain meant that in his influential attempt to disentangle the causes for the declining size of middle-class families in late nineteenth-century Britain, *Prosperity and Parenthood*, J. A. Banks could only cite the opinions of medical specialists, novelists, and other writers, yet for all their evidence he was left with 'no idea' whether it could be taken as

'specifically representative of the actions and words' of wider
social groups, or 'how most members of the middle classes . . .
had begun to think'. Historians nevertheless attributed the
spread of family limitation to middle-class influence. Subsequently the oral history work of Diana Gittins on married
life and birth control between the wars showed this assumption
also to be socially condescending. She was able through interviewing to discover why parents chose whether or not to have
children, and how they learnt about the contraceptive means
which they used. She demonstrated that working-class women
got their knowledge from each other at work rather than
through their middle-class contacts, and thus that the diffusion
theory, whereby family limitation was held to have spread to the
working classes through middle-class influence, was seriously
misleading.[36]

Her findings first appeared in a special *Family History Issue*
of *Oral History*, which also included articles on child-rearing,
courtship, and conflict between adults and adolescents. These
aspects of family history have been further developed since, as
in John Gillis's account of courting and marriage ceremonies,
For Better for Worse, and Steve Humphries's provocative explanation of working-class delinquency as a form of family self-
help in *Hooligans or Rebels?* More recently life-story interviews
have shown their subtlety and strength in exploring the consequences of marital break-up and children's experience of
Growing Up in Stepfamilies: highlighting both the pain of loss
and inadequate communication, but also long-term resilience.[37]

The impact of the new evidence is especially powerful in two
directions. The first is the interaction between the family and
the economy. A notable instance, indeed a masterpiece of micro-
history, is *The Seed is Mine*, Charles Van Onselen's painstaking
reconstruction of the life of a South African sharecropper and
his extended migrant family. Equally important has been the
work of Tamara Hareven on the mill people of Manchester,
New England. She was able to demolish another more widespread sociological assumption, that the nuclear family cor-
responds to the needs of industrialized economies, by showing

the continuing effectiveness of the extended family, both as an instrument for migration and the supply of labour over long distances, and as a buffer in crisis. But she builds on other theories to draw out the complex way in which the family and economy interact, and how the relationship between family structure, tensions between generations, and class-consciousness is continually reshaped by the moment in the cycle of economic boom and slump when each generation starts paid work: by the crossing of *Family Time and Industrial Time*. Her book has been a conceptual landmark.[38]

A second, equally fertile theme has been that of relationships between generations. Here earlier sociological research had highlighted the extent of isolation of the old, and this was interpreted as a consequence of the weakening of the extended family. But life-history studies such as *I Don't Feel Old* and *Between Generations*, in which two or three generations in each family were interviewed, have re-emphasized the mutuality of social visiting, caring, and influence. Life-history research on stepfamilies also shows the key role in caring and support provided by grandparents. Equally crucially, through her long-sustained oral history research on three Lancashire towns, in which she has investigated the whole family cycle from childhood through marriage to old age, Elizabeth Roberts has decisively refuted earlier sociological suggestions that the exchange of help within families, including caring for the old, can be explained principally as a calculated response based on self-interest. She shows how help was frequently given where no return was possible, and how the carers, who were above all women, were much more influenced by social values about poverty and independence, and by their affection for those who turned to them in need. Roberts's work is indeed primarily about women; and it leads us directly to women's history.[39]

Here again, the potential of oral evidence is enormous. Women's history was ignored by most historians up to the 1970s, partly because their lives have so often passed undocumented, tied to the home or to unorganized or temporary work. Sheer neglect has given this whole field the excitement of a

voyage of discovery. From the start one strong current has been
the publication of testimonies in order to bring out the hidden
voices of women. Notable early instances include Sherna
Gluck's *From Parlor to Prison* on the lives of American suffragettes, Mary Chamberlain's *Fenwomen*, or the looser collection
in Sheila Rowbotham and Jean McCrindle's *Dutiful Daughters*.
Many of the more recent collections have been from other
cultures: Brazilian, Moroccan, and Egyptian women, Latin
American feminists, or the migrant *Women of Phokeng* in South
Africa. Given the radical aims of these collections, it may seem
surprising that the most popular of most recent women's testimonies has in fact been the confessional tape-recorded life-story
of Princess Diana, published by Andrew Morton as *Her True
Story In Her Own Words*. But Diana was seen as breaking out of
a royal palace silence. She could have fitted into some of these
collections, which range from the very poor to wealthy women.
And a continuing explicit aim of this kind of work has been to
reassert the 'dignity' of women in their varying cultures and
contexts, and to 'break that ancestral silence', whether in the
Middle East or the West.[40]

More interpretative women's oral history has focused especially on four overlapping themes: on work, on war and politics,
and on sexuality. On both sides of the Atlantic there have been a
whole series of studies on women at work—in fields, in factory
assembly lines, in the fishing industry, in domestic service, in
wartime, on the frontier—on which we have already partly
touched. But as essays like those in *Our Work, Our Lives, Our
Words* show, or Anna Bravo's writing on solidarity and loneliness among peasant women, this new history also challenges
basic assumptions about social structure and inequality, gender
roles, the 'nature' of men and women, the roots of power
between them, and the moulding of consciousness through
both home and work.[41]

War has interested women's historians especially as a time of
change, when gender roles could be more flexible as women
replaced men in the factories and fought with them in the
resistance. In *Rosie the Riveter Revisited* Sherna Gluck showed

how the influence of wartime experience depended crucially on the woman's age at the time. Perhaps more surprisingly, the more politicized women who joined the wartime resistance as freedom fighters usually found themselves in a context of continuing clear gender roles, even if for those whose upbringing had been particularly restricted 'the joy of a new literacy and freedom of movement' is especially strongly recalled. Penny Summerfield contrasts two types of women's war narratives: on the one hand the 'heroic' narratives of those who welcomed the war effort, and strove to participate 'as close to the front line as a woman could get'; on the other, the 'stoic' narratives of women who saw war as something to be endured and 'just got on with it'. The stoics, unlike those with heroic memories, did not take up any new opportunities which the war offered, nor did they remember it as changing them personally. Other political studies of women range from Spanish anarchist feminists to the racist *Women of the Klan*. Approaching the Ku-Klux-Klan as a women's historian brought a new perspective on political activism to Kathleen Blee, leading her to contrast the highly publicized roles of men—like night riding, electoral corruption, and gang terrorism—with the quieter but perhaps more influential activities of women, such as consumer boycotts of shops or 'poison squads' spreading rumour and slander: 'traditional (and male-centred) definitions of politics that focus on workplaces, electoral contests, courts, and organized voluntary association ignore the political effects of actions and organizing in neighbourhoods or through kin and informal networks'.[42]

Sexuality has been approached from a number of angles, including the liberating influences of war, and the position of the single umarried woman within the family. There have also been a number of substantial oral history studies of lesbian and gay sexuality. An outstanding instance is the account of working-class lesbians in the bar culture of Buffalo, New York, from the 1930s to the 1960s, *Boots of Leather, Slippers of Gold*, for which the interviews ranged widely, both in terms of ethnicity and of orientation, 'butches' and 'fems', 'rough and tough' and upwardly mobile lesbians. The book maintains, contrary to the usual view that gay liberation originated entirely from middle-class homosexuals, that this working-class bar culture represented a pre-political phase of the liberation movement. Equally striking is Luise White's history of prostitution in Nairobi since the 1920s. She has a broad canvas, relating prostitution to migration, urban housing, labour migration, and family, but at the same time through her interviewing drawing a subtle view of prostitution from the inside, sharply contrasted with the typical outsider depiction of prostitution as degraded social pathology. She shows how, contrary to outsider views, the most prestigious prostitutes were the streetwalkers, *watembezi*, whom the women thought of as faster earners and safer, yet more adventurous, by contrast with *waziwazi* room-girls, or the *malaya*, who would give men a bath, tea, and food, and even an overnight stay: these were seen as too much like passive married women. This evaluation linked with their overall attitudes. There were no pimps in Nairobi, and prostitutes earned well. Many of them became house-owners in the city, or sent back valuable remittances to family farms in the countryside, so that indeed 'the work of prostitutes was family labour'. Thus in contrast to the typical outsider stereotype of prostitutes as social degenerates, helplessly exploited victims condemned to a despicable fate, she found the women proud to have led active and independent lives, and conveying their sense of self-respect and dignity. As Kayaya Thababu, a *malaya* woman from the 1920s, put it, 'At home, what could I do? Grow crops for my husband and father. In Nairobi I can earn my own money, for myself.'[43]

The limitations of written documentation apply equally to other social groups at the margins of power. This is most obvious with deviant subcultures, which sociologists have long explored through collecting life-stories: the Chicago classics run from boy crime in *The Jack Roller* and drug addiction in *The Fantastic Lodge* to *The Professional Fence*. In Britain Tony Parker ranged similarly from the professional thief of *The Courage of His Convictions* to the incompetent institutionalized ex-soldier in *The Unknown Citizen* and the eight sex offenders of

The Twisting Lane. He has also talked to solitary lighthouse-keepers, soldiers, and Northern Irish terrorists. Others have investigated the changing experiences of the police. And the historical insights which can be won through this approach are vividly demonstrated through Raphael Samuel's extraordinary record of the slum childhood and violent criminal adulthood of Arthur Harding in *East End Underworld.*[44]

There have been two forms especially in which the history of minority groups has been influenced by oral evidence. The first is the study of immigration. The example here was provided by the interview field-work of sociologists from the Chicago school onwards, but originally the intention was to examine the problems of immigration as if they constituted a form of social pathology. More recently both sociologists and historians using oral sources have moved towards a more balanced approach in historical work, examining the ordinary experience of immigration, the process of finding work, the assistance of kin and neighbours, the building of minority community institutions, the continuance of previous cultural customs, and the creation of new mixed hybrid cultural forms and identities including mixed marriages, as well as problems of racial tension and discrimination. In particular, oral evidence can explore the images of another country, the local tips and stories, and the receiving network at the other end of the journey, which explain why people do not move randomly, but follow particular migratory paths: so that, for example, nine-tenths of those running Indian restaurants in Britain come from the single town of Sylhet in the Ganges delta. It can also suggest—particularly by setting the direct evidence of personal experience against the generalized message of the community's own oral tradition— how distorted are some of the commonly held explanations of immigrant social patterns in terms of racial or cultural inheritance rather than the simple economics or class factors. It can show how importantly the migration experiences of men and women differ, and how this can be crucial in deciding whether or not to return home. And especially it can explore the role of the web of family connections in migration: the migratory images transmitted between generations—'our family love to travel'—the grandmothers caring for children left back home, or the suffering of a mother who encourages her children to leave, yet cries every day for the loss of them.[45]

The second form is black history: in Britain, perhaps still a branch of the first, but in the United States decidedly distinct. It offers a cluster of outstanding works with which to conclude our exploratory survey of the achievement of oral history. We may usefully at this point step back and ask, what is distinctive about them as history? What do they do which could not otherwise have been done? Three things. First, they penetrate the otherwise inaccessible. They give voice to the great city ghettos of urban America. Paul Bullock's *Watts, the Aftermath* is an account of a mass confrontation in Los Angeles; while Alex Haley's *Autobiography of Malcolm X* has few equals for conveying the bitter richness of city life or as a powerful portrait of an individual leader. They delineate the bitterness of black-white relations in terms of individual lives: Bob Blauner's *Black Lives, White Lives* on northern California, Studs Terkel's *Race*, Chicago-based but more diffuse. Terkel especially brings out the antagonism with which whites thought of blacks: 'I hated them'; 'when the niggers start breakin' in on the neighbourhood, I'm gonna start shooting'; 'negroes, they're animals'. Some of his black informants described prejudice more subtly: 'being Black in America is like being forced to wear ill-fitting shoes'. Nor did the illiterate rural black communities leave records for future historians. William Montell's *The Saga of Coe Ridge* is the leading American example of a serious fully documented community study, by its subject largely dependent on oral evidence: an account of a black colony, settled on a remote hill spur after emancipation from slavery, surviving at first through subsistence farming and lumbering, but degenerating through lethal fights with neighbouring whites over women, and driven as natural resources became exhausted into moonshining and bootlegging, so that eventually it was broken up by the county sheriff's revenue men.

Secondly, where records do exist, oral evidence provides an

essential corrective to them. This is especially true of the old rural South where history matters, as nowhere else in America, because it is employed to justify or deny the claims of white supremacy. It was thus no mere accident that the rich interview material which had been collected in the 1920s and 1930s from former plantation slaves and their dependants remained unused by historians for more than three decades. This has now been remedied, not only by full publication of the slave narratives in eighteen volumes edited by George Rawick—thus constituting the most important collective autobiography yet published— but also by the admirable interpretative essay, *From Sundown to Sunup: The Making of the Black Community*, which constitutes an introductory volume. And similarly, to narrow the focus to a single case study to which we will need to return, Lawrence Goodwin was only able to discover, through oral evidence, the true story deliberately concealed by contemporary newspapers and records of how the white upper class used systematic violence to destroy the inter-racial populism of one Texas county in the 1890s.[46]

Finally, oral evidence can achieve something more pervasive, and more fundamental to history. While historians study the actors of history from a distance, their characterizations of their lives, views, and actions will always risk being misdescriptions, projections of the historian's own experience and imagination: a scholarly form of fiction. Oral evidence, by transforming the 'objects' of study into 'subjects', makes for a history which is not just richer, more vivid, and heart-rending, but *truer*. And this is why it is right to end with Theodore Rosengarten's *All God's Dangers*, the autobiography of Nate Shaw, an illiterate Alabama sharecropper born in the 1880s, based on 120 hours of recorded conversations: one of the most moving, and certainly the fullest, life-story of an 'insignificant' person yet to come from oral history. By fruits such as these, one would gladly see the method judged.[47]

4

Evidence

How reliable is the evidence of oral history? The question will be familiar to any practising oral historian. Our first task here will be to take it at face value, and to see how oral evidence stands up when 'assessed and evaluated in exactly the same way that you evaluate any other kind of historical evidence'. But as we shall see, the question poses a false choice. Oral sources can indeed convey 'reliable' information; but to treat them as 'simply one more document' is to ignore the special value which they have as subjective, spoken testimony.[1] We shall come back to that. But let us first take the question in the straightforward, or sceptical, manner in which it was intended.

We can begin by looking over the shoulder of 'The Historian at Work', as described by Arthur Marwick in his *The Nature of History* (1970). First he lists the 'accepted hierarchy' of sources: contemporary letters, informers' reports, depositions; parliamentary and press reports; social inquiries; diaries and autobiography—the last usually 'to be treated with an even greater circumspection' than the others. In considering these sources, the historian must first ensure that the document is authentic: that it is what it purports to be, rather than a subsequent forgery. Next follows the crucial problem:

How did the document come into existence in the first place? Who exactly was the author, that is, apart from his name, what role in society did he play, what sort of person was he? What was his purpose in writing it? For example, an ambassador's report . . . may send home the kind of information he knows his home government wants to hear . . . Does a tax return give a fair account of real wealth, or will there not be a tendency on the side of the individual to conceal the extent of his possessions . . .?

Or in using 'an exciting on-the-spot account' from an author or newspaper reporter, 'how can we be certain that in fact he ever left his hotel bedroom? These, and many others, are the sort of questions historians must ask all the time of their primary sources: they are part of his basic expertise.'[2] We may note that the authors of documents, like historians, are assumed to be male. More importantly, many of the questions which have to be asked of the documents—whether they might be forgeries, who was their author, and for what social purpose were they produced—can be much more confidently answered for oral evidence, especially when it comes from a historian's own field-work, than for documents. But little indication is given of how any of these questions, either of identification or of bias, can be answered. It is only in the case of medieval forgery that a specific expertise is mentioned. Otherwise the historian's resources are the general rules in examining evidence: to look for internal consistency, to seek confirmation in other sources, and to be aware of potential bias.

These rules are in practice less observed than they should be. The oral historian has a considerable advantage here, in being able to draw on the experience of another discipline. Social investigators have long used interviews, so that there is an abundance of sociological discussion on the interview method, the sources of bias in it, and how these may be estimated and minimized. Discussion of the bias similarly inherent in all written documentation is by comparison sparse. There are few guides to be found to the faults in any of the modern historian's favourite quarries.

Newspapers present a characteristic example. Few historians would deny the bias in contemporary reporting or accept what the press presents at face value, but in using newspapers to reconstruct the past much less caution is normally shown. This is because they are rarely able to unravel the possible sources of distortion in old newspapers. We may know who the owner was, and perhaps identify his political or social bias, but whether the normally anonymous contributor of a particular piece shared that bias can scarcely ever be more than guessed. Thus the evidence which historians cite from newspapers suffers not only from the possibility of inaccuracy at its source, which is normally either an eyewitness account or an interview report by the journalist. It is also selected, shaped, and filtered through a particular, but to the historian uncertain, bias. For example, when Bonar Law made his famous speech to a vast Conservative rally at Blenheim Palace in July 1912, declaring he would support Ulster in resisting Irish Home Rule by force, there were slight differences in the reports of the exact words which he chose to use in its key phrases. These reporting differences may have been accidental or intended. Not all modern historians use the version which *The Times* printed next morning. Nor, however, is it the custom to point out such variants, even in a book of 'documents', or a biography of Bonar Law.[3] This instance tells us more about the historian's normal practice than its consequences, because the historical effect of Bonar Law's words was more through the newspaper reports than through their direct impact at Blenheim. But another example may show how newspaper evidence can be systematically misleading as well as inaccurate. Lawrence Goodwin has used newspapers and other written sources in combination with interviews in a political study of a county of East Texas, in which a whites-only Democratic party ousted the inter-racial Populists from power in the 1890s. It was impossible to tell from the local Democratic press either how this happened or indeed how the Populists had maintained support in the first place, and who most of their political leaders had been. Goodwin was able to discover three separate oral traditions from different political standpoints in the community which, when linked with press reports, showed that the Democratic countercoup had been based on a systematic campaign of murder and intimidation. Not only had the newspaper deliberately omitted the political significance of what it did report, but some of the 'events' reported had not happened and were published as part of the intimidation. One politician who was reported dead, for example, in fact escaped his murderers and lived another thirty years.[4] But Goodwin's refusal to rely on newspaper evidence is rare among historians—and it has an interesting basis, as in an earlier career he was a journalist himself.

Most historians would feel themselves closer to the heart of things with correspondence. Certainly letters have the advantage of often being the original communication itself. But this does not free them from the problem of bias, or ensure that what letters say is true, or even conveys the real feelings of the writer. They are in fact subject to the kinds of social influence which have been observed in interviews, but in an exaggerated form, because a letter is rarely written to a recipient who is attempting to be neutral like an interviewer. Yet historians rarely stop to consider how far a particular letter has been shaped by the writer to meet the expectations of its envisaged recipient, whether a political enemy or a political friend, or a lover, or perhaps even the tax inspector. And if this is true of letters, it is much more so of such other primary sources as paid informers' reports, or depositions—the statements of evidence made in anticipation of a possible court hearing.

Printed autobiographies are another very commonly cited source. Here the problems of reliability are more generally acknowledged. Some are shared with the life-history oral interview. In A. J. P. Taylor's view, 'Written memoirs are a form of oral history set down to mislead historians' and are 'useless except for atmosphere'.[5] But they lack some of the advantages of the interview, for the author cannot be cross-questioned, or asked to expand on points of special interest. The printed autobiography is a one-way communication, its form usually following the conventions of a literary genre and its content selected with the taste of the reading public in mind. It cannot be confidential. If it is intimate, it is more in the self-conscious, controlled manner of an actor on the stage or in a film. As a public confession, it rarely includes anything which the author feels really discreditable. In those cases when it is possible to compare a confidential interview with a life-story written for publication, there seems a consistent tendency to omit some of the most intimate detail, to forget the trouble with unruly children further down the street, for example, which can be much more revealing than the rosy generalization that 'Children had more respect for their elders then'. Nevertheless, just because it is is printed rather than recorded on tape, many historians would feel happier citing a published autobiography than an interview.

Many of the classic sources for social historians, such as the census, registrations of birth, marriage, death, public inquiries such as Royal Commissions, and social surveys like those of Booth and Rowntree, are themselves based on contemporary interviews. The authoritative volumes of Royal Commissions rest on a method which was shaky even when a Francis Place or a Beatrice Webb was not at work manipulating witnesses behind the scenes. They used a peculiarly intimidating form of interview, in which the lone informant was confronted by the whole committee—just like a widow seeking out-relief who faced the Board of Guardians.

Most basic social statistics are also derived from human exchanges and consequently rarely offer a simple record of mere facts. Émile Durkheim believed, when he wrote his classic study of *Suicide*, that it was possible to treat 'social facts as things': as immutable, absolute truth. But it is now accepted that the suicide statistics which he used vary as much with the degree to which suicide was regarded as a social disgrace to be covered up, as with the rate at which people killed themselves.[6] Similarly we know—from other, retrospective interviews—that the marriage registers of the late nineteenth and early twentieth century grossly underestimate the marriage rates of those younger age groups who should have obtained parental consent to marry. Those who thought their parents might object simply misstated their ages to the registrars. The later figures show that the younger true rates were *double* those recorded at the time. Very much in the same way, in the 1990s when the National Child Development Study's cohort, who had been followed from their birth in 1958, were reinterviewed at the age of 33, the results showed up twice as many retrospectively remembered instances of parental separation or divorce in their childhood as could be traced from re-examining the earlier interviews: a clear reflection of the degree of shame which had been felt during their childhoods by their parents.[7]

Other statistics turn out, on closer investigation, to be equally influenced by social attitudes of their period. Food statistics, such as those of the consumption of different kinds of fish, were distorted by the need to market new types of fish under old names: it was common practice, for example, to sell cat-fish, weaver, task, or gurnett as haddock or filleted haddock. Figures for the proportion of the workforce which was skilled show startling discrepancies which are only explicable as social points of view: thus the census statistics, based on self-report, have remained high and slightly rising while those from employers' returns have plummeted. Similar problems affect even the recording of physical facts such as housing. The census definition of 'a room', used for measuring overcrowding, was a social one, which determined the exclusion of sculleries, and how substantial a partition was required before one room was counted as two. But social historians, perhaps because they have come to statistics relatively recently, much too easily fall into Durkheim's trap of treating them as 'things'.

This is true even of historical demography. Here surely, one might hope to find historians dealing with hard facts. But take the table of 'Completed Family Size By Year of Marriage' from 1860 to 1960 confidently printed by E.A. Wrigley in his *Population and History*. This is based on various sets of retrospective interviews with mothers, and assumes their accuracy in remembering the number of live births which they had. But no allowance is made for the numbers of those children born who died in infancy or early childhood, so that the table does not measure the average number of children actually reared—the 'completed size' of family as experienced by its members. Because of high child mortality, the average size of family before 1900 was much smaller than the table suggests, and never actually as high as the so-called mean completed family size of the tabulation. In other words, 'completed family size' is a demographer's abstraction, not a social or historical fact. Statistically minded historians and sociologists have ignored this. They have displayed no awareness that while the trend in the table is beyond dispute, the actual figures—however critical for population studies—are not. They are estimates, which have been subject to significant revisions in recent years by the Registrar-General, even for the years before 1914.

Social statistics, in short, no more represent absolute facts than newspaper reports, private letters, or published biographies. Like recorded interview material, they all represent, either from individual standpoints or aggregated, the *social perception* of facts; and are all in addition subject to social pressures from the context in which they are obtained. With these forms of evidence, what we receive is *social meaning*, and it is this which must be evaluated.

Exactly the same caution ought to be felt by the historian faced, in some archive, by an array of packaged documents: deeds, agreements, accounts, labour books, letters, and so on. These documents and records certainly do *not* come to be available to the historian by accident. There was a social purpose behind both their original creation and their subsequent preservation. Historians who treat such finds as innocent deposits, like matter thrown up on a beach, simply invite self-deception. It is again necessary to consider how a piece of evidence was put together in the first place. Thus, for example, official information from School Board and County Council records does not suggest that women teachers were required to resign on marriage before the 1920s, when this became an official policy; but thereafter, records this as the consistent practice. Yet individual life-stories document quite frequent requests to resign on marriage before 1914, as well as appointments of married women to posts during the operation of the bar. The official reports of the Poor Law Commissioners of the Labour Migration Scheme of the 1830s can similarly be shown, through alternative sources, to have grossly exaggerated the figures for the numbers of paupers removed, and to have quite falsely claimed that all of those removed had found work, in order to suggest that the scheme was succeeding.[8]

At another level, even such apparently accidental social documentaries as photographs and films are in fact quite carefully constructed. So much so that, for example, almost *all* the sound background to Second World War film is faked. With photographs, on rare occasions one can discover how for the 'casual' family snapshot, everybody in the picture was forced to change out of their normal clothing. Equally important, social images of 'respectable' or 'happy families' determine what photographs are *taken*. Not merely this, but a similar decision is made about what is *kept* for the album. And the same kind of weeding shapes the public archive. The process of discarding and confusing memories to fit modern needs, which has been identified as a form of genealogical conquest in African tradition, has its equivalent in the systematic, if half-conscious, doctoring of the record sets which is the practice of Western countries. One can only refute, as thoroughly misleading, Royden Harrison's assertion that written archive sources, 'the type of evidence upon which historians set the highest store', possess a special superiority over oral material, because they constitute 'a kind of primary evidence which takes the form of pieces of paper which have been bequeathed to us unintentionally, unselfconsciously; secreted by institutions or by persons in the course of their practical activities'. Contrary to his assertion, this *is* 'a matter of some superstitious prejudice in favour of the written over the spoken word'.[9]

The true distinctiveness of oral history evidence comes from quite different reasons. The first is that it presents itself in an oral form. It is important to remember that the conventional one-to-one interview is but one of a variety of possible oral forms. Drawing in *Narrating Our Pasts* (1993) on her own West African field-work experience, Elizabeth Tonkin has shown how the content and form of memory is strongly influenced by the social context in which it is produced, including particularly the type of performance or genre, and the expectations of the audience. Her call for us to look equally closely at the range of Western contexts of oral communication—from pub stories and funeral reminiscences to academic perorations—indicates a particularly promising new path for oral history work.

Whatever its original context, an oral form of record brings both drawbacks and also advantages. It takes far longer to listen than to read and if the recording is to be cited in a book or article, it will need to be transcribed first. On the other hand, the recording is a far more reliable and accurate account of an encounter than a purely written record. All the exact words used are there as they were spoken; and added to them are social clues, the nuances of uncertainty, humour, or pretence, as well as the texture of dialect. It conveys all the distinctive qualities of oral rather than written communication—its human empathy or combativeness, its essentially tentative, unfinished nature. Because it will remain exactly the same afterwards, a printed text cannot be permanently refuted; that is why books are burnt. But a speaker can always be challenged immediately; and unlike writing, spoken testimony will never be repeated in exactly the same way. This very ambivalence brings it much closer to the human condition. Paradoxically, even through freezing speech in a tape recording—as well as more obviously through transcribing it onto paper—some of this quality is lost. Nevertheless, the tape is a far better and fuller record than can ever be found in the scribbled notes or filled-up schedule of the most honest interviewer, or still less in the official minutes of a meeting. We have seen earlier how the 'doctoring' of official records has become so accepted that even the Cabinet Minutes document less what happened in the Cabinet, than 'what the Civil Service wishes it to be believed happened'. This is equally true at the humblest level of the parish council. George Ewart Evans first became 'sceptical of official records' while he was himself a local councillor. 'Not that there was any blatant inaccuracy . . . But since the time of the meeting so recorded, a selective intelligence had been at work, omitting almost everything that did not contribute to fortifying the main decisions reached.' The result was a set of minutes 'streamlined to the point of appearing to be the record of a different meeting'.[10] In the same way, the notes of the interviewer seek to contribute to the survey's hypothesis, to fill in the blanks in the schedule. Or the record of an 'exchange of views' between politicians is purged of its damaging passages and slips. The uniquely telling accuracy of the recorded tape, as evidence, needs less arguing since first Nixon tripped himself with it over Watergate, and then Princess Diana and Clinton were successively caught by taped phone calls.

Clearly in these instances, since the original communication was oral, the oral recording provides the most accurate document. Conversely, when the original was itself a written communication, as in a letter, that written letter must remain the best record. However, the distinction is commonly less clear, because we communicate through both means. Sometimes a 'sacred' moment defines a particular form as authoritative: the judge pronounces sentence, but the death warrant is signed; the priest says mass from the book, but the international agreement is signed as a treaty. But what of a letter, originally dictated to a secretary, checked through reading back, discovered by a historian in the recipient's private papers, and quoted aloud to students attending a history lecture? Or the private recollections of a person, widely read in recent history, recorded at an interview, transcribed, and returned with written comments? Or the particularly puzzling practices of the lawcourts, where proof is argued out through oral testimony and debate, and written documents are read aloud; yet, quite inconsistently, their own proceedings are never taped, but recorded in paraphrase by a clerk, and judges tend to take more account of written than oral evidence, as if the oral performance was a merely rhetorical drama justifying truths conveyed on paper?[11] Certainly in each case there are both oral and written links in the chain of transmission; and either can modify or corrupt the original. And in none is it obvious which the original document is.

For some historical eras one can be more confident. Thus

even after the Reformation in Europe the principal means of communication was oral. People in general perceived the world as much through the sound of fellow human beings, or animals, and also through smell, as with their eyes. For this era, the document is normally a subsidiary record. With the spread of literacy, and the increasing use of the letter, the newspaper, and the book, the dominant means of communication became the written or printed word. The paper document could then be primary; word of mouth a subsidiary form. Today the printed word has again been displaced by a more powerful means of audio-visual communication, in television and film. The visual-verbal form has thus in turn become subsidiary; and as the telephone has generally replaced the letter, the original in most key exchanges between individuals—the Internet notwith-standing—has become once more the oral communication. There are of course, in each of these stages, differences between social classes, and between subjects of communication. But the main point is that the original of evidence is sometimes oral, and sometimes not, and equally may or may not present itself, after transmutations, in the same form; and neither oral nor written evidence can be said to be generally superior: it depends on the context.

The evidence of oral history is, however, also distinctive in being normally retrospective over a longer time span. This is not because its sources are spoken. On the contrary, the tape recorder makes it possible to take statements during or immediately after an event, while writing almost always demands more of an interval. And most written sources—whether from newspapers, court hearings, Royal Commission interviews, or committee minutes—are also retrospective. Neither contemporary nor historical evidence is a direct reflection of physical facts or behaviour. Facts and events are reported in a way which gives them social meaning. The information provided by interview evidence of relatively recent events, or current situations, can be assumed to lie somewhere between the actual social behaviour and the social expectations or norms of the time. But with interviews which go back further, there is the added possibility of distortions influenced by subsequent changes in values and norms, which may perhaps quite unconsciously alter perceptions. With time we would expect this danger to grow. In the same way, over time the reliance on memory apparently becomes more salient. To understand the extent of these problems we can fortunately turn to the literature of the social psychology of memory, and also of gerontology, for help.

It is generally accepted that the memory process depends on that of perception.[12] In order to learn something, we have first to comprehend it. We learn it in categories, seeing how the information fits together, and this enables us to reconstruct it on a future occasion, or to reconstruct some approximation of what we comprehended. As F. C. Bartlett argued in his pioneering discussion *Remembering* (1932), it is in fact only through this basic process of ordering that the human mind has overcome the tyranny of subjection to chronological memory. If we could not organize our perceptions, we would only be aware of what had most recently happened to us. Immediately after an event it does seem that we can remember a great deal more than later on. For a very short time we have something close to a photographic memory. But this only lasts for a matter of minutes. It is of crucial significance that this first phase is extremely brief. Then the selection process organizes the memory and establishes a durable trace by a biochemical process, fixing changes in the signalling connections between the nerve cells of the brain. Biochemical research on the brain has not only begun to identify these processes, but equally important, has established that human memory is not held in fixed boxes like a computer, but rather as a dynamically alive system operating across quite large areas of the brain. Unfortunately despite its recent rapid advances scientific research has little to tell us about the processes by which memory is recalled, and is therefore not yet able to answer the particular questions which a social scientist would wish to ask about the remembering process. However, a change takes place in the microstructure of the brain, which is certainly capable of resisting gross suppressions of mental activity like anaesthetics. Then, when the material is recovered, some kind of reverse process takes place: another situation is recognized, and the brain picks out the material and to a certain extent reconstructs it.[13]

The process of discarding, which is the counterpart of selection, does continue over time. This clearly presents a problem for oral history. But the initial discarding is by far the most drastic and violent, and it affects any kind of contemporary witness. This can be demonstrated from the few studies over time that exist. Let us consider first an artificial laboratory experiment conducted by Dallenbach with pictures in 1913 (see below). Because it is artificial, like most laboratory tests it provides a poor index of the reliability of social memory. It is nevertheless striking that the number of errors remains more or less stable after the first few days. It suggests what may be a quite typical 'curve of forgetfulness'.

There are comparable findings from more recent Norwegian and American research on patterns of child-rearing, for which mothers have been reinterviewed over periods of up to six years. In each of these studies memory proved least reliable in recalling past attitudes, and best about practical matters such as feeding methods (95 per cent accurate after three years). Even after a few months, a mother's picture of childbirth and early infancy will differ a little from her original account. But when the time span is increased to six years, the inaccuracies show no significant increase. Similarly, for a later stage in life, it is now possible to juxtapose information given by the same person to oral historians over intervals as long as twenty years, and while differences of emphasis can be shown, the degree of consistency is the more notable feature.[14] Most significant, however, is the

Dallenbach's picture experiment, 1913

Fifteen students scrutinized picture and asked sixty questions on details				
Days since saw picture	0	5	15	45
Number questions answered (av)	59	57	57	57
Number wrong answers (av)	8	10	12	13

Source: Ian Hunter, *Memory*, rev. edn. (London, 1964), 175.

conclusion of an experiment devised to test, over a period of almost fifty years, the memories of 392 American high-school graduates for the names and faces of their contemporaries in classes of ninety or more students. They were first given eight minutes to list in unaided 'free recall' the names of all those who belonged to their class. They were then asked to pick, within eight seconds each time, first a series of names of their own classmates out of others; and then, similarly, pictures of their faces; and then, again with time limits, to match names to pictures and pictures to names. The findings are set out below.

It is clear that on all counts the loss of memory during the first nine months is as great as that during the next thirty-four years. Only beyond this do the tests suggest any sharp decline in average memory; and even this may be more due to declining speed in tests timed over seconds, and also to the effect on average performance of 'degenerative changes' among some of those in their seventies. Of equal importance is the finding that for those classmates who were considered friends, *no* decline in accuracy of recall can be traced, even over an interval of more than fifty years. The more significant a name or face, the more likely it is to be remembered; it is the others which a 'very slow forgetting process' gradually discards from the memory.

The memory process thus depends, not only upon individual comprehension, but also upon interest. This is the most likely explanation for the frequently observed tendency in Western

Classmates' names and faces recalled (%)

Time since graduation	Free recall	Name recognition	Picture recognition	Name matching	Picture matching
3 months	52	91	90	89	94
9 months	46	91	88	93	88
14 years	28	87	91	83	83
34 years	24	82	90	83	79
47 years	21	69	71	56	58

Source: H. P. Bahrick, P. O. Bahrick, and R. P. Wittlinger, 'Fifty Years of Memory for Names and Faces', *Journal of Experimental Psychology*, 104/1 (Mar. 1975), 54–75.

societies for women to remember family events better than men. Accurate memory is much more likely when it meets a social interest and need. It has been shown that illiterate Swazis, who might be thought to have particularly good memories because they can write nothing down, are no more capable of remembering messages for Europeans than Europeans are, but when they are asked about the exact descriptions and prices fetched by cattle sold a year previously, they can recite this, while the European who bought the cattle and noted their prices in his accounts cannot. Similarly, an 80-year-old Welshman in 1960 was asked for the names of the occupiers in 1900 of 108 agricultural holdings in his parish, and when his answers were checked against the parish electoral list, 106 proved correct. Reliability depends partly on whether the question interests an informant. It is lack of any intrinsic interest which vitiates many of the early laboratory experiments with memory—as well as some outside it. For example, Ian Hunter describes an experiment in which a meeting of the Cambridge Psychological Society was secretly tape-recorded. A fortnight later all the participants were asked whether they would set down what they remembered happening. On average they remembered under one in ten of the specific points made, and of those which they did recall, nearly half were incorrect. They incorporated statements from other meetings and occasions elsewhere. But the experiment demonstrates not so much the normal unreliability of memory, as the fact that this scholarly group, which relied on written material for its scientific progress, was meeting together chiefly for the social benefits of debate, interaction, and self-exhibition.[15]

Memory is a social as well as an individual process as these instances suggest. Another early but still crucial contribution to present understanding of memory was the work of the French sociologist Maurice Halbwachs in arguing the extent to which individual recollections operate within the framework of a collective memory. In studying well-defined social groups, whether rural villages or urban neighbourhoods or groups at work or an extended family, this is a very fruitful perspective for exploring group consciousness, and where collective perceptions are the issue the accuracy of memory is no longer the main focus. Indeed, as Pierre Nora's impressive multi-volume *Realms of Memory* (1996–8) demonstrates, it is possible to reconceptualize a whole range of historical evidence, from buildings and street names to rites and traditions, so that they become considered primarily as expressions of collective identity. On the other hand, for our purposes here it seems important to warn against any suggestion that collective memory not merely stimulates or influences individual memory, but determines it. Collective memory is not an independent essence and its meanings must always be transmitted by individuals; and in practice the boundaries of most groups, and therefore of their collectivity of memory, are uncertain. The context of remembering is also crucial: in a group situation, such as a local celebration, or a memorial service, or in a pub, collective perspectives of memory are likely to exercise much more power than in more private reflections at home. Thus Alastair Thomson found that among Australian First World War veterans, who were lionized in public as the heroes who had first crystallized Australian identity, some accepted the legend of loyalty, courage, and self-sacrifice, while others felt uncomfortable and inadequate with such images, remembering how often they had been shocked or afraid. Similarly, the essays in *The Myths We Live By* show not only how readily social groups create the myths which they need, but also how even the most powerful and universal myths, such as that of the wicked stepmother, can either be taken up as images to confirm experience, or ignored in the telling of an alternative individual memory.[16]

In any context recalling is always an active process. Bartlett wrote, perhaps with exaggeration: 'In a world of constantly changing environment, literal recall is extraordinarily unimportant. It is with remembering as it is with the stroke in a skilled game. Every time we make it, it has its own characteristics.'[17] He had in mind particularly how a story may be retold differently to various audiences in different situations, and how its recall can be stimulated by remeeting an old acquaintance, or revisiting the scene of some past event. A willingness to remember is also essential: a feature of memory which is especially relevant to interviewing.

Conversely, recall can be prevented by unwillingness: either a conscious avoidance of distasteful facts or unconscious repression. It is of course a particular interest of psychology to revive these suppressed memories through the therapeutic interview. In recent years the reliability of suppressed memories, for example of sexual abuse within the family, have become an important legal controversy. Experiments have shown that it is relatively easy to generate false memories by feeding people with a mixture of genuine and misleading stimulants to memory such as photographs. It seems on balance highly unlikely that the memories recovered through therapy are either all true or all false.[18] But they must be seen as a relatively doubtful source of memory, and it is therefore perhaps fortunate that the potential influence of an oral history interviewer over an informant is so much more muted.

Thus although laboratory experiments have succeeded in establishing the main elements of the memory process, they provide a poor guide to its reliability, because they take place in a social vacuum isolated from the needs and interests which normally stimulate remembering and recalling. One of Bartlett's classic experiments, for example, was to ask a group of ten Cambridge students to repeat to each other, in sequence, a Red Indian tale, 'The War of the Ghosts'. The final version retained no more than a few scraps of the original. But these students had no intrinsic interest in a story from another culture; for them it was just an experiment, whose outcome proved more interesting, as it happened, because of their own lack of accuracy. But there are epic tales among the illiterate peoples of Africa which have been passed down orally for at least 600 years. These tales are subject to variation when the social needs of their tellers and audiences have changed, but can be consistent enough for the original elements to be identified by studying the structure of different versions. And nearer at hand, Iona and Peter Opie have found very remarkable chains of transmission in their study of *The Lore and Language of School Children*.

Because of the very rapid turnover of children in school, the links in the chain of transmission are much shorter than with adult oral traditions, so that a school jingle in 130 years will have passed down twenty generations of children, perhaps 300 tellers—equivalent to more than 500 years among adults. It is extraordinary, in view of this, how much survives. For example, in his *London Street Games in 1916*, Norman Douglas reported 137 child chants, and forty years later the Opies found 108 of them were still being chanted. And among the 'truce terms' used by children—whose accuracy is presumably especially important to them—are words like 'barley' and 'fains' which go back to the Middle Ages. They originated in adult vocabulary, but have been preserved only among children. 'Tiddly Winks the Barber' is a rhyme which children still repeat as it was originally composed in 1878. The Opies have many nice examples of both survival and change.

On rare occasions one can show in an ordinary life-story how a telling phrase has been retained. One of my own first interviews was with Bob Jaggard, an Essex farm worker born in 1882, who started work in 1894 on a farm, leading horses. Early on in the interview he said:

Men got 13 shillings a week and when I started work I went seven days a week for three shillings.

Can you remember at that time whether you thought that was bad or good money?

I knew it was bad money. Yes, they were put on.

Did you feel there was anything you could do about this to get more money at that time?

No, we didn't, that was just that. I can tell you right start, the old farmer what I worked for, he said a man carry a sack of wheat home every Saturday night was thirteen shillings . . .

Later on in Rider Haggard's *Rural England* I discovered that he had visited Bob Jaggard's village, Ardleigh, in 1901. A week's wages by this date had risen by eighteen pence. In Ardleigh he visited a Mr T. Smith, farming 240 acres, who had been there for fifty-one years. 'How could farmers get on', he asked Rider Haggard, 'when each man took the value of a sack of wheat; that is 14s. 6d. per week?'[19] Seventy years after Haggard's visit it was still possible to record the Ardleigh farmer's grumble, stuck in Bob Jaggard's mind.

One can of course match examples of recall with instances of misremembering; and individuals certainly differ in their ability to remember. But let us return to the normal memory process. How far is memory usually affected by increasing age? Young children, from birth up to the age of 4, have very little long-term memory at all. This is followed by a transitional stage up to the age of 11. Many children—more than half—retain a photographic type of memory, and also a great capacity for rote learning of a kind which is very unusual later in life, although it is retained by a small minority of adults. Some psychologists argue that the disappearance of photographic memory is connected with the onset of 'logical' thinking, although there are difficulties in demonstrating this. However, after the age of about 11, and especially after the age of 30, the immediate memory begins to show a progressive decline, so that it becomes increasingly difficult, for example, to retain a whole set of complex numerals in the head. On the other hand, the total memory store is increasing; it is as if one pushes out the other. Studies of vocabulary retention have shown that while for the most intelligent groups there is very little decline at all, for the average group tested a decline of memory sets in by the age of 30 and continues very slowly, but is never drastic before either terminal illness or senility is reached. Thus the problem of memory power is not much more serious for interviews with old people in normal health than it is with younger adults.

With this process of declining power in all adults the recent memory is first affected. Hunter writes: 'If there is, in the elderly person, an impairment of central nervous functioning, this favours recall of earlier as opposed to more recent events. With progressive impairment of a general neurological kind, recalling activities undergo progressive disorganization. That is, recall of recent events is impaired first.' There have indeed been statistical memory tests which, although in some respects methodologically doubtful, do suggest that if word associations are examined, nearly half go back to childhood or youth, and only a very tiny proportion are recent.[20]

The final stage in the development of memory commonly follows retirement, or some other traumatic process, such as widowhood. This is the phenomenon recognized by psychologists as 'life review': a sudden emergence of memories and of desire to remember, and a special candour which goes with a feeling that active life is over, achievement is completed. Thus in this final stage there is a major compensation for the longer interval and the selectivity of the memory process, in an increased willingness to remember, and commonly, too, a diminished concern with fitting the story to the social norms of the audience. Thus bias from both repression and distortion becomes a less inhibiting difficulty, for both teller and historian.

Interviewing the old, in short, raises no fundamental methodological issues which do not also apply to interviewing in general—and consequently to a whole range of familiar historical sources, as well as to those of the oral historian. It is to these issues which we must now turn. We shall explore approaches to interviewing more fully in a later chapter. Our concern here is with the degree of influence which the interview as a social relationship will inevitably have on the material which is collected through it.

The minimization of variance in answers due to differences of style between individual interviewers has long been the aim of social method. In the sociological handbooks this concern is often taken to self-defeating extremes. Ken Plummer, after charting all the possible errors listed, concludes that 'to purge research of all these "sources of bias" is to purge research of human life'. The real aim of the life-history sociologists or the oral historian should be to *reveal* sources of bias, rather than pretend they can be nullified, for instance, with 'a researcher without a face to give off feelings'.[21] But in precisely this sense, there is much we can learn from the experience of survey research. The key issue is how to introduce sufficient standardization without breaking the interview relationship through inhibiting self-expression. One approach has been to begin with a freer form of interviewing in order to explore the variety of responses obtainable, and then to follow up with a standardized survey, in which the exact words of questions and their sequence is predetermined. An alternative is to mix the two methods in each interview, encouraging the informant to free expression, but gradually introducing a standard set of questions in so far as these are not already covered. This protects the interview relationship, but makes the material less strictly comparable.

Since, in contrast to oral history, very little of this large-scale social survey interviewing is recorded, it is difficult to know how exactly interviewers normally follow such survey instructions. The rare tests which have been reported suggest that a third of the questions may be regularly altered in unacceptable ways. In one extreme instance, an experiment was carried out in New York during a survey of racial attitudes. Of the fifty respondents, eight were 'planted', and their interviews were secretly tape-recorded. Fifteen interviewers were employed, none of them full-time professionals. When the recorded interviews were analysed it was found that, out of the fifty questions supposed to be asked, on average each interviewer committed fourteen asking errors (that is, changing or omitting the questions); thirteen probing errors; eight errors when recording the answers on the sheets; and then four simple 'cheats' (that is, putting down an answer when none was given). One planted respondent acted as a 'hostile bigot', a type which could be expected to occur in most random samples. When faced by the bigot, half the interviewers invented half of what they put down on the questionnaire. Clearly this is not the kind of raw material which makes up the typical random sample questionnaire survey, but the experiment does bring home the vulnerability of survey questionnaire interviews. We may well feel that the openly recorded interviews of an oral historian are likely to be as reliable as most conventional survey evidence.[22]

It is certainly also clear that interviewers carry into the interview both their own expectations and a social manner which affect their findings. For example, in one questionnaire survey interviewers asked women whether their husbands helped in purchasing house furnishings. The results differed depending on whether the interviewer's own husband helped or not. Those interviewers helped by their own husbands found this also the case for 60 per cent of their informants, while the other set, whose husbands did not, found only 45 per cent. Some of the pressing and misinterpretation which went into these results would have been revealed in tape-recorded interviewing.[23] There does not seem to be much doubt that much of the 'predictive' reliability of the contemporary social survey rests on the informal workings of both interviewers and analysts, who try to adjust their results towards what they themselves feel are credible conclusions. When nearly all of them are similarly mistaken in their expectations, as in the famous case of the 1948 Truman election victory, it is more likely to be these informal workings rather than defects in the method itself which produce the wrong prediction.

Recording can help to expose and assess this kind of social bias. But the interviewer has a social presence, even when not revealing any explicit opinions which could influence the informant. There is a widely held image of an interviewer as a middle-class woman; and most informants have some idea of what her views are likely to be. This has some advantage, because the consequent bias in response can be more easily allowed for; and it can also be to some extent countered, by showing respect for the informant's own views. But there are interesting consequences when the image is unequivocally altered. Thus American surveys have long recognized that black informants can give substantially different answers to some questions—for example, doubling the likelihood of expressions of social dissatisfaction or criticism—when asked by black rather than white interviewers.[24] A parallel caution between races has been noted in Africa where, Vansina tells us, the White missionaries are expected to be interested in traditions. But they must not be told traditions that go against their teaching, because then they will criticize them, which will harm the prestige of the narrators, and will fight against them, which will harm the whole community.[25] In Europe an interviewer with a strong working-class accent, or a man rather than a woman, can expect to vary the social effect in—one hopes—a less drastic, but comparable manner.

It should be emphasized that it is not necessarily true that an interviewer of the same sex, class, or race will obtain more accurate information. If the social relationship in an interview becomes, or is from the start, a social bond, the danger towards social conformity in replies is increased. Nor does increased intimacy always bring less inhibition. It is remarkable, for instance, how many people, when stopped anonymously in the street by Mass Observation and asked questions about sex, were prepared to answer with a candour which is rare in the most intimate home interview.

The presence of others at an interview also has a marked effect. Boasting and exaggeration may be reduced, but the tendency to conform will be greatly increased. Howard Becker, when interviewing American medical students in groups, found that cynicism was the norm, but in private most students expressed idealistic feelings.[26] Sometimes a group meeting may be helpful, for example in bringing out conflicts in tradition about particular figures in a community's past from informants with different standpoints. And in a more personal interview, a husband or wife sometimes stimulates the other's memory, or corrects a mistake, or offers a different interpretation. An account of the division of domestic responsibilities given in such a situation, however, would usually be much less critical of the other's part. Equally it is noticeable that a group of old people will often emphasize a common view of the past, but if subsequently seen separately much more individual pictures may emerge.

Even when others are not present at the interview itself, their unseen presence outside may count. This is a particularly important influence in any tight-knit community. The insider and outsider have different difficulties here. The insider knows the way round, can be less easily fooled, understands the

nuances, and starts with far more useful contacts and, hope-
fully, as an established person of good faith. All this has to be
learnt and constructed by the outsider who, in the extreme case
of a European student of African history, may not originally
know the language, ethnography, or geography of the community. But there can be good in this too, for the outsider can ask
for the obvious to be explained; while the insider, who may in
fact be misinformed in assuming the answer, does not ask for
fear of seeming foolish. The outsider also keeps an advantage in
being outside the local social network, more easily maintaining
a position of neutrality, and so may be spoken to in true confidentiality, with less subsequent anxiety. The insider's social
situation is brought out by the experience of a student collecting
information on her own Suffolk village. One retired horseman,
explaining 'how hard things was in them days', told of how,
when he had a child a few days old die, he carried the coffin to
the churchyard himself in the early morning but had to pay a
man to bury the child as he was due to start work at 6. Due to
the extra walk he reached work at 6.30,

and in his pay at the end of the week the money had been taken off
for the half-hour he was absent. The son of the farmer who deducted
this money from his pay still farms in the same farm in the village
today and a few days after that interview with the horseman he sent a
message to me to say that he hoped he had not given me an unfa-
vourable impression of the present farmer, as . . . 'times was hard
then just after the (First World) War, there wasn't nothing else he
could do really, can't expect him to pay a man for work he harn't
done'.[27]

Andrew Roberts has emphasized the parallel handicaps of
belonging to an African community:

Relations with the local people may well be more difficult than those of
a white student. In so far as African students have kept up links with
the land of their fathers, they come back to it as a full social personality, far more subject than a mere foreigner to the moral constraints of
the society. If they ignore local custom in the cause of research, they (or
their relations) will have to answer for the consequences. Through the
web of kinship, they may well be caught up in conflicts which cause

people to withhold information they might readily impart to a transitory white visitor. Besides, since independence, African students are rather more likely than whites to be suspected of being agents of central government.[28]

This is the extreme case of the problem, closer to the fieldwork situation of the anthropologist. One suspects that here in the long term the disadvantages of the European outsider may prove decisive. The social codes and layers of expressive meaning have to be penetrated as well as formal language itself. Even the very structure of conceptualization may be fundamentally different, and Western notions of time and space misleading. 'The scholar struggling to understand a foreign culture', Elizabeth Tonkin suggests, 'may eventually realize that what appear to be answers to the question "where did we come from?" are actually explaining "why we are here".'[29] The disadvantage of the insider in interpretation, on the other hand, is rather in the ease with which a community myth can be accepted at face value. Those others often at the top and bottom end of the social scale, who carry a different viewpoint are not noticed. Nor can the social function of the myth be detected. For interpretation, as we shall see, this may prove much more revealing than the explicit messages which it conveys.

The message may also differ, depending on just where it is heard. Thus an interview at home will increase the pressure of 'respectable' home-centred ideals; an interview in a pub is more likely to emphasize dare-devilry and fun; and an interview in the workplace will introduce the influence of work conventions and attitudes. Linked with these changes in emphasis will be changes in language. A recording in a pub, for example, will often be festooned with swear-words; cross the home threshold, and the vocabulary will be transformed. Each might again vary if the interview was transformed from a confidential exchange to, at the other extreme, a television recording with technicians, glaring lamps, and a public audience beyond.

These then are some of the main influences from the interview situation. They are crucial: for they underlie the difficulties of any historian or sociologist in penetrating social reality, past or present. For the historian it is hardly possible to measure the extent of these difficulties, except when past errors come to light. But there are a number of sociological repeat surveys, which suggest how far any historical or contemporary evidence derived from interviews needs to be treated with care. In one study carried out by G. L. Palmer in Philadelphia in 1943, it was found that after only ten days 10 per cent of respondents reported their age differently by one year. Again, the Opinion Research Centre in 1949 made a comparison in Denver between interview survey material and local official records. It was found that once more 10 per cent of the answers were incompatible on age, 10–15 per cent on the possession of objects like library cards, cars, and the make of car, and 5 per cent even on the possession of a telephone. Such findings also call into question the reliability of many contemporary official statistics.[30]

With this in mind, let us look at some cases in which the accuracy of retrospective material collected in large-scale surveys can be assessed. One of the first is the sociological study by P. M. Blau and O. D. Duncan of *The American Occupational Structure* (1967). The authors carried out a pre-test of 570 men in Chicago and tried to match their names against the census. They were only able to match 137, and in less than half of these did they find complete agreement of occupation and industry between the two sources. Tucking away as an appendix this rather damaging assessment of the foundations of their sophisticated statistical analysis, they argue that the discrepancies are partly due to high labour mobility in America (in 1945–6 this peaked at 12 per cent of all workers changing jobs), and partly—scarce comfort for historians—to the inaccuracies of a census at least as unreliable as their own survey. They cite a post-enumeration survey carried out by the Bureau of the Census to check its own results, which found that 17 per cent of the men were classified in a different major occupational group in the two surveys. This is a finding which might well be better known among statistically minded historians. Blau and Duncan were also able to show the differences between the census and their own survey were systematic. There was a tendency for labourers who appeared in the census to be described as craftsmen or technicians in their own questionnaire, but there was not a comparable error in the opposite direction. It was, on the other hand, reassuring to discover that the discrepancies, and so presumption of inaccuracy in retrospective interviewing, became *less* as the time interval increased. Men were more likely to describe correctly their father's occupation fifty-five rather than twenty-five years ago. For example, according to the census Blau and Duncan ought to have found that in 1940 12 per cent of the fathers were professional or managerial, and 17 per cent were farmers; but in fact far too many professionals and too few farmers were reported—20 per cent and 13 per cent respectively. But for 1910, when the census had recorded 11 per cent and 40 per cent, their own findings were much closer: 14 per cent and 38 per cent.[31] The reason for this retrospective increase in reliability is that an older man has fewer social reasons for wishing to misdescribe his father's occupation than a younger man. On some subjects it is therefore possible for the historian to get more reliable information from interviews than the contemporary sociological investigator.

Since then there have been many reports of the accuracies and inaccuracies of recall of earlier events in survey research, with very varied results, some much more negative than others. These studies tend to be about relatively short-term recall, but they re-emphasise that the problem of memory is not peculiar to the oral historian, but basic to social research; and also that restrospective data does have a potential validity. And it is certainly possible to find strikingly encouraging instances of long-term recall. Thus another large-scale retrospective survey is provided by David Butler and Donald Stokes's study of *Political Change in Britain* (1969). The historical information here is less closely analysed, but their tables of how each generation remembered their fathers' political views are clearly compatible with the broad picture which we have from other historical sources of a Labour Party rising rapidly at the end of the nineteenth-century to oust the Liberals as the main contenders for power with the Conservatives. So are other figures showing that the Conservatives relied chiefly on the middle classes and the Church of England for their supporters, while their opponents depended upon Nonconformity and the working classes. Charles More's detailed statistical comparisons between oral history interviews and contemporary reports and census figures on skill and apprenticeship at the turn of the century are equally reassuring. Such confirmations of established historical accounts clearly suggest that the retrospective survey can provide social information which in its broad divisions is reliable.[32]

If we accept that memory is not so subject to error as to invalidate the usefulness of information gathered from retrospective interviewing, how do we overcome a rather different criticism—that our informants cannot be taken as typical or representative? Social surveys are normally based on carefully chosen samples, designed to secure as representative a group of informants as possible. They confront the oral historian with a dilemma. A survey whose informants are predetermined, and interviewed according to an inflexible schedule, will collect material of intrinsically lower quality. Some of the best potential informants will be missed, and others often less willing chosen in their place; while the interview itself cannot be sufficiently flexible to draw the most from them. On the other hand, one of the great advantages of oral history is that it enables the historian to counteract the bias in normal historical sources; the tendency, for example, for printed autobiography to come from the articulate professional or upper classes, or from labour leaders rather than the rank and file. Because of this, it is important to consider how far the oral historian could make use of some of the techniques of representative sampling developed by the sociologists.

The historian starts with a difficulty not shared by the sociologist. If the old people alive today were themselves a balanced cross-section of their generation in the past, in principle we should only need to draw a random sample from a list of their names. There would remain the practical difficulty of obtaining a fully reliable list which, unlike electoral registers, is rarely available. But we can be certain that such a 'random sample', even although providing the most certain form of present representativeness, would distort the past. It could take no account of migration, local or national, or of differential mortality. We know that people die much faster in some occupations than in others. Death rates can also be affected by personal losses, such as widowhood; by personal habits, such as smoking or drinking; perhaps by personality itself. Until a whole cohort of people has been studied from youth to age, we cannot be sure how far the cumulative effect of all these factors distorts the representativeness of the surviving group. But we do have measures of some of the most important differences between present and past, such as occupational and population distribution. This makes it possible for a large oral history project to rest on a frame which is, at least in some of its key dimensions, reliable.

For our own research project for *The Edwardians*, we recorded some 500 men and women, all born by 1906, and the earliest in 1872. Thea Vigne and I wanted to select a group representative as far as then possible of the Edwardian population as a whole, so that we designed a 'quota sample'—a list of categories of various proportions into which people had to fit in

Occupational and sex sample

	Men		Women	
	Occupied	Unoccupied	Occupied	Unoccupied
Professional (n=18)	4	3	4	7
Employers and managers (n=54)	16	10	4	24
Clerks and foremen (n=28)	10	2	2	14
Skilled manual (n=142)	48	24	14	56
Semi-skilled manual (n=160)	48	25	30	57
Unskilled manual (n=42)	16	8	4	14
Total (n=444)	142	72	58	172
	214		230	

Geographical sample

Rural 144	Urban 200	Conurbation 100	
⨉	⨉		London
		⨉	South East
		⨉	East Anglia
		⨉	West
		⨉	South West
		⨉	South Wales
		⨉	North Wales
			Midlands
			Lancashire
			Yorkshire
		⨉	North West & North East
			Lowland Scotland
		⨉	Highland Scotland

order to be counted. The sample was based on the 1911 census and it totalled 444 persons (see below). The proportion of men and women was as in 1911; so were the proportions who had then been living in the countryside, the towns, and the conurbations; and so too the balance between the main regions of England, Wales, and Scotland. We tried to ensure a proper class distribution by dividing the sample into six major occupational groups, taken from the adjusted census categories of Guy Routh's *Occupation and Pay*, 1906–65 (1965). Those informants who were not working in 1911 went in as dependants of the chief breadwinner in the household, normally the father or husband (see below). We had to carry out more interviews than the total 444 in order to fill the quotas, partly because some turned out to belong to a different classification than expected, and partly because not all were sufficiently complete.

Our aim was to present the people of Edwardian Britain who were alive in 1911, partly through those who survived, and partly through their children. And as a whole, the survey does succeed in this way, for the patterns which it produces by region and by class make sense. Some of the faults in the design of the quota itself could, on another occasion, be corrected. For example, we orginally failed to take account of the fact that because Edwardian women normally ceased working at marriage, the proportions of women working was far greater in some adult age groups than others.

It is all too possible to fill a category in the frame locally from a single social network which might, for example, exclude the less respectable. We therefore used a variety of means to find informants: personal contact, doctors' lists, welfare centres, visiting organizations, essay competitions, newspapers, and even chance encounter. We tried to notice the social bias which particular methods of contact could introduce, and counteract them. And there can be no doubt that the presence of the sample frame itself served to push the search for informants well beyond what would have otherwise seemed sufficient. In oral history work, as in any social research, it is too easy to miss the people at the margins: the very rich and the very poor, the disabled, the homeless and so on. And we certainly found ourselves that the wholly unskilled, the 'rough' and 'unrespectable', for example, were again and again almost to the last moment socially invisible.

The quota sample carries one undeniable advantage over the random method. Since the choice of individual informants is not predetermined, there is no longer any need to force an interview on a respondent who remains unwilling, even after the purpose of the research and potential value of their contribution has been explained. Everything is to be gained from avoiding an interview which is likely to generate false material.

But while it is clearly desirable to record only willing informants, there is another possible danger of going too far in the opposite direction, and recording only the exceptionally confident and articulate. Even within a particular social group or occupation, these may be a distinct stratum of leaders with their own culture and intellectual attitudes. Such informants are not merely unrepresentative, but can often prove less reliable. The more people are accustomed to presenting a professional public image, the less likely their personal recollections are to be candid; politicians are therefore particularly difficult witnesses. So are those who, through reading, have fixed upon a view of the past which they propagate professionally—such as historians and teachers. They can be the most insightful, but equally the most misleading sources. Indeed in African history Vansina originally suggested that the testimony of amateur collectors of oral tradition should always be avoided as 'quite worthless, because it is second-hand . . . "Listen to the words of the smith, do not listen to what the man who works the bellows has to say", as the Bushongo put it'. His ideal informant is a person still living the customary life, middle-aged or elderly, 'who recites traditions without too much hesitation, who understands their content but is not too brilliant—for if he were, one would suspect him of introducing distortions'.[33] The point—if not the patronizing tone, which he later very much modified—may be held relevant in Britain, too. If oral history is to be effectively representative, at all social levels, it is not just the unusually articulate and overtly reflective who must be recorded. Its essence is in conveying the words and feelings of ordinary people. The ideal choice is a broad one, but firmly grounded on the centre.

We may be certain in wishing to avoid interviews with unwilling informants. But what of those who are not so much unwilling as laconic, withdrawn? They will give the bones of a life-story to a sympathetic interviewer, but never the most rewarding material. While they should clearly be included in any representative survey, what is lost if they are not deliberately sought out? This can be partly checked by observing whether their stories vary in any consistent direction from those of ordinary informants. We can secure a very rough indication from one American research project, which examined how far personality changed as people passed retirement and grew old: B. L. Neugarten's Kansas City Study of Adult Life. This categorized fifty-nine respondents before and after retirement as shown below.[34] Although such findings must be treated with considerable caution, they do suggest that neither the withdrawn nor the unwilling informant is essential to secure a representative picture of earlier life experiences. The first, well-integrated group would present no difficulties. For the second and third groups, little would be lost by taking informants from only one of the two post-retirement subcategories in each case. The incidence of widowhood, for example, is not consistently related to earlier life experience. And the last group would make unreliable informants in general. Of course this tentative study gives no measure of the similar changes in personality during childhood, youth, and earlier adulthood. If we are seeking evidence from childhood, we can assume with some confidence that there is *no* kind of family life which produced exclusively a single, uninterviewable type of personality, and is therefore inaccessible to the oral historian. Differences in personality type need to be taken into account, with, one hopes, perhaps eventually a more sophisticated measure of

Kansas Study of Adult Life: Personalities of 59 respondents categorized

Before retirement	Afterwards
(a) 19 well integrated	16 socially active, 3 socially disengaged, but calm, self-directed, contented
(b) 16 of 'armoured', 'defended' personality type, ambitious with high defences	11 holding on—'I'll work until I'll drop'; 5 constricted, closing themselves off from experience
(c) 13 of passive dependent type; rely on one or two people for emotional support	8 satisfactory; 5 apathetic, collapsed (widowed etc.)
(d) 11 of unintegrated type	7 dissatisfied isolates, 4 senile

normal distributions, but they do not present an insuperable difficulty.

To meet the various problems raised by retrospective representativeness, the oral historian needs to develop, rather than the standardized random battery sample, a method of strategic sampling: a more tactical approach such as the 'theoretical sampling' advocated by Glaser and Anselm Strauss in their *The Discovery of Grounded Theory* (1967). Various different approaches are worth considering. For many projects, as on an event, or about a small group of people, the issue is not representativeness, but who knows best; above all, participants and direct witnesses. As the sociologist Herbert Blumer puts it, the search ought to be for *validity* rather than for reliability: 'a half dozen individuals with such knowledge constitute a far better "representative sample" than a thousand individuals who may be involved in the action that is being formed but who are not knowledgeable about that formation'. One very fertile way of looking at long-term intergenerational change in work and family life, and also migration, which can be carried across periods of tumultuous political change too, is to take a cross-class sample of families, and interview two or three generations in each family: this was the technique which Daniel Bertaux and I used in *Pathways to Social Class* (1997). For other projects the whole objective might be to focus on a restricted group, for example interviewing several members of the same extended family group; or interviewing married couples and 'snowballing' by following up with their neighbours and friends. This would construct a picture of their social networks, attitudes, myths and memories, for which the very circularity of the enclosed group would be a strength rather than a weakness: as for instance in Yves Lequin's study of the collective memory of the metal-workers of Givors on the Rhône.[35] For a broader local study, the most appropriate method might be the 'community stratified sample', in which the aim is not to secure a mirror of its broad distributions, but to ensure the representation of all significant social layers within it. Or both aims might be met, by simultaneously working with two separate samples, the second devised on the 'quota sample' method which we used for our own national survey. No method of sampling can claim to be the best for all situations.

Concern for representativeness is essential if oral history is to realize its potential. The worst kind of oral history is that which begins and ends with the daily help. But it is equally important not to become obsessed with this issue, and lose sight of the substantive issues in developing methodology. And also of when they are best just forgotten. One of the deepest lessons of oral history is the uniqueness, as well as representativeness, of every life-story. There are some so rare and vivid that they demand recording, whatever the plan. In a flash, we may be in another world, normally beyond even the most painstaking researcher: as in the experiences of a Glasgow girl, daughter of a proud artisan, a boilermaker who would sketch designs on the linoleum floor, but forced her and her brother—aged barely 4 and 7—out to sleep on the street to please their stepmother:

She just told us to get off, that's all. Yes, yes, shut the door on us. Gave us nothing . . . (for food), we used to steal the workmen's pieces to begin with. And then at other times, when we got too well known . . . we used to gather scrap and go to the rag store, get coppers and then go to these eating houses and get, maybe a bowl of soup . . . and then other times, Tommy and I used to go to a grocer's shop or a dairy, and I would ask the time while he was pinching scones off his table. That's how you lived. Between that and begging from door to door . . . (for clothes and shoes), we stole them in the cloakroom of the school . . .

I've slept under bridges. I've slept in people's doorways, with their carpets and cats on the landing, and I've slept in watchmen's huts. I've slept in school shelters . . . In the dockyards, I've slept in the sheds, with the rats running round . . . I was nearly down the hold of a boat. In a truck of coal . . . I put the tarpolin over me, you see . . . They were just going to tip it into the hold of a boat—when the crane man saw me . . .

And then this old auntie . . . she used to chase my step-mother, because of what she was doing to me . . . She'd get a hold of us and take us away and wash our faces and soaped us all and do what she could for us. But she had to work. And always when she come back at night she couldna find us you know . . .

And this particular night, I'm asleep on her doorstep . . . But along came a lady, and I was sound asleep on this doorstep. She wakened me up, and asked a lot of questions . . . took me to her house, she carried me up, and she washed, cleaned me and put me in her own bed . . . She put me out the next morning, she had fed me, put all nice clothes on me . . . And she give me I think it was a penny . . . My father was in a close, in an entry, right facing . . . He whistled, and I looked . . . I thought that was great. And I goes to my daddy. You wouldna guess what happened. He struck me of everything I had . . . He went to the first pawn shop, pawned them. Pawned them. There I was left in the street again . . . I went back up to the woman. And I telled her my daddy had taken all off me . . . Next thing I knew I was in court . . .

In the end—although not until the age of 8—she was taken into a church home, and her brother sent to a training ship.[36]

In weighing up the reliability of a particular example of remembered evidence, just as in the selection of informants to record, it is important for oral historians to accept that there are no absolute rules, but rather a number of factors to be taken into account. Ultimately there are only useful guidelines to indicate when oral sources can be most reliably used, and to give us a reasonable strategy for when to doubt most, just as there are for other historical sources. The basic tests of reliability which we shall consider in detail in the final chapter—searching for internal consistency, cross-checking details from other sources, weighing evidence against a wider context—are just the same as for other sources. All are fallible and subject to bias, and each has varying strengths in different situations. In some contexts, oral evidence is the best; in others it is supplementary, or complementary, to that of other sources.

Recent analyses of retrospective survey interviews are interesting in this respect, for they indicate that information can be collected 'with a reasonable degree of accuracy' of employment histories, health and education, and marital and fertility histories and family characteristics.[37] This fits in well with the strengths which have been found in oral history evidence where they can be tested against other sources. But they can be of still greater value especially for fields for which little other evidence exists.

In the field of family history, for example, internal patterns of behaviour and relationships are generally inaccessible without oral evidence. The same is often true, in studying a strike, of the details of informal local organization, or of deviant behaviour such as blacklegging, or the normal devices like stealing fuel which helped families to survive with no income. The extreme case is the history of underground movements, such as the secret Jewish organizations in Nazi territory at the time of the Second World War. Yad Vashem, the great Archive of the Holocaust in Jerusalem, has collected, besides some thirty million written documents relating to the persecution and exterminaton of Jewish communities in the Fascist period, more than 25,000 oral testimonies. Collection was begun as early as 1944, and, immediately after the end of the war, offices were set up in many parts of Germany and elsewhere for collecting evidence. Several of these centres are still active. They have collected a wide range of material on social and cultural life, partly in order to preserve some record of communities whose history would otherwise have died with them. Much more remarkable has been the ability to reconstruct, step by step, with the exactness and the patience which is needed for evidence which may need to be proved in court—and has regularly been tested in this way—accounts of both the persecution and resistance to it. When a large part of the Nuremberg trial evidence was sub-sequently lost by the Russians, Yad Vashem was able to reconstruct three-quarters of the missing documents. As one of the archive's pioneers, Ball-Kaduri, knew from first-hand experience in Berlin, official documentation could not possibly provide an adequate record of the activity of Jewish leaders and their sympathizers who, in order to evade detection by the Gestapo, were forced always to meet in private, and to use spoken communication only. Yad Vashem has indeed suc-ceeded in preserving a history which, as he argued, written documents could never represent: 'Was nicht in die archiven steht'.

More often, the role of oral evidence is less dramatic, complementary or supplementary, reinterpreting and filling in gaps and weaknesses in the documents. The census of occupations, for example, is a very unsatisfactory record of secondary and part-time occupations. Through interviews it is possible to discover how a tradesman combined his craft with running a public house, or a casual worker took a series of occupations in a seasonal cycle, or many women described as housewives took in work at home or went out to part-time jobs. The labourer, 'that catch-all title favoured by the Census enumerators, turns out in many cases not to have been a labourer at all, but a man with a definite calling—a holder-up in the shipyards, a winch man at the docks, a well-digger or drainer in the countryside, a carrier or a freelance navvy'. Conversely, as a Divisional Inspector of Mines observed in 1912, 'You may have a perfectly good quarryman working three weeks or a month in a quarry, and another time he is a farm-labourer or working on some other work altogether.' Such complexities could not be caught by the single entry of the census record, even if the enumerator was sensitive to them. And since for more recent periods the individual entries are anyway not available, in the meantime it may also be more accurate in a quantitative as well as a qualitative sense to use oral evidence:

Of what value would be the knowledge that 30 per cent of the workers in a particular plant were Polish, if we knew from previous investigations that this geographical unit was far too large to be meaningful? On the other hand, the response of an informant that a single department, say metal-finishing, possessed a work force that was 90 per cent Polish might be off by a few points, or even by as much as to 10 or 15 per cent, but it would be far closer to the truth than the census estimate, which would be unable to go any further than specifying that 30 per cent of the workers in the plant were Polish.[38]

Similarly, while court records and newspapers might provide

the best evidence for a dispute over common rights, or the numbers of poachers convicted month by month, oral sources could be essential to discover how the commons were normally used, or how the poaching system with its receivers, regulars, and casuals was actually organized. In his study of Headington Quarry, Raphael Samuel found oral history most useful in explaining the social structure and pattern of everyday life, least helpful in understanding a crisis, such as a political riot, and a prolonged dispute over school discipline, for which the contemporary documentation was richer. Interviews nevertheless probably do offer the best method for assessing the normal means used by teachers across the country for maintaining discipline in class. One critic of *The Edwardians*, contending that 'interesting reminiscences ought not to be offered as a substitute for a clear understanding', asserted that

it is quite misleading to say that Edwardian teachers resorted *en masse* to corporal punishment. The debate over corporal punishment in State schools had begun in the 1890s, if not before, and many School Boards had begun to restrict its use even if the NUT protested at its complete abolition. A knowledge of the NUT's journal. *The Schoolmaster*, would have indicated this.

This journal does indeed show that there was debate. And one could also learn from the *School Board Chronicle* that teachers were demanding the right to use the cane. But it is certainly not possible to gain from these documents any kind of evidence of the extent to which corporal punishment was normally tolerated anywhere, as it is from the witness of the children themselves.[39]

As every experienced oral historian knows, however, the simple assertion and counter-assertion that oral history sources are reliable or not, true or false for this or that purpose, obtained from this or that person, obscures the really interesting questions. The nature of memory brings many traps for the unwary, which often explains the cynicism of those less well informed about oral sources. Yet they also bring unexpected rewards to a historian who is prepared to appreciate the complexity with which reality and myth, 'objective' and 'subjective', are inextricably mixed in all human perception of the world, both individual and collective.

Remembering in an interview is a mutual process, which requires understanding on both sides. The historian always needs to sense how a question is being answered from *another* person's perspective. For example, general questioning on the good—or bad—old days will encourage subjective and collective myths and impressions; while detailed questions can draw out the particular facts and accounts of everyday life which the social historian may be seeking. But this does not mean that the myths and impressions lack any validity. The misunderstanding comes partly just because the historian is attempting to see change from another angle: the experience of one generation following another, rather than that of a single life cycle. When old people say that they enjoyed themselves more as children, or that neighbours were more friendly then, they may be perfectly properly evaluating their own lives, whether or not children find neighbours just as friendly today. Similarly historians too easily forget that most people are less interested in calendar years than themselves, and do not arrange their memories with dates as markers.

In general, one of the keys lies in mutual interest. Thus a man might be fascinated by the technological evolution of the motor engine through his years as a garage mechanic, but considerably less well informed about the upbringing of his children. But it is also true that over-interest can also present problems. An excessive concern with justifying the part they themselves played, as well as too much second-hand knowledge is, no doubt, one reason why politicians are apt, especially when not cross-questioned, to give somewhat casual accounts of major incidents. 'My experience is that memories are very fallible as a rule on specific events,' comments R. R. James; 'very illuminating on character and on atmosphere, matters on which documents are inadequate.'[40] But if personal pride and political interest make caution necessary in evaluating the recollections of politicians, with ordinary people sheer lack of interest is likely to affect their memories of national events. Melvyn Bragg, for example, discovered that it was pointless trying to collect information on important but historic events like Acts of Parliament or international incidents which to Wigton people were remote:

A man will talk of the Second World War, not in terms of Rommel or Montgomery or Eisenhower, but in a way in which everyone who served under those generals would understand. And poverty in the Thirties to a woman with six children would not be in terms of coalition governments and social legislation and trade union demands, but soup-kitchens, shoes for the family, the memory of a day's outing to the seaside—the common body of daily life.[41]

It is partly due to less interest, but also to a much briefer opportunity for incorporating them in the memory, that one can observe a *general* tendency for recurrent processes to be better remembered than single incidents. Thus a farm worker, in recalling an angry exchange with a farmer, may find the incident hard to place in time, and perhaps confuse the details with those of another similar occasion. But ask him about precisely how he handled his horses while ploughing, and it will be very, very rare for him to be wrong. A child's memories of King Edward VII's Coronation Day are likely to be much less substantial than those of regular playmates and play places. In many events, people did not know at the time what was happening, so that their retrospective accounts will be as much based on what they learnt from the news or from others as from their own participation. Indeed, just because such second-hand impressions may be more powerful than their own direct experience of the original fleeting incident, especially if they become a well-established part of community memory, some people come to believe that they actually saw an incident, such as an air raid, which they in fact experienced at second-hand, through the newspapers or local talk. As David Jenkins observes of the village communities of south-west Wales, 'what is most accurately remembered is what has been periodically recalled and this is usually material concerning people; memory is much less reliable when it concerns events that neither recurred nor were consistently recalled'.[42]

It is certainly possible to reconstruct an event with oral evidence. But it is likely to prove a more difficult task, and unless this general tendency is understood, it may lead to serious misunderstandings. In his study of Henry Ford's development of the popular, mass-produced motor car, Allan Nevins was able to make rich use of oral evidence in giving body to the story which he found in the company's documents. Nevins comments, as a veteran oral historian, that 'any man's recollection of past events is untrustworthy'. But he knew how to use evidence effectively. For example, he could use it to establish Ford's own personal methods of working in the factory, like his avoidance of office work and letter-answering; and to separate the various roles in the team-work which went into the crucial Model T design. But in dating the introduction of the moving assembly line, he found that some Ford workers confused the first 'genuine attempt' of 1912 with an 'episodic . . . rope-hauling experiment' of four years earlier. Others correctly confirmed that there had not been a regular moving assembly line before the later date.[43]

This telescoping of two separate events into one in the memory is a very common phenomenon. For some purposes, the historian's task will be to try to separate them, delicately probing deeper; but for others, this very reorganization of the memory will be a precious indication of how a people's consciousness is constructed. Thus when Sandro Portelli interviewed Dante Bartolini, a veteran militant of the industrial town of Terni, north of Rome, he told him how in 1943 the workers broke down the munition factory gates, seized all the weapons, and escaped to the mountains to join the Partisans. Many of the workers had indeed joined the Partisans, where they established their own liberated zone, but they did not sack the factory in 1943; although Bartolini himself was one of those who seized arms in the factory after the arrest of the Italian Communist leader Togliatti in 1949. For Bartolini the resistance and the post-war industrial struggle are all part of a single history, eloquently conveyed in his symbolic story. In a similar spirit, almost half the steelworkers whom Portelli interviewed told the story of the post-war strikes with the killing of a worker by the police placed in 1953 rather than in 1949; and they also shifted its context from a peace demonstration to the three days of barricades and street fighting which followed the firing of 2,700 men from the steelworks. In fact nobody was killed in those three days in 1953. But as Portelli argues, the facts are not the interesting point about the episode. 'The death of Luigi Trastulli would not mean so much to the historian if it were remembered "right". After all, the death of a worker at the hands of the police in post-war Italy is not such an uncommon event . . . What makes it meaningful is the way it operates in people's memories.' Thirty, forty years on, in the 'longue durée' of memory, Trastulli's death still echoes in popular imagination. 'The facts that people remember (and forget) are themselves the stuff of which history is made.' The very subjectivity which some see as a weakness of oral sources can also make them uniquely valuable. For 'subjectivity is as much the business of history as the more visible "facts". What the informant believes is indeed a *fact* (that is, the *fact* that he or she believes it) just as much as what "really" happened.'[44]

We may illustrate this with a memory from British labour history which is again 'false', but nevertheless significant. Lindsay Morrison and Roy Hay were investigating a strike which took place in 1911 at the Singer factory in Glasgow. With the help of the only surviving worker from the workforce of the time (aged over 100) and his son:

we did piece together a story about how the Singer Company tried to break the strike. According to their version, which we subsequently heard from other independent sources, the company paid the Post Office to make a special delivery of postcards to all those on strike. The delivery was carried out on the Sunday evening and the postcards announced that all those who failed to report for work at starting time on the Monday morning would be considered to have left the employ of the company . . .

Now, we checked this story as far as we could from written sources, newspapers, a manuscript history of the company, and contemporary accounts. We found that there was a delivery of postcards but that they were made in the normal way and that the message they contained was somewhat different. The company said that when 60 per cent of the postcards they sent out had been returned, signifying the willingness of the workers to return on the previous terms, then the factory would be reopened. Obviously the pressure is here too and the firm was making a clear attempt to by-pass the union. But perhaps in a less underhand way. Nevertheless, and this is the point I want to stress, subsequent labour relations in Singer's seem to have been conditioned more by the first version, which seems to have circulated widely and been believed, than by the second. For some purposes, the fiction captured in oral evidence may be more important than 'the truth'.[45]

Rumours do not survive unless they make sense to people. Seen in such a light, as Portelli puts it,

there are no 'false' oral sources. Once we have checked their factual credibility with all the established criteria of historical philological criticism that apply to every document, the diversity of oral history lies in the fact that 'untrue' statements are still psychologically 'true', and that these previous errors sometimes reveal more than factually accurate accounts . . . The credibility of oral sources is a *different* credibility . . . The importance of oral testimony may often lie not in its adherence to facts but rather in its divergence from them, where imagination, symbolism, desire break in.[46]

As a further instance, Portelli recounts the story of Alfredo Filipponi, a former factory worker and tram driver, who had been secretary of the Communist underground in Terni under Fascism and a military commander of a Partisan brigade in 1943–4. As an older man Filipponi had been bitterly disappointed by the failure to achieve a socialist society in Italy, and he believed that the crucial mistake had been the decision of the Communist leader Togliatti to participate in a democratic post-war Italy, rather than continue an armed struggle for revolution. 'At that time, with the partisan struggle, we should almost have made it.' In support of this view, he gave Portelli a graphic account of a meeting of Partisan commanders in Terni which Togliatti addressed, and Filipponi challenged him: 'I disagree because, as Lenin said, when the thrush flies by, then it's the time to shoot. If you don't shoot when it flies by, you may never get another chance. Today the thrush is flying by: all the Fascist chiefs are in hiding and running away . . . This is the time: we strike, and make socialism'. Now this confrontation, and the meeting itself too, were purely imaginary. Nor did Lenin ever use the metaphor of shooting the thrush: the image comes from a popular local hunting proverb. But the value of the story for Filipponi is in allowing him to conclude triumphantly, 'they got the warning; they had to admit that I was right later'. And for us, it gives an invaluable insight into the way of thinking of a militant Communist of his generation; not only about political tactics, but also in subsuming local popular culture and imagery through relabelling it as Marxist.[47]

History, in short, is not just about events, or structures, or patterns of behaviour, but also about how these are experienced and remembered in the imagination. And one part of history, what people imagined happened, and also what they believe *might* have happened—their imagination of an alternative past, and so an alternative present—may be as crucial as what did happen. This is the focus of the essays collected in *The Myths We Live By*. They show how a variety of myths and images can shape experience in many different contexts. Thus the male descendents of Admiral Byng, who was shot for alleged cowardice in 1754, two centuries later still seem driven to reckless displays of bravery; immigrant Puerto Rican women in New York find models of the strength they need in idealized images of their mothers and grandmothers; or—within hours of the dispute beginning—small children who participate in an Italian school strike create stories of heroic boys leaping from the upper floors and a villainous headmaster monopolizing all the heaters.[48] And on a grander scale it is clear that the building of collective memory can result in a historical force of immense power in its own right; as the epic struggles of the miners, or the repeated persecution of the Jews, or the obstinacy of the Boers, or the three centuries of religious battle in Northern Ireland, so eloquently and tragically testify.

The constructing and telling of both collective and individual memory of the past is an active social process, which demands both skill and art, learning from others, and imaginative power. In it stories are used above all to characterize communities and individuals, and to convey their attitudes. An old Ulsterman, Hugh Nolan, put it nicely 'Well, do you see, the way it is, *all* good stories and good novels, they're all fiction . . . But even they're fiction, there bes a warning. And there bes information in them too.' As John Berger has remarked, the function of the stories of past and present which are told in a small community, 'this gossip which in fact is close, oral, daily history', is to define itself and its members. 'Every village's portrait of itself is constructed . . . out of words, spoken and remembered: out of opinions, stories, eyewitness reports, legends, comments and hearsay. And it is a continuous portrait; work on it never stops.'[49] Individual autobiography is less rich in resources. It draws, in a finite span, on what one person has experienced and learnt; and the core of it must be direct experience. But stories are also commonly used in the telling of individual lives, in order to convey values; and it is the symbolic truth they convey, and not the facts of the incident described, which matters most. The encapsulation of earlier attitudes in a story is a protection, which makes them less likely to represent a recent reformulation, and therefore especially good evidence of past values. And this remains so when—as quite commonly in collective oral tradition, and also sometimes in individual life stories—the narrative draws not only on the reconstruction of direct experience, but on older legends and stories. One of my own first interviews was with a Shetlander, born in 1886, Willie Robertson. I asked how much contact the people had with the lairds (the landowners)—a question bearing on their degree of class-consciousness. He told me, as a true story, naming a particular laird. a burial folktale which is quite widespread in Scotland:

That was Gifford of Busta. He was one of the county property owners—the laird. And before he died, he'd left instructions that there were to be nobody to attend his funeral except his own kind, the lairds. Well all these people had to come a long distance to funerals and there was no conveyance except they came on horseback. And I have been at a funeral in my time where they give you refreshments: gave you whisky, a glass of whisky, or you could take a glass of wine. Now these lairds that came to Gifford's funeral got refreshments: liquid refreshments; maybe some other. Then they had to carry the remains, the funeral, four or five miles to the cemetery. Well they were always stopping and having more refreshments. And one dropped out; two dropped out; till latterly there were only two; and they lay alongside the coffin. So they were out for the count. And an old crofter come by, and he saw Mr Gifford's remains in the coffin lying there, and these two men. He went across to his house and got a big rope; he took the coffin up on end and put the rope round him; and he took him to the grave and buried him himself. And his kind weren't to be allowed at the funeral. And he buried the laird.

Willie Robertson may have been mistaken in believing his story to be literally true; but this cannot diminish its symbolic force as an answer. Funerals in the island communities of small farmers (crofters) and fishermen were normally occasions for the demonstration of the fundamental equality of all before God, and in the long walk to the cemetery every man would take his turn in bearing the coffin. In some it was even the convention for the better-off to be deliberately paired with the poorest. But as he tells the story he draws not only on a folk tradition, but on his own political and religious ideas. Willie Robertson was an Elder of the Kirk, with a strong belief in temperance. He was also a shoemaker-Socialist: a member of the SDF converted by outdoor speakers who came up north with the East Anglian herring boats. So his story is also a parable of the Good Samaritan; infused with a flavour of Marxist class-consciousness.

Although such a complex instance is relatively unusual in an ordinary life-story, it does suggest the need for understanding the different forms and conventions which shape not only how we tell our stories when *Narrating Our Pasts*, but also enable *any* communications between people. Just as in a book the needs of argument, of shape and length, press for the inclusion of some details and the omission of others, so in the telling of an ordinary story: the symbolic meaning and factual details must hang upon a form. 'No utterance whatsoever falls outside a *literary genre*', Vansina urges: study 'form and structure first, because they influence the expression of the content'. Such forms in oral sources have been principally analysed by anthropologists, and by folklorists interested in oral literature, rather than historians. In oral 'literature' distinctions are made between characteristic major genres, such as the group *legend*, the individual *anecdote*, the family *saga*, and the folk*tale*. Thus there is an international type-list of several hundred folktales, which enables archivists all over the world to recognize a tale. and see how the version they have collected varies from the basic type, and what influences have contributed to these changes. Vansina can not only sift out the familiar stereotypes, 'fillers' and 'formulas', from the parts of a narrative which convey significant messages, but also confidently assert, for instance, from the systematic analysis of narratives from a whole region, that 'all migrations in the upper Nile are caused by a quarrel between brothers over an item of little value'. Most European oral historians must work without such a cumulation of experience to help them. The individual anecdote and the family history can be subjected to the same formal analysis, as indeed is shown in the recent volume *Genre and Narrative*—but much more such work is needed.[50]

The way in which the story is learnt also needs to be more closely studied. In France, for example, village children are taken by their parents or grandparents to the cemetery to teach them the history of the family. A wedding photograph hung on the wall or a reunion of war veterans or workmates are all mechanisms for the reconstruction of memory. But these mechanisms vary significantly between different social groups and localities. Among the French Protestant minority in the Alpine foothills of Drôme, memory of the past is not of a timeless rhythm of life and work, as for their Catholic neighbours, but of a long, tragic history, a history of struggle and persecution, clandestinity, exodus, and resistance. Here children are shown the secret assembly-places in the woods, the beams from which martyrs were hanged. 'A Protestant—had no right to be born, or to marry, or even to die.'[51] And so deep was the mark of seventeenth- and eighteenth-century persecution, that the more recent past has come to be remembered in just the same mould: the 1851 insurrection not for its marches and clashes, but in its repression; and similarly, the Second World War.

The study of the differing processes of transmission has been carried furthest among the anthropologists and historians of Africa, due to their special dependence on oral sources. A clear distinction must be made between personal oral histories—eye-witness accounts—which are relatively easy to evaluate, and oral traditions—which are handed down by word of mouth to later generations. This latter process can be quite different in two adjacent societies. In northern Ghana Jack Goody has found a sharp contrast between one centralized tribal society, in which a relatively fixed, brief myth is handed down by official utterers; and another society, decentralized, in which perfor-mance of the collective myth (the Bagre) is *intended* to be local and creative, so that it continually changes, and different ver-sions from different groups have astonishingly little in common. Other Africanists have tried to disentangle the process by which immediate memory is transformed into formal tradition. This can sometimes be quite rapid: the lives of African prophets, for example, can be transformed into myths within a space of two or three years. But Joseph Miller, on the basis of field-work in Angola, suggests that in some societies there may be a point in time, as events pass beyond the reach of first- and second-hand memory, when recollections undergo a marked change. Accounts of the Angola War of 1861 (which is also known from Portuguese documents) are sometimes relatively accurate, with details of guns and so on, without much moral comment, rather like written documentation; but are sometimes presented as a stylized, mythical event in the traditional war-narrative manner—the style of the official tradition-bearers, the profes-sional oral historians of Angolan society, whose task was to collect oral information and present it in public performances.

Possibly memory of the Angolan War is undergoing transition as it passes beyond informal memory. Once none of an audience can remember details of an event, or have their own perceptions and opinions about it, what is needed is a simplified, stylized account which concentrates on the meaning of the story. The time limit thus marks a great sorting-out process, in which some stories are discarded, and others are synthesized, restructured, and stereotyped. The official tradition-bearers are highly concerned with standards of professional accuracy, but they are not the standards of Western historians. Thus beyond that time limit, historians of Angola can best use oral traditions as evidence of values, rather than of facts; and in doing so take account of the completely different African perceptions of time, and of the nature of change, which they embody.[52]

It is hardly surprising, since dates are rarely a strong point even of immediate memory, to find that 'weakness in chronology is one of the greatest limitations of all oral traditions'. Not all is always lost: Paul Irwin has been able to show, for instance, that the sub-Saharan Liptako in Upper Volta correctly remember their Emirs and also the wars of succession between them, at least back to the 1820s. Both here, and in other comparisons from the Pacific between written records and oral tradition, the inaccuracies are far from one-sided. But equally interesting are the distortions: the incorporation of European motifs into traditional history, like the 'wild blackfellow image' of a free past which is now recounted by the North Australian Ngalakan Aborigines, the upholding of false claims to distinctiveness in customs from neighbouring people, the dropping of undesirable rulers from king lists, and the manipulation of genealogies in order to claim land or property which is 'a very common use of genealogies all over the world'.[53]

Above all, consciously and unconsciously, memories which are discreditable, or positively dangerous, are most likely to be quietly buried. 'Forget that story; if we tell it our lineage will be destroyed', exclaimed a Tanzanian in the Nango royal capital at Vugha: his family had a history of conflict with the rulers. Few Germans wish to explore their own family's contribution to the liquidation of the Jews. Even the survivors of such massacres often want to forget, to put the memory behind them, as much as to tell what they had suffered; as Quinto Osano, Fiat metal-worker, survivor of the Mauthansen concentration camp, put it, 'Yes, we always want it to be told, but inside us we are trying to forget; right inside, right in the deepest parts of the mind, of the heart. It's instinctive: to try to forget, even when we are getting others to recall it. It's a contradiction, but that's how it is.' Perhaps this is why the oral traditions of the Australian Ngalaka omit all mention of their decimation by European massacres. Similarly in Turin, stronghold of the Italian working-class movement, the humiliating phase of Fascist dom-ination is typically skipped in factory workers' spontaneous life-stories: a self-censoring silence which Luisa Passerini sees as a deep 'scar, a violent annihilation of many years in human lives which bears witness to a profound wound in daily experience'. The extreme instance was Soviet Russia, which became a society wrapped in silence for seventy years. In the essays collected in *Trauma and Memory*, the ambivalence in memories bringing acute pain, and yet need to remember is explored in other contexts, from the experiences of Argentinian veterans of the Malvinas war whom everyone wanted to forget, or Black Jews who fled from Ethiopia to a Promised Land which did not want them, to the Guatemalan Indian widows forbidden to mourn their men by the army which had massacred them.[54]

Family traditions are also well-known for their silences and secrets. Carolyn Steedman never learnt that her parents were unmarried and she was illegitimate until after her father had died. Jan Vansina, who came from a Belgian village rich in oral tradition, and was first struck by its value when he found the villagers rejected the official version of history taught at school, later found out, after sixteen years of consistent checking, that his own family history was only half reliable. The basic eco-nomic story of how his grandfather, in a situation of developing industrialization, went in for growing cauliflowers, is quite cor-rect. But there are more peripheral parts which have either been forgotten as less creditable, or, like the family's distant origins in

Milan, created from mis-memories of a visit to north Italy. 'Half these stories are not true. They are an image setting. They are necessary for the pride of someone.'[55]

The discovery of distortion or suppression in a life-story is not, it must again be emphasized, purely negative. Even a lie is a form of communication; and it may provide an important clue to the family's psychology and social attitudes. But in order to read these clues, we must develop a sensitivity to the social pressures which bear on them. A spontaneous, unchallenged life-story, Vansina argues, will tend to present a consistent self-image or a logical self-development, and events will be 'retained and reordered, reshaped or correctly remembered according to the part they play in the creation of this mental self-portrait. Parts of such a portrait are too intimate or too contradictory ever to be revealed. Others are private but, depending on mood, can be told to the very near or dear. Others are for public consumption.' Thus a typical autobiography may be quite open about family tensions in childhood, but will very rarely reveal difficulties in the writer's own marriage; and less sharply, the same contrast is found when interviewing. Sexual experience is particularly likely to be censored or not told at all. A good interviewer is scarcely likely to be content, however, with the merely public story, and is only likely to find real difficulty in getting beyond this in exceptional cases. One study of deprived families, for example, found that it took several interviews for their informants to move from presenting the answer they thought was socially desirable to one which represented their own views. 'When Elsie Barker was asked how many brothers and sisters she had, her answer in the second interview was that she was the third child out of six. It was only much later that she explained that the three younger children were in fact the daughters of an elder sister, Brenda, who had committed suicide. Because they were brought up with her, she had always thought of them and continued to think of them as sisters rather than nieces. Elsie had at first omitted all mention of Brenda.'[56] The full story was not merely too complicated for a simple answer, but introduced a painful, shameful family memory. Yet it was hidden, rather than irrecoverable. The combination of facts given at different times, through this process of recovery, gives us much more significant information than the bare facts themselves.

The possibility of recovery, of gradually unpeeling the layers of memory and consciousness, is a crucial distinction between direct personal memory and an oral tradition several generations old. Interestingly, in recent years oral traditions have become accepted as a legal form of evidence in relation to indigenous people's land claims in the courts of Canada, the United States, Australia, and New Zealand. However, earlier there have been a good many anthropologists who have argued that oral traditions are so malleable under social pressures, so continually shaped and reshaped by changing social structures and consciousness, that their value is not only purely symbolic, but that only for the present. Jack Goody, for example, would interpret traditions through a theory of 'dynamic homeostasis', whereby any alteration in social organization or practice is immediately reflected in a reshaped tradition. Vansina vigorously rebuts such extreme functionalism: while it is true that 'all messages have some intent which has to do with the present, otherwise they would not be told in the present and the tradition would die out', the notion that traditions retain no messages at all from the past is an absurd exaggeration. Social changes lead as often to additions, leaving older variations and archaisms intact, as to suppression; and suppressed items usually leave traces. If nothing from the past were left, 'where would social imagination find the stuff to invent from? How does one explain cultural continuities?' Researchers on oral tradition have indeed most recently assumed this mix of continuities and invention, as well as the interaction with printed sources, and interestingly, in recent studies for example on praise poems in southern Africa or on Indian historical traditions in the Colombian Andes, have identified 'reinvention' and creativity as signs not of cultural pollution but of social adaptiveness and vigour. Vansina cogently sums up the debate:

Yes, oral traditions are documents *of the present*, because they are told in the present. Yet they also embody a message *from the past* at the same time. One cannot deny either the present or the past in them. To attribute their whole content to the evanescent present as some sociologists do, is to mutilate tradition; it is reductionistic. To ignore the impact of the present as some historians have done, is equally reductionistic. Traditions must always be understood as reflecting both past and present in a single breath.[57]

Such a vigorous defence is scarcely needed for direct personal memory, although the argument would apply here too; the balance of influences is clearly different. Quite often the myth-makers turn out to be not the direct participants, but the reporters, even the historians. The 'classic' southern Spanish anarchist rising in the village of Casa Viejas, seen by Eric Hobsbawm and other historians as a revolutionary response to hunger, 'utopian, millenarian, apocalyptic', has been shown by Jerome Mintz from direct testimony of the villagers themselves—with whom he lived for three years—to have been a conscientious, but ill-conceived insurrection following the call from Barcelona militants during the 1933 general strikes in the cities. The village had not been a well-organized anarchist stronghold; the rising was brutally suppressed before its people had time even to divide up the land, let alone inaugurate a Utopian society; and the man who held out longest was not its charismatic leader, but a heroic and unpolitical charcoal-burner. The myth of Casa Viejas survived because it suited the beliefs of both the Fascist authorities and the left, providing scapegoats and heroes. And through the Franco decades the survivors had to keep quiet too: 'It's right and natural that not knowing someone well, one would lie. One has to protect oneself.'[58] But they still knew.

For direct memory, the past is much closer than in tradition. For each of us, our way of life, our personality, our consciousness, our knowledge are directly built out of our past life experience. Our lives are cumulations of our own pasts, continuous and indivisible. And it would be purely fanciful to suggest that the typical life-story could be largely invented. Convincing invention requires a quite exceptional imaginative talent. The historian should confront such direct witness neither with blind faith, nor with arrogant scepticism, but with an understanding of the subtle processes through which all of us perceive, and remember, the world around us and our own part in it. It is only in such a sensitive spirit that we can hope to learn the most from what is told to us.

The historical value of the remembered past rests on three strengths. First, as we have demonstrated, it can and does provide significant and sometimes unique information from the past. Secondly, it can equally convey the individual and collective consciousness which is part and parcel of that very past.

More than that, the living humanity of oral sources gives them a third strength which is unique. For the reflective insights of retrospection are by no means always a disadvantage. It is 'precisely this historical perspective which allows us to assess long-term meaning in history', and we can only object to receiving such retrospective interpretations from others—provided we distinguish them as such—if we want to eject those who lived through history from any part in assessing it. If the study of memory 'teaches us that *all* historical sources are suffused by subjectivity right from the start', the *living* presence of those subjective voices from the past also constrains us in our interpretations, allows us, indeed obliges us, to test them against the opinion of those who will always, in essential ways, know more than ourselves.[59] We simply do not have the liberty to invent which is possible for archaeologists of earlier epochs, or even for historians of the early modern family. We could not have presumed that parents did not suffer deeply from the deaths of their children, just because child death was so ordinary, without asking.

We are dealing, in short, with living sources who, just because they are alive have, unlike inscribed stones or sheaves of paper, the ability to work with us in a two-way process. So far we have concentrated on what we can learn from them. But the telling of their story can also have its impact on them too. We need to turn to that next.

5

Memory and the Self

Every historical source derived from human perception is subjective, but only the oral source allows us to challenge that subjectivity: to unpick the layers of memory, dig back into its darknesses, hoping to reach the hidden truth. If that is so, why not seize our chance, unique to us among historians, ease our informants back on to the couch, and, like psychoanalysts, tap their unconscious, draw out the very deepest of their secrets?

It is a beguiling call. Psychoanalysis is the magic of our time. The strange power of psychoanalysts to hear and to heal, to release trapped anger and shame from pasts we had forgotten and, through expression, to put it to rest; to win our love through listening to us and then to give it back to us as a new strength in our own self-confidence—in short, through penetrating to the deepest intimacy that we have shared with anyone, to change our most secret, inner selves—by its nature cannot be fully anticipated or logically comprehended. That alone makes it as threatening as it is compelling. Add a mysterious theory of the unconscious built around our personal sexuality, which is both the taboo and the altar of our culture, and it is no wonder that their power makes pyschoanalysts—and still more psychiatrists, with their battery of drugs in the cupboard to tamper with the mind—the witches, and also the oracles, of the twentieth century. And for historians in particular they present the double challenge, professional as well as personal, of alternative professions manipulating the past according to different rules.

Like it or not, however, few oral historians are going to be able to practise psychoanalysis. It requires years of a different

training. Equally important, oral history interviews are based
on the assumption of other purposes: our informants cannot be
asked to lie on their backs, to open their minds in free association, to talk while the interviewer keeps silent, or to report daily
with notes on their dreams and fantasies. But oral historians
certainly can learn a good deal from psychoanalysis about the
potential of their own craft—both for themselves, and for their
informants. Indeed, thinking about the implications of psychoanalysis has undoubtedly provided one major stimulus for the
advances in our understanding of oral memory as evidence over
the past ten years.

The most direct way in which this interest has arisen has often
been through a personal experience of therapy. We are fortunate
to have one account of this by a leading oral historian, in
Ronald Fraser's *In Search of a Past* (1984). This is a rare,
original, and fascinating book which would have made a mar-
vellous piece of social history in itself. Fraser interviewed his
own parent's servants. Through their sharp eyes he reconstructs
the Home Counties upper-class social world of the 1930s, and
the transformation wrought when the hunting ceased and the
social fences came down in the Second World War. The servants' words give us, tellingly, the complex mixture of loyalty
and hostility which bound both servant to servant and servant
to employer; and also, chillingly, the emotional emptiness at the
heart of the manor-house family—the loveless couple, and their
lonely, snooty son. But Fraser's courage and originality is to
bring together and interweave these painful childhood memories with two other dialogues: with his father, once daunting,
now pathetic and bewildered, his mind disintegrated to a blur in
which patches of memory float loose, on the way to his end in
an old people's home; and in discussion about his own memories with his psychoanalyst. The result is a completely new
form of autobiography, confronting the great issues of time
and class, yet intensely intimate.[1]

It is also a fugue on the nature of memory. The apparently
straightforward life-story evidence of the servants is shown, by
juxtaposition, to have its own silences and evasions, for example

on the sexual relations between them; it is set against the severely eroded memory of the old man, which may be the fate of their minds too; and it provides material for Fraser's unpeeling of his own unconscious memory in his psychoanalysis. It was his nanny, for instance, who told him how he was fed and changed on the clock, and potted from the age of four months: 'Later, I tied you on your pot to the end of the bed until you produced.' And through his therapy, Fraser not only gives vent to his anger against his parents, but comes to understand how the social division between employers and servants in his childhood home was also an emotional split which he carried into adulthood. His tough, practical nanny was as much a mother to him as his elusive, beautiful mother; while it was the resentful gardener who so hated his father's silent arrogance that became the lonely boy's closest daily companion, listened to him, taught him to plant, to value working with his hands—a second father. It was the gardener who, through emotionally attaching him to a working man, unknowingly opened the political path which Fraser took much later, when he rejected the values of his class along with those of his rejecting father.

Thus while at the start, the psychoanalyst seemed to be looking for something quite different from the past than Fraser's own interest as a historian, brushing aside abstract theorizing, the material world, what really happened, to concentrate on *feelings* about the past, on relationships between people, by the end of his 'voyage of inner discovery' through analysis the two dimensions of understanding had become part of a single interpretation.[2] This does not mean, however, that such an interpretation could only have been reached through psychoanalysis. It would have been an equally typical outcome of the group discussion which takes place in family therapy, drawing out underlying feelings through direct confrontation with other family members in a situation where expressing them is safe, indeed expected. The specific techniques of free association and dream analysis are not part of this therapeutic approach. Nevertheless, it is as effective in uncovering the complexity of contradictory emotions, of intertwined love and anger, which are typical of intimate relationships; and still more so, through the insights brought from a family systems theory which looks for the structuring of relationships, in pointing to the equally characteristic intergenerational influences in emotional patterns.[3]

Take the case of a north Italian small businessman's beautiful teenage daughter, who was slowly starving herself to death. What was her protest about? The family could not understand and the school, where she was working hard and doing well, could offer no clues. Desperate, they came for help to a charismatic family therapist in the big city. Their first accounts of each other were typically restrained: the children thought their mother could perhaps be a bit more independent, while she spoke of her husband as a good man whose only problem was that he never laughed, he was always so serious and sad. But it took scarcely an hour in the consulting room to lift the veil from the family secrets which had paralysed them all. The husband came from a well-to-do family, but had married one of his father's maids after getting her pregnant. For him the affair had been a rebellion against his own father, who dominated his 'saintly' depressed mother; for her a release from family poverty. But instead of escaping, they trapped themselves in the grandparents' problems, imposing them on their own children. He had done the honourable thing, but he had never forgiven his wife for seducing him and spoiling his life. He preferred to spend his free time with his own parents, sharing a common scorn of 'la serva'. The wife found him always severe, hard with her, unable to listen to her problems, and his scarcely concealed anger had driven her into recurrent depression; the husband found her intolerably over-emotional, was sick of her family's problems; the children complained of her crying and shouting. Emotionally, rather than committed to each other as a couple, both husband and wife remained primarily attached to their families of origin. Her family were not only socially inferior to his, but had remained much poorer, and her bitterest complaint against him was his refusal to give money to help her sisters; while he saw her family as a recurrent drain on his resources, always asking for more. Yet he insisted that each Sunday she must cook a family meal for his own parents who shared his resentment against her and her people. In this deadlock of emotional and class antagonism, the Sunday cooking was a form of hatred. Even though none of them had understood before, it was clear enough now that the girl's refusal of food was a cry against the hidden but intolerable conflict between her parents. Her action was its mirror opposite: rather than food as hatred, starvation as love.

Family therapy is another special situation in which inner truths quite often emerge more quickly than in psychoanalysis. It has the advantage of interpreting individual needs not in isolation, but in a social context. Through its perspective we can explore just why in one family each generation of sons quarrels with its fathers, while another hands down both the skills and ambition to succeed in just the same family profession; why in one family neither fathers nor sons can commit themselves to a single, sustained love relationship, but must always keep mistresses, while in another it is the strong women who call the tune and the men flit through like marginal episodes, and in yet another depressed mothers are followed by depressed daughters. This exploration of the diversity of ordinary experience is far more rewarding than the crude applications of individual psychoanalytic theory to whole cultures which has unfortunately typified 'psychohistory'.[4] It is also much closer to the extraordinary variety in individual lives which oral historians typically discover and need to explain. One of the principal lessons to be drawn from both kinds of therapy is the need for an enhanced historical sensitivity to the power of emotion, of unconscious desire, rejection, and imitation, as an integral part of the structure of ordinary social life and of its transmission from generation to generation.

Similarly, it is not the specific techniques of psychoanalysis in the interpretation of dreams which matter most, but the attention which it has drawn to the pervasiveness of symbolism in our conscious world. We could well ask for dreams from our own informants, their nightmare fears, or their fantasies while day-dreaming on the assembly line; and to learn the most from such expressions of their inner wishes and anxieties we should obviously need to spot the typical tricks of 'dream-work', its condensation of messages, reversals, substitutions, metaphors, word-play, and visual images, through which dreams convey their symbolic messages. These tricks are one reason for the frightening power of fantasy and nightmare. But it is equally rewarding to know that these devices are also normal clues to the symbolic meaning of consciously conveyed messages: of social customs like rough music, or of jokes, or of traditional myths and personal stories.

More directly, the reinterpretation of Freudian psychoanalysis by Jacques Lacan has brought special attention to the fundamental role of language as part of the symbolism. He believed that the unconscious is structured like a language, and he saw the acquisition of sexual and personal identity as a simultaneous and always precarious process, whose foundations are laid as the human infant enters language, through being spoken to, listening, and learning to talk. Masculinity and femininity are therefore imposed on the infant's inner psyche, long before sex differences have any immediate meaning, through the unconscious cultural symbolism of gender embedded in language. Lacan's reformulation of Freud's essentially male perspective on the development of human personality is less radical than those of Klein and Chodorow earlier; and, partly because he has put it forward in such wilfully incomprehensible 'symbolic' language, as a theory it stands up much less well to logical criticism.[5]

Nevertheless, it has undoubtedly helped feminists to show the inadequacies of straightforward deductions from the differences between male and female social achievement, and the hollowness of policies for equal opportunities which ignore the weight of culture. Right from those earliest moments of developing social consciousness, the little girl learns that she is a female entering a culture which privileges masculinity and therefore privileges men, just as in language itself the masculine form always takes priority as the norm and the feminine only enters as the exception. To take a positive place in the world of culture she must fight from the start; but it is an unequal fight. In cultures with pictorial scripts the same lessons will be internalized for a second time, as she learns to read her language: a Chinese girl will discover that the character for a man is made from the symbols of field and strength while that for a woman from loom or womb.

The internalization of such attitudes is equally clearly revealed in the different ways in which men and women recall their pasts. It is not only that their memories tend to focus differently, men more readily talking about work, women about family life, and also that women are likely to find it easier to talk about remembered feelings than men. They also use words differently. Even in childhood, girls are much more likely than boys to report what others said in detail. And among older men and women, Isabelle Bertaux-Wiame has observed how among migrants to Paris from the French countryside, 'the men consider the life they have lived as *their own*', as a series of self-conscious acts, with well-defined goals; and in telling their story they use the active 'I', assuming themselves as the subject of their actions through their very forms of speech. Women, by contrast, talk of their lives typically in terms of relationships, including parts of other life-stories in their own; and very often they speak as 'we', or 'one' (*on* in French), symbolizing the relationship which underlies that part of their life: 'we' as 'my parents and us', or as 'my husband and me', or as 'me and my children'.[6] Read in this light, life-stories reveal unsuspected and important new messages.

Lastly, we can understand more from what is not said. Again it is not the specific theories of psychoanalysis which prove most useful, so much as a new sensibility, an ability to notice what might have been missed. Freud's own original belief in total memory looks now more like a nineteenth-century fantasy wish to recapture the past, and has certainly no scientific basis, even though it has been so influential that most people apparently 'believe all memories potentially retrievable'.[7] Freud was almost certainly wrong in explaining the absence of memories of infancy through repression: it is much more probable that infant experience is forgotten because the long-term memory is not yet organized than that it is suppressed because shameful. Nor will it help us much to consider whether or not the typical 'resistance' of the analysand—secretive, hidden, obdurate—might be understood through the analogy of childhood refusals to be fed or weaned or to defecate in the right place. The important lesson is to learn to watch for what is not being said, and to consider the meanings of silences. And the simplest meanings are quite likely to be the most convincing.

In short, what we may hope to gain through the influence of psychoanalysis is an acuter ear for the subtleties of memory and communication, rather than the key to a hidden chamber. What is typically repressed is also typically present—such as sex. What the unconscious holds may differ in proportion, and in power, but not in kind: it is simply human experience, accidentally or actively forgotten for all the reasons which we have seen. Concentration camp survivors dream about food and torture. The real world moulds even the delusions of the wholly mad. Victorian schizophrenics wove their fantasies around religion, while contemporary schizophrenics fantasize about sex; but both take off from the everyday concerns of their time. Fantasy and the unconscious are in the end no more than the reordering of lives. Sometimes they may present the world upside down; and they certainly have the power to change how people act in reality. The unconscious is there as a force behind every life-story. But the mould of civilization and its discontents is clear enough, from whichever side of consciousness we perceive it.

There is however another dimension of psychoanalysis which demands equal attention from oral historians. This is its primary therapeutic process through the releasing of memory. Many oral historians have come to realize this by chance, through their own practice. They will learn—often through a third person—how being interviewed gave an old person a new sense of importance and purpose, something to look forward to, even the strength to fight off an illness and win a new lease of life. They may also have found that it is not always so simple.

Most people hold some memories which, when recalled, release powerful feelings. Talking about a lost mother or father may evoke tears, or anger. Usually an unembarrassed, sympathetic response is all that is needed in this situation: expressing the feelings will in itself have been positive. Practice has also shown that it is normally possible, and indeed helpful, for an oral historian to listen to seriously traumatic experiences, for example of rape, or of imprisonment in a concentration camp. But for some people these memories may tap such deep, unresolved pain that it demands more sustained reflection with the help of a professional therapist; and clearly in such cases the best that the oral historian can do is to suggest how this could be found. There are warning signals to watch for, such as general incoherence, long silences, repeating the same story of shock and horror, or bursts of rage or sobbing, trembling, or a hunched posture. Such haunting memories arise, typically, from family experiences which are violent, shameful, or especially entangled and perplexing; or from the atrocities of war and persecution.[8]

Donald and Lorna Miller have recorded the memories of survivors of 'the first genocide of the 20th century', the massacre of over a million Armenians—half their entire population in the Ottoman Empire—in the years from 1915 to 1922. Some were burnt alive; others used as pack animals, maimed, tortured, or starved to death. The bellies of pregnant women were torn open, and other mothers forced to leave their straggling infants to die on rocks in streams, or sell them to passing Arabs; not a few mothers and families committed suicide together. What has this unimaginable horror left in the memory of survivors? Some will never speak of it. In some, anger has now given way to political explanation, or resignation that nobody cares; or even to forgiveness. But in others hatred of the Turks burns fiercely on: they dream at night about being chased: 'I wake up sweating', 'They stab you in the back.' And yet others still hope for revenge: in 1973 one 78-year-old survivor, who had lost almost all his family in the massacre, shot two Turkish consular officials dead in a cafe in Santa Barbara, California.[9] His rage was a memory which spanned over fifty years in another culture and another continent.

The memory of the still more systematic degradation, humiliation, and extermination of the Nazi concentration camp victims is equally haunting. Two hundred Italian survivors have testified how many of them kept it to themselves, because they felt its full horror would be incredible to others, inexpressible in words, and too painful for those close to them to hear: how they had been separated from all they knew, robbed of all their possessions, stripped naked, shaven of all their hair, given numbers instead of names, made to eat with their mouth and hands 'come una bestia'; lived every day within the sight and smell of death, smelling the burning bodies, seeing the human ashes used for road cinders, seeing piles of corpses; how they learnt, in order to survive, to eat grass to keep down hunger, to steal from anybody, to trust nobody but an intimate, to sleep undisturbed next to a corpse of a fellow inmate after stripping it of clothes to keep warm themselves, above all to think of death as ordinary, even when guards hacked another prisoner to death in front of them by beating their heads open . . . No wonder even today, the price of the telling may be weeks of renewed nightmare terror. And such memories may be almost as intolerable indirectly. Claudine Vegh found similar fears, nightmares, nervousness, anger, and paralysis when interviewing French Jews whose parents were killed in the Nazi period. 'Many of those who were left orphans never talk about their past, it is taboo . . . They do not want to, above all, they cannot, talk about it.' Many who did talk were very reluctant, spoke in hoarse whispers, or burst into tears. They had not been able to mourn at the time of their separation from their parents because there had been no time, no ceremony, and they had not been sure until long after that the parent had died. No reconciliation had been possible. They had carried into old age an open wound, a confusion of loss, shame, anger, and guilt, still as real today as ever: 'mute agonies' which had 'haunted them all their lives, . . . a hurt so painful, so omnipresent, so all-encompassing, that it seems impossible to talk about it even a lifetime later'.[10]

Such memories are as threatening as they are important, and demand very special skills in the listener. They are thankfully exceptional. For most people the pain of the past is much more manageable, lying alongside good memories of fun, affection, and achievement, and recollecting both can be positive. Remembering our own lives is crucial to our sense of self; working on that memory can strengthen, or recapture, self-confidence. The therapeutic dimension of life-story work has been a repeated discovery. Thus Arthur Ponsonby, the literary critic and anthologist of *English Diaries* (1923), noted how many of his authors used their diary pages for the purpose of 'self-analysis, self-dissection, introspection, . . . for clearing their minds, for threshing out human problems, for taking stock of the situation . . . They may even derive from it the same sort of relief as others find in prayer.' Sociologists have also noted the confessional dimension to life-story interviewing, and partly because much of their work has been with deviants who are often personally isolated, have especially encountered unexpectedly warm responses to a 'sympathetic ear'. Annabel Faraday and Ken Plummer vividly illustrate this from one series of letters they received: 'If my reactions have been impulsive, it is because you have unexpectedly breached the wall of my isolation and I cannot help thinking of you as a friend in a special category. Hoping you can think of me in a similar way.' And from a later letter: 'I found great relief in talking to you today. Thank you for being such a sympathetic audience and for making me feel so relaxed'. And again, several months later: 'I feel I am overburdening you and using you as an outlet for my personal troubles, but it has been a case of opening a valve . . .' As researchers, they did indeed find their shift from sympathetic observer, 'through sounding board to confessor and emotional prop', was a burden which could have consumed indefinite energies, given the severe problems of many of the sexual deviants they were recording. But the positive changes which they saw in some informants were equally striking: the transvestite, for example, who suggested he was now 'strong enough to "come out" publicly—a move which he felt would inevitably result in the final breakdown of his shaky marriage and which he suggested could be done through the publication of his life history'.[11] The changes which oral historians may notice in their subjects are certainly unlikely to be as colourful, but they may be as important. Their growing realization that not only were people good for history, but history might be good for people in themselves, has been one major source for the reminiscence therapy movement which has spread so strikingly in recent years.

Its other growing point has been a noticeable change in attitudes to ageing in the caring professions. Earlier gerontologists actively disapproved of reminiscence. They saw 'living in the past' as pathological, a withdrawal from present reality, denial of the passage of time and ageing, even evidence of organic brain damage or psychological 'regression to the dependency of the child'. The idea that reflection on the personal past, and through it acceptance of change, might be essential to the maintenance of self-identity through the typical transformations of the life-cycle, is a logical inference of basic psychoanalytic thinking, and was already being argued by Erikson; but psychoanalysis of older people was in practice uncommon. The key influence came from an American research psychiatrist, Robert Butler, who began tape-recorded interviews to investigate the mental health of the old in 1955, and through interviewing stumbled on the 'quite apparent . . . therapeutic benefit in reminiscence'. Beginning with a now classic paper on 'The Life Review' (1963), he has argued for the need to view reminiscence as normal and healthy, part of a universal process for re-evaluating past conflicts to re-establish self-identity, and a means of helping the elderly to help themselves. Through either an individual interview or a group discussion 'they can reflect upon their lives with the intent of resolving, reorganizing, and reintegrating what is troubling or preoccupying them'. The old as much as the young need the chance to express their feelings, talk through their troubles, work out their regrets; to reconsider, for example, at a time in life when they want to hand on their moral experience to a younger generation, the painful lessons of parenting, and 'to express the guilt, grief, uncertainty, fear, and uneasiness which are tied to their concern that they have not been effective parents'.[12]

Butler's influence was spread both through a guide to *Living History* (1970) published by the American Psychiatric Association and also a series of papers by researchers and therapists attempting to test his ideas. Partly because of disagreement over what exactly was meant by normal reminiscence, and also through insufficient consideration of the distorting effects of loss of self-identity through institutionalization, nothing sufficiently conclusive emerged from this research.[13] The eventual practical breakthrough in Britain has come rather from the social workers and hospital staff who have provided the front line in caring for the rapidly growing numbers of older people in need today.

There were already some precedents in social work practice, such as the use of 'life books' of documents and photographs first developed for children in care, to help them keep or recover a clear sense of self after bewildering transfers between institutions or while settling in with foster-parents. Life books have been more recently used with the adult mentally handicapped. There were also instances of the casual use of reminiscence in social work with the elderly. The crucial point, however, was a growing realization of 'the huge arrogance', as Malcolm Johnson has termed it, of professionals—of a different class and generation, and a different life experience—presuming that they could define the needs of their clients without first understanding their own diagnosis of their condition. That meant looking at the problems of old age in the perspective of the ageing person's own life experience: listening to them, 'to identify the path of their life history and the way it has sculpted their present problems and concerns'. In this way the individual's own *priorities* for the later phases of life would emerge, the outcome of a lifetime of 'losses and triumphs and fears and satisfactions and unfulfilled aspirations'. Many social workers stumbled on this relevance of the past when it proved the clue to a particularly puzzling case: the old man, for instance, unable to look after himself, yet stubbornly reluctant to go into a home. His resistance became immediately understandable once it was learnt that he had been a child in an orphanage. And in more recent years the use of the life-story approach in negotiating choices for housing and care has been increasingly emphasized. Listening, in short, has proved to be professionally useful.[14]

In the mean time a government architect for old people's accommodation, Mick Kemp, disturbed by the low quality of life he had seen in the many homes he had to visit, had been enabled to develop experiments in the use of images to stimulate withdrawn old people to talk and respond. The first images were artistic, but then he found that old pictures of scenes and events—like domestic interiors, the abdication of Edward VIII, the General Strike, or the Jarrow March—were still more effective. So was old music, linked to the pictures. From 1980 the *Recall* project was taken over by Help the Aged Education Department, where Joanna Bornat was able to bring to it her own experience as an oral historian. Within a year a series of six tape and slide sequences combining music, singing, and spoken memories of the past was issued for practical use with groups of old people.

Cheap and simple to use, needing only a tape recorder, a slide projector, and a white wall to get started, the *Recall* packs have proved immensely successful, an immediate and practical demonstration of the effectiveness of Butler's ideas. In a whole variety of situations, ranging from old people's day centres and clubs for the active elderly living at home to the chronic sick in danger of institutionalization, the severely depressed, dementing, or even psychotic hospital patients, reminiscence has been reported as having remarkable effects. In a normal group of rather bored, withdrawn old people, there will be a sudden change of atmosphere: as the tape-slide show goes on, they start to talk, and to sing the songs, and then they go on talking afterwards—and the others listen to them. Still more remarkably, old people who have been mute for months suddenly speak to others; someone normally totally inert can be seen tapping a foot to music; an old woman who has seriously neglected herself starts to take an interest in her appearance; an old man, silently withdrawn into acute depression, exchanges a memory with a former workmate—and he smiles. Equally important is the impact of this changing atmosphere on others. Staff can see that something can be done; relatives begin to visit more often, and stay longer. Put simply, *Recall* sparks a common talking-point; and once communication is restarted, people rediscover each other as human beings.

The first series of *Recall* packs—on 'Childhood' in the 1900s, 'Youth' in the 1920s, 'The Thirties', the two wars, and so on—sold 1,500 in three years. Since then many districts have produced their own local packs. There are regular training courses in the use of reminiscence for nurses, social workers, occupational therapists, and other professional and voluntary workers with the old. Reminiscence therapy has become a reinvigorating wave, a catalyst for change in the care of the older people which can alter attitudes in a host of small but cumulatively significant ways. John Adams put up old posters in a continuing care ward in a south London hospital and found these too got both residents and visitors talking: 'patients can be overheard explaining to their visitors, with the aid of an Imperial War Museum poster, how they distinguished German from British airships in World War One'. Wards should be given names which mean something to old people, after a music hall star, rather than after a saint or a local landowner, and they should be decorated with the same intention, so that 'reminiscence ceases to be a special event and becomes simply part of the general fabric of ward life'. Andrew Norris and Mohammed Abu El Eileh took out a group of frail elderly psychogeriatric patients from a Dartford hospital, following a suggestion in a group therapy session, on a tour of places of interest which they had mentioned, visiting former workplaces, homes, schools, and pubs: 'the response of our reminiscers was staggering'. Group discussion also resulted in the discovery of three former musicians among the patients, for whom they were able to buy instruments to entertain the ward. More active groups have gone on to produce local booklets and exhibitions.[15]

It is still far from clear how useful, in a strictly medical sense, reminiscence may be. Certainly it cannot cure conditions like dementia: 'it may just make living in hospital a little more bearable and meaningful'. Equally clearly its application and its effects must differ, depending on whether the context is social work with old people living in their own or residential homes, or in a range of hospital situations; and between individuals. Peter Coleman emphasizes that reminiscence does not suit everyone equally. His own research is exceptional, for he has been able to follow up the eight survivors of a group of fifty-one old people whom he had interviewed in sheltered housing in London ten years earlier. Originally he had found that twenty-one were 'happy reminiscers' who enjoyed talking about their pasts; but there were also sixteen who saw no point in reminiscing, because they were actively coping with life in other ways. The 'happy reminiscers' proved the most resilient group, but the active non-reminiscers only included a few with low morale, such as a lonely ex-prisoner: more typically, they were busily active and reminiscence seemed to them a waste of precious time. The more striking contrast was with two other groups. Eight were 'compulsive reminiscers' whose 'brooding in the past' was 'dominated by regretful memories': they talked a lot, but felt bad about it. Their prognoses proved bad, showing increased psychological disturbance. Such people might actually be harmed by group therapy: what they needed was skilled personal counselling. The prospects were equally bleak for the six who avoided reminiscing because it made them more depressed, since the present seemed to them so much worse than the past. Typically they had suffered a severe loss, such as recent bereavement, and could not manage the difficult adjustment to widowed, single life without their lifetime companion. Again their need was more likely for individual therapy, which they did not receive: those who had not died were still depressed ten years on. There are, in short, no automatic solutions: 'each person needs to be considered in a special way.'[16]

The key is in precisely that. Reminiscence therapy is no more a panacea than psychoanalysis. The basis of its transforming power, as with oral history itself, is quite simple: listening seriously to what old people have to say. It is through this that a miserable, difficult, moaning old white person can become a whole person, even one with some similar experience, to a young West Indian nurse. When care staff do not get to know their patients they too easily become mere bodies to be fed and watered, managed and maintained in existence. Communication can make them people again.

What do you see nurses, what do you see,
What are you thinking when you look at me?
A crabbit old woman, not very wise,
Uncertain of habits with far-away eyes,
Who dribbles her food, and makes no reply
When you say in a loud voice, 'I do wish you'd try' . . .
Is that what you are thinking, is that what you see?
Then open your eyes, you're not looking at me . . .
I'm a small child of ten with a father and mother,
Brothers and sisters who love one another.
A young girl at sixteen with wings at her feet,
Dreaming that soon now a lover she'll meet . . .
At twenty-five now I have young of my own,
Who need me to build a secure happy home . . .
At forty my young now will soon be gone
But my man stays beside me to see I don't mourn . . .
Dark days are upon me, my husband is dead:
I look at the future, I shudder with dread . . .
I'm an old woman now and nature is cruel,
Tis her jest to make old age look like a fool . . .
But inside this old carcase a young girl still dwells,
And now and again my battered heart swells,
I remember the jobs, I remember the pain,
And I'm loving and living life over again . . .
So open your eyes nurses, open and see,
Not a crabbit old woman, look closer *see* me.[17]

6

Projects

Oral history is peculiarly suited to project work. This is because the essential nature of the method is itself both creative and co-operative. It is true that oral evidence once collected can be used by the traditional independent scholar who works only in the library. But this is to miss one of the key advantages of the method—the ability to locate new evidence exactly where it is wanted, through going out into the field. And field-work to be successful demands human and social skills in working with informants, as well as professional knowledge. This means that oral history projects of any kind start with unusual advantages. They demand a range of skills which will not be monopolized by those who are older, expert, or best at writing, so they allow co-operation on a much more equal basis. They can bring not only intellectual stimulation, but sometimes, through entering into the lives of others, a deep and moving human experience. And they can be carried out anywhere—for any community of people carries within it a many-sided history of work, family life, and social relationships waiting to be drawn out.

Oral history projects can take place in many different contexts, both as individual and as group enterprises: in schools, colleges, and universities; or in adult education or literacy groups, from museums, or from community centres. They can involve all kinds of people: schoolchildren, unemployed young adults, working parents, or the old retired. Although sharing many features, each context provides a distinctive emphasis which carries its own advantages and its own problems. We shall therefore look at them in turn. And because the discussion is meant to be a practical one, we shall recount the particular experience of several projects which have been carried out successfully. The ideas which follow are not just ideal suggestions, but have been shown to work.

Let us begin with schools. Since an oral history project is a complex and time-consuming operation, the first question any teacher is likely to ask is why give it a place in the curriculum at all? The educational arguments can be summarized briefly. A concrete objective and a direct product are provided for project work. Discussion and co-operation are promoted. Children are helped to develop their language skills, a sense of evidence, their social awareness, and mechanical aptitudes. For history teachers oral history projects have the special advantage of opening up locally relevant history for exploration. But they have also been successfully used in teaching English, social studies, environmental studies, geography, religious studies, or integrated studies; and, in varying forms, at any stage of social and intellectual development between the ages of 5 and 18. It is perhaps most suitable of all for primary school teaching, and at the other end of the school for A level students whose course includes a 'personal study' and therefore allows individual research. For history teaching the use of oral evidence in teaching was specifically endorsed by the National Curriculum's History Working Group: 'The reminiscences and reflections of people provide one of the richest sources of information for the recent past. If used carefully and selectively, oral history can add colour and depth to historical studies. Memories of family, friends and members of school communities can add a new dimension to pupils' understanding.'[1]

Any school project in oral history should assist children towards a much sharper appreciation of the nature of evidence, because they will be directly involved in its collection. This may come as an undesirable idea to authors and publishers who dislike school projects which create their own resources, or indeed to some professional historians. But at a simple level, in collecting anecdotes and memories of how people lived in the past, how they dressed, children's games, the changing landscape—however primitive their interviewing or recording technique may be—children are collecting evidence. At the same time, they become creatively involved in assessing it. They face basic issues: when to trust or to doubt information, or how to organize a set of facts. They experience, through active involvement at a practical level, history as a process in the re-creation of the past. Like young archaeologists, they are given spades in the place of lectures—taken to the coal-face to hew as historical researchers. And because they are collecting from sources which professionals have not used, they have a chance of putting this new evidence together in a piece of history of their own—a great-grandfather's memories of the First World War, or a neighbour's memories of a street fifty years ago—which is unique, and so brings a very special motivating force and sense of achievement.

During this process, several types of skill may be developed. First, there are inquiry skills. Once pupils have started to interview, the desire to find out more from other sources can be very powerful, leading into searches of the school or local libraries for books, and through this into techniques like using book indexes or the library cataloguing system. They learn through a range of techniques, not just by interviewing.

Next, it can provide important assistance in the development of language skills. This concerns both written and spoken language. Before interviewing, children have to discuss together the best wording of the questions which they might ask. When tapes are played back, they can also criticize the way in which questions are asked. While themselves interviewing, they have to learn to listen to other people, and grasp exactly what they intend to convey. This can demand intense concentration. Without realizing it, they are confronted with the problems of comprehension and interpretation which the English textbook comprehension exercise attempts to simulate. At the same time, through interviewing, or through being themselves interviewed, children can gain confidence in expressing themselves in words. This can be transferred from the spoken to the written word, for example, by getting them to write down what they can hear from a tape; or, conversely, by using a duplicated version of a transcript as a starting-point for discussions. They could perhaps discuss the differences between written and spoken language. At a later stage in the project, they can go on to reading in library work, and to a presentation of the project, including transcript material, in written form.

Technical skills will also be acquired in the handling of machinery when computers and tape recorders are used. Although these are not absolutely essential in school projects, they are highly desirable and can often be borrowed locally; and similarly a video camera can be an important additional resource. These skills can be carried further in the presentation of the project: for example, by editing extracts from recordings into a tape sequence, or by combinations of slides and sound, or by printing a booklet combining photographs and transcripts, or by an exhibition which makes use of all these means together. All this can also help to build links with the community, especially when interviewees are also asked to lend old photographs, postcards and other documents for the exhibition or booklet.

Finally, fundamental social skills can be learnt. Through interviewing itself, children may develop some of the tact and patience, the ability to communicate, to listen to others and to make them feel at ease, which is needed to secure information. To interview you have to behave as an adult; you cannot giggle. Children can be helped to learn to move in an adult world. At the same time, they may gain not only a vivid glimpse of how life was in the past, but a deeper understanding of what it is like to be somebody else; and how other people's experience, in the past and today, is different from their own—and why this might be. They can thus be helped both to understand and feel empathy with others, and to face conflicting values and attitudes to life.

So much for the theory. What about the practice? We can best turn to some examples of projects which have worked. The first is from a primary school.

At a county primary school in Cambridge, Sallie Purkis used

oral history with the younger age groups. She began with a
project, carried out over half a term on two afternoons a
week, with a class of twenty 7-year-olds. It was a diverse group:
some of the children came from abroad, and while nine children
could not read, others were very bright. The project was to be
their first ever experience in learning history. One of its objec-
tives was to make this first encounter exciting and interesting,
and to get the children to feel that they could collect historical
evidence, and that history was real, and relevant to their own
present. It was an advantage that the project was carried out in
a school without subject boundaries, so that the teacher could
launch easily into art work, English, and outside visits.

She chose as a concrete starting-point a photograph, suggested by a local librarian, of the school itself sixty years earlier,
just opened, with its first pupils standing among the builders'
rubble. The children were immediately interested by this, commenting on the pupils' clothes. They worked out where the
photograph had been taken from, and how old these first children would now be—in other words, as old as their own grandparents. Following this, 'grandma' was chosen as the key
symbolic figure of the project (aunts or other relatives could
be substituted) and it turned out that it was a novel experience
for *grand*parents to be involved in the school. Tape recorders
were not used, but a written questionnaire was sent out. It was
composed after discussion with the children, and, in retrospect,
was too long, for it produced more material than could be
organized satisfactorily—a few questions would have been quite
sufficient. Most but not all of the grandmas responded, and one
child, who called himself a 'historian' by the end of the project,
interviewed three people. Another produced a typescript. There
was thus an abundance of good material.

Sallie Purkis made a reading book for the class by selecting
extracts on particular topics and writing them out herself. The
first topic was 'What Grandma Said About Clothes': men's
clothes, women's clothes, and shoes—one child's grandfather
was a shoemaker. The children drew these. They also brought
in photographs, often very precious, so that they had to be

protected in plastic; these made a big show, and the children
proudly identified with them. Then objects began to be brought
in—garments, irons, and so on. Some of them were rather overwhelming, like 'the hat my father wore at grandfather's funeral',
in a big box marked NOT TO BE OPENED. Some of the children went
on to reading. Other children made a model clothes shop out of
shoeboxes. The class went on a museum visit. All the children
wrote essays: on shopping for clothes, on washing day; and on
'Grandma Day'. For the climax of the project without doubt
was Grandma Day: the afternoon when, to their own very
apparent enjoyment, the grandmas were invited up to school
for talk and tea with the children.[2]

Another imaginative primary school project—one of many
reported in the news columns of *Oral History* in the 1970s and
1980s—was at an inner London school in Notting Hill. For this
Alistair Ross chose a history of Fox Primary School itself,
focusing particularly on the school's wartime evacuation to
the countryside. This enabled the project to include a school
journey with the two classes of 7–10-year-olds to Lacock in
Wiltshire, where they interviewed villagers who remembered
the invasion of London children from their own school over
thirty years earlier. The whole project was notably successful in
stimulating the children to develop collaborative discussion
with adults, and also to use what they learnt in their own
creative writing.[3]

Next, let us look at some projects with older children. In this
context both the constraints and the opportunities are heightened. The interdisciplinary and investigative nature of oral
history requires some flexibility in the school's timetabling,
and also the adoption of the project-based examination schemes
now available, for realizing its full potential: but given this
scope, a project with older children can reach more ambitious
levels. Many schools have been able to publish projects for their
own centenaries or on local history as booklets; others have
organized local exhibitions. At Thurston Upper School in
Suffolk, Liz Cleaver used some form of oral history with all
the years: constructing family trees with the younger classes,

and then moving on to comparisons of health provision before and after the welfare state by questioning grandparents, and finally to a series of sixth-form projects on 'Life in Suffolk Between the Wars'. The sixth formers set up a committee to run these projects themselves and used them to produce special magazines for local sale. Each year a minority went on to individual A-level projects for their school-leaving examinations.[4]

It is, however, to the United States that we must look for the most widespread use of oral history in secondary schools: for there has been nothing in Europe to approach the extraordinary success for many years of the Foxfire project. Despite its unfortunate later demise, its example remains very relevant. Eliot Wigginton went straight from college to Nacoochee School, a small town high school at Rabun Gap in the mountains of Georgia. He soon discovered that the teaching methods he had been taught simply did not work. In the teachers' room the talk was utterly pessimistic: these kids could not do anything, they could never write. Wigginton saw that their essential problem was *boredom*: they were 'just ordinary high school kids' with a hunger to do something. Once they got the chance to create their own material they were transformed. They found it in the *Foxfire* school magazine project. Originally started as an optional course in 'Creative Writing', it became the core of a cluster of courses which allowed credits in filming, building and other crafts, and even science. The children collected information through interviews, photography, and measured drawings, and they learnt not only to produce a magazine, but technical crafts, taking apart and reconstructing machines and old buildings, and organizing old people's get-togethers.

The magazine became a phenomenal success, not only locally, but nationally right across the United States. Selections published in book form from 1972 as *Foxfire One*, *Two*, and *Three* had already sold more than four million copies by 1978, with the first volume proving the best-selling book ever published by Doubleday. Partly through its own foundation with its regular training workshops and newsletter *Hands On*, the influence of *Foxfire* spawned more than 200 similar high school magazines, such as *Sea Chest*, published by the Cape Hatteras High School at Buxton, North Carolina, and *Loblolly*, from Gary High School in the ranching-lumbering, gas, and oil countryside of Texas.

Wigginton was in constant demand as an adviser all over the country, especially from demoralized inner-city high schools. I heard him describe a typical visit to an Indianapolis high school with 5,000 pupils and 350 teachers who had 'just given up'; only the twenty school guards, armed with guns, maintained a bare semblance of order. His message there, as always, was that responsibility must be placed, not on the children, but on the teachers. If children were given the chance to be creative, they would respond. He would abolish textbooks altogether if he could.

Certainly the school's location helped to create *Foxfire*'s wider appeal. Over the years, the project has built up a group of trusted informants, to whom the school pupils return again and again for new information. Their southern voices speak of regional crafts—log-cabin building, cooking, making quilts, soap, straw mattresses ('Best sweet smellin' bed you ever slept on. We changed th'straw every year at threshin' time')—and of customs and beliefs around childbirth, work, sickness, and death, which take one straight back into the world of the early Puritans, in which religion and witchcraft were still inextricably intertwined. Of curing burns and bleeding by faith healing they say, 'Stoppin' blood's just like drawin' out fire . . . You do it with th'same verse and th'same words.' And of planting by the moon:

Take taters. On th'dark of th'moon or th'old of th'moon—that's th'last quarter, they make less vine; and on th'light of th'moon they makes more vine and less tater . . . Th'Lord put th'signs here for us t'go by. It's all in th'Bible: th'signs of th'stars, moon, sun, and all. You've got to follow all these signs if you do right. Don't you know the signs?

Yet to get schoolchildren to bring together material of this quality in a regular quarterly magazine, even after winning the confidence of the people of old mountain communities, took great organizing skill and imagination over several years—especially when it remains, as any oral history project must, just one aspect of a school's programmes, exciting some pupils, but by no means all.

Eliot Wigginton's practice was to start with a relatively brief preparation for interviewing in the classroom:

We illustrate, for example, the need for a tape recorder by telling a short story in the class, and then the next day without telling them the reason for telling the story at all come into class and say, 'Let's take out a piece of paper and a pencil and retell that story that I told you yesterday.' I use a few details; say it's a hunting story, I can say, 'When I caught that bear, I took a stick about six-and-half feet long, and I did this with it, and then I took a couple of rawhide thongs and I did this and I . . .'— that kind of thing. I tell a story that's got some details in it that a kid would be forced to remember. You'd be amazed how off the kids are in their repetitions of that story.

This led on to a discussion of how to get a good interview. The key was genuine curiosity:

The kid should not be wandering around and looking out of the window and drumming on the floor . . . You may get into an interview situation that you expected to take a half an hour and it may in fact go into four hours if somebody gets cranking. They've got to be curious . . .

You tell them that the cardinal sin of interviewing is to get into a question-and-answer pattern . . . get one sentence or two sentence responses and then ask another question on a totally different subject . . . What you want an informant to do is to get on to a topic and then begin to expand, and inside that expansion all kinds of things happen. You try to get the kids to ask the same question a hundred different ways. You know, 'How did you do so-and-such? Well, did anybody else in your house do it differently?' You keep them beating around inside that topic as much as possible—'Have you ever heard of it being done in another way?' Then if possible you give the kids some information before they go out on a topic that they can carry with them, like other alternative means of doing something . . . (And) you have to remind the kid that he can't cut off the people once they get going. If they start telling stories . . . bear hunting stories, the worst thing you can train a kid to do is cut him off and say, 'No, wait a minute! I don't want bear stories. I want how to tan a hide . . .'

This preparatory stage was kept quite short. As soon as possible pupils were sent out into the field for their first interview. They went for the first time either with a staff member, or another more senior and experienced pupil. Initial interviews were set up in advance, to make sure that the experience was with a sympathetic informant. Once the children became more confident, they went out into the field on their own without any staff members. And they began with relatively small topics— 'how one woman made soap, smaller things of that sort'—and gradually worked up to bigger topics.

Eliot Wigginton's most remarkable achievement, however, was in devising an organization for publication which made the fullest possible use of the material which the pupils collected:

We do many kinds of articles. I'll give you a few illustrations. We got a call from another magazine one time that said, 'We're doing an article on various ways that you can tell what the weather is going to be like this year . . .' We had six or eight in a file, and we said, 'Okay, I'll tell you what. You call us back at 3.30 this afternoon and we'll have something for you.' You take two class periods and just about every kid who is working on the magazine—fifty-five kids—and you say, 'Okay, you guys right there, you take Kelly's Creek. You guys take Betty's Creek, etc., and you go out and ask everybody you run into what weather signs, what specific weather signs they can remember, and you be back here in an hour and forty-five minutes.' We got something like 110 weather signs in an hour and forty-five minutes that we never even suspected existed, and those appeared on three or four pages inside *The Foxfire Book*.

Another kind of interview we do is the personality type interview. We usually feature one person in each issue. In this particular issue it's a woman named Ada Kelly, who's a grandmother that lives in our section. The kids who are responsible for the Ada Kelly article go back and interview her at least three or four times . . . The kids will organize all that together and present it. Meanwhile, if the folklorist wants to see all of the original material, we have all the original transcripts plus all the original tapes . . .

With an ongoing organization, it became possible for each successive year of pupils to help not only each other, but following years. They were encouraged to choose their own subjects. But very often they collected much more than they needed for their own purposes:

He may have gone out for ghost stories and come back with fifteen hunting stories also. When a kid gets the transcriptions all made and you have a carbon, he cuts out of the carbon the material that he needs for his article, his ghost stories . . . but somebody else in the class may be collecting hunting stories . . . He puts those together and says, 'Here, you can add these to your article.' The guy that's collecting hunting stories may do the same for the ghost-story article; in other words, they all plug in with each other. We get twenty or thirty articles usually going at the same time. If a kid comes back with a chunk of information that is not being dealt with at that time, we have what we call an 'Articles-in-Preparation File' . . . Then next year, if a kid wants to pick up that subject and carry it on . . . he can pick up that interview and go on with it. So all the material gets utilized; all of it gets used in one way or another.

Eliot Wigginton's *Foxfire* project was undoubtedly a remarkable enterprise, an example which needs to be thought about very closely. There can be no doubt that for many pupils involvement in it proves a transforming experience. As one puts it:

I've learned through *Foxfire* . . . to express myself and communicate. Then by actually teaching a younger kid how to do something I've learned to appreciate the value of teaching and become excited when I see the kid's eyes light up . . . Then more significant than that, I've learned to appreciate the value of people working together, people being dependent on each other . . . It's made a difference in my life.[5]

So much for examples of projects which have worked. But for the teacher who is considering just starting, this very success may seem daunting. What about the normal problems which can be expected in an oral history project?

First, there are those of organization. Oral history work is essentially a small-group activity, and difficult to organize in large classes. There can be no doubt that projects benefit greatly from situations in which teaching is organized on a team basis, or the curriculum favours interdisciplinary work—and it is perhaps an argument for them that they point to fundamental issues in school organization. But many problems can be overcome by advance preparation: for example, by making pre-interview contact with old people, groups of children can be sent out interviewing while others are discussing material already collected in the class. For this and other purposes it is vital to draw as fully as possible on outside resources, starting with the children's own parents and the Parent-Teacher Association, and using the community networks provided by the local paper and local radio, clubs, firms, and libraries. If the school is in an area of high unemployment there will also be many skilled middle-aged people who could help the project.

Secondly, there is the question of equipment. Oral history work does not depend on the existence of recorders or video cameras, although it can be much more fully developed with them. If the school's policies towards equipment and its use are not generous, you will again need to rely on the support you can win from outside, beginning with parents. There should certainly be enough homes which can lend you the tape recorders to make a start.

Thirdly, subjects have to be well chosen. They must interest each particular group of children. For younger age groups, family history is particularly suitable. It helps a child-centred approach, drawing on the child's own access to family memories and documents, and at the same time encourages parents or grandparents to participate in the work of the school. A whole variety of themes can start from developing family trees with different kinds of information. With older groups there are many more choices: homes and houses, food and clothes, work including domestic work, family life, games or leisure—and any of these can be made comparative with memories from other countries. A project can be about a local event. But perhaps one idea may be given a special mention at this point: a project which focuses on the story of a particular street. It is not always easy to see any boundaries or shape to local or community history in a big city. But a single street can offer a microcosm of some aspect of its history: of changes in working-class community life, or shops and trading, or of successive patterns of immigration. With the help of a local newspaper, in some cases it may even prove possible to trace some representative of most of the families who lived there forty or sixty years ago. It will certainly provide the teacher with a physical basis for a class project which could combine photography, the collection of records and topographical data, searches of archives and newspaper files, as well as interviewing.

Next, the children must learn some of the personal skills needed in the interview, which is not always easy. They can practise by interviewing the teachers themselves, or members of their own family. Or old people can be asked up to the school, although this normally proves much more successful in an informal small group, rather than in front of a whole class. Indeed there is a danger of leading children through such a demonstration to think of old people as historical objects, rather than as valued for themselves. Children can also be asked to write their own autobiographies, partly from family documents, and be interviewed by another child—making sure that this does not lead into too deep a probing of personal situations, which could prove a damaging experience. They must also be taught how to formulate different kinds of questions. This can be helped by criticizing other interviews, like the teacher's own. And it is particularly important that the children's first interview recordings should be listened to and commented on, to give support as well as advice.

Special sensitivity is needed for projects in racially mixed schools. Clearly, both black and white children need to learn about their own and each other's historical cultures, and there has been much recent curriculum work with this objective, some of it including mutual interviewing. But for historical work it must be remembered that many immigrant children have no nearby grandparents; and their families speak either altogether different languages, or in accents which English children find hard to understand. Getting prior support from the community will be more than usually important, and the mechanics of interviewing need to be thought through especially carefully. For example, while old white people can be interviewed by black children in clubs, racial tension and apprehensiveness may make it very difficult to arrange for this in their homes. There is also a special need in this situation for an integrating theme—such as the relationship between industrialization and migration. It is undoubtedly an area in which more experimentation is needed.

What can be done with the fruits of oral history projects afterwards? As we shall see with community projects, they can be combined with photographs, letters and documents, clothes, tools, and other objects to mount an effective exhibition, either in the school or a local centre. They can be published as local booklets or newspaper articles. More ambitiously, they can be developed into a video presentation. Afterwards, recordings can be deposited in the public library or museum. Wherever possible, a continuing, active relationship with the local community should be built up through returning to it the material collected in some form.

Finally, we need to beware of too easy success. Oral history projects can only be carried out successfully by skilled teachers in carefully considered contexts. Careless exercises could lead to considerable offence being caused, for example, by the tactless release of damaging (or libellous) information. And the advantages of the approach are largely destroyed if over-prepared, centrally produced materials are imposed. Hence the final product should not aim for a technical standard beyond the reach of the children. It is essential for them to be involved at every stage in the process, and to recognize their own contribution at the end. If oral evidence becomes just another source material in teaching, its hold on the imagination will be lost.

Two more specialized forms of life-story work also need to be mentioned: literacy work and reminiscence drama. A special autobiographical method has been developed for remedial teaching in reading and writing, both in schools and also for adult literacy groups. For many of the illiterate or scarcely literate adults— now estimated at two million in Britain—and children, shame and secrecy at their disability are the first hurdle which needs to be overcome if they are to be helped. Many face the added disadvantage of being first-generation immigrants, attempting to communicate in a second language. Beginning from oral work enables them to start where they are most confident and build from that point. Typically a group will first discuss some personal experiences of common interest: family, work, migration, or whatever. The tutor will record this discussion and transcribe parts of it. At the next session students will attempt to read part of the transcript of their own words, and then discuss the ideas, words, and grammar they have used, with the tutor suggesting possible changes to make the passage clearer. Gradually they move on from reading what they have spoken to writing independently, and to reading generally. But throughout the clue to success is beginning with their own language, as it is spoken, with its personal phrases and speech rhythms, about familiar people and experiences. It is this which eases each leap forward. Often the end result may be a personal autobiography, and some of these have later been published in booklets like the London collection *Our Lives*, which included the migration story of Mohammed Elbaja, a Moroccan boy at Shoreditch School. Many more were able to see their own words printed in the magazine *Write First Time*, which developed its own special format, with the lines broken to reflect points of sense and rhythmic phrases within each sentence, as in the example shown below.[6]

Another specialized form of educational work is reminiscence drama. This is again practised with various age groups. One of the most successful dramatic companies has been Age Exchange, led by Pam Schweizer, which for over twenty years has created theatre from old people's memories, which they play back primarily for audiences of old people, in clubs, community centres, or homes. There have also been less specialized one-off experimental uses of drama for particular projects: a nice instance is the fifty-year celebration of the Flint Sit-Down Strike in Michigan carried out by the Labor Theater Project, aiming to give back local people a sense of their own history by

This short piece by Terry Collins, which appeared in *Write First Time*, was written as an angry response to being made redundant. The first idea, which was two sentences long, was typed up and duplicated. Then everybody in the group discussed the issue and Terry added to it. He was then given some advice on spelling and setting before the piece appeared in the form printed below.

Made redundant

by T.A.P. Collins

This man at work
told the boss that I was too slow for him.
He sent my mother and dad a letter
so we went to see the Disabled Resettlement Officer.
I told her that he threatened me with the sack.
She telephoned him as she was very angry about it.
Me and this other boy, we were pushed around,
out of the door like criminals
and could not say anything about it.
But according to him, the time and motion man,
I was too slow.
He made me redundant.
I had been there eleven years and nine months.

drawing on their own memories. Particularly notably, in the 1980s the Royal Court Young People's Theatre worked especially with London schools, and its director Elyse Dodgson drew on her own remarkable experience in creating and producing theatre with West Indian girls in an inner south London comprehensive school. Three of their plays reached the London stage, culminating in *Motherland*, a deeply moving but beautifully controlled drama of West Indian experience—hopes and dreams, reality and rejection—in coming as migrants to Britain. The starting-point was a set of interviews with the girls' mothers and others of their generation in Brixton, collected by a former pupil with the help of a special grant. This personal testimony fired the girls' imagination and sustained them through the long period of working together as a group, for six hours a week over several months, to create the play. The emphasis was on group work rather than individual performance, with all expected to participate in every rehearsal, each playing a variety of roles, and all decisions taken through mutual discussion. The drama was developed through experimental role play: responding to themes taken from the recorded testimonies, the girls developed expressive mimes and wrote the words and music of songs to match the individual words. At a later stage the mothers were drawn in to see rehearsals and make their own suggestions. Ultimately *Motherland* interwove three levels of expression: the remembered real experience of the text from the interviews, spoken by narrator or chorus, the children's own imaginative songs, like 'Searchin' for housing, and the symbolism of group mime. Thus the experience of asking a landlady for accommodation and being turned away was expressed through a ritual of the whole group, walking, knocking, and freezing, which became a central image of the whole play. It is this combination of creative but highly disciplined group expression with the words of individual life experience which makes this children's drama so unusually compelling.[7]

Less need be said at this point on projects in higher education, in colleges and universities, where there has again been much successful work in oral history. In Britain, North America, and Australasia there has been a steady growth both of individual oral history research for undergraduate projects or postgraduate theses and also of taught courses at various levels. An evaluative survey of British courses in 1997 found over a hundred, primarily in history but also in sociology, English, and other disciplines.[8] In some of these courses students chose their own themes, but it seemed to be more usual for a common research topic to be decided by the tutor. The choice of topic will clearly be a crucial factor in the practical difficulties which may be encountered: whether, for example, the informants needed would be either hard to trace or very busy public persons; or whether the theme would demand travelling to distant or strange places. But for most themes the problems will be those typical of oral history work, and also of writing individual projects or theses, in general. For group work too the basic approach is the same. As a starting-point, for example, I have found that constructing family trees and talking about them, or interviewing in pairs and reporting back, will immediately involve and draw out almost any student group.

There are, however, two particular difficulties at this level. As many courses indicate, it is possible to go beyond learning together to carry out a joint research project. With pooled effort, this can go further faster. But group projects are much more difficult if an assessment on an individual basis for each element in the course has to be returned. And even individual projects become very difficult when, because of an inflexible system which only admits closed written examinations, they cannot make a contribution to the final degree result. It is encouraging that a third of the courses are able to include an assessment of project work.

A more special danger is in allowing the teaching of the method to shift too far from the practical to the abstract principle. Such academicism is largely responsible for the recurrent unpopularity of 'methodology' courses in the social sciences. Discussion of theory needs to be interwoven with practical experience, and it also needs to be directed towards specific historical issues. At the University of Essex, where the MA in Social History includes a course in the interview method, we have taught through a workshop approach. Students are plunged as quickly as possible into interviewing each other, and then seeking out an informant to interview on a topic of their own choice. These interviews are played back and discussed in the group. They invariably raise questions of the accuracy of memory, suppression, interviewing technique, and the experience of being interviewed. They also bring out examples of the kinds of historical material which can be collected, and the complexity of attitudes which it reveals. These practical sessions are interwoven with others discussing the principles of oral history from reading, so that the two approaches cross-fertilize each other.

This need to learn by practice as well as theory is cogently argued by Janis Wilton for her Australian distance-learning courses.

> At the core . . . is the requirement that students should practice and apply oral history method and theory . . . They must get out there and interview. They must prepare for and process the interviews they conduct. They must do something with the interviews . . . They must explain and analyse both the oral history process and the product which they have created.

This also seems to be an outcome especially valued by students: a British group, for example, 'all thought that the most significant part of our project was becoming "active" learners in the field of oral history'.[9]

As in many courses, at Essex the students then go on to mini-projects of their own, conducting a series of interviews and writing up an evaluation of their method and findings, including a model list of questions which could be used in a more extended project involving more than one interviewer. In many cases these small exploratory projects have proved the starting-points for full graduate research dissertations.

The choice of the topic is clearly critical. We have found it possible for a single student, undergraduate or graduate, working alone on a vacation project, to make a real contribution to historical knowledge through new field-work. It is best (although not essential and for some subjects intrinsically impossible) if interviews can be combined with research in archives or on local newspapers. It is also important to choose a subject which is relevant to wider historical issues as well as a sufficiently defined and *localized* theme. It will fail if potential informants are too scattered to be traced relatively quickly. Some examples of subjects which have proved creative, but manageable, are studies of various East Anglian village communities; neighbourhood and class relations in a Nottingham slum and in fishing ports; migrant hop-pickers, the recruitment of school-teachers, and the Essex military tailoring industry; young Bengali women's migration to Britain in the 1970s; London's Italian community; domestic economy among farm labouring families, and the spreading use of birth control among various social groups; Colchester engineering workers in the First World War, and the experience of the General Strike of 1926 in the town.[10] The possibilities, however, are limitless. And the gains are equally clear: the personal fulfilment, co-operative spirit, and deeper understanding of history itself which can result—and beyond that, the breaking down of the isolation of academic study from the world without.

It is no doubt here—for history in the community—that the oral history project has its most radical implications. It can contribute to many different enterprises—an adult literacy programme, an evening class in history, a local history society or a community group project, a scheme for retraining the young unemployed, a reminiscence therapy group for old people in a home or a hospital ward, a museum exhibition, or a radio programme. For each its essential merits will be to encourage co-operation, on an unusually equal footing, in the discovery of a kind of history which means something to ordinary people. Of course these are tendencies which have to be nurtured; and they can create problems.[11]

The first issue concerns the choice of topics. For many of these purposes the best topic may seem simply one which will catch immediate interest. By contrast the local history society's notions may be more severe, and indeed possibly too limited by the traditional conventions of documentary history. But the broadening perspectives of social history have meant that, with imagination, a topic can certainly be found which satisfies both. Thus Raphael Samuel argued for a re-mapping of local community history

in which people are as prominent as places, and the two are more closely intertwined. He or she can then explore the moral topography of a village or town with the same precision which predecessors have given to the Ordnance Survey, following the ridge and furrow of the social environment as well as the parish boundaries, travelling the dark corridors and half-hidden passageways as well as the by-law street. Reconstructing a child's itinerary seventy years ago the historian will stumble on the invisible boundaries which separated the rough end of a street from the respectable, the front houses from the back, the boys' space from the girls'. Following the grid of the pavement you will come upon one space that was used for 'tramcars', another for hopscotch, a third for Jump Jimmy Knacker or wall games. 'Monkey racks' appear on the High Street, where young people went courting on their Sunday promenades, while the cul-de-sac becomes a place where woodchoppers had their sheds and costers dressed their barrows . . . (And similarly in) particular woods or fields . . . here mushrooms could be found or rabbits trapped; there potatoes were dug or horses illegally grazed, or long summer days were spent at haymaking or harvest . . .

Or again, instead of taking a locality itself as the subject, the historian might choose instead as the starting point some element of life within it, limited in both time and place, but used as a window on the world . . . It would be good to see this attempted for nineteenth-century London. A study of Sunday trading in Bethnal Green, including the war waged upon it by the open-air preachers; of cabinet-making in South Hackney, or of Hoxton burglars . . . would take one closer to the heart of East End life than yet another précis of Hector Gavin's *Sanitary Ramblings* . . . Courting and marriage in Shepherd's Bush, domestic life in Acton, or Roman Catholicism among the laundrywomen and gasworkers of Kensal Green might tell one more about the growth of suburbs than logging the increase of streets . . . The study of social structure, too, might be made more intimate and realistic if the approach were more oblique, and focused on activity and relationships. A study of childhood in Chelsea (of whom you could or couldn't play with, of where you were allowed to go), masculinity in Mitcham, the journey to work in Putney, or of local politics in Finsbury, would tell us a great deal (more) about the way class differences were manipulated and perceived, and social allegiances expressed in practice . . . than a more flat-footed approach taking the Registrar-General's fivefold divisions as markers.[12]

It is this approach of seeking for 'a window on the world' which initially allowed Raphael Samuel to catch the imagination of trade unionists on adult education courses at Ruskin College, Oxford, by getting them to explore the histories of their own occupations, and subsequently to stimulate the History Workshop movement which spawned local groups through the districts of London and the provincial cities. The movement's half-yearly journal, *History Workshop*, should provide sufficient reassurance to those pessimistic enough to fear that enthusiasm must prove incompatible with scholarly standards.

Its early activities nevertheless presented a challenge to professionalism as such, 'dedicated to making history a more democratic activity', and attacking a situation in which '"serious history" has become a subject reserved for the specialist ... Only academics can be historians, and they have their own territorial rights and pecking orders. The great bulk of historical writing is never intended to be read outside the ranks of the profession.'[13] A similar opposition to this view underlies the activities of many oral history groups, such as the collection of songs and interviews from north Italian factory workers by the Istituto Ernesto di Martiro in Milan, the joint work of the Brighton Trades Council and Sussex Labour History Society in the Queen Spark Books series, or other co-operative life-story publishing groups such as Peckham People's History, Bristol Broadsides, and the People's Autobiography of Hackney from East London. There is a parallel too in the neighbourhood committees which were set up in fifteen districts of Boston to produce, from library research, locating photographs, and collecting memories from all kinds of people, a bicentenary series of history booklets. There can be no doubt that these booklets, which were distributed free to residents in the Boston Bicentenary series or sold several thousand copies in the case of Hackney, brought local history to an exceptionally wide audience. But the spirit in which they have been produced by co-operative work can be equally striking. In the Hackney group there was an insistence that anyone can record anyone else, and all should contribute to the process of presentation. The purpose was as much to give people confidence in themselves, and their own memories and interpretations of the past, as to produce a form of history. In this context the professional, confident in self-expression and backed by the authority of higher degrees, can become a positive menace, tearing at the roots of the project. Of course a complete absence of the wider historical perspectives of an experienced historian can be equally damaging to a group's work. It will lead to the creation of one-dimensional historical myths rather than to a deeper social understanding. What is needed is a dynamic relationship, with interpretation developing through mutual discussion.

The success of the local group project will thus depend partly upon how it makes use of the differing talents which each will bring to the work: their own life memories, ability as technicians, knack with organizing, or skill in getting others to talk, will be as important as a reservoir of historical information. In some projects roles can be best divided up within a normal committee structure, while in others a professional will be the informal leader of an egalitarian group.

The level of equipment will also determine what can be achieved. As we shall see, both interviewing and archiving demand good equipment to get the best results. Certainly a life-story group can run very successfully on no more than pencil and paper. But if you want to record for local radio or set up an archive, you need to buy good quality equipment. Hence before starting any project it is essential to know that you can either buy or borrow workspace, desks, chairs, filing cabinets, at least two good cassette or digital tape recorders, and a computer. You need to think about a video camera too.

The next choice is whose memories to record. This is of course critical for any oral history project: and the underlying principles remain the same. First, there is little point in recording people whose memories are confused or impaired, or who are too withdrawn to talk about them. Secondly, what matters is the *direct* personal experience that somebody has, rather than their formal position. This is a particular trap for local historical societies or public libraries. It can mean that the people chosen to record are those very local dignitaries, such as mayors and council officials, who have the most need for caution and thus the least to give. It is 'almost axiomatic', as Beatrice Webb very correctly observed,

that the mind of the subordinate in any organization will yield richer deposits of fact than the mind of the principal. This is not merely because the subordinate is usually less on his guard . . . The working

foreman, managing clerk, or minor official is in continuous and intimate contact with the day-to-day activities of the organization; he is
more aware of the heterogeneity and changing character of the facts,
and less likely to serve up dead generalization, in which all the living
detail becomes a blurred mass, or is stereotyped into rigidly confined
and perhaps obsolete categories.[14]

Thirdly, it is necessary to be constantly aware of the social
balance of the accounts which are being collected. Thus there is
always a tendency for projects to record more men than women.
This is partly because women tend to be more diffident, and less
often believe that their own memories might be of interest. It is
also because men are much more often recommended as informants by others. Even when this is recognized as a problem, it
may prove difficult to solve. For example, if the subject is a local
industry, it will be easy enough to find men who worked in it;
indeed they may still meet together as old workmates at a pub or
a club. But their wives, or women workers in the same industry,
although equally vital to its functioning, will be much harder to
trace, because they will not normally be locally known by their
occupation, and their social networks will be those of the
neighbourhood rather than the workplace. Similarly, there is
an equally strong tendency for a community project to record
its central social stratum—normally the respectable working
class and the lower middle class—at the expense of both top
and bottom. There are difficulties in tracing the retired works
director to Cheltenham Spa. And again and again, the very
poorest, the 'rough' elements which were a vital part of the
community, prove equally elusive. They are not suggested as
informants because the more 'respectable' old people either
positively disapprove of what they would say, or simply regard
them as too pathetic or unintelligent to have any worthwhile
memories at all. Yet they are often precisely those whose different views, richly expressed in dialect stories, can provide the
most valuable recording of all. And it is the juxtaposition of live
experience, from all levels of society, which makes the most
telling and thought-provoking local history.

Finding a sufficient range of informants is thus a key task. A self-selected group, responding to a public notice or a local newspaper or radio appeal, can certainly provide the best start for some projects, but it will rarely be representative enough. People can be located in many other ways: through personal contacts; at old people's workshops or clubs; through trade unions or political parties; appeals in the local paper, a shop window or on the radio; through welfare workers or doctors, churches or visiting organizations; even by chance encounters in a shop or a pub or a park. It is always much easier when you can approach them with a personal recommendation from somebody else. Although there will be refusals, which can be disheartening, provided that you keep a clear idea of who you are searching for, this part of the project depends above all upon persistence. But it will be worth persisting.

Lastly, what about the outcome? For the future, your tapes and transcripts must be deposited, along with photographs, documents and other material you have collected, as a resource for future public use: and the best place for this is likely to be your city library or county archives. More immediately, you can draw on them to produce educational packs for use in local schools, including cassettes of interview extracts; to stage small travelling exhibitions, again combining sound with photographs and text; and to make a tape and slide show for use with old people to stimulate their own memories of the community's past. You may be able to find a drama group with whose help you can develop some of your material into a stage production. You can publish your material in printed form: as newspaper features, as local booklets, or—like Island History in London's Isle of Dogs—as annual calendars of old photographs. You could set up a Website through your computer to make extracts from the text and also from the sound of your recordings available to a worldwide audience through the Web.

Another possibility is to use your tapes to make programmes for local radio. The simplest, and often most effective form, may be a collage of extracts with a minimal linking by a narrator. However there are more complex possibilities, particularly if you have your recordings in digital form, so that you can do your own editing on a computer. There are now numerous software packages available on the market—and some free ones on the Web—which you can use on your own computer. This will allow you, for example, to produce a tape for radio or educational use which mixes field-work recordings—including your questions—with atmospheric background sounds including music, fading in and out, and as a third layer, your own reflections on the meaning of the tapes. This can give much more variety to the sound character of the tape, while crucially opening up the decisions behind the editing process, and so presenting in a single form both experience and its interpretation.

An equally ambitious outcome is a video documentary. If well done, this can be a particularly compelling form for presenting oral history. With a handheld miniature video camera it is possible for a lone interviewer to film every interview recorded, but this is likely to prove a mixed blessing. As an end product a video documentary is technically demanding, because it has to look good as well as sound good, and that implies close-ups and changes of angle on the person talking, and also the use of other visual material to conceal the awkward jumps where cuts are made. All this means that it is usually better to record in sound first, choose what you think is best for your video, and only at that point film, with the technical subtlety needed.

Quite often, as in a printed calendar or in a museum display, only the caption may betray its origin in oral recording work. Thus many museums have used oral history projects for reconstructing, correcting, and interpreting material displays, from the Smithsonian's black tenant house in Washington, or the Schneider steel furnaces which once lit up the company town of Le Creusot in France, to the 1920s Durham dentist's surgery at Beamish; but using the oral evidence from the project in the display itself, as in the fishing family's kitchen at Lancaster Maritime Museum, is still strangely rare, though equally effective. Thus at the Gloddfa Ganol slate mine in Blaenau Ffestiniog, North Wales, you can watch and hear miners themselves in a tape and slide show in the old stables before entering the vast caverns cut within the mountain. Elsewhere visitors may be lent cassettes to carry round the building themselves. The extract is best when very brief, less than a minute. A labourer can speak about ploughing, or a weaver explain a loom. In the Imperial War Museum you can hear the sound of marching and guns as you look at exhibits from the trenches, or enter a recruiting booth where an old soldier's voice recounts what it was like to be signed on.

It is also possible for museums to make oral material available through interactive multimedia computer screens, a form of display which will become increasingly common. In the longer run multimedia offers dramatic possibilities for research, archiving, and publication. In principle it will be possible to organize digitally recorded material so that as you read a transcript you can switch over and hear the sound of the same passage and the expressions of the speaker. This would be an immense gain. For the moment, however, disc space is limited, especially for sound and still more for film, so that multimedia oral history has had to take the form of much more limited CDs of extracts, or of programmes installed for museum displays and accessible through computer screens in the exhibitions. To be successful, multimedia museum programmes need to be easy to understand, fastmoving, and elegantly designed. The attraction is in seeing what you can find. Thus at the São Paulo football club's museum you can start with the 1940s, choose famous goals, see a snatch of film in which a goal is scored to the roar of the crowd, find a witness, read his story, listen to half a minute of it, see his photographs, a map of his migrations through his life, and so on, constantly flicking from one bit of information to another. In some cases you may be able to choose one of a list of questions to put to a witness. But nothing will last very long. These programmes are much more akin to dictionaries or other reference works. They do not allow, and are not intended for, any sustained or in-depth study of either the texts or the sounds. They must be seen as a new kind of publication, which will gradually develop its own style, and may indeed succeed in hooking in the attention of poeple who would not be attracted by more conventional forms. Thus while multimedia displays, some brilliant and many dull, are likely to play an important role in future museums and exhibitions, they need to be seen as additional rather than replacing other ways of using oral sources.

Some of the most effective instances of community oral history have been from temporary initiatives. Both Coventry and Southampton museums organized exhibitions from their projects which included tea dances to jazz bands, at which old couples spun the floor in rejuvenated delight to the sound of long-lost tunes; and these occasions also proved catalysts for the reunion of old workmates, and even of two sisters who had not seen each other for forty years. In other projects, old people's reminiscence groups have contacted local schools as well as vice versa. In Harlow New Town, Jewish teenagers ran an old people's club inside their own club; while in the Cambridgeshire village of Burwell a project for a documentary film including recorded memories led to a 'drop-in club', again within the youth club, for old people collecting their pensions from the post office on Thursday afternoons. They chatted with some of the youth group over tea, leading on to recordings, articles published in the community magazine, and so more offers of information.

A small number of community projects are much more ambitious—or succeed beyond expectations. Thus the New York Chinatown History Project aimed to help build a democratic community structure precisely by a highly politically conscious but sensitive interpretation of older and newer immigrants, community bosses and sweated laundry workers, to each other. In Sweden a project in the condemned slum neighbourhood of Nöden in the city of Lund in the 1960s so revived local community feeling that Nöden was permanently saved from the motorway project which would have destroyed it; and in the 1980s the 'Dig Where You Stand' factory history tent toured the country stirring the solidarity of old industrial communities in a similar way. And a British project, by evoking very different memories, succeeded in turning the local radio into a two-way channel. For this Dennis Stuart of Keele University's Adult Education Department conceived a project in local Methodist history, working with Arthur Wood of Radio Stoke-on-Trent. A set of eight chapel study groups was formed, each examining their own records and carrying out interviews, and this material was brought together, linked by narration and live recordings of singing and preaching, in a series of broadcast programmes. The programmes, and an exhibition linked with them, stimulated more recording work—and also a new programme series consisting of weekly fifteen-minute programmes, each composed of a patchwork of voices with no narrative, mostly on aspects of social life before the First World War, which proved very popular, and lasted altogether eighty weeks. This again stimulated very active local participation, with people sending in comments, offering to be interviewed, and bringing in essays about their own memories.

We can end with a still more striking instance of local participation, which brought about the creation of a whole new museum in Italy. This is not an oral history project as such, so much as a community history project in which the role played by oral memory was of vital importance. It also provides a very striking instance of the co-operation possible between workers and university scholars, taking place in the context of a wider Italian political movement for the re-evaluation of working-class culture. As Alessandro Triulzi, in describing the project argues, the Museum of Peasant Civilization—the Museo della Civilta' Contadina di S. Marino in Bentivoglio—must be understood not just as a collection of objects from the past, but as 'the workers' own answer to the cultural appropriation they have been subjected to by the dominant classes', and a step towards 'the re-appropriation of values and contributions that have long been ignored or trivialized and distorted by the state official culture'.

The museum stands some miles outside Bologna, in the hot, flat, rain-swept countryside of the Po valley. It is a superbly documented and socially very penetrating display, set out in the elegant baliff's house of a former landed estate, of the life and work of the peasant sharecroppers of the surrounding countryside. Opened in 1973, it was the fruit of a campaign which had lasted nine years. It began in 1964 when a former peasant, Ivano Trigari, discovered an old farming tool half-buried outside a friend's house, locally known as a *stadura*:

The stadura is a round iron bar, fifty or sixty centimetres long, which was used in old Bolognese ox-carts both as a brake and as an ornament. The top of the bar was usually embellished with a cross or other decorations, and it had one or more iron rings which gave each cart when moving its own characteristic sound.

Trigari cleaned and polished this *stadura*, and put it on show in the window of the agricultural co-operative where he worked in the little town of Castelmaggiore. The result was astonishing: a 'fever for *stadure*' seized the town, a competition to produce the best specimen, schoolchildren bringing in examples sent by their fathers wrapped in paper, news of discoveries coming from every corner. Within a few days some twenty had been amassed, the most beautiful on display in the front of the shop, the rest piled in a corner. The collection became the talk of the town, drawing crowds of old peasants from the bar and the workers' club, the Casa del Popolo. As they stood there looking and commenting, Trigari listened to their memories, questioning them for details he did not know. He realized, as he puts it, that these oral memories could provide 'a general fresco of an epoch which had disappeared already, or was soon to disappear'. The comments varied:

Some cursed the tools which reminded them how hard they had worked in the past; others were excited, reminded of their youth. They said that times were better now, and started exchanging memories of the past, of times when they had to rise at two in the morning to go ploughing; of how they had to take their ox-carts to the rice fields to collect forage and the rice-straw which was used then as litter for the animals . . . And again of when they used to take all the hemp to their landlord's mansion or how they carried the huge grape baskets on their heads; or of the great bundles of firewood which were carried to the baker; or finally, of when, with the best cart and oxen, the *stadura* all shining, the bridegroom went to the bride's house to take her dowry.

Before long, other tools were coming in too: old looms, hemp tools, yokes, hoes, ploughs, and so on. Out of this grew the idea of a systematic local collection of old working implements. It was taken up enthusiastically by the peasants, who hunted through their houses and in disused depots, and persuaded their friends to do the same. A *festa della stadura* was started to win support, which has become an annual occasion. An association was set up, the *Gruppo della stadura*, which organized a travelling exhibition, an ancient cart drawn by a tractor with samples of tools, putting them on show in nearby villages at fair and carnival times, or at the celebrations of local saints' days, and appealing for support. 'Peasants would listen, and often contributed on the spot tools, money, advice, and suggestions where further material could be found.' By the time that, after years of searching, the association won the present home for its museum from the provincial administration of Bologna, almost 4,000 objects had been assembled. 'Based on an unfailing faith and pride in their own sense of history', the movement had developed into 'a collective effort that involved almost everybody in the community'.

A key factor in winning official support had been the backing of a group of university students and researchers gathered around Carlo Poni, Professor of Economic History at Bologna. With the first stage of the project brought to success with the opening of the museum, the close contact between historians in the university and the community was intended to continue. The museum has collected a substantial archive of labour contracts, estate papers, the records of peasant organizations, and photographs. It acts as a centre for seminars and for research in agrarian history. At the same time it draws in thousands of local visitors, especially schoolchildren, who are encouraged to write their own term papers using the museum material. It is also providing training for others who wish to start similar ventures elsewhere: some fifteen new agrarian museums in Emilia alone, and the idea is spreading to other provinces. Perhaps most interesting, for the oral historian, is the encouragement of local historical memory. Schoolchildren collect interviews from their own villages as well as using the museum's records. The interview method has also been developed by university students. And above all, peasant-historians within the community have found a renewed confidence. One instance will suffice to conclude: that of Guiseppe Barbieri of S. Giovanni in Persiceto.

Aged 78, Guiseppe Barbieri, now a retired peasant, has a poor scholastic record (he didn't get beyond third grade) but a considerable record as a local historian. His first work, a 300-page manuscript titled 'My memories in war and peace. Some family remembrances', was written in 1936. In it the then 39-year-old peasant described at length this war experience, the peasants' working conditions in pre-WWI Emilia, the agrarian struggle of 1919–20, and peasant reactions to national events, like the rise of Fascism, or to local tragedies, like the earthquake of 1929. Written in ungrammatical Italian (almost a foreign language to him since, like most peasants in the area, he speaks the local dialect both at home and work), his exercise book manuscript lay idle in his house until 1975, when news of the peasant museum spread in the region . . . Guiseppe Barbieri decided to take up pen again . . .

Barbieri's new book was to be on rural traditional structure and daily labour. It was to offer, in Triulzi's words, 'a working man's answer to the scholars' false dichotomy between the little history of daily life and labour and the Great History of official textbooks'. And Guiseppe Barbieri certainly entered his task with enthusiasm; for he hoped, in his own words, 'to continue it quickly, while my memory is still good, since I have passed my 77th year already and I feel proud to express our past'.[15]

The spirit in which to undertake an oral history project could hardly be better put.

7

The Interview

To interview successfully requires skill. But there are many different styles of interviewing, ranging from the friendly, informal, conversational approach to the more formal, controlled style of questioning, and good interviewers eventually develop a variation of the method which, for them, brings the best results, and suits their personality. There are some essential qualities which the successful interviewer must possess: an interest and respect for people as individuals, and flexibility in response to them; an ability to show understanding and sympathy for their point of view; and, above all, a willingness to sit quietly and listen. People who cannot stop talking themselves, or resist the temptation to contradict or push an informant with their own ideas, will take away information which is either useless or positively misleading. But most people can learn to interview well.

The first point is the preparation, through reading and in other ways, of background information. The importance of this varies a good deal. The best way of starting off some pieces of work may be through exploratory interviews, mapping out a field and picking up ideas and information. With the help of these a problem may be defined, and some of the resources for solving it located. The 'general gathering interview' at the beginning of a local project, like the 'pilot interview' of a big survey, can be a very useful stage. And of course there is no point in having any interview at all unless the informant is, in some sense, better informed than oneself. The interviewer comes to learn, and indeed often gets people to talk in just this spirit.

For example, Roy Hay has found in his research with the Clydeside shipbuilders that quite often, 'one's own ignorance can be turned to good use. On many occasions older workers have greeted my naïve questions with amused tolerance and told me, "Naw, naw laddie it wasn't like that at all," followed by a graphic description of the real situation.'[1]

It is nevertheless generally true that the more one knows, the more likely one is to elicit significant historical information from an interview. For example, if the basic narrative of a political decision, or a strike, has been established from newspapers, it will be possible to place the informant's own part within the events exactly, to identify where he or she may have special direct experience and observations; which recollections are second-hand, and to spot elisions of memory between similar events at different times—like the two 1910 general elections, or the strikes of 1922 and 1926. This background information may itself have been built up very fully through earlier interviews, as with the systematic reconstruction of Jewish persecution and resistance during the Second World War, or of the local Partisan movements in Italy, where the point of a testimony may be to corroborate and fill out in precise detail the hourly events of a day in 1944 when a man's family was destroyed.

A similar command of detail can be built up for a life-story interview, when the subject is a public personality, or a writer, or possesses sufficient personal papers. Although some of the material—like the subject's own writings—will be available before the start of interviewing, more may be produced as a result of the first interviews, leading to correspondence, the discovery of further documentation, and eventually more interviews at another level of questioning. Of course not all prominent informants are willing to be subjected to a step-by-step research process. Thomas Reeves found that interviewing American liberal intellectuals required exceptionally painstaking and thorough preparation. They were often too busy to grant more than brief interviews, so that 'specific, highly-informed questions' were essential. Worse still, should he appear hesitant, or seem to be fishing blindly, the relationship between the participants in an interview can be quickly destroyed. Liberal intellectuals seem especially interested in testing your credentials to be an oral historian by probing your knowledge of the subject under discussion. I have often felt, particularly at the beginning of an interview session, that they were interviewing me . . . These sort of queries are ploys in status games.'[2]

Such demanding informants are rare. Nevertheless, even with a more general historical study of a community or an industry, it is important to pick up a knowledge of local practices and terminology as quickly as possible. John Marshall, for example, points out how misleading the question 'At what age did you leave school?' could be in the Lancashire cotton towns. A former millgirl would answer, at 14; and it was only because he knew that the majority had been half-timers in the loom-sheds long before leaving school—a fact which they took for granted—that he then went on to ask, 'When did you begin work?'[3] Many oral historians have found that a basic knowledge for work terms is useful, as a key to establishing mutual respect and trust. And Beatrice Webb, decades earlier, made the same point with a characteristic sharpness:

To cross-examine a factory inspector without understanding the distinction between a factory and a workshop . . . is an impertinence. Especially important is a familiarity with technical terms and a correct use of them. To start interviewing any specialist without this equipment will not only be a waste of time, but may lead to more or less courteous dismissal, after a few general remarks and some trite opinions . . . For technical terms . . . are so many levers to lift into consciousness and expression the more abstruse and out-of-the-way facts or series of facts; and it is exactly these more hidden events that are needed to complete descriptive analysis and to verify hypotheses.[4]

Nor is this true only of the specialist. It is an equal 'impertinence' to subject numbers of working people in a community or an industry to questions, without first ensuring, as far as possible, that they are historically relevant and correctly phrased for the local context.

A broader study of social change, depending on a relatively

wide spectrum of informants, also demands particularly careful preparation of the form of questions before interviewing. Asking questions in the best way is clearly important in any interview. This is, however, an issue which can raise strong feelings among oral historians. A contrast may be made between so-called box-ticking 'questionnaires' whose rigidly structured logical patterns so inhibit the memory that the 'respondent'— again the choice of term itself suggestive—is reduced to monosyllabic or very short answers; and, at the other extreme, not so much an 'interview' at all, but a free 'conversation' in which the 'person', 'tradition-bearer', 'witness', or 'narrator' is 'invited to talk' on a matter of mutual interest. There have also been important discussions of the issues of control in the interview relationship which underlie these choices by feminist oral historians and ethnographers. Sharing a belief that their research should be not only about women but also for them, some have gone on to reject any hierarchy in the research process, and argue that those researched should become partners and collaborators. The interview thus becomes either non-directive or co-negotiated in form and themes.[5]

The contrasting merits and drawbacks of the 'two schools of interviewing' are nicely summarized by Roy Hay:

Firstly there is the 'objective/comparative' approach usually based on a questionnaire, or at least a very highly structured interview in which the interviewer keeps control and asks a series of common questions to all respondents. The aim here is to produce material which transcends the individual respondent and can be used for comparative purposes . . . In the hands of flexible, sensitive interviewers, who are prepared to abandon the script when necessary, this approach can generate very useful material indeed, but it can be deadly. Promising lines of inquiry are too easily choked off and, worse still, people are forced into the predetermined framework of the interviewers and so large relevant areas of experience are never examined at all.

At the other extreme is the free flowing dialogue between interviewer and respondent, with no set pattern, in which conversation is followed wherever it leads. This method occasionally turns up the very unexpected and leads to completely new lines of inquiry but it can very easily degenerate into little more than anecdotal gossip. It can produce miles and miles of useless tape and impossible problems of selection and transcription.[6]

The truth is that when interviews are well carried out the contrast between the 'two schools' is much less drastic. For one thing, the principles are always mitigated by the effect of the personalities involved in each particular interview. Some interviewers are naturally more chatty than others, and can draw out an informant this way (although this is relatively unusual, and a more common effect of chattiness can be to shut people up). And informants vary from the very talkative, who need few questions, just steering, or now and then a very specific question to clarify some point which is unclear; to the relatively laconic, who with encouragement, broad open-ended questions, and supplementary prompts, can reveal much richer memories than at first seemed possible.

Secondly, no oral historian, even when using an interview guide, would want to go for a caricature of the classic survey's search for 'objective' evidence, with its instrument a rigid inflexible questionnaire style of interview carried out by a dehumanized interviewer 'without a face to give off feelings'. As Pierre Bourdieu puts it in his reflections at the end of *La Misère du monde* (1993), the innumerable writings on survey methodology, while useful in describing unintended effects which an interviewer may produce,

almost always miss the point, not least because they remain faithful to old methodological procedures, often derived from the desire to imitate the external signs of the rigour of the best established scientific disciplines. It does not seem to me, at any rate, that they do justice to what has always been done—and known—by those researchers who are most respectful of their object and attentive to the almost infinitely subtle strategies that social agents deploy in the ordinary conduct of their existence.

In his life-story research Bourdieu has therefore aimed 'to instigate a relationship of *active and methodical listening*, as far removed from pure laissez-faire of the non-directive interview as from the directiveness of the questionnaire survey', in which 'a *reflex reflexivity* based on a sociological "feel" or "eye" enables one to perceive and monitor *on the spot*, as the interview is actually being carried out, the effects of the social structure within which it is taking place'.[7] This fits well with the typical technique of the oral historian. Those oral historians who use interview guides do so not in order to introduce rigidity to their research, but principally because some types of research make advance planning of questioning essential—for example, in any project where interviewing work is shared in a team, or where paid interviewers are used; or wherever material is to be used for systematic comparisons.

Thirdly, the free form may also mislead. Alessandro Portelli, while favouring a flexible interview form which he calls a 'thick dialogue' or 'deep exchange', is equally against 'the myth of non-interference' which would push this to the extreme of non-interaction to avoid distortion. For it takes great deftness, and a well-chosen informant, to be able, like George Ewart Evans, to get outstanding material from an apparently free-flowing interview while remaining 'relaxed, unhurried', and giving the informant 'plenty of time to move about . . .': 'Let the interview run. I never attempt to dominate it. The least one can do is to guide it and I try to ask as few questions as I can . . . Plenty of time and plenty of tape and few questions.'[8] Those few questions are based on years of experience, combined with a clear idea obtained in advance of what each particular informant may tell.

The strongest argument for a completely free-flowing interview is when its main purpose is less to seek information than to record a 'narrative interview', a 'subjective' record of how one man or woman looks back on their life as a whole, or part of it. Just how they speak about it, what they miss out, how they order it, what they emphasize, the words they choose, are important in understanding any interview; but for this purpose they become the essential text which will need to be examined. Thus the less their testimony is shaped by the interviewer's questions, the better. In the approach developed by Gabriele Rosenthal and her group, the interview follows three phases.

The interview is opened by a wide, non-contentious question, and in the first phase the interviewer simply offers non-verbal encouragement; in the second phase details may be drawn out by asking the interviewee to say more about themes already mentioned; only in the third can new topics and missing themes be raised.

However, it is questionable whether a fully subjective narrative interview could exist. In order to start at all, a social context must be set up, the purpose of recording explained, and at least an initial question asked; and all these, along with unspoken assumptions, create expectations which shape what follows. Some researchers have reported that simply to ask, 'Tell me the story of your life', produced results which were generally disappointing: 'it tended to result in a brief, even terse account', Janet Askham found, simply because 'they did not know what I was interested in'. Stories flowed much more freely once she started to ask questions. In a strange way the 'narrative interview' tends to suppress the interviewer just as much as the survey instrument. Hence other oral historians also favouring the narrative form of analysis have argued instead for a form of 'interactive interviewing' which gives more explicit weight to the interviewer's contribution and explicitly sees interviews as co-constructed.[9]

There are a few basic principles in the phrasing of questions which apply in any interview. Questions should always be as simple and as straightforward as possible, in familiar language. Never ask complex, double-barrelled questions—only half will usually be answered, and it usually won't be clear which half. Avoid a phrasing which points to an unclear answer: for example, ask, 'How often did you go to church?', rather than, 'Did you often go to church?' Of course occasional hesitation does not matter at all, and may even win a little sympathy from the informant. But frequent apologetic confusion is simply perplexing, and is especially to be avoided as a style of asking delicate personal questions since it only conveys your own embarrassment. A careful or indirect question, previously worked out and confidently put, is much better. It shows you know what you're doing, so the atmosphere is more likely to stay relaxed.

You will need a different kind of phrasing to establish specific facts and to get description or comment. The latter demands an 'open-ended' type of question, like 'Tell me all about . . .', 'What did you think/feel about that?', or 'Can you describe that to me?' Other cue words for this sort of question are 'explain', 'expand on', 'discuss', or 'compare'. If it is a really important point, you can encourage at length: 'All right, so you're in —. Shut your eyes, and give me a running commentary—what you see, hear . . .' A physical description can also be suggested as a lead into an evaluation of a person's character. Right through the interview whenever you get a bald fact which you think might be usefully elaborated, you can throw in an inviting interjection: 'That sounds interesting'; or more directly, 'How?', 'Why not?', 'Who was that?' The informant may then take up the cue. If, after some comment, you want more, you can be more emphatic ('That's very interesting'), or mildly challenging ('But some people say that . . .'), or try a fuller supplementary question. In most interviews, it is very important to use both kinds of questions. For example, you may be told, as a general comment, that 'we helped each other out', 'we were all one big family in the street', but if you ask a specific question such as who outside the family helped when the mother was ill, it may become clear that neighbourly aid was less a practice than an ideal. Getting behind stereotyped or non-committal generalizations to detailed memories is one of the basic skills, and opportunities, of oral history work.

Leading questions must normally be avoided. If you indicate your own views, especially early in an interview, you are more likely to get an answer which the informant thinks you would like to hear, and will therefore be unreliable or misleading as evidence. There are some exceptions to this. If you know somebody has very strong views, especially from a minority standpoint, it may be essential to show a basic sympathy with them to get started at all. Also, in order to allow the possibility of some responses which would be conventionally disapproved by most people, it may be best to ask a loaded question: 'Can you tell me of a time when you had to punish severely . . .?', 'Were most people taking home materials from the works in those days?', or 'I hear the mayor was a very difficult man for his immediate employees to get along with'—which is much more likely to provoke a clear reaction than a bland form like, 'I know the mayor was a very generous and wise person. Did you find him so?'[10] But such questions are dangerous on most occasions, and are not normally appropriate. Most questions should be carefully phrased to avoid suggesting an answer. This can be quite an art in itself. For example, 'Did you enjoy your work?' is loaded; 'Did you like your work or not?', or 'How did you feel about your work' are neutral.

Finally, avoid asking questions which make informants think in your way rather than theirs. For example, when dealing with concepts like social class, your information is much stronger evidence if you encourage them to produce their own basic terms, and then use these in the subsequent discussion. And try to date events by fixing the time in relation to their own age, or a stage of life, such as marriage, or a particular job or house.

Even if you are going to carry out only a small oral history project of your own, it is worth thinking about the sequence of topics for the interviews and the phrasing of questions. The strategy of the interview is not the informant's responsibility, but yours. It is much easier to guide if you have a basic shape already in your mind, and questions can lead naturally from one to the other. This also makes it easier, even when you digress, to remember what you still need to know about. In addition, for most projects you will need some basic background facts from all informants (origins and occupations of mother and father, own birth, education, occupations, marriage, and so on), and you will also find a recurrent need for basic and supplementary questions on many topics. If you have already worked out these questions in your head, and can toss them in when needed, you can more easily concentrate on what the informant is saying, instead of trying to think of how to get in yourself.

In deciding on the possible shape for your interview, a

fundamental issue is whether to focus overwhelmingly on a single theme—for example, an event, a period like wartime, a particular industry or sport—or to aim for a full life-story, beginning with family background and running on through childhood and education to work, later personal and family life, and so on. Because one of the greatest strengths of oral history evidence is its potential to connect up different spheres of life, the life-story approach, while more time-consuming, is more likely to bring new insights. It also makes a fuller use of the opportunity in recording the memories of someone who may never have been previously recorded, nor will be recorded again. For both reasons, the life-story form is worth considering seriously for most projects.

While for your own purposes when working alone a skeleton list of headings, along with wordings for key questions, may be sufficient, certainly for team-work, or for a comparative project on any scale, a more fully elaborated interview schedule is desirable. Provided such a schedule is used flexibly and imaginatively, it can be advantageous; for in principle, the clearer you are about what is worth asking and how best to ask it, the more you can draw from *any* kind of informant. With relatively reticent people, who say right at the start, 'It's all right as long as you use the questions', this is obvious enough: and such informants are quite common. You can then follow the lines of the schedule more or less methodically. With very talkative people the schedule should be differently used. If they have a clear idea of what they want to say, or the direction the interview should take, follow them. And wherever possible avoid interrupting a story. If you stop a story because you think it is irrelevant, you will cut off not just that one, but a whole series of subsequent offers of information which *will* be relevant. But sooner or later, they will exhaust their immediate fund of recollections, and they too will *want* you to ask questions. With this kind of informant several visits will be needed, and afterwards you can play back your recordings, checking against the schedule what has been covered and what is worth asking in later sessions. The printed form of the schedule in this case becomes particularly useful. But normally it is much better to know the questions, ask them directly at the right moment, and keep the schedule in the background. Essentially it is a map for the interviewer; it can be referred to occasionally, but it is best to have it in mind, so that the ground can be walked with confidence.

Certain other decisions need to be taken before the interview. First, what equipment should be taken? In a minority of contexts, the best answer is none. Even note-taking, let alone tape recording, may arouse suspicion in some people. Fear of tape recording is quite common among professionals whose work ethic emphasizes confidentiality and secrecy, like civil servants, or bank managers.[11] For different reasons it can also be found among minorities who have experienced persecution, and fear that any information on tape might get into the hands of the police or authorities, and be used against them; or in close-knit communities where gossip is feared. Some people may object to recording, but not to note-taking. Even if neither is possible, a skilled interviewer can learn to hold enough of the main information and key phrases to jot down soon afterwards, and make an interview worthwhile. Indeed, before tape recording made such a method seem by comparison impressionistic, this was the commonest sociological practice.

Most people, however, will accept a tape recorder with very little anxiety, and quickly lose any immediate awareness of it. The recorder can even help the interview. While it is on, people may be a little more likely to keep to the point, and other members of the family to stay out of the way. And quite frequently, when it is switched off, some highly significant additional facts may be given, which could have been held back if there had been no recorder at all; information which is meant to be known to the researcher as background, but in confidence (and must of course be treated in this spirit).

It is worth thinking very seriously about your choice of machine because this will be crucial for the quality of recording, and also for the editing process. For a really good recording, of the quality needed for a radio programme, you will need to come with good equipment and to use it properly. At present the technology is evolving rapidly with the introduction of digital audio recording making choices difficult, since equipment could become rapidly obsolescent: hence, before buying, you would be wise to check the latest opinion with the National Sound Archive. Digital recording has the double advantage of enabling processing and editing on a computer; and also of perfect copying. MiniDisc field recorders are now available which are cheaper, more compact, and acoustically better than a good cassette recorder. It is not yet clear, however, how good MiniDiscs are for long-term archival purposes: from this point of view DAT may be preferable, although much more expensive. A more conservative but safer choice would be a high-quality cassette machine, but a cheap cassette with a built-in microphone will be hopeless. You will certainly need a separate microphone and some extra money spent on quality in this will be especially worthwhile. When using a tape recorder it is important to avoid drawing attention to the machine, and diverting one's own attention, by fussing about it. If it is a new one, make sure you have read the manual which goes with it, and practised operating it and setting it up. Check before you set out that it is functioning, and that you have all the parts and tapes you may need, including batteries.

You can also take with you various aids to memory. An old newspaper cutting or a local street directory can help. George Ewart Evans often took a work tool.

In the countryside I often take along an old serrated sickle. With that there is no need of any abstract explanation of what you are going about. He sees the object, and if you choose well he won't need any prodding to open up. We are both right into our subject from the beginning. In the same way if I was going to see an old miner, I'd take a pair of yorks or a tommy-box.[12]

Since the focus of his interviews was the work process, such a tool was an ideal starting-point. If it was to be childhood in the family, a piece of clothing might be better; or for a political life story, an early pamphlet. These might also stimulate the production of old letters, diaries, cuttings, and photographs, which is particularly worth encouraging and could be an especially valuable by-product of an interview.

Next, where should the interview be held? It must be a place where the informant can feel at ease. Normally the best place will be their own home. This is especially true of an interview focusing on childhood or the family. An interview in a workplace, or in a pub, will activate other areas of memory more strongly, and may also result in a shift to a less 'respectable' style of speaking. A trip round the district can also prove rewarding, and stimulate other recollections.

Nearly always, it is best to be alone with the informant. Complete privacy will encourage an atmosphere of full trust in which candour becomes much more possible. This is usually true even of an old married couple who are particularly close to each other. Of course it is not always easy to find a tactful way of seeing them apart. (It is easier if you interview both of them; and particularly if two of you arrive together at the couple's home, and then pair off in different rooms.)

The presence of another person at the interview not only inhibits candour, but subtly pressurizes towards a socially acceptable testimony. Fortunately, however, this is not all disadvantage. An old couple, or a brother and sister, will often provide corrections of information which are positively helpful. They can also stimulate each other's memory. This effect becomes still more marked when a larger group of old people get together. There will be a much stronger tendency than in private to produce generalizations about the old days, but as they argue and exchange stories among each other, fascinating insights can emerge from these forms of collective memory. To a more marked extent than in an individual interview these stories, many of which are likely to be about *other* people, even more than usual, need to be understood in the first place as narrative art forms, conveying symbolic meanings. But sometimes a group, for example in a public bar, may also offer the only way to get good information about a hidden world of a common work-experience, such as sabotage or theft, or the secret devices of poachers in the countryside.

The group can also be a useful device in other situations. John Saville and a research student met with three leaders of the Manchester Unemployed Workers Movement of the 1930s, and in five hours of co-operative discussion reconstructed many of the gaps in the newspaper evidence which they had previously assembled. With more self-defended public figures, such as Canadian politicians, Peter Oliver has found cross-examination by two or even three interviewers effective, and David Edge used a triangular interview for his work on radio-astronomers. Beatrice Webb, although strongly favouring privacy for the normal interview, also developed a technique of 'wholesale interviewing' in the more relaxed atmosphere of social occasions, once with a party 'even telling fortunes from their hands, with all sorts of interesting results!' At the dinner-table or in the smoking-room she found that 'you can sometimes start several experts arguing among themselves; and in this way you will pick up more information in one hour than you will acquire during a whole day in a series of interviews'.[13]

Once the preliminary decisions have been made, you have to make contact with your informant. You can call in person, but it is usually better to write (enclosing a stamped addressed envelope), and follow this up by telephone. You have to convince them in simple, straightforward terms that your project is worthwhile, and you should emphasize its relevance to their own experience. It will also always be much easier if you can say that somebody else in the informant's own social network has recommended them. You need to explain briefly too how you want to use the interview. Suggest a possible time for a first visit, but always leave the informant the chance to propose another, or to refuse altogether. Don't be disappointed by a refusal: you are in fact likely to have as many as acceptances. With a minority of informants, like politicians or professionals, it may be wise to send your research proposal and put in writing the use you intend for the interview. This will help them to decide whether to see you, and will help to clarify your future right to use of the material (see below, Chapter 8). Some may begin thinking about the topics which interest you and search out some old papers before you come.

Most people would be more likely to find a long letter forbidding, so it is best to wait until your first meeting. Then start by explaining the subject of your project or your book, and how the informant can help you. Many people will protest that they have nothing useful to tell you, and need reassurance that their own experience is worthwhile, that it is unfamiliar for younger people whose lives have been very different, and essential for the making of real social history. Some may be genuinely surprised at your interest, and you will need to be more than usually encouraging in the early stages of the interview. Some will explicitly raise the question of confidentiality, and not want their names given. Be open about your intentions, and honour any promises you make. Most people will trust you to be discreet with what they tell you—and this trust must be respected. Do not attach their names, without their explicit consent, to potentially damaging quotations about themselves or their neighbours.

The start of this first meeting is also normally the best time to ask whether the interview may be tape-recorded, although sometimes this can be suggested in the initial approach. Some oral historians believe in using the first meeting as a brief, exploratory visit, for preparing and getting to know an informant, without using a tape recorder. The drawback is that, even in trying to establish basic facts about the informant's background, it is difficult not to tap the essence of the memory. You can go over the same ground on a second visit, but it is likely to be presented in a much more stilted way. In my own experience, it is best to get the recorder going as quickly as you can once you start talking.

Before starting you also need to consider possible acoustic problems. Too many oral historians are in such a rush to get on at this point that they fail to take sufficient trouble over the sound quality of their recordings. But it is well worth knowing how to get the best out of your machine, just as there is no special virtue in driving badly or typing with two fingers.

First of all, try to use a quiet room where you will not be

disturbed by others talking, and there are no loud background noises, or acoustic problems like those caused by hard surfaces. Traffic outside can be dulled by drawing curtains, but a spitting fire will sound surprisingly loud on the tape, especially if the microphone is not close to the speaker's mouth. In his experience with recording dialect in ordinary homes, Stanley Ellis has found that radio and television, a ticking clock, or a budgerigar, could 'spoil a recording completely . . . The acoustics of the room itself should be observed. A tiny room, well stuffed with furniture and with washing airing on a clothes-horse can be an excellent studio. A large quarry-tiled kitchen with plastered walls may give a tremendous reverberation sufficient to spoil the whole recording.'[14]

Next, consider where to put the recorder and the microphone. Never place them close together, or you will record the machine's own noise. The recorder is best placed on the floor, out of the informant's view but where you can watch it yourself and glance from time to time to see if the tape is nearly exhausted without drawing attention to it. The microphone should not be placed on a hard, vibratory surface, nor several feet away from the speaker. Don't record across a hard-topped table. Ideally the microphone should be a foot away from the informant's mouth. With a firm hand, if you choose to sit side by side, you can hold it; or you can place it on a stand; or you can use two clip-microphones, one on your informant and one on your own clothing. All this can be done very quickly. You can stress that it is the informant's voice you need, not the clock or the bird or the radio. And make sure at the same time that the informant is sitting comfortably, and has not given up a favourite chair. Until all this is completed, you need to avoid talking about the subject which you want to record. Then switch on the recorder and let it run, while chatting. Play this back to test that the recording level is correctly adjusted. If the level is too low, the background noise will swamp the recording; if too high, the sound will become distorted. Then set the recorder running again and, apart from changing tapes, leave it running while the recording session continues. It is a bad practice to keep switching off when the informant wanders off the point, or during your own questions. And never begin with a formal announcement into the microphone, 'This is—interviewing—at—'; it is a formalizing, freezing device. You could leave some spare tape at the beginning to add this afterwards if you wish—but do not add it before, or it may boom out in your playback test.

You are now ready to launch your opening question. What follows will vary greatly depending on the kind of informant, the style of interview you favour, and what you want to know. But again, there are some basic rules. An interview is a social relationship between people with its own conventions, and a violation of these may destroy it. Essentially, the interviewer is expected to show interest in the informant, allowing him or her to speak fully without constant interruption, and at the same time to provide some guidance of what to discuss if needed. Lying behind it is a notion of mutual co-operation, trust, and respect.

An interview is *not* a dialogue, or a conversation. The whole point is to get the informant to speak. Your role is above all to listen. You should keep yourself in the background as much as possible, simply making supportive gestures, but not thrusting in your own comments and stories. It is not an occasion which calls for demonstrations of your own knowledge or charm. And do not allow yourself to feel embarrassed by pauses. Maintaining silence can be a valuable way of allowing an informant to think further, and drawing out a further comment. The time for conversation is later on, when the recorder is switched off. Of course you can go too far in this direction, and allow an informant to falter for lack of come-back. To grind to a halt in silence at the end of an exhausted topic is discouraging, and a firm question is needed before this point. But in general you should ask no more questions than are needed, in a clear, simple, unhurried manner. Keep the informant relaxed and confident. Above all, never interrupt a story. Return to the original point at the end of the digression if you wish, with a phrase like 'Earlier you were saying . . .', 'Going back to . . .', or 'Before we move on . . .' But it is axiomatic, if the informant wants to go on to a new line, to be prepared to follow.

Keep showing that you are interested, throughout the interview. Rather than continually saying 'yes'—which will sound silly on the recording—it is quite easy to learn to mime the word, nod, smile, lift your eyebrows, look at the informant encouragingly. You must be precisely clear where the interview has gone, and especially avoid asking for information that has already been given. This demands a quick memory and quite intense concentration. You may find you need to take rough notes as you go along, although it is best to do without this aid if you can. At the same time you should be watching for the consistency of the answers, and for conflicts with other sources of evidence. If you are doubtful about something, try returning to it from another angle, or suggesting, tactfully and gently, that there may be a different view of the matter—'I have heard' or 'I have read that . . .' But it is particularly important not to contradict or argue with an informant. Beatrice Webb observes with characteristic pungency: 'It is disastrous to "show off" or to argue: the client must be permitted to pour out his fictitious tales, to develop his preposterous theories, to use the silliest arguments, without demur or expression of dissent or ridicule.' And certainly, the more you can show understanding and sympathy for somebody's standpoint, the more you are likely to learn about it. Bourdieu puts this particularly vividly:

At the risk of shocking both the rigorous methodologist and the inspired hermeneutical scholar, I would willingly say that the interview can be considered a sort of *spiritual exercise*, aiming to obtain, through *forgetfulness of self*, a true *transformation of the view* we take of others in the ordinary circumstances of life. The welcoming disposition, which leads one to share the problem of the respondent, the capacity to take her and understand her just as she is, in her distinctive necessity, is a sort of *intellectual love*: a gaze . . .[15]

Discussion of the past can recall painful memories which still evoke strong feelings, and very occasionally these may distress an informant. If this happens, don't be embarrassed by the tears, or apologize: just be gently and naturally supportive, as you would be to a friend; and after an interval ask whether they would like to continue. With some informants it may be wiser to leave the more delicate questions to a later stage in an interview. If it is absolutely essential to get an answer, wait until the end, and perhaps switch off the recorder. But never press too hard when an informant seems defensive or reluctant to answer. It is generally best to try to steer towards a more open conclusion, asking for a summing up of feeling about an experience, or whether anything needs to be added. An interview which ends on a relaxed note is more likely to be remembered as pleasant, and lead on to another.

You need always to try to be sensitively aware of how informants are feeling. If they seem fidgety and are only giving rather terse answers, they may be feeling tired or unwell, or watching the clock for some other engagement: in which case, close the recording session as quickly as possible. While avoiding glancing at your own watch, always fit in with their times, and turn up punctually when you are expected, or they may become tense waiting for you. In normal circumstances, an hour-and-a-half to two hours will in any case be a sensible maximum. An old person, in the interest of the occasion, may not realize the danger of becoming overtired, but will certainly regret it afterwards, and may not want to repeat the experience.

Do not rush away after the recording session. You need to stay, to give a little of yourself, and show warmth and appreciation in return for what has been given to you. Accept a cup of tea if it is offered, and be prepared to chat about the family and photographs. This may be the moment when documents are most likely to be lent to you. It is a good time for fixing another visit. You may find that you can give something in return with some immediate practical help, lifting or fixing something, or some advice about how to set about solving a worrying problem. Indeed, as Ann Oakley has cogently argued, it may sometimes be 'morally indefensible' to hold back from helping in this way, and sharing experience, by talking gently about yourself and your own ideas.[16] Just now and then, this will be the beginning of a friendship which will last. But go forward with tact and caution. Do not get into an argument on subjects likely to be controversial such as teenage behaviour or politics, which is more likely to make for reticence later on.

In some interview situations grander hospitality may be given—an ample lunch with drink—which can perhaps emphasize the normal problem of mutual obligation, bringing a pressure to produce an 'official' version of history. But in most cases you can show sensitivity in making use of the material which has been given, even if it contributes to a conclusion of your own which your informant would not share. Beatrice Webb had no doubts here:

Accept what is offered . . . Indeed, the less formal the conditions of the interview the better. The atmosphere of the dinner-table or the smoking room is a better 'conductor' than that of the office during business hours . . . A personally conducted visit to this or that works or institution may be a dismal prospect; it may even seem a waste of effort to inspect machinery or plant which cannot be understood, or which has been seen *ad nauseam* before . . . But it is a mistake to decline. In the course of these tiring walks and weary waitings, experiences may be recalled or elicited which would not have cropped up in the formal interview in the office.[17]

Her comment is based on research work of her own in which the normal interview situation was uncommon in two ways: both interviewer and informant were drawn from the top levels of society, and they were roughly the same age. Usually interviewers, whether professional historians or the married women typically employed for survey work, are middle-class, and in their thirties or forties. Their informants are normally ordinary working-class or middle-class people, and in oral history work often considerably older. Thus to their normal modesty, or even undervaluation of self, may be added the fragility of old age, and a special vulnerability to discomfort or anxiety.

Changing this social balance can have implications for interviewing method which need considering. For example, an interview between the sexes will often help to encourage sympathy and response; but there are some kinds of confidence, for example about sexual behaviour, which are probably much more easily exchanged between married people of the same sex. A very young person, or somebody with a very superior manner, may have more difficulty in gaining trust. Race can provide another kind of barrier: surmountable, but complex. Portelli recounts how a black Kentucky minister's wife at one point, after talking to him for hours in depth about her life, told him, 'there's always gonna be a line' between them, because, as a white person, 'I don't trust you'.[18]   On the other hand, a person from the same working-class background and community as an informant will win an initial rapport, although later on may find difficulty in asking questions because of a common social network, or because the answer (often mistakenly) seems obvious. Similarly, considerable problems of reticence may be encountered if you interview a member of your own family. Differences in social background have to be recognized, and where possible met by variations in interviewing style.

The most recurrent problem is presented by the public personality as informant. Such people are generally tougher and fitter, and perhaps even younger, than the typical informant. They may have such a strong idea of their own story, and what matters in it, that all they can offer is stereotyped recollections. They often also, 'in the course of long careers in public life will have developed a protective shell by which they ward off troublesome questions and while seeming to say something worthwhile in fact give away as little as possible'. This can have become such a habit that 'the subject, even if trying to be frank and open, almost without thinking may reply with the clichéd responses which served so well on other occasions.. It is this defensive veil that the interviewer must penetrate.'[19]

One way of getting off the prepared script is to ask about something quite unexpectedly mundane and everyday, rather than challenging. Once more spontaneous talk has started, it becomes easier to shift to more significant themes. Occasionally innocence itself can penetrate the shell. 'Politicians have the right experience to be able to deal very cleverly with a young innocent historian', observes Asa Briggs. But 'a very young man can . . . get a lot from a very old man that members of his own generation don't get'. More usually, there is no alternative but to try to be 'sensitive *and* tough at the same time'. Some of the basic rules still apply: the danger of breaking up the interview through too challenging cross-questioning, and also the positive advantages of, for example, an informal discussion over the dinner-table. Nevertheless, several oral historians, such as James Wilkie in Mexico, Lawrence Goodwin in the southern United States, and Peter Oliver in Canada, have argued for the need to 'cross-examine' in a much more vigorous manner. The oral historian, according to Peter Oliver, while avoiding an openly 'adversary' posture,

should not hesitate to challenge the answers he receives and to probe . . . 'Come on now, Senator, surely there was more to it . . .? Mr So-and-So claims that . . .' Most politicians are pretty worldly and hard-skinned types; few will resent being pushed to re-examine their initial responses if it is done with some tact and skill, and often it is only by doing so that the interviewer will uncover truly significant material.

Portelli similarly suggests that 'a (respectfully) antagonistic interviewer may induce the narrator to open up', and he describes how he took a frank approach especially with informants to whose position he felt opposed: 'One cannot expect informants to tell the truth about themselves if we start out by deceiving them about ourselves. Fascists and capitalists who knew which side I was on often gave me much more vivid and motivated accounts and explanations than if they had blandly assumed I shared their party or class line.'[20]

A comparable instance is provided by the leading radio-astronomers interviewed by David Edge. They combined a very idealized image of science and what was important to its history with the defensiveness needed for success in the competitive grant-aided politics of the scientific world. He developed a triangular method, in which the radio-astronomer was interviewed at the same time by Edge, who as a former scientist and perhaps personal friend, and already in possession of inside secrets, was equipped to challenge on technical issues, and by

Mike Mulkay, a scientifically naïve sociologist, waiting to pounce on wider inconsistencies and points of interest. David Edge normally led the interview, chasing detailed points, challenging, and arguing; Mike Mulkay came in as an 'outsider', and there was often a notable change in the informant's voice when a question came from him. This argumentative technique clearly depends partly on some sort of common membership of a social group, and partly on knowing exactly how far the challenge may be pressed.

At the opposite end of the spectrum one may contrast the special skills which are needed for interviewing in situations where meanings are only exchanged with difficulty, such as interviewing people with learning disabilities, or in another culture in which not only language but also basic concepts differ sharply from those in the West. These situations present particular difficulties in negotiating consent to the interview and its use. In drawing out information in such contexts visual cues, such as time lines or life maps, friendship network diagrams or family trees, can be especially helpful.[21]

We must return, however, to the ordinary oral historian who was left chatting over a cup of tea. If you have completed the whole interview, this may be a suitable moment for getting a copyright signature. And then after leaving, three things remain to be done. First, record as quickly as possible any comments of your own on the context of the interview, the character of the informant, additional remarks made off the tape, and what may *not* have been said. Next, label the tape, disc, or box. Later on, play back the recording to check what information has been obtained and what you still need. In particular, make sure that you have the basic facts about the informant which any social historian would want to know in order to use it as evidence: the informant's age, sex, home, and occupation, and also his or her parents' occupations. At the same time you can make a list of any names whose spelling needs to be checked with the informant. Finally, if this was your last visit, you can verify these points (providing a stamped addressed envelope again) along with your thank-you letter. This letter can usefully restate the general purpose of the interview, and again if appropriate go into questions of confidentiality or copyright. But it is in any case a courtesy which will be valued. And it is on such personal care, just as much as historical expertise, that success in interviewing depends.

8

Storing and Sifting

The recording has been completed: but how then should the tapes be kept? And how can they be used to make history? We need first to consider the problems of storage and indexing, and then the stages in writing and presenting history with oral evidence.[1]

The last twenty years have seen a series of radical shifts in recording technology, which have brought with them parallel changes in archival opinion. Because even magnetic tape recording is a relatively recent technique, it remains far from certain how long it can last and what are the ideal conditions for its storage, and with digital recording the uncertainties are still greater. Up to the mid-1980s the most favoured equipment for high-quality recording and archiving was based on open reel tapes. The quality of cassette tapes has, however, gradually improved, so that archivists no longer advise that for long-term preservation cassette recordings should be transferred to open reel tapes. Basic advice on storage considerations has also changed. Good modern tapes no longer have a backing which is likely to disintegrate. The chief problem now is the avoidance of 'print-through', or sound echoes, which can develop during storage. Some experts recommend various means of reducing the risk of print-through, such as running the tape through a recorder once a year so that it is respooled, but it is not clear that this is a worthwhile safety measure—indeed, it may on balance create worse risks of other damage. For the moment, there are only two certain rules.

First, the quality of tape to be used for storage should be

carefully chosen. Never use extended play cassettes, which because they are thinner tend to get stretched or broken when in use on the machine. If you are using a digital recorder, get up-to-date independent technical advice, for example from the British Library National Sound Archive.

Secondly, the place for storing the tape needs to be considered. The tape can be damaged by dust, or by excessive damp or heat. It should never be exposed to temperatures much higher than normal room temperatures by, for example, being stored up against a heating pipe. Modern tapes do not require artificially controlled temperatures or humidity, but the optimum for storage is now considered to be a temperature of 15 to 20°C and a relative humidity of 40–50 per cent. Tapes can also be damaged, and even completely wiped of their recordings, by interference from a powerful magnetic dynamo. This risk needs to be taken into account in some buildings, as well as when travelling with them. But in practice, for most oral historians it will suffice to store tapes in a cupboard, boxed or wrapped, away from the sun or fire or heating pipes, in a room comfortable for working in. And do not smoke or eat near them.

Every tape or disc, as soon as used, needs to be well labelled, using a permanent marker rather than a biro or felt-tip. It is best to label the case as well as the tape or disc itself. It is much better if the original is kept as a master, and a copy made from it when it is required for use; and for a public archive such precautions are essential.

Exactly what you put on the label will depend on how you develop your system of indexing. If you have only a few interviews, it is enough to put the informant's name, 'Tape One, Side One', 'Tape One, Side Two', and so on. Corresponding to this, you can keep on your computer the names in alphabetical order, in each case with a list of the tapes or discs made with them. It is a great time-saver, if you also have transcripts, to add in which pages of transcript cover each side of tape or track of the disc. This list then constitutes an index and catalogue of your collection. The tapes, discs, and transcripts can themselves also be kept in alphabetical order to help finding. The disadvantage of this is that each new interview has to be inserted within the existing sequence, rather than added to it. After a while it becomes much easier to store the interviews in order of accession, giving each new informant a number, and adding the number to the index card. You will also need a numerical index giving the name for each interview number. Similarly, if you decide it is more useful to keep your main index in number order because, for example, this conveniently separates two different parts of your collection, you will still find that you need an alphabetical index which at least gives the number of each informant's interview.

As the collection grows, and especially as more people contribute to making and using it, it becomes increasingly important to use a database system for the index on your computer and to add more information in some systematic form. First, it is desirable to add to the informant's name, when and where the recording was made, who was the interviewer and what equipment was used.

Secondly, it is worth extracting some of the basic background details about the informant which are essential for evaluating the interview and should thus be found within it. They will of course vary to some extent, depending on the focus of the project. Thus a political collection might include specific entries for elections fought or offices held; and the Imperial War Museum lists details such as 'service', 'arm of service', 'rank', 'decorations and awards', which would be inappropriate in a different context. But most historians need at least to know when an informant was born, his or her parents' occupations, where they lived, whether or not there were brothers and sisters, the informant's own education, occupational career, religious and political affiliation if any, whether he or she married, and if so, when, to whom, and whether they had children.

All the information can be condensed, and some of it codified, if the suggested form seems too long. At the end of *Speak for England*, Melvyn Bragg added a very helpful index of 'The People' set out in this form:

160 Joseph William Parkin Lightfoot *b*. Bolton Low Houses 13th December 1908 *br*. Two *s*. Two *pl*. Fletchertown 1938, Kirkland 1942, Wigton 1954 *f.j*. Coalminer *o.j*. Retired, previously coalminer 1922, farm labourer 1924, labourer on pipe-tracks, part-time gardener 1930s, driver Cumberland Motor Services 1942–68, own shop in 1950s *e*. Bolton Low Houses until 14 *r*. Methodist *p*. Labour *m*. Married *ch*. Two

The abbreviations are self-explanatory, except perhaps for *pl*., which means 'places lived in'.

A third possibility is to create summaries of interview contents. For some projects, which are organized to follow a definite interview schedule, this may be superfluous; all the necessary clues will be in the basic background of the informant. But the larger and more diverse a collection, the more summaries become an essential part of the catalogue. One of the most fully developed examples is provided by the BBC Sound Archives. These entries provide a particularly full summary of the contents of each item in the archive, but they begin with a briefer heading. A summary, depending on the time which is to be spent on it, can aim to be brief or full. But it ought at least to indicate the principal places, social groups, occupations or industries, political or other ideologies, personal or family matters, and (more clearly than these cards) time periods covered.

CAMPBELL, Beatrice, Lady Glenavy (Wife of 2nd Baron Glenavy)   AA
LP28463   D. H. Lawrence And His Circle: the first of two   29.1.64.
             programmes in which she recalls some impressions of
             her friendship with
19' 12"   Katherine Mansfield, John Middleton Murry,
             D. H. Lawrence, and Frieda Lawrence.
             Producer: Joseph Hone
    Copyright: PF   CTIR 38700A
    Annots: None
    Trans: TP 30.3.64
    Script.
Note: This talk was recorded in Ireland and is taken from her
    autobiography Today We Will Only Gossip, published by Constable,
    9.4.64.

/continued . . .

CAMPBELL, Beatrice, Lady Glenavy (Wife of 2nd Baron Glenavy)   AA
LP28463   29.1.64.
Recalls first meeting Katherine Mansfield and Middleton Murry, who were
great friends of her future husband, Gordon Campbell: Katherine's
appearance and manner; felt Katherine regarded her as an interloper into
their circle, and tried to shock her with daring conversation; Katherine's early
struggles as a writer; sufferings from unhappy marriage and love affairs;
devotion and care of her friend Ida Baker; how her hostility to Beatrice
overcome by incident during visit to Paris; the 'psychological dramas' and
discussions during evenings at Parisian cafés.
Gr.90: Through them met Lawrence and his wife, and Koteliansky, known
as 'Kot'; qualities which made him a friend of Lawrence; Kot's first meeting
with Katherine arising out of quarrel between Lawrence and Frieda, and
their subsequent friendship; Katherine's association with Murray.

–2–   /continued . . .

CAMPBELL, Beatrice, Lady Glenavy (Wife of 2nd Baron Glenavy)   AA
LP28463   29.1.64.
Gr.145: Katherine's complex character and varying moods: two occasions
when she 'put on acts'; a week-end the Campbell's spent at the Murry's
country cottage which was 'not a success'.
Gr.220: Reminices about time Katherine and Murray spent on visit to
Cambell's cottage in Ireland; Murray sorry to leave, but Katherine glad to
return to London.

–3–

Finally, especially with a large public collection, it will be
necessary to create a general system of indexing linking with
the other series. Now that most properly equipped public
archives have computerized their indexes, there is a good choice
of models. Go for an off-the-peg programme which is user-
friendly and flexible: the worst mistake is to get a specialized,
tailor-made system individually designed for the collection,
because when its designer goes you will be left helpless.

In principle the general index can give access not only to the
brief entries about each informant, but also to the summaries.
The brief entries could be indexed so that it was possible to

Accession no.: C410/004/01–7
Accession no.: F94–F100 (Playback)
Collection title: Living Memory of the Jewish Community
Contents note: Barbara Stimler interviewed by Jennifer Wingate
Performer name: Stimler, Barbara, 1927 Feb. 5–, (speaker, female; interviewee)
Performer name: Wingate, Jennifer, (speaker, female, interviewer)
Recording date: 1988.11.17
Location: interviewee's home
Recordist: Wingate, Jennifer
Recording equipment: Marantz CP430 audio cassette recorder, 2 lapel mics
Carrier description: tape 7 cassettes (C60) stereo
Documentation: typed transcript and summary, 1 photo
Original or copy: original
Item copyright: NSA
Access restrictions: none
Copy condition code: a
Dubbing ref. no.: F94–F100

Subject: Holocaust, Jewish
Subject: World War 2 – Poland
Subject: Auschwitz (Concentration camp)
Subject: Lodz Ghetto

Interview summary:
Born in Alexandrow-Kinjawski, Poland. Private Catholic school, accepted by nuns. Jewish high school. Father owned shop. Kosher household. Remembers beginnings of anti-Semitism. When war broke out, their's was the first town to be bombed. Evacuated to uncle's in Lubraniec. Then forced to move on; stopped in Kutno. Remembers having to wear Yellow Star. Sent to work camp in Kutno, no food. Released; father taken away, never seen again. Lodz/Litzmannstadt Ghetto where she worked with sick children. 1943 taken to Auschwitz; knew nothing about concentration camps; horrified. Describes conditions, friends, singing Polish and Jewish songs, entertaining Germans. Winter 1944, work camp in Pirshkow. Russian advance. Death march to Odra. Escape and return home. All close family dead. Went to London, factory work, sewing. Married Edward Stimler from Kracow. Two sons (interview with eldest son see C410/113/01–03). Nervous breakdown. Applied for reparations from German government, 1956/7; lump sum for loss of education & injury to health, monthly pension. Family life, illnesses, feelings of bitterness, anger, appalled by signs of anti-Semitism in England.

RECORDING CALL NUMBER	COPY MATERIAL	LOCATION
1) C410/004/01–07	1 RECORDING	MIC
2) F92–F100	1 RECORDING	STP

A sample entry from the British Library National Sound Archive, Cadensa Catalogue search for informants, for example, under year of birth, occupation, or region. It would also be possible to include names of people or places. Important events could perhaps be listed. But what about indexing the summaries, or even the transcripts themselves? There are no easy solutions to this. Key-word-in-context systems may create more problems than they solve, because the concepts which will need indexing can be conveyed by many different words, or indeed by indirect innuendo, or even avoidance and omission. Since computers think with rigidly narrow-minded consistency, the key words will in practice have to be edited into the text before they can be picked up, as is indeed possible with the transcript, and easy enough with the summaries if a standard format has been imposed. This means that with most oral history collections, even with a computer, indexing is likely to be a process closer to the name and subject indexing of an ordinary book, including the development of a cross-referenced series of subject headings. Whatever system is chosen, above all it should be designed to help, rather than replace, human imagination, understanding, and intuition. In practice this means that the best cataloguing and indexing systems will tell the historian which parts of the collection will repay further investigation, and which will not. Ideally it should be made possible to eliminate, as quickly as possible, all those main sections, or individual items, which are concerned with a different time, place, or general subject-matter from the historian's theme.

Before a recording enters a public archive, or indeed before anyone attempts to use it in some form of publication, a key point needs to be clarified: that of control of the right to access and use. This is not, however, a simple issue, partly because the law of copyright is itself uncertain, varies between different countries, yet as regards oral history has never been tested in the courts in most of them; but equally because it raises wider ethical questions of responsibility towards informants.[2]

The general legal principle is that there are two copyrights in a recording. The copyright in the recording as a recording is normally the property of the interviewer or of the institution or person who commissioned the interview. The copyright in the information in the recording—the informant's actual words—is the property of the interviewee. These copyrights can only be transferred in writing. However, short extracts may be used for reviews or research, including theses. Perhaps more importantly, a licence to quote the informant is implied by a consent to be interviewed. Thus a person who, knowing that a historian is collecting material for a research study, agreed to be interviewed, would appear to have little legal ground for complaint if he found himself quoted in print. And in practice he would be very unlikely to attempt to prevent, or to seek compensation for, the publication of any quotation unless he considered it substantially damaging.

A bonafide scholar is unlikely to have committed an actionable libel through the interpretation of interviews, but it is important to remember that reproducing defamatory statements made in an interview does open the possibility of a court action. To be actionable the statements must be false and the plaintiff's reputation must have been damaged; the dead cannot be libelled. But short of this it would be foolish anyway to provoke a publicized complaint. It is always important to consider carefully whether the publication of identifiable confidences could not cause local gossip or public scandal. In any case, apart from ethical considerations, you also have a legal 'duty of confidentiality' to respect any assurance you may have given that the information will be 'confidential'.

Equally, an informant could reasonably complain if information was used in a significantly different context from that suggested; and also, if it proved the making of a best-seller, could claim a share of the earnings. If the publication is a single life-story, the authorship of the book, and the names on the cover, certainly ought to be decided jointly.

There is much to be said for this balance of rights. At the very least, however, it is crucial that before or after the interview a letter should be sent to the informant explaining the project and making clear not only its immediate object, but also the potential value of their information to wider historical research. This means that the licence to use the interview becomes general, rather than confined to the first researcher. Although British copyright law is now more restrictive than it was up until 1989, it is worth noting that informal understandings have proved a satisfactory basis for the writing of innumerable sociological studies, as well as all the oral history publications which we have discussed earlier. Similarly, the fact that in theory some copyright must also exist in most unpublished manuscript material has rarely produced serious obstacles to the free access of scholars to the holdings of local and national record offices. An insistence on a formal transfer of legal rights through explicit, written consent may not only worry an informant, but could actually reduce quite proper protection against exploitation.

There are, nevertheless, good reasons why formal agreements have increasingly become the standard practice, especially where interviews are to be archived and made accessible to other researchers. This was early the case in broadcasting, where observation of copyright has to be particularly careful because of the frequent involvement of public figures, and also due to the influence of the financial complexities of musical copyright. It has also been advised for many years by the Oral History Association of the United States, where standards were originally set for the recording of eminent public figures and a precise agreement was therefore necessary, not only as to copyright, but also as to whether particular pages of the transcript should be closed until a certain date, or accessible only by specific permission. In Britain the Imperial War Museum obtains a precise written agreement from its informants, who are often not only eminent public figures, but especially security-conscious. The formula advocated in Willa Baum's booklet for American local historians was relatively simple:

I hereby give and grant to the Central City Historical Society as a donation for such scholarly and educational purposes as the Society shall determine the tape recordings and their contents listed below: (signed) . . . . (informant).

To this riders may be added restricting access for a time period, or to specified pages of the transcript.[3] The 'Clearance Note' used by the British Library National Sound Archive is also brief, stating that the material will be preserved 'as a permanent public reference resource for use in research, publication, education, lectures and broadcasting', offering the opportunity to restrict access for a maximum of thirty years, and asking the interviewee to sign, 'I hereby assign the copyright in my contribution to the National Sound Archive'. More elaborated agreements are now the standard practice in the United States. Thus the University of California at Los Angeles uses an Interview Agreement, signed by both parties before the interview, covering both recordings and transcripts, by which the interviewee, in return for 'no remuneration or compensation', 'irrevocably assigns' copyright to the interviewer, conveying 'the right to use the interview for research, educational, and other purposes, including publication', and also to 'donate any and all materials' elsewhere at the end of the research. Here again an option to restrict use is included.

The Imperial War Museum, which has found that 'it is frequently more difficult to obtain assignments and settle other conditions of deposit and access with executors or heirs than with the informants themselves', seeks a quick exchange of letters 'to tie up all the legal loose ends' along the following lines:

I am now writing to formalize the conditions under which the Museum holds your recordings. The questions which I have already put to you verbally are listed below. I should be grateful if you would let me have your written answers in due course.

1. May the Museum's users be granted access to the recordings and any typescripts of them?

2. May the recordings and typescripts be used in the Museum's internal and external educational programmes?

3. May the Museum provide copies of the recordings and typescripts for its users?

4. Would you be prepared to assign your copyright in the information in the recordings to the Trustees of the Imperial War Museum? This would enable us to deal with such matters as publication and broadcasting, should they arise, without having to make prior reference to you. If you agree to this assignment it does not, of course, preclude any use which you might want to make of the information in the recordings yourself.

Whether or not such a formal agreement is reached, there remains an ethical responsibility towards the informant which is probably more important. First of all, you have an ethical obligation to obtain 'informed consent' for the interview. This implies a responsibility to explain clearly and meaningfully what your research is about, the various forms in which it might be published, whether any royalties might come to them, and whether the interview might be made available to other researchers. Informants should understand the potential uses to which the material might be put, and the extent to which confidentiality will be maintained. If the recording has been made with an implicit assumption of confidentiality, that must be respected. Any quotation from it which might embarrass the informant must be made either anonymously or with subsequent permission.

Occasionally you may be recording people whose views you strongly oppose, but you can still follow the same basic principles in explaining the research and in quoting them. Your work will be more powerful if you set out their views straightforwardly, rather than antagonistically. You may also discover a more positive side in such informants, which can provide important clues to understanding the appeal of their views. Thus before interviewing women who had been activists in the Ku-Klux-Klan, Kathleen Blee 'was prepared to hate and fear my informants. My own commitment to progressive politics prepared me to find these people strange, even repellent . . . What I found was more disturbing. Many of the people I interviewed were interesting, intelligent, and well informed . . . Many were sympathetic persons.' It was this surprising normality which became the basis for her new interpretation of the movement.[4]

With any informant, permission should always be sought for the use of material in a different manner from that originally understood: for example, instead of a history book, for a biographical collection or a radio broadcast. Moreover, when informants have a right to a royalty fee, as for a broadcast, or a biographical collection, this should be secured for them. They should be warned of the broadcast time well enough in advance to tell friends. And if they are quoted at length in a book, try to ensure that they receive their own free copy. As far as possible— and admittedly there are some legitimate forms of scholarly publication for which this might be counter-productive—informants' attention should be drawn to the use made of their material. Indeed, an oral historian who does not wish to share with informants the pleasure and pride in a published work ought to consider very seriously why this is so, and whether it is socially justifiable. There may perhaps be a case for publishing the material collected in a more popular form such as a local pamphlet as well as in some academic mode. One accepts that only the outstanding oral historian can reach the range of readership of a Studs Terkel with a single book. But it remains an overriding ethical responsibility of the historian who uses oral evidence to ensure that history is given back to the people whose words helped to shape it.

It should be added that the depositing and preservation of recordings needs to be seen in the same light. They can be of interest and use to far more people than the historian who made the recording. All too many oral history tapes remain with the secretary of a local society, or in an academic's private study, effectively inaccessible to a wider public. This may be reasonable while they are being actively used for personal research, but commonly continues beyond this, partly because national and county record offices have only slowly organized facilities for storing and listening to tapes. But the offer of the original recordings, or copies, to a local record office or a public or university library, besides being desirable in itself, may stimulate the provision for those needs, and prove the seed for a significant collection—an asset which will find many different uses within the community.

For the same reason there is a strong argument, whatever the immediate use envisaged for them, for the full transcription of recordings as the first stage in the writing and presentation of history. Transcribing is undoubtedly very time-consuming, as well as being a highly skilled task. It takes at least five hours, and for a recording with difficult speech or dialect up to twice as long, for each hour recorded. Voice recognition software is now beginning to offer a quicker alternative. But unless the tape or disc is fully transcribed, anybody but the person who made the recording—and so has quite a clear idea of what it contains—will be severely hampered in using it. A summary is at best only a rough guide for the visiting researcher: listening to more than a few interviews takes several hours, where skimming through transcripts might take minutes. But the person who makes the recording is also best able to ensure that transcription is accurate. Because this task is so lengthy, and, apart from other claims on time, new recording always seems more urgent, transcribing nearly always falls behind. In a research project supported by a grant, this can be avoided only by making a full estimate of the transcribing time and equipment needed at the start. Allowance ought to be made for your computer discs, headphones, so that the transcriber is not distracted by background noise, and for a variable speed memoscriber or tape recorder with a reverse foot-pedal for play-back: all essential for transcribing at a reasonable speed.

It is equally important to recognize that transcribing work can only be carried out by a person with particular skills, working on a regular basis. Part-time agency audio-typing will either be incomprehensible or prohibitive in cost. A transcriber needs to be interested in the tapes, intelligent in making sense of them, especially in the key art of turning verbal pauses into written punctuation, and a good speller with an unusually quick ear. It is also isolated work. These are not necessarily the qualities which make a successful secretary. The only way to know whether somebody can transcribe well is to give them a recording and let them try.

Most oral history projects will not have the resources to pay for a transcriber, and will need to carry out the work themselves. For a very small group, or for a researcher's own tapes, the process can, however, be quite markedly shortened, even if at the expense of long-term satisfaction. The best 'shortened transcript' lies between a summary and a complete transcription. For the most part, the content is summarized in detail, but actual quotations are only used when the words are so well or vividly put that they are worth considering for extracts or quotations in the finished presentation.

With cassettes there is no easy way of moving from the transcript to the tape, although finding devices can be added to the transcript (either by using the numbers in the counter-setting on the machine, although these unfortunately vary even between machines of the same make, or by noting the time intervals every five or ten seconds). One of the great advantages of digital recordings is that they can be structured to make the shift between sound and text easy.

Ultimately, however, there can be no substitute for a full transcript. Even the best shortened version is like an intelligent historian's notes from an archive rather than the original documents. Nor can the historian today know what questions will be asked by historians in the future, so that any selection will result in the loss of details which might later prove significant. The full transcript should therefore include everything, with the possible exception of diversions for checking that the recorder is on, having a cup of tea, or present-day chatting about the weather. All questions should go in. Fumbling for a word may be left out, but other hesitations, and stop-gaps like 'you know' or 'see', should be included at this stage. The grammar and word order must be left as spoken. If a word or phrase cannot be caught, there should be a space in the transcript to indicate this. These are all quite straightforward guidelines. But the real art of the transcriber is in using punctuation and occasional phonetic spelling to convey the character of speech.

Even a complete transcript is an interpretation of the recording, and the version suggested here is best seen as a practical compromise between two other possibilities. The first is the much neater, condensed transcript, cutting out pauses and distracting hesitations or false starts in the interests of readability, which is the most likely form be used for publication. The second is the more elaborate attempt to convey the complexity of speech on paper through elaborate systems of notations indicating intonation, emphasis, pauses, and so on, which has principally grown from anthropological approaches to oral history such as the 'ethnopoetics' of Dennis Tedlock. Unfortunately this second approach not only arises from, but also fails to solve, the basic problem that orality can never be adequately conveyed in print. The very elaborateness of the notation systems used brings this home by creating texts which are exceptionally hard to read. As Michael Frisch comments, 'The more completely we strive to make the voice audible on the page, the more we risk making it illegible'.[5]

Whatever approach is chosen, the transcript is inevitably a literary form and the problems which it raises are inseparable from those of subsequent quotation.[6] The spoken word can very easily be mutilated in being taken down on paper and then transferred to the printed page. There is already an inevitable loss of gesture, tone, and timing. Much more serious is the distortion when the spoken word is drilled into the orders of written prose, through imposing standard grammatical forms and a logical sequence of punctuation. The rhythms and tones of speech are quite distinct from those of prose. Equally important, lively speech will meander, dive into irrelevancies, and return to the point after unfinished sentences. Effective prose is by contrast systematic, relevant, spare. It is therefore very tempting for the writer, wishing to make a point effectively, to strip a spoken quotation, re-order it, and then, in order to make it continuous, slip in some connecting words which were never in the original. The point can be reached when the character of the original speech becomes unrecognizable. This is an extreme, but any writer, unless continually aware of this danger, may at times reach such a level of decadence in transcription.

The difficulties may be illustrated by taking as an example one of the first passages in Ronald Blythe's *Akenfield* (1969), an old farm worker's account of a domestic economy in the years before 1914. The picture he gives is very bare, highly effective— but so terse in detail that one wonders how far the original interview has been tidied up:

There were seven children at home and father's wages had been reduced to 10s. a week. Our cottage was nearly empty—except for people. There was a scrubbed brick floor and just one rug made of scraps of old clothes pegged into a sack. The cottage had a living-room, a larder, and two bedrooms. Six of us boys and girls slept in one bedroom and our parents and the baby slept in the other. There was no newspaper and nothing to read except the Bible. All the village houses were like this. Our food was apples, potatoes, swedes and bread, and we drank our tea without milk or sugar. Skim milk could be bought from the farm but it was thought a luxury. Nobody could get enough to eat no matter how they tried. Two of my brothers were out to work. One was eight years old and he got 3s. a week, the other got about 7s.[7]

There is in these lines an unremitting logical drive. Every word stands with evident purpose in its proper place. Every phrase is correctly punctuated. There are no ragged ends, no diversions to convey the speaker's own sense of a childhood home, or the bitterness or humour felt in poverty. Some phrases read like the author's own comments: 'skim milk . . . was thought a luxury'. There are no dialect words, no grammatical irregularities, no sparks of personal idiosyncrasy. The passage may convince but, unlike many others in the same book, it does not come alive. One wishes to know, but is provided with no indication of, where the interview has been cut, and what has been put in to sew it up again.

We can turn for a contrast to George Ewart Evans's *Where Beards Wag All* (1970), also about Suffolk villagers, some of them from the same community. This is a book with more direct argument than *Akenfield*, but supported by substantial quotations in which we seem to hear the people themselves talking, even thinking aloud, in their own, very different style, as this old man:

It's like this: those young 'uns years ago, *I said*, well—it's like digging a hole, *I said*, and putting in clay and then putting in a tater on top o' thet. Well, you won't expect much will you? But now with the young 'uns today, it's like digging a hole and putting some manure in afore you plant: you're bound to get some growth ain't you? It will grow won't it? The plant will grow right well. What I say is the young 'uns today have breakfast afore they set off—a lot of 'em didn't used to have that years ago, and they hev a hot dinner at school and when they come home most of 'em have a fair tea, don't they? *I said*. These young 'uns kinda got the frame. Well, that's it! If you live tidily that'll make the marrow and the marrow makes the boon (bone) and the boon makes the frame.[8]

We have to pause here to listen, accept the difficult rhythm and syntax of his speech, ruminating, working round to the parable image which he has held all the time in store. This quotation certainly requires more adaptation by the reader. But that may be needed, and if so will become generally learnt, as the qualities of speech become more understood.

George Ewart Evans is using artistry in his quotation as much as Ronald Blythe. Probably some hesitations, pauses, or repetitions have been eliminated from the recorded speech, and he has put in punctuation. But he has done this in a way which preserves the texture of the speech. Italics are used to indicate unexpected emphasis, and punctuation to bring the phrases together rather than to separate them. The syntax is accepted; the breaks in the passage left. And occasionally a word is spelt phonetically to suggest the sound of the dialect. Too much phonetic spelling quickly reduces a quotation (from whatever social class) to absurdity, but the odd word to convey a personal idiosyncrasy, or a key tone in a local accent like the Suffolk 'hev' and 'thet' used here, help to make a passage readable as speech without losing any of the force of its meaning.

In transferring speech into print the historian thus needs to develop a new kind of literary skill, which allows his writing to remain as faithful as possible to both the character and meaning of the original. This is not an art normally needed in documentary work. But the analogy with documentary quotation in other ways sets a useful standard. It is unfortunately not the usual practice in sociological studies quoting interviews to indicate cuts and other alterations. Historians can, however, insist on the care normal in their own discipline, showing excisions by a dotted line, interpolations by brackets, and so on. A reordering cannot be acceptable if it results in a new meaning, unintended by the speaker. And the creation of semi-fictional informants, by exchanging quotations between them, or dividing two from one, or creating one out of two, must always be by the standards of scholarship indefensible. An oral documentary which does this may gain in effect, but it becomes imaginative literature, a different kind of historical evidence.

Finally, oral historians in the United States have introduced an additional standard in their practice. After transcription, typescripts are sent to the informant for correction. This clearly has advantages in picking up simple errors and misspellings of names. It can also result in stimulating new information, and political historians who use the interview method often send transcripts for this purpose. But it has drawbacks too. Many informants find it impossible to resist rewriting the original conversational speech into a conventional prose form. They also may delete sentences and rephrase others to change the impression given from some particular memory. Since the original tapes are rarely consulted in American archives, and the transcript rather than the tape is regarded as the authoritative oral testimony, the process of correction can weaken the authenticity of the oral evidence in use, unless the original and corrected versions are both made available. In addition, while some informants, like retired public figures, may have the time and confidence for correcting a lengthy transcript, there are probably many more for whom it would simply be a worrying imposition. For many informants it is therefore usually better to write asking only for a few clarifications of confusions, uncertain names, or vital details missing—which will usually be gladly supplied.

Meanwhile, simultaneously with transcription, the sorting of the material for use should be begun. There are many computer programs now available which can help you with this.[9] You need to keep the material in at least two different forms. The first should be the transcript as a complete interview as recorded, a series parallel to the tapes or discs themselves.

Provided you have indexed for this, these whole interviews can then be regrouped as you choose: for example, by place, by social group, or by occupation. The second form is the interview re-sorted, and divided up between different subject or thematic files, depending on what use is in mind. If you have stuck fairly consistently to your original research plan, these computer files may well follow the sequence of the original schedule of questions. Alternatively, especially if your ideas have been changing, it is better to sort according to the sections you intend for writing up your findings. Either way, if a question has been asked, for example, about church attendance, or how people met their husbands or wives, and these are themes which concern you, you can ensure that all the relevant material is put in the same file, so that when you come to write it can be quickly found together. But it is crucial that the precise choice of method in re-sorting should reflect the form of analysis and presentation intended. It is to this essential, final question that we must now turn.

9

Interpretation
The Making of History

The evidence has now been collected, sorted, and worked into an accessible form: the sources are at our disposal. But how do we put them together? How do we make history from them? We shall have to consider, first, what choices may be made in the manner and shape of presentation. Next, how do we evaluate our evidence? Thirdly comes the heart of the matter, interpretation: how do we relate the evidence we have found to wider patterns and theories of history? How do we construct meaning in history? And finally, we shall take a concluding look ahead, at the impact which we might hope for from oral evidence on the making of history in the future.

The interpretation of history with oral evidence opens many new possibilities. In the broadest sense, all testimonies normally carry within them a triple potential: to explore and develop new interpretations, to establish or confirm an interpretation of past patterns or change, and to express what it felt like. As a whole, most of the essential skills in judging evidence, in choosing the telling extract, or in shaping an argument, are much the same as when writing history from paper documents. So are many of the choices: between, for example, audiences of other historians, of schoolchildren, an old people's club, local newspaper readers, or television viewers nationally. Oral history does, however, highlight the need for some of these choices, simply because it can be effective in so many different contexts. There are, however, always three basic issues which need to be decided. These are: who is the author or editor; what is the medium to be used, and what form of interpretation or analysis is intended.

First, the question of authorship or editorship arises naturally from the origin of oral evidence in the co-operation of an interview—and sometimes also the carrying out of field-work by a group. Especially with a single life-story, there is an ethical obligation for the narrator of the story to be on the title-page as well as the researcher: whether as an author, or in the title itself. And with some printed publications there may be a case for recognition of the co-operation in the form of joint editorship. For a school project, or a community oral history, the collective work in putting together oral material may be as valuable an experience as the recording itself. In a community project a group of old people may record each other's reminiscences, discuss them together, decide what to choose for publication, correct and elaborate the scripts, and so on. In a school project the co-operation will be more likely over production: choice of the best extracts, design, and printing. The recognition of all those who contributed through joint editorship will be an important form of symbolic validation.

The second choice is the medium, for its techniques and conventions will shape and limit the message which can be conveyed. Technically it is now possible to combine text with sound and film or photographs, and some oral history projects have issued their own multimedia discs, but as we have seen (Chapter 6), the possibilities here remain still rather limited and exploratory. It is also common for booklets and printed programmes to be sent out as an aid to broadcasting, using two media in parallel. On the other hand, it is surprisingly rare for a sound tape or disc to be issued to accompany a book. Thus in practice, for the moment oral history is still normally presented in one of a number of separate forms.

The first is sound alone. The most elementary way in which you can use sound yourself is in giving a talk about your oral history work. However, this does require some careful preparation. Since the accent may be a little hard to catch at first (and the tape recorder very likely does not amplify well enough) it is best to choose a few, clear, quite long extracts—four or five minutes each. It will help if you supply the audience with duplicated copies of the transcripts. For a more elaborate lecture, where extracts are used to illustrate an argument which may be quite complex, this solution is less easy. In this case you must have good recordings in the first place, and they will need to be copied from the original recordings onto a single tape of extracts. You must also make sure that a reliable amplifying system is available in the lecture room. You can then lecture standing next to the play-back machine, flicking the quotations on and off with the pause control. Still better is to convert your cassettes to digital extracts in the form of a CD compilation, which allows you to skip examples and restart exactly where you wish. Without such preparation, as most oral historians by now know to their cost, an audience is likely to be puzzled by incomprehensible voices, distracted by intervals while the right place is found on the tape, and irritated by a gross over-running of time.

A much more complex possibility for using recordings is the radio broadcast. There is a whole range of possibilities here, from the raw material itself in an autobiographical interview to the illustrated academic talk. Broadcasting has also developed a very special art of conveying scenes and messages in sound. Original recordings can be not merely clarified by cutting out hesitations and pauses, but heightened by rearrangements of words. Some of this amounts to a tampering with evidence which a historian ought not to accept, but the fine editing which becomes possible with the technical resources of broadcasting can certainly make quotation briefer and more effective. The sound needs to be varied and this can be done partly during recording, so that some voices are more close up than others, some are recorded outside or in a room with an echo, but especially through adding background sounds and music. A programme also has to be built around a strong narrative, but at the same time the pace will fluctuate between, at one extreme, the long anecdote, and at the other, the brief conclusive one-line quip. Sound can also make some clues superfluous, so that a series of extracts in different regional or class accents can be directly juxtaposed. Indeed a whole programme can be designed as a collage of sound, with very little or no connecting narrative at all, and 'footnotes' perhaps supplied by the programme notes. In this way a historical picture of a community can be built up, such as a fishing town, interweaving the sounds of the herring gulls and the auctioneers at the quay, with old people's accounts of how the men caught fish, how the women gutted it and mended nets, stories, singing in the pubs, hymns, and preaching in church. Programmes can be built around a very few people, or many; and all sorts of themes are possible—for example, the rediscovery of a forgotten story of how child emigrants were sent to Australia without their parents' knowledge, a disappearing world like the pre-electronic steelmakers, the hopes and dreams and myths of an Andean Indian mountain community, or how we got it wrong in idealizing past village life.

When pictures are added to sound, as with film, video, or television, there is a radical shift not in potential themes but in how they can be conveyed. Oral historians have been slow to incorporate the visual, partly for the good reason that it makes much higher technical demands to be at all successful, and therefore too often leaves them feeling at the mercy of professionals who insist on subtly changing their message. Another problem may be that the range of possible informants shifts: the articulate witness whose body language jars may have to be dropped for another, who says much less, but with a compelling expression. Because the visual effects tend to dominate, the ideal solution is to film the whole theme professionally on location, so that the backgrounds and the angles on the speakers become much more varied. Most oral history programmes, however, are made of 'talking heads', only varied by close-ups. Furthermore fine cutting is not possible in an interview unless a separate visual sequence such as an extract from old film is introduced, because otherwise there is likely to be a jump in the interviewee's physical position at each cut. But a separate visual sequence is distracting, conveying its own meanings. The same problems apply with a collage. Since the verbal messages conveyed can be less easily clarified, and the pictorial meanings tend to be symbolic rather than precise, television presents argument in a more diffuse form than radio. It makes a sharp argument difficult to sustain: thus Michael Frisch criticized the major American series 'Vietnam: A Television History' for its 'tendency to defuse specific political analysis in favor of a more general, vaguely tragic view of the war'. Nevertheless, film and television are extremely powerful forms of historical presentation drawing mass audiences. And there is no doubt that seeing the informants themselves, their expressions and gestures and body postures, along with old photographs of their families, homes, and workplaces, does brings an important added dimension of historical immediacy.[1]

The third fundamental choice is the form of interpretation or analysis. There are essentially two parallel questions here. The first is whether you essentially want to present testimonies—with no more than minor comment—or primarily you want to argue for a historical interpretation. The second is whether you prefer to approach history through biography or through a wider social analysis. Oral evidence, because it takes the form of life-stories, brings to the surface a dilemma which underlies any historical interpretation. The individual life is the actual vehicle of historical experience. Moreover, the evidence in each life-story can only be fully understood as part of the whole life. But to make generalization possible, we must wrench the evidence on each issue from a whole series of interviews, reassembling it to view it from a new angle, as if horizontally rather than vertically; and in doing so, place a new meaning on it. We are thus faced with an essential but painful choice.

There are broadly four ways in which oral history can be put together. The first is the single life-story narrative. For an informant with a rich memory it may well seem that no other choice can do the material full justice. Nor need a single life narrative present just one individual biography. Indeed most interviews are not just about the informant: 'far from dealing only with ourselves when we tell about the past, we incorporate the experiences of a multitude of others'.[2] And in outstanding cases a single interview can be used to convey the history of a whole class or community, or become a thread around which to reconstruct a highly complex series of events. Thus the auto-biography of Nate Shaw in *All God's Dangers* is powerful just because it stands for the wider experience of the black people of the southern United States. A story of such power asks for no more than a brief explanation of its context; others, especially if intended to be read as in some sense typical, will require a much fuller introductory discussion and interpretation if they are to reach beyond the anecdotal.

The second form is a collection of stories. Since none of these need be separately as rich or complete as a single narrative, this is a better way of presenting more typical life-history material. It also allows the stories to be used much more easily in constructing a broader historical interpretation, by grouping them—as a whole or fragmented—around common themes. Thus Oscar Lewis explores the family life of the Mexican city poor in *The Children of Sanchez*, by taking for one family the different accounts of parents and children and bringing them together into a single multidimensional picture. On a larger scale, a group of lives may be used to portray a whole community: a village, as in *Akenfield*, or a town, as in *Speak for England*. Or the collection may focus upon a single social group or theme, like *Fenwomen*, or *Working*, or *Blood of Spain*. It may be organized as a collection of whole lives, or stories about incidents, or as a thematic montage of extracts: *Blood of Spain* interweaves all three. And here again the character of the introduction will also shape the impact of the stories.

The third form is narrative analysis. This is most characteristically of a single interview, but may also be carried out with a group of interviews depending on the method chosen. The focus of this approach is on the interview itself as an oral text, and what can be learnt from its language, its themes and repetitions, and its silences. It is above all concerned with how the narrator experienced, remembered, and retold his or her life-story, and what light this may throw on the consciousness of the wider society. It does not normally aim to evaluate the typicality of the narrator or his or her experiences.

The fourth form is that of the reconstructive cross-analysis:

the oral evidence is treated as a quarry from which to construct an argument about patterns of behaviour or events in the past. It is of course possible within one book to combine analysis with the presentation of fuller life-stories. In my own *The Edwardians*, a series of family portraits, chosen to represent the varied social classes and regions of Britain, is interwoven between the more directly analytical chapters. But wherever the prime aim becomes analysis, the overall shape can no longer be governed by the life-story form of the evidence, but must emerge from the inner logic of the argument. This will normally require much briefer quotations, with evidence from one interview compared with that from another, and combined with evidence from other types of source material. Argument and cross-analysis are clearly essential for any systematic development of the interpretation of history. On the other hand, the loss in this form of presentation is equally clear. Because of this, these basic forms are not so much exclusive alternatives as complementary, and in many cases the same project needs to be brought out in more than one of them.

In any of these forms, writing a book which uses oral evidence, either alone or with other sources, thus does not in principle demand many particular skills beyond those needed for any historical writing. You will need to create a system for citing your interviews. You also need to check that you have got your quotations correct, as you would citations from written sources. Oral evidence can also be evaluated, counted, compared, and cited along with the other material. It is no more difficult, no easier. But in some ways it is a different kind of experience. As you write, you are aware of the people with whom you talked; you hesitate to give meanings to their words which they would wish to reject. Humanly and socially, this is a proper caution; and indeed anthropologists have shown it equally essential to scientific understanding. In writing, too, you strongly wish to share with others the insights and vividness of the life-stories which have held your own imagination. Moreover, this is material which you have not just discovered, but in one sense helped to create: and is thus quite different from another document.

This is why an oral historian will always feel a specially strong tension between biography and cross-analysis. But this is a tension which rests on the strength of oral history. The elegance of historical generalization, of sociological theory, flies high above the ordinary life experience in which oral history is rooted. The tension which the oral historian feels is that of the mainspring: between history and real life.

Whatever form you have chosen, you will need to evaluate your interviews in three ways: as texts, as types of content, and as evidence. Every interview needs to be read through as a text, so that you can listen to what it says, pick up its overall meanings, its repeating comments and images, and so that you can watch for and note the well-told story or telling phrase. Secondly, for any purpose, you will need to disentangle different types of content in the interview, contrasting the parts which are more 'objective' with those which are primarily 'subjective': in particular, to distinguish information about the biographical life path (birth, education, marriage, work, and so on), from expressions of how that life experience felt, and also from more general comments on personal life and social change. Thirdly, you also need to evaluate your interview as source material in terms of reliability. This matters even if you are only concerned with how people remember rather than how the past was, because you will need to know to what extent their memories are censored or mythologized.

In this evaluation of reliability, first, each interview needs to be assessed for internal consistency. It must be read as a whole. If an informant has a tendency to mythologize or to produce stereotyped generalizations, this will recur throughout an interview. The stories in it may then be taken as symbolic evidence of attitudes, but not as reliable in factual detail as they might be with another informant. Similarly, suppression of information can be revealed by a repeated avoidance of discussion of a particular area (such as the war years), or through unresolved contradictions of detail (such as the date of marriage, and the birthdate and later age of a first child, which was conceived before marriage). Any extensive suppression or invention will produce extremely obvious inconsistencies, contradictions, and anachronisms. On the other hand, some inconsistencies are quite normal. It is very common to find a conflict between the general values which are believed true of the past and the more precise record of day-to-day life; but this contradiction can be in itself highly revealing, for it may represent one of the dynamics of social change.

On many points a cross-check can be made with other sources. This can of course be a cumulative process as material is gathered in: a series of interviews from the same locality will provide numerous factual cross-checks between each other. Details can similarly be compared with manuscript and printed sources. '*Any* evidence,' as Jan Vansina puts it, 'written or oral, which goes back to *one* source should be regarded as on probation; corroboration for it must be sought.'[3] This dictum may, however, be of more general relevance to oral tradition handed down over several generations than to direct life-story evidence. Where there are discrepancies between written and oral evidence, it does not follow that one account is necessarily more reliable than another. The interview may reveal the truth behind the official record. Or the divergence may represent two perfectly valid accounts from different standpoints, which together provide vital clues towards the true interpretation. Very often, indeed, while oral evidence which can be directly confirmed proves to be of merely illustrative value, it is fresh but unconfirmed evidence which points the way towards a new interpretation. Indeed, much oral evidence, springing from direct personal experience—like an account of domestic life in a particular family—is valuable precisely because it could come from no other source. It is inherently unique. Of course its authenticity can be weighed. It cannot be confirmed, but it can be assessed.

Lastly, the evidence can be evaluated by placing it in a wider context. Thus a folklorist or literary scholar might be able to pick out stories which are versions of known tales, distinguishing the elements in them which are unaltered and those which are new. Similarly an experienced historian will already have learnt enough from contemporary sources about the time, place, and social class from which an interviewee comes to know, even if a specific detail is unconfirmable, whether as a whole the words ring true. General absence of reliable detail, anachronistic attitudes, and incongruous linguistic phrasing will all be obvious enough.

At this point the forms of analysis begin to divide, depending on whether our approach is based on the narrative or reconstructive mode. Let us consider them in turn.

The narrative mode is in fact a cluster of perspectives, some much more specific than others, and with important differences in assumptions and method, ranging from the broad brush of traditional criticism to the tight disciplines of narrative analysis.

In the most straightforward approach the historian may seek to understand an interview in the sensitive, humanistic manner of the traditional literary critic who interprets the meanings intended by the author, often in a confused and contradictory text, from all the clues in it which seem helpful. Thus Ron Grele contrasts two interviews, each with a working-class Jewish New Yorker from the tailoring trade. Despite their similar backgrounds, they present history in fundamentally different ways. For Mel Dubin, an immigrant's son born in the city, skilled worker and union organizer, history is an uphill struggle for progress, chronological, and despite its setbacks, logical. In each dimension of his account—his personal story, the neighbourhood, the union, the garment industry—he constructs the same pattern of rise and decline, and gives the same explanation, the disappearance of the skilled immigrant Jewish and Italian tailors of earlier decades: just the skills on which Mel's own life was built. Mel's history, constructed from both direct experience and knowledge of the past, and also with the help of significant omissions and exaggerations, is a historical myth of progress, 'which functions in very particular ways to give a dynamic to the tale, and leads inevitably to certain very real conclusions about the nature of the world of the garment industry today'. Bella Pincus, on the other hand, also a militant, was herself an immigrant, coming to the city as a teenager from a village in Russian Poland; she worked before marriage as a semi-skilled machine operator, and returned again to work as a widow. Bella does not present history as the logic of change, but as a series of dramatic episodes, all exhibiting the same moral lesson of struggle: 'It's always the same. Ever since the world is it's rich and poor, struggling and well off. That's how it is.' It is indeed closer to her own history. And she tells it with the constant poetic use of paired images. For example, she describes her first impressions of New York in terms of the open-top buses, the flat roofs of the houses, and the washing in the street, in contrast with the closed buses, pitched closed roofs, and hidden washing of her Russian childhood: symbols which also give the sense of openness she felt in her own life when she was a young girl in New York, compared to her life in Russia, and to her life now. Thus in both these life-stories it is not only through the facts and opinions given, but perhaps still more through the imaginative and narrative skills with which they are put together, that we can perceive the speaker's deeper historical consciousness. This is all the more striking since they had to fight to be heard in the interview, returning 'again and again to the main thrust of his or her story, despite the sometimes strained efforts of the interviewers to control the situation and to divert them to other questions'. The need to 'Listen to their Voices', both in the interview and afterwards, is here put conclusively.[4]

This is an equally good approach for identifying the images in interviews which alert us to the presence of *The Myths We Live By*: the everlastingly long hot summers of a golden childhood, the angelic devotion of a mother, the witch-like evil of a step-mother, the ogrish bullying of an employer, and so on. Thus Vieda Skultans finds that elderly Latvians, whose social world was first destroyed by the Soviet invasion of 1940 and then again by the collapse of Communism in 1991, look back on their childhoods as sensually miraculous. One older woman says of herself, 'we lived as if in a fairy tale'. She remembers the market as full of southern fruits: 'there were such beautiful cherries with such a miraculous taste'. The nearby fields were also abundant with 'wonderfully scented' meadow flowers. And above all she recalls the shrubroses in her grandmother's garden as 'heavily scented'. As her mother put it to her, 'You were born in the rose era'. Such images stand out very clearly: to spot them you do not need a special technique, but simply to be on the watch.[5]

A much newer and more technical approach is to evaluate an interview in terms of genre, which can throw light both on how the story is told, and how the form in which it is told may shape its contents. Genre is a long-standing form of literary analysis. From the 1970s it became increasingly used in studies of popular culture, and also by Africanists such as Ruth Finnegan researching on oral literature, but it was the call by Elizabeth Tonkin for us to study Western oral genres—jokes, 'sob-stories', radio announcers, ghost stories, TV comedy, pub stories, the psychoanalytical confession, as well as forms of interview—which generated the recent volume on *Narrative and Genre*. As the contributors there show, it is clear that oral interviews may incorporate other genres, most notably proverbs, jokes and anecdotes, family stories, sexual stories, (mainly men's) war stories, or (mainly women's) hospital stories. These genres within oral interviews need to be identified and much more studied. It is also possible for written forms to draw on oral genres; and in terms of content the differences between the oral and the written may also reflect not only the form but also the degree of confidence established in a particular interview. Beyond this, as Alessandro Portelli observes, oral interviews not only may contain other genres, they are a special genre which it is our task to understand: 'The life story as a full, coherent oral narrative does not exist in nature; it is a synthetic product of social science—but no less precious for that.'[6]

There are now some suggestive studies of the oral telling of war stories, sexual stories and medical stories in English.[7] There is still, however, nothing to emulate the sustained work of Philippe Lejeune on forms of autobiography in France. He has evaluated and compared a whole series of different genres including the autobiography in the third person, the radio interview, the 'document vécu', and the oral history interview. He is particularly illuminating in his discussion of the modern 'document vécu': the candid autobiography 'from the horse's mouth', which reveals the hidden story of a prison or hospital, a murder or sexual scandal, of war or resistance, or simply the unknown lives of ordinary people like peasants or fishermen, which French publishers have brought out in series with titles such as 'Témoignages', 'Elles-mêmes', or 'En direct'. He shows these are shaped partly by opposition to other forms: the nurse's own experience, for example, is an answer to romantic hospital novels with doctors as the heroes—'the men in white'—and also to the official literature of her own profession. More generally, they are assumed to contrast with the self-conscious literary autobiography, and presented as direct, readable, even artless: but in practice they repeatedly use the same devices, such as the present tense, the diary form, and direct dialogue, and are organized dramatically as a clear story told through a series of scenes. Tantalizingly, Lejeune fails to follow this with an equivalent analysis of the forms and devices found in oral history interviews, a challenge that therefore remains open.[8]

A fundamental issue which needs to be much more explored is the extent to which genre shapes what can be told. Luisa Passerini found among the Turinese workers whom she interviewed that the majority spoke of themselves as fated, 'born socialists', born rebels, born to poverty, and so on. She sees these messages, however, as often not consciously intended, but reflections of the ideas in an earlier, archaic popular culture surviving in spoken language: as for instance with the woman who explains her childhood pranks, her marriage without the permission of her parents, and her insistence on being a working wife, by saying 'I had the devil in me'. She contrasts such interviews with a minority—mostly men—who portrayed their lives in terms of choice, decision, acquiring skills, searching, and sacrifice. Interestingly, however, these too drew on a historical genre. Paradoxically she found that not only some active Catholics but also socialist militants adopted a traditional form of life-story similar to that used for saints, with a stage of 'seeing the light', and some of them even referred to this 'self-hagiography' as 'my confession'.[9] No doubt these contrasting ways of shaping the telling of life-stories also influenced what was mentioned in detail.

The influence of genre is especially suggested by a comparison made by Stefan Bohman of diaries, written memoirs, and interviews from the same Swedish working men. He found the diaries, small printed pocket-books crammed with tiny writing, still traditional journals of events, mainly about the weather and work: none took up the form of the private reflective diary. Memoirs and interviews were more alike, using the same stories and even phrases, but with important differences too. The written memoirs focused on early life, and they used a more public, abstract language. Thus one man writes: 'My father died in Stockholm on 2nd August 1933. He died in extreme poverty after a long illness, patiently borne. What can I have done to deserve such suffering he said—and poor Mother.' He even uses the stock phrase of public memorial announcements, 'after a long illness patiently borne'. His account in the interview is much more personal and detailed—and as a result, significantly different in what it conveys:

Yes, he died at home. I came home one day the last year, I came home when I was out of work. He was lying there on an iron bedstead. We were incredibly poor. It was in the afternoon, three or four o'clock. I saw there was blood and a bloodstained handkerchief on a chair by the bed . . . He'd taken a razorblade and cut both his wrists, hacked at them. But he hardly bled at all, he was so thin. He thought he was a burden on the family.

'What have I done to deserve to suffer like this?' he said.

Another man writes of his own later years in his memoir:

As a result of the conditions now prevailing, the summer home or my 'life's work', if I may thus express myself, has if anything become a burden in the financial sense, now that I have retired. Unless I sell it, which I do not wish to do. I am not altogether satisfied with the taxable values stated above. I regard this as a construction making it possible to collect money from a hard-working and perhaps somewhat naive citizen.

What he really wants to say is trapped in the conventions of the style of writing which he believes appropriate for a public memoir. The interview releases the same message in quite a different manner:

Djurö is my life's work. I worked and slogged and hammered away like hell, and I scraped and saved to do it. But the taxable value, you see, it's hard to keep it on, I could sell it if I wanted to . . . It's rather a smack in the teeth. Somebody in the same position could have blown the money and lived it up. Then he can go on the welfare. I've never got a penny-piece that way, and I don't want to either.[10]

Another approach is to look for the often half-conscious meanings which can be discerned in the formal qualities of language itself. These hidden meanings can be read whether or not one accepts the view of some linguistic and psychological theorists that grammar itself moulds the infant consciousness. The general contrasts between oral and written forms are in themselves striking. Written language is grammatically elaborate, linear, spare, objective, and analytical in manner, precise yet abundantly rich in vocabulary. Speech on the other hand is usually grammatically primitive, full of redundancies and back-loops, empathetic and subjective, tentative, repeatedly returning to the same words and catch-phrases. But these contrasts are not absolute within either speech or writing: there are marked differences between individuals in vocabulary and grammar, tone and accent, which reflect regional origin and education, social class and gender. William Labov's pioneering formal structural analyses of storytelling by urban black Americans first brought out their technical artistic sophistication, and very interesting contrasts have been shown between manners of talking in almost adjacent white and black settlements in the South. Labov seemed less interested in the symbolic implications of such language structures, but sometimes this is clear enough. Thus as Isabelle Bertaux-Wiame first observed, when ordinary people tell life-stories, the men are more likely to use the direct, active, subjective mode, the 'I', and women the indirect, reflective 'we' or 'one'. And choices of particular key words and catch-phrases, for instance when conveying moral attitudes, will again vary, both between speakers and with the same speaker in different contexts, and can be equally telling of assumptions, often unspoken, and sometimes deeply buried.[11]

Reading interviews for their images, identifying their genres and examining their linguistic structures are all ways of taking them apart, but there are other forms of narrative analysis which examine them as a whole. One approach is to look at the interview, not simply as the story of the teller, but as the outcome of the interaction of interviewer and interviewee: so that, as Elliot Mishler has cogently argued, the interview should be interpreted as a joint product between *two* people, 'a form of discourse . . . shaped and organized by asking and answering questions'. His own experience comes from medical interviews, where the asymmetry of power between questioner and respondent is especially marked, because it is only the former who has favours to offer: the right information makes a cure more likely. Mishler shows how quickly the patient keys in to the doctor's responses—either meaningful silences or requests for more detail—and cuts out circumstantial comment, often ending up with simple 'yes' and 'no' answers. He alerts us to the need to watch the questions as well as the answers in interpreting an interview. In 'the mainstream tradition' of social science surveys this mutual exchange of meanings is suppressed, both at the interview stage and also later in the process of coding, but with recorded evidence there is the chance to examine the whole dialogue, although few have done so. Anthropologists, however, have become increasingly sensitive to the issue of authorship, partly because of the extreme imbalance of wealth and power between them and their informants. The conventional anthropological life-story has typically been divided between, first, an interpretative introduction by the anthropologist and, second, the text of the informant's story, from which all traces of the researcher's questions have been removed. We can contrast this with the alternative academic model of Pat Caplan's *African Voices*. Her book tells the story of a Tanzanian islander, Mohammed, her part-dependant and close friend, whom she has known for thirty years. She uses the diaries he kept for her earlier on, his letters to her, and the life-story interview which she recently recorded with him. All these are set out separately, along with her questions, and also her comments for the book itself. But particularly strikingly, she also includes at the start a recording of their discussion about the purpose of the book and how they intend to share the royalties, followed by his prayer for her; while at the end there is no conclusion—'a tidy ending would be spurious'—but instead, another prayer from Mohammed. While perhaps overinhibiting the interpretative voice of the anthropologist, Caplan's approach certainly reveals the interaction between researcher and narrator exceptionally fully.[12]

A much more formal method of narrative analysis, drawing particularly on Labov, was developed by Catherine Riessman for a study of men's and women's accounts of divorce, in which she had been originally frustrated to discover that many of her informants avoided giving direct answers to her questions, and instead told her stories. But how was she to understand these? She describes the process which she eventually used as beginning with the rough transcript of the interview as a whole. From this she strips out the non-narrative elements—asides, interactions with the interviewer, false starts, and so on—seeking to focus on the 'embedded narrative segments within an overarching narrative that includes non-narrative parts'. Next, following Labov's example, the selected text is divided up into clauses, each given a numbered line. While Labov groups and names the lines according to their function in the narrative (orientation, complication, resolution, etc), Riessman groups them by content. She also differs in choosing to divide the text into lines according to the speech 'poetics' with which they are enunciated: 'intonation contours, rising and falling pitch, pauses and discourse markers ("well", "and", "so", nonlexical expressions like "uh") . . . ' Once the text is divided in this way, Riessman's aim is to identify the key features in stories which recur through each interview, and from that to compare these features in different groups of interviews, contrasting, for ex-

Rough Transcription	*Retranscription*

This is actually a crucial incident because I finally got up and went into the other room. She was [talking to her lover on the phone] in the laundry room with the door closed. I knocked on the door and said, "When are you going to be done with this?" 'Cause we were going to talk. And she held her hand like this and went "No." And I got absolutely bullshit. I put my fist through the door, which is not the kind of stuff that I do, you know. I'm not a real physically violent person at all.

30 and (p) finally, ah it's, this is actually a crucial incident [A]

31 because I *finally* got up and (p) [CA]

32 and (p) went into the other room [CA]

33 (p) she was in the laundry room with the door closed and [O]

34 (p) knocked on the door and said [CA]

35 "When are you going to be done with this?" [CA]

36 'cause we, we were going to talk. [O]

37 And she kind of held up her hand like this and went "no." [CA]

38 And I got absolutely bullshit [E]

39 I put my *fist* through the door (I: uh-huh) [R]

40 which is not the kind of stuff that I, that I do, you know [E]

41 I'm *not* a real physical violent person at all. [E]

Catherine Reismann, *Narrative Analysis*, 1993, p. 58. Reprinted by permission of Sage Publications.

Retranscribed Version of Story I	*Core Narrative of Story I*

001 L: uh (1) the way I've usually started these is to ask	Abstract
002 how you found out you were a DES daughter,	002 L: how you found out you were a DES daughter
003 and what was it like	003 and what was it like
004 N: (1) um, it's funny because the, details are fuzzy, in my head,	Orientation
005 what I, think happened, was um (1) (tch)	006 N: when I was around 19,
006 when I was around 19,	008 I was in college
007 I we—	
008 I was in college	Complicating action
009 and I went, to a, a gynecologist to get birth control	009 and I went, to a, a gynecologist to get birth control
010 and, I happened to be lucky with my first exam	011 he was, he knew that I was a DES daughter because I had adenosis (1) um,
011 he was, he knew that I was a DES daughter because I had adenosi (1) um,	012 so he told y'know he told me (2.5)
012 so he, told y'know he told me (2.5)	016 I think shortly after that
013 and I don't remember how it became (laughs) clear between my mother and I,	017 [my mother] told me,
	018 um and I either said "I know already" or, (inhale)

014　that (1.5) that uh 'cause she didn't
　　　know I was going to the gynecologist
015　that she (1)016　I think shortly after
　　　that,
017　she told me
018　um and I either said 'I know already'
　　　or, (inhale)
019　um (1) but I didn't learn from her
　　　directly first
020　um I learned from this doctor (1.5)
021 L:　uhm
022 N:　and I was so concerned at the time
　　　about getting birth control,
023　that I think I sort of didn't, um,
024　it never really, became the major part
　　　of my life
025　it sort of f'flitted in and out (tch)

Resolution/coda
022　and I was so concerned at the
　　　time about getting birth control,
023　that I think it sort of didn't,
　　　um,
024　it never really, became the
　　　major part of my life (tch) (1.5)
　　　it sort of f'flitted in and out

Catherine Reismann, *Narrative Analysis*, 1993, p. 62. Reprinted by permission of Sage Publications.

Retranscription	*Analysis of Poetic Structures*
01　About (p) things that are hard?	**FRAME**
02　Well um I don't know what's hard (laughs)	03　I've been walking around
03　I've been walking around	04　in this for the last month or so
04　in this for the last month or so	05　feeling that things are very hard
05　feeling that things are very very hard	06　like I have a cloud over me and I'm
06　like I have a cloud over me	very *confused*
07　and I'm very *confused*	
08　and I can't (P)	**AFFECT AND CONFLICT**
09　I feel like	**Stanza 1**
10　I am too burdened	09　I feel like
11　and I can't imagine how	10　I am too burdened
12　to be less burdened	11　and I can't imagine how
13　I feel like	12　to be less burdened
14　I I *need* to be doing everything I'm doing	**Stanza 2**
15　(P) and so I don't know how to	13　I feel like
16　take some of the burden	14　I *need* to be doing everything I'm
17　off of myself (P)	doing
18　*Int.*: Why do you think you need to be doing everything?	15　and so I don't know how to
19　*Cindy*: (P) Well ah I I need to work	16　take some of the burden
20　in order to earn a living.	17　off of myself
21　(p) I need to ah	
22　go to school	**ENDURING ROLE STRAINS**
23　so that I won't always have to work for nothing.	**Stanza 3 (money)**
24　I need to	19　Well I need to work
25　be a good mother	20　in order to earn a living
26　'cause that's very important to me.	**Stanza 4 (school)**
	21　I need to
	22　go to school

27 (P) And (P) I'd like to
28 find a little free time
29 if I can (laughs).

23 so that I won't always have to work
    for nothing
Stanza 5 (care of children)
24 I need to
25 be a good mother
26 'cause that's very important to me
Stanza 6 (time for self)
27 And I'd like to
28 find a little free time
29 if I can

Catherine Reismann, *Narrative Analysis*, 1993, p. 63. Reprinted by permission of Sage Publications

ample, those of different gender or political persuasion. A sceptic would question whether such an elaborate process is really needed in order to make judgements which could equally be reached more informally. Perhaps the most important justification is that both the multiple stages of analysis and the poetic form in which the transcript is set out allow much deeper concentration on the text. The meanings in oral testimonies grow each time they are read or spoken. Setting out parts of a transcript as lines of poetry can be a rewarding way, both for contemplating and also for presenting the testimony: for 'the poem is a way of walking slowly through the text'.[13]

A final, more sociological, technique of narrative analysis, again markedly formal, can claim comparable strengths. This has been developed in Germany especially by Fritz Schütze and Gabriele Rosenthal, partly as a response to the particular difficulties in interviewing and interpreting ex-Nazis. In the interview itself, 'a set of non-interfering techniques' are used in the belief that an unfettered narration 'comes closest to the experience itself'. Typically this means that the interview begins with a completely free life-story, which the interviewer simply encourages without interruption or comment, allowing the narrator to develop his or her own motifs and interpretations and overall theme, 'the red thread'. When this narration has concluded, amplifying questions may be drawn from it to encourage more stories and details; but only in the third stage may independent questions be introduced about themes not previously mentioned—perhaps, for example, about a phase of years skipped over, or about the narrator's father, and so on. The analysis is through a group discussion of the interview transcript, and is 'reconstructive', so that hypotheses are generated from the text rather than imposed from without—although of course they do draw on the researchers' wider knowledge. The first stage is to separate out the basic biographical information, which will also help to identify significant omissions and silences. Then the entire transcript is read as a whole in sequence, distinguishing the key elements of description, narration, and argument, looking for the narrator's own interpretation of his or her life, and seeking for both open and hidden meanings. Hypotheses are then debated by the group, always in relation to alternative hypotheses. Next, to test the interpretations which have been generated, shorter sections of text—a page, or just a sentence—are analysed in greater detail, again in sequence, and hypotheses and counter-hypotheses are again debated by the group. Finally the life-story is reconstructed in a dual form, on the one hand a year-by-year biography of what happened, on the other the narrator's personal and subjective interpretation of his or her life experience. Every case, however, is presumed to represent aspects of a wider field. Thus when the project involves a group of interviews it is then possible, on the basis of comparison and contrasting differences, to create a range of types or models of life-story. It is, however, even so, difficult to move from the small number of cases to convincing generalization about the larger society. The approach is also very demanding in terms of time, particularly because the method of analysis requires a group rather than a lone researcher. Nevertheless it has certainly proved a very effective method both in elucidating and in unravelling the often reluctant and highly ambivalent memories of older Germans about the Nazi and war eras. And a British group who led a European project on social exclusion, and who adopted this same method, also concluded that even though very lengthy and somewhat 'ponderous', the formal analysis was astonishingly rich in generating hypotheses from a single case of relevance to the wider social structure. They were convinced that 'only in-depth interrogation brings out the full value of an interview for revealing the intersection between culture, the social structure and the individual'.[14]

Despite the variety of forms of narrative analysis, ranging from the literary to the sociological, from the formal to the poetic, from the inclusion to the exclusion of the interviewer, some possible to combine and others incompatible, they have one crucial quality in common. They force the reader to slow down and look closely at both the whole text and its details, its images, forms of language, themes, its manifest and latent meanings. Ultimately, perhaps the greatest strength of narrative analysis, whatever its precise form, is to encourage an acuter and more sensitive listening.

Let us now turn to the reconstructive mode of analysis. Despite increasing interest in narrative approaches, this has remained the most characteristic method in published oral history. It is also close to the 'ethnosociological' approach for which Daniel Bertaux argues in his *Les Récits de vie*. The objective is to use life-story interviews to reconstruct in detail how a social context or element works and changes: for example a work environment, or a particular type of mobility, or a type of social situation such as a single mother or divorced father, or a homeless or disabled person. The ethnosociologist seeks to understand these contexts in terms of testimonies of day-to-day practice and knowledge, relationships, values and conflicts, special language, and so on, gathered through reflective accounts of practical lived experience.[15] This clearly echoes the aims of many social historians using oral evidence. It is therefore not surprising that there is much in common between such social historical and sociological forms of analysis.

To begin with, interviews, like all testimonies, contain statements which can be weighed. They weave together symbols and myths with information, and they can give us information as valid as that obtainable from any other human source. They can be read as literature; but they can also be counted. To start with, a group of interviews can be tested to see how the

% left school	Born			Father		
	before 1889	1890–9	1900–9	Owner	Deep-sea skipper	Deep-sea crewman
at 11 or 12	36	15	7	0	16	33
at 13	53	33	36	22	69	33
at 14 or 15	11	52	57	78	15	33

basic information they contain measures up against that known from other sources. Thus in his study of 'The Family and Community Life of East Anglian Fishermen', Trevor Lummis tabulated some of the information collected from sixty interviews.[16] Informants were asked the age at which they left school. Their answers fit neatly with known national trends, both with time and across social class.

Information had also been collected on the number of informant's brothers and sisters, and whether any died in childhood. Fishermen are known to have been unusually slow in reducing family size. When tabulated, the figures again prove compatible with national trends towards lower infant mortality and fewer children—as again they are with known differences between social classes. The historian with such test results at his elbow can move forward with some confidence into less charted terrain.

At this stage, some will be looking for patterns, clues towards

	Born			Father		
	before 1889	1890–9	1900–9	Owner	Deep-sea skipper	Deep-sea crewman
Number of brothers and sisters	9.9	7.0	7.9	9.1	8.5	9.5
% who died as children	15	14	7	11	15	25

interpretation, in the facts before them. Others will have started from a more definite theoretical standpoint, and probably some more detailed lesser hypotheses too—hunches which they wish to test. But both will eventually need to look for some form of proof. In general, a historical interpretation or account becomes credible when the pattern of evidence is consistent, and is drawn from more than one viewpoint. Great care needs to be taken with each of these conditions. Thus a single 'case study' is almost inevitably a weaker base for arguing general historical interpretations than a comparison between two or more groups, each with different characteristics, at the same period. A comparison between different groups over time is stronger still, although harder to achieve. The more that an argument can be shown to hold under varying conditions, the more convincing the proof. However, since history is made up of a multitude of cases, almost all of which are unique in more than one way, it is in practice often very difficult to make useful comparisons. The proof of the explanation must then be sought from within the single case; the evidence counter-checked as far as possible in detail, and the likelihood of overall bias in it weighed. For example, in a study of Frontier College, the great Canadian experiment in working-class educational self-help, George Cook found himself forced to accept that he was collecting within a single broad perspective:

Generally speaking, we are hearing from those who want to help the college. Although many felt that they had 'failed' as labourer-teachers, they remain convinced that it was a 'noble idea' and reflect favourably on their experiences. They have rose-tinted glasses . . . We have not been able to reach those who have negative views . . . the early employers . . . (or) any of the early union men who worked with the college. Most importantly, we cannot find any of the labourers . . . We shall probably learn little or nothing about what *they* thought.[17]

In the same way, it would be difficult, in a study of work experience, to obtain a critical view from long-service employees who had given their lives to the enterprise, and only done so because they were prepared to accept its conditions. The upper servants of a country house provide an example. Yet while such employees are relatively easy to locate, the transient workers who may even have outnumbered them are inevitably much harder to trace. Nor, it must be strongly emphasized, will the use of written documents necessarily compensate for such an imbalance in the oral evidence. John Toland founded his sympathetic portrait of *Adolf Hitler* as 'a warped archangel', a misunderstood, 'complex and contradictory' character, on interviews with 250 survivors of Hitler' s own circle.[18] He had no difficulty in buttressing it from the German archives. Oral history of this kind simply parallels the distortions of official history. It would have been a different matter had he chosen to encounter some of Hitler's opponents and victims.

A special caution is also needed if counting is to be used as part of the proof, because of the difficulties in retrospective sampling. Tabulation can be a very valuable way of classifying and disciplining one's impressions of the contents of a number of interviews. A careful scrutiny of interview material with a coding frame in mind can indeed force a much more precise consideration of what one is trying to show and what evidence the interviews can offer. On the other hand, even with interviews collected on a representative sample basis, it is best to stick to the simpler forms of analysis and not venture beyond straightforward percentages and strong correlation patterns. For example, Trevor Lummis analysed a set of thirty-five interviews for an Open University programme on 'Historical Data and the Social Sciences', concerning the decline of domestic

Household	Households where servants ate apart from employers (%)	Households where servants shared at least one meal a day (%)
One servant and children	8	92
One servant without children	80	20
Two servants and children	67	33
Two servants without children	100	0

service in the early twentieth century. It had been suggested that one reason for this decline might have been that middle-class employers wanted a more private family life, and that the presence of servants increased distance between family members. A first look at the interviews suggested, however, that the social gulfs within the household were less marked when it contained young children. Deciding to take daily eating habits as a test, he was able to produce the tabulation shown.

These figures show quite conclusively that within such households the presence of children does reduce social separation at mealtimes. They also suggest that the number of servants in the household may also be critical, but they do not prove this: it would require more figures from larger households to do so. However, provided that numbers are sufficient, and that sources of bias from the selection of informants has been allowed for, the historian can take comfort from the social scientist, for in quantitative studies the normal effect of misremembering is to lower all the correlations among variables, blurring all the patterns in a randomly confusing way rather than distorting them in particular directions. As Richard Jensen puts it, 'this means that the *true* values of correlations are higher than the observed ones. In other words, if the historian spots an interesting pattern using error-laden data, he or she can be confident that the time pattern was even stronger—certainly a happy result.[19]

Simple counting and percentaging can be done by anyone. There are now easy ways of carrying out these processes by computer, or if you have a small number of interviews you can just use a pocket calculator. The really time-consuming stage, whether or not you can use such aids, will be in the critical, detailed reading and categorization of your material.

Preliminary counting can suggest how an interpretation might be developed. But by raising new questions, it may also point to the need for further field-work. We cannot in fact make the neat separation which we have so far assumed. The ideal situation is very different: a continuous development through the to and fro of big theories, small hunches, and the practical strategy of field-work—in other words, of drawing on the strengths of *both* quantitative and qualitative research approaches. What was initially seen as the main problem may turn out to be a misconception, a dead end; so as the field-work continues, the emphasis is shifted to another area of questioning, or a different key group of informants is sought out. Alternatively, the original theory does not fit the facts discovered. Can the theory be modified? Or is it better to look at the facts from another quite different perspective? There is, of course, no set procedure by which such a developing search for interpretation can be carried forward. By definition it demands flexibility and imagination. Not all will succeed. Scaling the historical heights is dangerous. And few really interesting problems are ever *finally* solved. Nevertheless, in the imaginative combination of interpretation and field-work, the individual historian does have a particular advantage over the large-scale research project. Because the material can be looked at as a whole, and also in depth, from many perspectives, and because the field-work is under direct control, interpretive flexibility can be developed in a way which supports the overall objective. Indeed, the whole method is based on a *combination* of exploration and questioning in the dialogue with the informant: the researcher comes hoping to learn the unexpected as well as the expected. Hence the recognized effectiveness of life-story interviews in generating 'concepts, hunches and ideas, both at the local and situational level and on a historical structural level, and *within* the same field, and in relationship to other fields'.[20] By contrast it is a well-known defect of large-scale operations that, although they can encompass a much wider range of possible explanations and sources, they cannot be subjected to such subtle control and modification in detail. They set out from an established research design, team-work is organized on that basis, time is finite, and the field-work must be completed well before the first draft of the final report is written. Yet once the analysis of field-work is started, it becomes clear that much of the material is of little interest, but if only that particular area had been more deeply explored . . . The individual historian will not be satisfied without that further search.

One can put this in another way, by comparing the historian with a scientist. Scientific research advances through a meandering sequence of general theory, observations and hunches, experiments, working hypotheses tested by further experiments, dead ends, and further hunches and tests, until at last one hypothesis stands up to all conditions, and, if appropriate, a reformulation of theory is then sought. Any historical work suffers the inevitable disadvantage of having to work from the real cases available rather than from specially created experiments. As Edward Thompson has suggested, historians have to test their ideas with a logical process closer to that of proof in law, always vulnerable to the discovery of subsequent evidence.[21] But the big project using a field-work survey is doubly handicapped by telescoping into one all the experimental steps of the central stages of research development. It is therefore immobilized by any discovery important enough to challenge its own pre-set terms. Hence the tendency of survey findings to elaborate the obvious. They purchase their greater resources at the expense of—to use Jan Vansina's phrase—'the power of systematic doubt in historical inquiry': the very essence of creative advance in historical interpretation.

All this is somewhat abstract. Let us consider an example of the interaction between theory and field-work in practice. Peter Friedlander has set out unusually clearly, in the introduction to *The Emergence of a UAW Local 1936–1939: A Study in Class and Culture*, how his research proceeded.[22] He had at his disposal at the start certain facts, like gross census figures, dates, and a bare narrative from contemporary documents; and also various general theories, such as the Marxism of class struggle underlying labour history, and from Max Weber the concepts of rationality and individualism as essential to a bourgeois epoch. But the gaps were enormous. There was no documentary evidence of attitudes in the factory to authority and how this changed as the trade union was organized; of who made up the inner circle of union leaders and how they were related to social groups within the factory and whether these leaders led or reflected opinion; or of which were in fact the key social groups of workers in the factory, how their attitudes to the union struggle varied, and how it affected their personal lives and outlooks. Equally, the theoretical concepts failed to meet. This trade-union struggle took place not merely within a highly developed industrial capitalist society. The majority of the workers had migrated into the city where they worked from quite different social contexts. Their fight to unionize was thus also part of a much wider transformation of social cultures in migrant families and individuals: in this case religious-minded Slavs, revolutionary Croatian nationalists, Yankee and Scots artisans, Appalachian farm families and urbanized American blacks. These specific cultural subgroups were in the event to provide the key to interpretation. Yet, as Friedlander observes, 'labour historiography, which has tended to assume the presence of a modern, individuated, rational worker, has usually viewed the process of unionization in narrowly rational, institutional, and goal-orientated terms. The problem of culture and praxis is passed over in silence.'

Even where an explicitly Marxist framework is used in labour history, the tendency is for a whole section of society to be 'conceived of as an individual, and the problem is then to explain the institutional formation as the outcome of a rational process within the consciousness of this *quasi* individual'. But it is not always easy to locate this expected rationality; nor to explain its shortfall in a particular case in terms of general theoretical concepts such as, for example, 'false consciousness'.

At each juncture where a gap is seen between the abstractions of the political economy of work, and the concrete reality of individual, peer group, gang, clique, family, and neighbourhood—of character and culture—there appear *ad hoc* psychological notions invested with an astonishingly ubiquitous explanatory power. Such notions ignore one of the basic problems of historical thought: the nature of relationships among these many layers of social reality . . . the complex structure of cultures and relationships that develop and interact.

As the research proceeded, it emerged that only the older established American skilled Protestant workers could be described in classic individualistic and rationalistic terms. This group supplied most of the leadership, although it also included many who felt no interest in the union. The Appalachians also acted as individuals, but principally on a moral basis: they joined the union relatively late, when they believed that its cause was *right*, and once having joined were as utterly loyal as to their religious sects. The older East European migrants were much more concerned with what was right or wrong in social or ethical terms for the community, and acted explicitly as a group. Although personally cowed and submissive, they disliked the foremen and the management, and became dependable supporters of the union leadership. Their children, by contrast, were much more active and outspoken, and in particular a group of young Poles who belonged to neighbourhood gangs played a special role in the struggle. Like the older Slavs, they acted together, but with little social and political consciousness: they were pragmatic, opportunistic, the uncontrollable militant wildcatters willing to break a contract by striking, and then to man the flying picket squad. It was as if the union to them was 'a bigger and better gang'.

It was only when these groups and their attitudes had been identified, that the narrative of the struggle could be meaningfully reconstructed. Yet not only was none of this information available at the start, but it was not even known to be needed. The discovery of information and development of an interpretation went forward hand-in-hand as, over a period of eighteen months, Friedlander talked with the union leader, Edmund Kord. Kord had an exceptionally full and accurate memory, and indeed, remembered more as his mind became increasingly focused on these past years. Friedlander spent a full week with him three times, and each of these prolonged sessions produced drafts, comments, questions, and discussion. One of the two intervals between sessions included six hours of recorded telephone discussion; another produced altogether seventy-five pages of correspondence. They had to create between them not just the facts which were needed, but a mutual understanding and language of exchange. And if the 'thick description' into which Friedlander finally fuses both facts and interpretation does not allow him the last clear step into a new theory, he certainly laid the grounds for it in the marked differences which he shows between generations as well as between various social groups in the factory, in their particular roads from one consciousness to another.

The contrasting paths taken by different generations of the same workgroup are also demonstrated by Tamara Hareven's remarkable studies of Manchester, once the textile capital of New England. Founded by the Amoskeag Company in the 1830s, the city grew around its booming millyard and the promise of steady, well-paid work drew in successive waves of immigrants. By the early twentieth century its complex of thirty mills, employing 17,000 workers, made up the largest textile plant in the world. The giant works was so central to their lives that the people of Manchester believed it would stand for ever: 'You thought it would always be there.' Yet within two decades, undercut by cheaper labour and newer machinery in other regions, the giant was dead. Amoskeag closed its doors, bankrupt, in 1936. Smaller firms later revived parts of the millyard so that textile work struggled on for another forty years in Manchester, but the last mill finally shut in 1975. Even then, there were workers who left in tears: 'I'll miss the people I worked with, I'll miss the mill itself . . .'; 'it's like a second home'.[23] The industrial revolution had come and gone: a haunting allegory of the fate of much of the Western world.

Tamara Hareven has published two books about Manchester. The first, *Amoskeag* (1978), was a dramatic documentary built around Randolph Langenbach's photographs and the testimonies of former mill workers: about getting jobs and learning skills, the pleasures and tensions of work, larking about, company paternalism, and the bitter dying struggles with Amoskeag. It is a testament to industrial work, its centrality to people's lives, and the jeopardy in which that work now stands, told through the men and women of Manchester themselves—a book of rare power. *Family Time and Industrial Time* (1982), by contrast, is a reflective and analytical interpretation marshalling a much broader range of source material. Alongside extracts from the interviews, the arguments are backed by numerous tables from the local census and from a sample of the Amoskeag's workforce records. Hareven provides a more fully documented labour history of the Amoskeag's evolving policies of paternalism, scientific management, confrontation with labour, and company unionism, as well as analyses of career patterns and opportunities for promotion within the mills.

The most important insights of the book come however from the juxtaposition of this study of the factory world with the family lives of Manchester workers which is made possible through oral history. The result is to challenge many widely held views. She shows how it is not the 'modern' nuclear family which deals best with a catastrophe on the scale of widespread redundancy, but the more 'traditional' extended family, which can remain effective when scattered—indeed, *more* effective just because it is scattered. The extended family had been the channel of recruitment of migrant workers to the mill; and at the end, it was the safety net of the retreat. Or again, workers who had *not* had steady careers proved more likely to have the adaptability to face such a crisis successfully than those who had. Such findings are set, moreover, within a clearly articulated theoretical frame of 'family time' and 'industrial time': the cross-cutting struggle of family 'life plans' and industrial history. The clock analogy perhaps suggests too much certainty in the outcome, but it brings out well how, though some aspects of the life cycle were constantly repeated, the experience and the chances of each generation differed sharply. While to one the Amoskeag gave the security of a paternalistic family, and chances of promotion, to the next generation it offered a nightmare of tension; and to the last the hopelessness of a sinking ship. The twisting consciousness of the community—loyal, militant, despairing—reflected the historic moment at which the youth of each generation entered the factory gate.

This ability to make connections between separated spheres

of life is an intrinsic strength of oral history in the development of historical interpretation. In studying the transition from one culture to another, in time, or through migration, we can not only look at those cultures separately, but observe the paths that individuals took from one culture to another. And almost every individual life breaks across the boundaries between home and work. Escaping from these conceptual boxes can produce strikingly new hypotheses even from a small-scale study. In demography, for instance, it was long assumed that family limitation and the use of birth control spread by the 'diffusion' of attitudes from the professional middle classes down the social scale to the working classes. Some exceptions, like the low fertility of cotton workers, had been noted, but it was a pilot oral history project by Diana Gittins which first indicated that the basic 'diffusion' model was false: for working-class women changed their birth-control practices through independent influences—notably discussion at work—rather than direct middle-class influence. Indeed, those with the closest contact with middle-class families, who worked for them as domestic servants, received the least advice on family limitation; and even doctors and nurses were generally unhelpful, if not positively misleading, to working-class patients. This first exploratory discovery through oral history led to the substantial research, including statistical analyses of women workers' fertility rates and the use of early clinic records, which Diana Gittins published in *Fair Sex* (1982). Her reinterpretation is a typical outcome of oral history, for 'diffusion' theory gives credit to the middle classes for a social transformation which owes as much to the aspirations of working-class women themselves.

Yet if working women have played such a crucial part in the profound social change marked by the demographic transition from the 1870s to the 1920s, from which so much else, economic and social, has followed, why have they been so much slower than men in recognizing their collective self-interest in politics and trade unionism? Male politicians and historians have too often assumed it 'natural' for women to take a less active part in the labour movement; and when the problem has been considered at all, it has been in terms of the workplace, and women's shorter, more interrupted working lives. But Joanna Bornat's research on Yorkshire textile unions has shown how women's consciousness was shaped as much through subordination at home as in the factory. They found their jobs through family contacts, were trained by kin at the mill, and handed back their entire wage packets to their mothers; and it was their fathers who decided whether or not they should join the union. If they joined, collectors took their subscription at the doorstep, not on the mill floor.[24] In short, the male division of the worlds of work and home has obscured any adequate understanding of the class-consciousness of women workers. But a history which cannot account for them rests on flawed foundations.

It is undoubtedly a danger that oral sources, used on their own, can encourage the illusion of an everyday past in which both the cut and thrust of contemporary political narrative and the unseen pressures of economic and structural change are forgotten, just because they rarely impinge directly on the memories of ordinary men and women. It is essential to place them in this broader context. But as we have seen, oral sources can also help us to understand how that context is itself constituted. They offer the promise, moreover, of advancing this understanding in a fundamental way.

They suggest, first, a basic misconception in the dynamics of social change. These are almost always described in terms which reflect the experience of men: of collective and institutional rather than personal pressures, of the logic of abstract ideology, acting through the economy, through politics, through élite networks of unions and pressure groups. Behind are the deeper contradictions of social and economic organization which sometimes openly, sometimes unknowingly they express. But an equally crucial element is missing: the cumulative effect of individual pressure for change. It is this which immediately emerges through life histories: the decisions which individuals make—to move or improve a house, to leave one community and migrate to another; to leave a job which has become intolerable or to look for a better one; to put money into the bank, or shares, or a business of one's own; to marry or to separate, to have or not to have children. The changing patterns of millions of conscious decisions of this kind are of as much, probably more, importance for social change than the acts of politicians which are the usual stuff of history.

This becomes evident as soon as we look at the major long-term social changes of the Western world in the last century. Certainly the ebb and flow of political rights and civil liberties, and the growing state intervention in education and welfare, have been the outcome of collective pressure and political decision; and collective trade union pressure has kept up the working-class share in real earnings and cut the hours given to paid work. But this does not touch the two most startling changes: the rise in economic productivity and living standards, and the reduction in the number of children. Neither are the result of political intervention—indeed, no state has yet shown much ability to influence either, except through inducing unintended disaster. The truth is that the mechanics of change of both the economy and population, although basic to everything else, are very imperfectly understood.

They will remain so until we incorporate, as part of the structure of interpretation, the cumulative role of the individual. That implies recognizing that a high proportion of crucial individual decisions are as likely to be made by women as by men—not only in spheres like family-building, but also as migrants and as workers (women change jobs more frequently than men). Equally important, we need to know how public ideas, economic and collective pressures interact at an individual level—as in the seizing of economic chances, or in the shaping of attitudes through family and friendship and the media, and through childhood and adult personal experience—to form those myriad decisions which cumulatively not only give shape to each life-story but can also constitute the direction and scale of major social change. Or to put it another way, it becomes clear that the production of people is as much the powerhouse of change as the production of things.

An example may again help. When I began the research for *Living the Fishing* (1983) I assumed that the economy would shape family relationships, and it indeed proved true that women in fishing families in many parts of the world, because of the frequent absence of their men at sea, take a greater share of the responsibility and authority in the family; although this may range from the 'partnership' marriage common among inshore fishermen whose wives work with them in a joint enterprise gutting and marketing the fish, to the long-distance, deep-sea fishermen who are effectively absentee husbands leaving their wives as single parents. Untangling the variations in between revealed a complex of other influences too, in which economy, property, space, work, religion, and family culture all played a part.

But economic influence did not work in one direction only. In a wage-earning company port like Aberdeen life aboard became so rough and family life so battered by drink and violence that the next generation voted with its feet; mothers sent their sons to look for other work, and young women looked for husbands other than fishermen. Family culture was equally critical to the economic survival of family boat-owning communities, but in a very different way. Here the widespread encouragement of individual initiative among the fishermen was needed to ensure recurrent adaptability in the face of rapidly changing fish stocks, technology, and markets. Part of the secret of the most successful ports turned out to be the inculcation of an ideology of hard work, thrift, achievement, and independence from childhood. But this valuing of individual worth had to go with an acceptance of some eccentricity as the price of creativity. And the transmission of such values was encouraged by the affectionate gentleness typical of a Shetland upbringing, where children were encouraged to talk and reason for themselves in a relatively egalitarian home; while it was severely inhibited by the more authoritarian, punitive, hierarchical, male-dominated family characteristic of Lewis. With apparently equal chances, the fishing of one flourished, while the other withered.[25]

Certainly the constraints exercised by the economic system,

technology, and resources on how men and women live their lives are fundamental. But the economy is a social creation, and part of its making is in the family. The unpaid labour of women within the household not merely services it, but also, through the rearing of children, the workforce of the future, lays part of the foundations of the future. Clearly both the transmission of values between generations and the moulding of personality within the family are questions of critical importance to historical understanding, as they are also constant themes of both private gossip and public debate. Oral history interviews are a particularly powerful way of looking at these issues, both in terms of cultural patterns and also of emotional configurations which may repeat themselves over the generations in different families. In my own work with Daniel Bertaux on this theme we were able to look at families as a whole rather than as the typical father-son unit of purely statistical social mobility studies. It quickly became clear that women were as crucial family influences as men, and that families often had two or more occupational traditions, some passed down through the men, some through the women, and some through both. When mobility did take place it was as often a woman as a man who was seen as the push or model behind it. Thus one woman who achieved mobility only after separating from her lorry-driver husband saw her inspiration as an aunt who divorced. 'it was all the scandal at the time, no one got divorced. She just used to enjoy life, really enjoy it . . . She was always the gay one, always for a laugh. A right flirt, she was terrific. She was my favourite.'

We also found, contrary to popular assumptions, that a strong family culture tended to root people where they were, rather than to encourage upward mobility. Those who did move upward socially almost always had experienced the loosening of family ties, most typically through migration or through divorce (which was especially important in giving chances to women).

By contrast, the mechanics of familial transmission can be seen at their most powerful especially clearly in small business families. The Mullens, a four-generation family of Midlands silversmiths, were a rare classic instance. Sal's grandfather, two great-uncles, father and mother, brother, husband, father-in-law, and two sons have worked in the trade. 'My father used to work for his father, and his workplace was built at the top of the garden, so when I was old enough to go with my father, he used to take me down to work.' The grandfather who founded the firm is now a legendary example in the family story: 'My grandfather kept tight reins on everything until the day he died. He wouldn't even have a telephone put in the factory. He used to say, "If people want us and want our stuff, they'll come"—and they did. It had a very good name. They made spoons, cutlery . . . only spoon maker in Birmingham. Oh a very good living yes.' Nevertheless the transmission of the family occupation had been far from painless. Some family members had deliberately chosen to escape into other work, while one unlucky man, who had already started as a professional accountant, had been forced to return to rescue the firm when his father became ill. Indeed, Sal's father himself took a bitter resentment against her grandfather, and the trade into which he had been born too, to his grave: as he lay dying, he was heard to mutter, 'I never liked spoons'.

Yet were the Mullens so exceptional? In fact the culture of innumerable families conveyed, albeit less compellingly, similar beliefs in continuity. Just as the aristocratic family's pride centred on their country house, so a mariner's family home might be full of ships; or a mining family treasure a lump of coal they claimed to be the first hewn from the local pit.

As with the Mullens, family legends and myths are also important elements in the intergenerational transmission of many families. Sometimes they are positive, like the entrepreneurial builder who attributes his dynamism to 'Jewish blood in the family, going way back'; sometimes they are of lost riches; sometimes they haunt. Mystery is a catalyst of myth; and when the mystery is repeated in more than one generation, it can become a particularly powerful family script. In Eileen Moriarty's family unexplained parental separations have occured transgenerationally, and moreover, taken precisely the same form. Her father's mother had 'left when he was very young as well, and it was an exact repetition of the situation that I had', when Eileen lost her own mother. After her father's mother had gone, her father never knowingly saw her again. Only after she died did they discover, it is said, through an uncle who read gas meters, that she had lived 200 yards away for years: 'and he's never known, all his life'. Yet when his own wife, Eileen's mother, deserted him in turn, the breach was as absolute, the absence even more total than after a death. 'She left, she just walked out one day, one night, and that was it. She was gone. She never returned.' Eileen's father pushed her out of their lives, just as his father had his own mother.

It was never mentioned again, her family . . . It was something that was never talked about, once she was gone. Everything was banished from the house one night; and that was it. Just like that . . . It went straight to him. Just that day. And dad just—everything like, little photos, he cut her picture up and everything; it was just gone. Amazing. Strange.

Eileen is still haunted by the fear that her father will be the next to disappear. When she is away for any length of time she phones compulsively, not to talk, but to be sure he is still there. 'It's very strange, the same happened to him, as what happened to us. It's really awful to think that—I hope it will never happen again. Oh yeh, I often do [wonder], yeh; but to think that someone was so near . . .'[26]

As these instances show, transmission within families can take practical, cultural, and emotional forms. Hence to fully understand intergenerational transmission will also require a major imaginative leap in our use of theory. At present we can turn to one of two general types of theoretical interpretation. On the one hand there are the big theories of social organization, social control, the division of labour, the class struggle, and social change: the functionalist and other schools of sociology and the historical theory of Marxism. On the other hand there is the theory of individual personality, of language and the subconscious, represented by the psychoanalytical approach. They can be layered together, as in an individual biography, but no satisfactory way has yet been found of bonding them. Psychohistory has simply resorted to the crude device of 'analysing' whole groups—even whole societies—as if they were a single individual with only one life experience. The difficulties in any more subtle reconciliation have emerged very clearly in the debates on Marxism, feminism, and women's history. The fundamental problem lies in the fact that each type of theory turns its back on the other. Marxism, like sociological theory in general, is deliberately concerned with minimizing the role of the individual, as opposed to the social group. Psychoanalysis claims to be founded upon the elemental human personality, and so independent of history. Yet while Marxism rests on the belief that men and women create their consciousness through what they do, the archetypal Freudian psychoanalysis assumes that the fundamental shaping of personality is completed in infancy—before the limits of remembered conscious action. This leaves few clues as to how a bridge between the two types of theory can best be constructed. It is nevertheless an essential task if history is to provide a meaningful interpretation of common life experience. And in this task, oral history will have a vital role. Its evidence intrinsically combines the objective with the subjective, and leads us between the public and private worlds.

It is only by tracing individual life-stories that connections can be documented between the general system of economic, class, sex, and age structure at one end, and the development of personal character at the other, through the mediating influences of parents, brothers and sisters, and the wider family, of peer groups and neighbours, school and religion, newspapers and the media, art and culture. Only when the precise role of these intermediary institutions in, for example, socialization into sex and class roles, has been established, will a theoretical integration become a possibility. Until then we can only guess how far the economic and social system moulds personality, or the system is itself shaped by basic biological drives. A beginning to such work can be seen but it would be foolish to claim more than this as yet. It represents, nevertheless, for the future probably the greatest challenge and contribution which oral evidence may offer to the making of history.

Twenty years ago I ended this book with a brief look forward into that future. Much of what I then hoped for has come about. Oral history has been vindicated in a whole series of publications, both empirical and theoretical. While the most hidebound opponents continue to snarl, mostly in private, the main debate has shifted from whether to use oral history or not, to how best to use it. It has left a more general awareness of how all historical evidence is moulded by individual perception and, selected through social bias, conveys messages of prejudice and power. The nature of history in this double sense has been an issue too long evaded by historians.

More than that, entirely new uses of history have sprung up in the movements for reminiscence group work and drama. Oral history is far more extensively used in education, both in schools and universities. There has also been a growth in resources. Both at a local and a national level oral history archives are now well established, and the networking of catalogue information is gradually spreading. Before long it will become relatively easy to search nationally for a recording of a particular person, event, or on a theme in either political or social history.

Unique, often disarmingly simple, epigrammatic, yet at the same time representative, the voice can as no other means bring the past into the present. And its use changes not only the texture of history, but its content. It shifts the focus from laws, statistics, administrators, and governments, to people. The balance is altered: politics and economics can now be seen—and thus judged—from the receiving end, as well as from above. And it becomes possible to answer previously closed questions: extending established fields such as political history, intellectual history, economic and social history; adding to other newer areas of inquiry—working-class history, women's history, family history, the history of racial and other minorities, the history of the poor and of the illiterate—a whole new dimension. We have already in existing titles—*Akenfield, Where Beards Wag All*; *Working, Workless*; *Pit-men, Preachers and Politics, From Mouths of Men*; *Division Street, The Classic*

Slum; *Below Stairs*, *The Children of Sanchez*; *All God's Dangers*, *Blood of Spain*; *The Dillen*, *The Leaping Hare;Madness in its Place, Wild Swans*—the first swallows of a new summer. As others follow, history will be changed and enriched.

The new balance to the content of history, and the sources of its evidence, will alter its judgement, and so, eventually, its message as public myth. We shall find from the past a different set of heroes: ordinary people as well as leaders; women as well as men; black as well as white. History, which once could only weep for a King Charles I on the scaffold, can now share grief with the old illiterate widower, Nate Shaw, twice-arrested black Alabama sharecropper, at the loss of his wife Hannah:

I just felt like my very heart was gone. I'd stayed with her forty-odd years, and that was short, short—except bein pulled off and put in prison. I picked her out amongst the girls in this country and it was the easiest thing in the world to do . . . She was a Christian girl when I married her. And she was a woman that wanted to keep as far as her hands and arms could reach, all the surroundings, she wanted to keep it clean. And I've kept myself clean as I possibly could. But in past days, I've sneaked about in places, I did. I own to my part of wrongness . . . I liked women, but . . . I desperately kept clean of runnin too much to a extreme at other women when I had her. Regardless of all circumstances, I weren't a man to slip around at women and no matter what I said to another woman or what I done, I let my wife come first . . . I'm praisin her now, I'm praisin her for what she was—she was a mother for her children, she was a mother for her children—and when they put me in prison, the whole twelve years, she stayed by her children, she didn't waver. I loved that gal and she dearly proved she loved me. She stuck right to me every day of her life and done a woman's duty. Weren't a lazy bone in her body and she was strict to herself and truthful to me. Every step she took, to my knowledge, was in my favour. There's a old word that a man don't ever miss his water until his well go dry . . .[27]

There will be more biographies like Nate Shaw's. Whose, we can only guess. A London West Indian bus conductor; a British Leyland assembly-line car worker; a Belfast boiler-maker's wife; a supermarket checker-out; a Welsh sheep-farmer; a Pittsburgh steelmaker; a Californian telephonist; a New South Wales truck-driver . . . Who knows? Or what particular questions oral history will succeed in solving. The riddle of working-class political voting for the right? Whether the old family firm was an economic asset or a handicap? How far industrialization emancipated women, or confined them as housewives to still more limiting male domination? What makes some social groups prefer to educate, and others to beat their children? How some persecuted immigrant minorities prosper, and others not? In what social context are major scientific discoveries made? Why some people are concerned about the environment, and others not? To each of these problems, oral history could make a critical contribution. Which are chosen depends on who sees this first.

In principle, the possibilities of oral history extend into every historical field. But they are more fundamental to some than to others. And they provide an underlying current: towards a history which is more personal, more social, and more democratic. This affects not only published history, but the process by which it is written. The historian is brought into touch with fellow-scholars in other disciplines: social anthropology, dialect and literature, political science. The academic is prised out of the closet into the outside world. The hierarchy of higher and lower institutions, of teachers and taught, breaks down in joint research. Old and young are brought into exchange and closer sympathy. The classics of oral history will no doubt continue to be created by uncategorizable individuals. But there has been a quiet sea-change in the process of historical writing, scarcely noticed by the book reviewers. Increasingly small oral history groups have been bringing out their own publications. Certainly most would gain from more interpretation, and often only a local could make the most of all the detail. It may be a history of the street and its families; of a factory's workers and owner; about a strike, or a bomb explosion; recollections of past leisure, education, or domestic service. These local publications are gathering new historical material for the future, which would otherwise have been lost. They are tapping the river water at the sea's mouth. The far limit of the past recoverable through oral evidence recedes remorselessly through death, day by day. But the real justification of history is not in giving an immortality to a few of the old. It is part of the way in which the living understand their place and part in the world. Landmarks, landscapes, patterns of authority and of conflict have all been found fragile in the twentieth century. By helping to show how their own stories fit into the changing character of the place in which they live, their problems as workers or as parents, history can help people to see how they stand, and where they should go. This is what lies behind the present popularity of recent history in Britain. It also points to the key social and political importance of oral history. It provides a new basis for original projects, not just by professionals, but by students, by schoolchildren, or by the people of a community. They do not just have to learn their own history; they can write it. Oral history gives history back to the people in their own words. And in giving a past, it also helps them towards a future of their own making.

A Life-Story Interview Guide

These questions are *not* a questionnaire, but a schematic outline interviewer's guide for a flexible life-story interview, in the spirit of Chapter 7. The interviewer's directions are printed in *italics*. In many instances the full form of the question is given, but in others an expanded form is needed in use. In general the questions on work are particularly likely to need further specific detail, and for any project a much fuller development of questions on its specific key themes will be needed.

GENERAL INFORMATION

To be completed after the interview:

Interview number:

Name: Male/female:

Address:

Date and place of birth: Key moves between places
                                         and dates:

Present Occupation:

Single/with partner/married/separated/divorced/widowed?

If ever married/separated, dates of marriage and separation:

Number of children:

PRELIMINARY

First of all, can you tell me when and where you were born?

How many years did you live there? Where did you move to then? (*Trace key moves between places by rough dates.*) Can you remember why the family made those moves?

LONG-DISTANCE MIGRATION

NOTE: when appropriate, this section is to be inserted at whatever point in the narrative it occurs during the following sections.

When did you first think about going abroad? Why? Had anyone in your family gone abroad before you? Or friends? Did they write and talk about it? Were you going for work, education, to join family, for an adventure? How long did you think you would be away? What did you know about Britain? Who from? Did you have family or friends who were already there? Did you contact them before leaving? Did you have a job waiting for you? How did you raise the money for the ticket?

Did you leave a wife/husband/partner/children back home? How did you feel about that? Who helped look after them while you were away? When did you next see them? Did they come over later?

What was the journey like? What did you imagine Britain would be like? Were you disappointed/satisfied? What struck you most when you landed? Did you have any difficulty understanding how people spoke? Did any one bother you about your accent or your clothes? Would you say that people were generally friendly or hostile towards you?

Did you have anywhere to stay? Who met you? Did you stay with them? Did they help you in any other ways (money, loans, equipment, advice)?

How did you find your first proper accommodation? Can you describe it to me? What were the facilities (cooking, bathroom, etc) like? Did you have to share? How did you get on with the other people in the house? With the landlord? Did you make friends locally? Did you change your style of food or not? Did you join any local associations, sports clubs, or churches? Did you find a 'grapevine' for meeting people, or finding work/ housing? Who belonged to your grapevine?

Did you feel at home in Britain? Do you now? Have you had experiences of racial discrimination or abuse? Have you been back to your original home? How often? Have you thought of returning permanently? Or of moving somewhere else? Do you keep in touch with your family back home? How often do you see each other? How often do you write or phone? Do you exchange news, gossip, confidences, or advice? Do family members send presents, parcels, money, or other kinds of help to each other? Who would you say your family consists of now?

GRANDPARENTS' GENERATION

Now can we talk about your grandparents? Let's take your mother's parents first. Do you remember your grandmother? And your grandfather? Where had they lived? (*Details of where born; any migration story.*) What had been their occupations? Can you describe their characters? How much did you see of them? Did they help to bring you up? Did you ever stay with them? Has your mother helped them in any way (practically, or financially)? What do you think were their main interests? Were they religious? How did they get on together? Were you close to them? Was either of them a strong influence on you?

How many children did they have?

Now can I ask you about your grandparents on your father's side? *REPEAT as above. Also, ask in similar detail about any stepgrandparents.*

Do you remember any other relatives of the older generations in your family (great-uncles and aunts, cousins, stepkin)? What kind of work did they do? How much contact did you have with them? Were you close to any of them? Was anyone an important influence on you? *If yes: ask in detail.*

Were there any other old people who were especially important to you as a child? *If yes: ask for detail.*

PARENTS

Now I'd like to ask you about your parents. Let's start with your father. When was your father born? Where? How old was he when he died? When was that? Can you describe his character to me? Did he show affection? What about anger? Were you close to him? Was he easy to talk to?

What work did he do? Did he always do that kind of work? Did he sometimes do more than one job? Do you remember your father ever being out of work? *If yes:* How did you manage then?

Now I'd like to talk about your mother. When was she born? Where? How old was she when she died? When was that? Can you describe her character to me? Did she show affection? What about anger? Were you close to her? Was she easy to talk to?

What kind of work did she do (before and after children)? Did she always do that kind of work? Did she continue working after she had her children? *If yes:* Who looked after you while she worked? Was she ever out of work? *If yes:* How did you manage then?

How many children did she have? Can you remember when they were born?

Where do you fit into the order? Did all your brothers/sisters live with you? All the time? *If no:* Where did they live then?

Did your parents bring you up to consider certain things important in life? What kind of a person did they hope you would grow up to be? Did they hold up any examples to you? If you did something they disapproved of, what would happen? Was your father or your mother stricter with you? What sort of things was s/he strict about? Did either of them strike you physically? How would you compare your mother and your father as influences in your life?

Now can we think about your parents as a couple? Can you tell me the story of their relationship as you know it? *Check: How they met, how long together, whether married.*

What were the best things about their relationship? And the worst things? Do you recall any family violence when you were growing up?

If split: Why do you think that they split? Can you tell me the story of their break-up? Did you hear them quarrelling? Did they discuss it with you at all? Was there anyone else you could confide in?

How did life change for you then? Did you move house? Did your parents continue to quarrel after they broke up or not? How often did you see your (absent) father/mother? Where did you meet him/her? Did you miss him/her? Did you ask him/her for advice? What do you think you lost through not living with him/her? Were you in any way closer to your (co-residing) mother/father when s/he had no partner? Do you remember her/him crying? Were you criticized less or more now?

Were either your father or your mother involved in any subsequent relationships? *If yes:* How did that affect your own relationship with him/her? How did you get on with their new partner(s)? How did they treat you?

Did they have other children? How would you describe your relationship with your half-brothers/sisters? Were you close to them?

If relevant: Now I would like to talk a little bit about your stepfather/mother. When was s/he born? Where? Can you describe his/her character to me? What did s/he do? Did s/he always do that kind of work?

How were he and your mother (she and your father) as a couple? How long did s/he live with you? How were things changed by his/her joining the family? What about household tasks? How much of a role did s/he play in bringing you up (discipline, financial support, playing)? Did s/he bring in any new ideas or attitudes? How would you describe your relationship with him/her? Was s/he easy to talk to? Were you close to him/her? Has s/he been an important influence on you?

Did you know his/her parents and family? Did s/he have children of his/her own? Did they also move in or not? How did you get on with them? Were you close to any of them? Were there any difficulties between the children of different parents? Quarrels? When different people took sides, who was on each side? Did you ever all sit down and talk and try to sort things out together as a family? Who decided the rules in the house?

SIBLINGS/COUSINS/UNCLES/AUNTS

Let's talk now about the other people in your family (including any half-blood kin that you may know about).

First, what about your brothers and sisters? Growing up as children, how did you get along? Did you feel any differently about your half/stepbrothers and sisters? Where do your brothers and sisters live now? Are you in touch with them? Do you/can you visit them often? How many of them are married? What sort of work are they doing? Do you have a favourite brother or sister? Can you tell me more about him/her? Was he/she an important influence on you?

What about your uncles/aunts? Did they live near you or with you when you were a child? How much did you see of them? Did you have a favourite uncle/auntie? Was he/she an important influence in your life?

I imagine you may have had some cousins—did you spend time with your cousins? What sort of relationship did you have with them? Did you have a favourite cousin? Are you still in touch? Has this cousin been an influence on you?

Did you have godparents? Or family friends that you might consider an aunt or uncle? Have any of them been an important influence in your life?

Were there any times when you got together with the wider family (a wedding, funeral, festival, or big event)? Can you describe a typical family get-together for me? Who was there? Did the family always get on together? How many would stay overnight? Do you still have any big get-togethers?

How did members of the family living in different places keep in touch in the past? What about today? How common was it/is it to write letters or phone? What information was important to pass on by phone/letter (such as family news and local gossip; tips about work opportunities at home and abroad, housing, or travel; etc)?

DAILY LIFE IN CHILDHOOD

Now I would like to ask you some questions about your daily life in childhood.

Who owned the house? The land? *If rented*: What was your relationship with your landlord like? *If owned*: Do you think that owning your house is important? Does your family still own the house/land? Can you describe the house to me? How many rooms did it have? Where did you all sleep in the house? What was the furniture like? Did your parents improve it in any way?

Who lived in your home when you were a child growing up? Was there anyone besides your parents and brothers and sisters (e.g. other kin, lodger, domestic help: *if yes, probe for details of role, relationship with children*)?

Who did what around the house when you were a child: the cooking/cleaning/washing etc? Did you help around the house/garden? What kind of things did you have to do? Did your brothers/sisters have to help? Who made your clothes? Did your mother/father grow vegetables/keep animals? Did you help with this? Did your father help with the household tasks? In what way? Did he look after you on his own or play with you? Did your mother play with you? Did the family sit down together for meals? Were you allowed to talk then or not?

Who did you play with as a child? What sort of games did you play? Were you free to play with whom you liked? Did you keep pets/take part in sports/join any clubs? When your parents were not working, what kind of things did they do to enjoy themselves? Did they go out to clubs or pubs, sport, or cinema? Together or separately? Did you go out together as a family? Did you go on holidays?

Did you go to church as a child? Which religion or denomination? How often? How important was religion to you as a child?

Were any of you seriously ill when you were a child? What kind of help did they get? How did that affect your lives?

When you were a child was there any talk of politics or trade unionism in your family? Were any members of your family involved with a trade union or with politics?

COMMUNITY AND CLASS

Do you think of yourself as a rural or an urban person? What's better about living in the town or the country? Has the local environment changed since you were a child? How? Has that concerned you?

Can you describe your childhood neighbourhood to me? Did you have neighbours living close by? Did neighbours help each other? In what ways? Did anyone help your family when, for instance, a baby was born or someone was ill or died? Did neighbours sometimes look after you? Did they discipline you? What sort of things would they correct you over?

Did your parents have friends? Were your mother's friends different from your father's? Where did they see them? Did they visit your home? How did they entertain themselves when they got together? How often were you included?

Many people divided society into different social classes or groups. What do you think the different ones were at that time? Which did your family belong to? Do you think it was possible then to move from one to another?

In your neighbourhood, were you considered better off or worse off than your neighbours?

In what ways did this show up? Were there people richer/ poorer than you? Who were the best-off people there (*probe: occupations, ethnic groups*)? What was your relationship with them? Who were the poor people? What was your relationship with them? Who did you mix most easily with? Did one group feel itself superior to the other? Were there places your parents wouldn't let you go to or children they would not let you mix with? *If yes:* Why was that?

SCHOOL

Now I would like to ask you some questions about your schooling. When did you start school? What schools did you go to? When did you leave? What did you think of these schools? *If relevant:* Would you have liked to have stayed on longer? Did you leave school with any qualifications? Do you regret not having more? While you were at school, how well did you do in the class? Did your parents encourage you with your school work?

Can you remember the teachers? How did you feel about them? Were they strict? What about? Did you get into any trouble at school? Did they emphasize certain things as important in life? Did they encourage discussion? Was any teacher an important influence on you?

Did they treat children from different social backgrounds or races differently? What about the other children? Were there any gangs in the school? Who were your friends (e.g. occupations/race)? Did you go to each other's houses? Were you good at sports/games?

What were your own dreams and hopes on leaving school?

If went on to higher education: Subjects, new friends, new attitudes, influence of lecturers, clubs and leisure, position of women.

EMPLOYMENT

Now I would like to talk about your working life. While you were at school, did you have any part-time jobs? When you left school, what did you want to do?

Did you experience any difficulties getting work? Why do you think this was (economic situation, race, etc)? When you were growing up, did anyone talk to you about prejudice? Have you had other similar experiences—in work, or social services, or socially?

How did you get your first full-time job? Was it through family/friends/other connections? What did you do in that job? How did you feel about it? How did you learn?

Did you have to go to any courses? Were any practical jokes played on you? What hours did you work? Did you feel you were reasonably paid or not? How much of it did you give to your mother? How did you get on with the others at work? Did men and women work together? Could you talk or relax or have fun together at all at the workplace? Did you join any trade union or works associations? What contact did you have with your employers or managers? How did you feel about them? Did you have any chances of promotion?

How long did you stay in that job? What was your next job? How did you get it? What did you do in it? How long did you stay in it? (*For all significant jobs, repeat as above; for all main occupations, it is important to devise fuller questions specific to that occupation.*)

Did you ever have more than one job at the same time? What were the jobs? Why did you do more than one job? How did you manage the time? Did you ever work away from your home area? When and where? What do you think is the difference in work opportunities and experience between working here and abroad? How far has changing technology affected your working life? Your relationships with others at work? Your pride in the job? Which of these jobs do you think was the best? Did you ever think of changing to another occupation?

LEISURE AND COURTING

Now could we talk about your leisure activities, including courting when you were young? How long did you live at home? Did you have your own room where you could entertain your friends? Where did you live after you left home? Who did you share with? Describe house. Were you expected to help your family (brothers, sisters, parents) by earning?

During your leisure time, what did you like to do? Did your interests change? Were there any sports that you played regularly? Did you belong to any clubs, associations, or churches? Did you have any hobbies? Did you go to the cinema, dance halls, shopping, pubs, etc? What was a good night out in those days?

Do you remember doing anything which could have got you into trouble with the police?

Did you do anything that your parents would have disapproved of? What did they think of young people who got into fights, or pinching things? Gambling or drugs or smoking?

Did you make new friends after leaving school? How did you

meet? Did you stick to a group? What did you do together? Did you have any special friends at this time? Did any of them become an important influence? What about girlfriends/boy-friends? Do you remember your parents' attitudes towards sex? How would they have reacted to your having sexual intercourse when you were going out? Did they offer you advice on sex or on relationships? Who did you go to if you needed that kind of advice? What were your parents' views on having children before marriage? And your views on that? What did they think about inter-racial relations? About same-sex relationships? And you?

If not married and still single: Why do you think you have not married? Did you ever feel family/community pressure to be married or be in a relationship? How do you deal with this? What are the advantages in staying single? And the disadvantages?

If married or living together: Can you tell me the story of the main relationships you had before marrying/settling down? How did you meet? What did s/he do? How did the relationship develop? What was good and what was difficult about it? Why did it end?

MARRIAGE AND CHILDREN

Can we now talk about your later family life? Can you tell me how you and your partner first met? How old were you then? And s/he? Can you tell me about him/her (country of origin, social background, job, personality)? How do s/he and your parents get on? How much do you have to do with his/her family? What are they like?

Did you live together or marry first? Why did you decide that? How long had you been going out before you lived together? Where did you live? Can you describe it? Did your parents help you in any way in setting up house? Or did they help you later on? How long did you live there? Can you describe the subsequent homes you lived in together (*probe as above: for main homes describe rooms, furniture*)? Were they rented (*relationship with land-lord*) or did you own them? Why? Did you improve any of them?

If married, either to former or present partner: Why did you get married? How old were you then? How old was your wife/husband? How long did you know each other before you married?

Did you have children before you married? *If yes*: Who was their father/mother? What was the reaction of your mother/father when they learnt you were going to become a parent and were not married? Did they help you? What kinds of help did they offer?

Can you remember your wedding day? Can you describe it? Who came? Who helped? Who paid for the event?

Do you still live with your husband/wife?

If yes: How would you describe your relationship now? Do you talk together and share important things? What do you do if you disagree? How has your sexual relationship changed?

What kind of work has your partner done since you were together? Do you discuss money? Who would you say is in charge of the household budget? Do you share the household chores and responsibilities? Who does what?

If no longer together: How did that come about? What went wrong with your relationship? Can you tell me the story of the break-up? How do you and your ex-partner get on now?

Can you tell me about your subsequent partners? (*Repeat detailed questions.*)

Now can we talk about your children?

Did you want to have children sometime in your life? How many children have you had? Names and years of birth. Did you plan to have the number you did? Contraception. Where were your children born? *If man:* Were you present? How did you feel? What part did you play in caring for the baby?

If woman: Did you know what to expect in childbirth? Books; classes; medical care. How did you get on? Who else was there? How did you feed your first baby? Did you have any difficulties? If you needed advice, who did you ask? Did you punish it if it was naughty? How? For what? Did you continue working when the children were small? How did you manage care for the child?

(Neighbours/friends/creche; pay?) Did you get practical or financial help from the family?

All: When you were bringing them up, what did you think was most important to give them?

Did you think there was a right and a wrong way of bringing them up? How much did you talk to them? Who did you talk to if you were worried about them? How helpful were your mother and mother-in-law? Did you believe that girls and boys should be treated the same or differently? How much did you expect them to help in the home? Boys as much as girls? Did you bring them up to believe that certain things are important in life? If they did something you disapproved of, what would you do? Would you sometimes strike them? Did you or your partner play with them or take them out? Did you go on holidays together?

How has your children's education gone? What kind of schools did they go to? How involved have you been? Have they experienced any difficulties in school? As they grew older, how much freedom did you give them? Did you know their friends? How did you treat their boy/girlfriends? What did you think if they went out with someone from another race? What would have been your view of your son/daughter having children before marriage?

Do you have any other children we have not mentioned, for example by other relationships?

Where do all your children live now? What are their occupations? When do you see each other?

How do you think that your attitudes towards your children were any different from your parents' attitudes towards you when you were growing up? What are your hopes, dreams, and aspirations for your children?

If separated: How did becoming pregnant change your relationship? Did you feel that a father should help provide for a mother and child (financial/spiritual/practical)? How many children did you have together? Did he/you support them? In what way? With money? Did he/you visit them? How often? Do you think he/you did enough to support them? What do you think the role of a father should be? Do you think that children need a father around when they are growing up? What do you think are the qualities of good parenting?

If repartnered: Can you describe the relationship between the children and your new partner? Has s/he been an influence on them? How did things change when s/he moved in (roles, housework, discipline, leisure)? Have you (and your present partner) been bringing up children by different relationships? How have they got on together? Have there been any special difficulties? Quarrels? When the family takes sides, who is on which side? Do you ever sit down and talk and find solutions together as a stepfamily?

CHANGING DAILY LIFE

In your adult life, what have you (and your partner) most enjoyed doing for pleasure (*probe: watching TV, sport, music, pubs, hobbies, travel, etc*)? Together or separately?

How important have friends been to you in your adult life? Who have been your closest friends? What do you share with them? What do you do together? Do you help each other? Where do they live? How much contact do you have?

Can you describe how the experience of travelling has changed in your lifetime? How did you mostly get about when you were younger (bus, tram, bike)? Did you bike far? Do you remember how things were different when fewer people had cars? Is it still a pleasure to go for a drive? What about the experience of shopping, how has that changed—where you shop, what you buy? What about the food you buy? Can you describe how typical meals have changed since your childhood? *(Probe for continuities in orthodox religious or ethnic diets.)* How much variety was there in food when you were younger? Did it taste better? Do you cook yourself? How did you learn?

Can you describe the main neighbourhoods you have lived in as an adult? How much contact have you had with neighbours? Have any helped when you have been in difficulty? Can you describe the main social groups or classes in each neighbourhood? Do you think it is possible to move from one social class to another? Can you think of anyone who did? Which group/ class were you closest to? Do you have any friends from other groups? Was there any conflict between the different groups? Have you ever been active in politics? Have you belonged to any local clubs or associations? Or churches?

How has your health been in your adult life? Have you been satisfied with the care you have received? Have you or your family ever tried any alternative therapies or complimentary medicine? Can you tell me about anyone in your family or among your friends who has had experience of mental illness? How do you think social attitudes to dying have changed in your life-time? How have funerals changed?

LATER LIFE

Do you have grandchildren? How often do you see them? Do you help your son/daughter take care of them? What kind of things do you do? Do you think this is the kind of help grand-parents should give? Do they help you in any way (visiting/ caring/money)?

When did you decide to retire? Why? How did that affect you financially? What has been your main interest since retire-ment—inside and outside the home? How has your relationship with your partner changed? And with your children? And grandchildren? And your friends?

CONCLUSION

How would you describe yourself, your identity now (e.g as working class, a Yorkshireman, Black British, etc)? How has that changed since childhood? Have you changed differently from your family and friends?

What has been the best thing in your life? The worst thing? What would you most like to do in the time ahead?

I'd like to thank you for giving me such a full and helpful account of your life and experiences, which will be very valuable for our research/my project.

Further Reading and Notes

We may divide the key general books between those before and after the early 1980s. Two early classics are Jan Vansina, *Oral Tradition: A Study in Historical Methodology* (London, 1965; modified reissue, *Oral Tradition as History*, 1985), and George Ewart Evans, *Where Beards Wag All: The Relevance of Oral Tradition* (London, 1970)—the first based on historical fieldwork in Africa, the second in East Anglia. The earlier phase of life-history sociology is represented by Daniel Bertaux (ed.), *Biography and Society: The Life History Approach in the Social Sciences* (Beverly Hills, Calif., 1981); and of European oral history by Paul Thompson (ed.), *Our Common History: The Transformation of Europe* (London, 1982).

Subsequently Ken Plummer, *Documents of Life: An Introduction to the Problems and Literature of a Humanistic Method* (London, 1983), has provided an excellent introduction for social scientists; a crucial collection is Sherna Gluck and Daphne Patai, *Women's Words: The Feminist Practice of Oral History* (London, 1991); while key new interpretative approaches are highlighted in Raphael Samuel and Paul Thompson (eds.), *The Myths We Live By* (London, 1990); Elizabeth Tonkin, *Narrating Our Pasts: The Social Construction of Oral History* (Cambridge, 1992); and Alessandro Portelli, *The Death of Luigi Trastulli and Other Stories* (Albany, NY, 1991).

On methodology, especially useful books include Valerie Yow, *Recording Oral History: A Practical Guide for Social Scientists* (Berkeley, Calif., 1994); for Third World contexts, Hugo Slim and Paul Thompson, *Listening for a Change: Oral Testimony and Development* (London, 1993); and Ruth Finnegan, *Oral*

Tradition and the Verbal Arts (London, 1991); and for brief methodological booklets, Robert Perks, *Oral History* (London, 1992) and Robert Atkinson, *The Life Story Interview* (Thousand Oaks, Calif.,1998). On analysis, two contrasting approaches are in Trevor Lummis, *Listening to History: The Authenticity of Oral Evidence* (London, 1987), and Catherine Riessman, *Narrative Analysis* (Newbury Park, Calif., 1993).

A particularly useful general anthology is provided by Robert Perks and Alistair Thomson (eds.), *The Oral History Reader* (London, 1998). Lastly there are the journals: most notably, from England *Oral History* (1970–), the journal of the Oral History Society, and from the United States the *Oral History Review* (1973–) of the Oral History Association. The International Sociological Association's Biography and Society Research Committee publishes a *Newsletter* (1983–), and there are journals of national oral history associations in Canada, Australia, and Brazil, as well as the trilingual *Words and Silences* (1997—) of the International Oral History Asociation. Earlier the *International Journal of Oral History* (1980–90) and the *International Yearbook of Oral History and Life Stories* (1992–6) were also of special importance.

Notes to Chapter 1: History and the Community

1. On the social purposes and manipulation of history: David Lowenthal, *The Past is a Foreign Country* (Cambridge, 1985); Eric Hobsbawm and Terence Ranger (eds.), *The Invention of Tradition* (Cambridge, 1983); Jean Chesneaux, *Pasts and Futures: What is History For?* (London, 1978); Raphael Samuel and Paul Thompson (eds.), *The Myths We Live By* (London, 1990).

2. Notable examples of this type of oral history work include Hugh Brody, *Maps and Dreams: Indians and the British Columbia Frontier* (London, 1986); Nigel Cross and Rhiannon Barker, *At the Desert's Edge: Oral Histories from the Sahel* (London, 1991); Staughton Lynd, Alice Lynd, and Sam Bahour (eds.), *Homeland: Oral Histories of Palestine and Palestinians* (New York, 1994).

3. For a good introduction to recent oral history work in the community see Robert Perks and Alistair Thomson (eds.), *The Oral History*

Reader (London, 1998), parts III ('Advocacy and Empowerment') and V ('Making Histories').

4. *Oral History*, 1/2 (1972), 9.

5. Produced by Ann Paul (see Gloria Wood and Paul Thompson, *The Nineties* (London, 1993).

6. *Oral History*, 1/4 (1973), 57.

Notes to Chapter 2: Historians and Oral History

1. Michelet, *Histoire de la Révolution Française* (Paris, 1847), ii. 530: 'la tradition orale'; James Westfall Thompson, *History of Historical Writing* (London, 1942), ii. 241.

2. Reissued as *Oral Tradition as History* (London, 1986), expounding a similar viewpoint, although more cautiously. For an autobiographical account, see Jan Vansina, *Living with Africa* (Madison, Wis., 1994). His first recording was in the Congo in 1953, of a Bushong poet-historian who had told him, 'we carry our newspapers in our heads' (p. 17). On oral tradition and history, see also David Henige, *Oral Historiography* (London, 1982); and Joseph C. Miller (ed.), *The African Past Speaks: Essays on Oral Tradition and History* (Folkestone, 1980).

3. D. T. Niane (ed.), *Sundiata: An Epic of Old Mali* (London, 1965), 1.

4. A. Haley, 'Black History, Oral History and Genealogy', *Oral History Review* (1973), 14–17.

5. On the transition to literacy, see Walter Ong, *Orality and Literacy* (London, 1982); and Ruth Finnegan, *Literacy and Orality: Studies in the Technology of Communication* (Oxford, 1988). A sustained critique of both oral and printed sources over three centuries on a single topic, the Protestant defiance of the French state in the Cévennes, is in Philippe Joutard, *La Légende des Camisards: Une sensibilité au passé* (Paris, 1977).

6. Trans. L. Shirley-Price (London, 1955), 34. On the Spanish friars in Mexico, Georges Baudot, *Utopie et histoire au Mexiave* (Paris, 1977).

7. Bishop Burnet, *History of His Own Time* (London, 1724), 89.

8. Voltaire, *Works*, trans. W. F. Fleming (New York, 1927), v. 62, xi. 9, and xviii. 6, 8, and 15; Westfall Thompson, *Historical Writing*, ii. 67. An alternative account, focusing more on popular oral tradition than on the oral sources which Voltaire trusted, contrasts the extensive use of oral sources by the antiquary John Leland in the 1540s with a growing scepticism, even mockery, of oral traditions

'comming from the mouths of rustics' in the 17th cent., partly as a result of growing class difference: D. R. Woolf, 'The Common Voice: History, Folklore and Oral Tradition in Early Modern England', *Past and Present*, 120 (1988), 26–52.

9. Samuel Johnson, *The Rambler* (13 Oct. 1750); James Boswell, *Journal of a Tour to the Hebrides with Samuel Johnson* (London, 1785), 425–6.

10. Trans. R. Rawlinson (London, 1728), 276–8.

11. Westfall Thompson, *Historical Writing*, ii. 67.

12. Macaulay, *History of England* (London, 1848–55), i. 382–4, 418.

13. David Vincent, 'The Decline of Oral Tradition in Popular Culture', in R. D. Storch (ed.), *Popular Culture and Custom in Nineteenth-Century England* (London, 1982), 20–47; Marilyn Butler, personal information.

14. George Ewart Evans, *From Mouths of Men* (London, 1976), 179; Sir Walter Scott, *Tales of My Landlord* (Edinburgh, 1816).

15. Oliver Lawson Dick (ed.), *Aubrey's Brief Lives* (London, 1949), p. xxix.

16. Richard Gough, *Human Nature Displayed in the History of Myddle* (London, 1968), 1 (Hoskins); David G. Hey, *An English Rural Community: Myddle under the Tudors and Stuarts* (Leicester, 1974).

17. James Everett, *Wesleyan Methodism in Manchester and its Vicinity* (Manchester, 1827), 1; and the London Baptist minister Josiah Thompson was compiling testimonies on early dissenting congregations in 1772–84, now in Dr Williams Library, London (information from John Walsh); Antoine Court among French Protestants in the 1730s.

18. *The Working Man's Way in the World, Being the Autobiography of a Journeyman Printer* (London, 1853); also, Eleanor Eden (ed.), *The Autobiography of a Working Man* (London, 1862)—especially remarkable for its lively, almost spoken style. The *How I Became a Socialist* series of the 1890s illustrates the conversion testimonial in reverse. See the full listings, including over 1,000 19th-cent. authors, in John Burnett, David Vincent, and David Mayall (eds.), *The Autobiography of the Working Class: An Annotated Critical Bibliography*, i–iii (1750–1945; London, 1985–7). For discussions of autobiography in England, see David Vincent, *Bread, Knowledge and Freedom: A Study of Nineteenth-Century Working-Class Autobiography* (London, 1981), and Laura Marcus, *Auto/biographical Discourses* (Manchester, 1994); for the earlier religious

autobiographies, Owen C. Watkins, *The Puritan Experience: Studies in Spiritual Autobiography* (New York, 1972).

19. Anthony Oberschall, *Empirical Social Research in Germany 1848–1914* (London, 1965), 81. For a selection, see Alfred Kelly (ed.), *The German Worker: Working Class Autobiographies from the Age of Industrialization* (Berkeley, Calif., 1987). In France working-class autobiography began with militants and the 1848 Revolution and the Paris Commune of 1871, but remained a rarity: Philippe Lejeune, *Je est un autre: L'autobiographie, de la littérature aux médias* (Paris, 1980).

20. *The State of the Poor* (London, 1797), p. ii. On the development of survey research in Europe and America from the 1830s onwards, Martin Bulmer and Kevin Bales (eds.), *The Social Survey in Historical Perspective* (Cambridge, 1991).

21. Eileen Yeo, 'Mayhew as a Social Investigator', in E. P. Thompson and E. Yeo (eds.), *The Unknown Mayhew* (London, 1971), 54–63; Henry Mayhew, *London Labour and the London Poor* (London, 1851).

22. Mary Higgs, *Glimpse into the Abyss* (London, 1906); Jack London, *The People of the Abyss* (London, 1903); George Orwell, *Down and Out in Paris and London* (London, 1933); Robert Sherard, *The White Slaves of England* (London, 1897), 41–3; Harold Wright (ed.), *Letters of Stephen Reynolds* (London, 1923), 109, to Tom Woolley, 25 Oct. 1908, and *Daily News* (22 May 1923). See also the perceptive preface to *Seems So!* (London, 1911).

23. *Our Partnership* (London, 1948), 27 and 158; Margaret Cole, *Beatrice Webb* (London, 1945), 59.

24. *Economic Journal*, 16 (1906), 522.

25. Michael Twaddle, 'On Ganda Historiography', and Robin Law, 'Early Yoruba Historiography', *History in Africa*, 1 (1974), 85–100, and 3 (1976), 69–89; J. W. Caughley, *Hubert Howe Bancroft Historian of the West* (Berkeley, Calif., 1946); Willa Baum, 'Oral History: A Revived Tradition at the Bancroft Library', *Pacific North West Quarterly* (Apr. 1967), 57–64.

26. F. W. Maitland, *Domesday Book and Beyond* (1897), pp. v, 3, 520.

27. William Robertson, *History of Scotland* (1759), pp. iv–vi, 1, 5, and 11. David Hume and Edward Gibbon worked with similar care.

28. *Meaning in History*, ed. H. P. Rickman (London, 1961), 85–6.

29. Langlois and Seignobos, *Introduction to the Study of History*, trans. G. G. Berry (1898), 17.

30. Acton's letter to contributors: Fritz Stern, *The Varieties of History* (New York, 1956), 247.

31. Langlois and Seignobos, *Introduction*, 129, 134, 155, 175, 196; R. G. Collingwood, *The Idea of History* (London, 1946), 131.

32. *The Struggle for Mastery in Europe, 1848–1918* (Oxford, 1954), 569–72.

33. *Listener* (1 Feb. 1973), 148; *English History 1914–45* (Oxford, 1945), 609; *Struggle for Mastery*, 574.

34. Walter Lowe Clay, *The Prison Chaplain: A Memoir of the Rev. John Clay* (Cambridge, 1861). For perceptive discussions of Chicago life-story sociology, see especially James Bennett, *Oral History and Delinquency: The Rhetoric of Criminology* (Chicago, 1982), and Philip Abrams, *Historical Sociology* (London, 1982), ch. 9.

35. H. L. Beales and R. S. Lambert, *Memoirs of the Unemployed* (London, 1934).

36. B. Malinowski, 'Myth in Primitive Psychology', in W. R. Dawson (ed.), *The Frazer Lectures* (London, 1932), 97; cf. *Sex and Repression in Savage Society* (London, 1927), 104; Paul Radin, *Crashing Thunder* (London, 1926), p. viii. For the American anthropological tradition, see Plummer, *Documents of Life*; Gordon W. Allport, *The Use of Personal Documents in Psychological Science* (New York, 1942); L. Gottshalk, C. Kluckhohn, and R. Angell, *The Use of Personal Documents in History, Anthropology, and Sociology* (New York, 1947). Outstanding examples include Walter Dyk, *Son of Old Man Hat: A Navaho Autobiography* (New York, 1938); Sidney Mintz, *Worker in the Cane: A Puerto Life History* (New Haven, 1960); Oscar Lewis, *Pedro Martinez: A Mexican Peasant and his Family* (London, 1964); Helen Hughes, *The Fantastic Lodge* (London, 1961). An early instance of representing a culture through a woman is Ruth Underhill, *Autobiography of a Papago Woman* (Menasha, Wis., 1936). The rare British anthropological contributions to the method include the more interpretative use of life-stories in Geoffrey Gorer, *Himalayan Village: An Account of the Lepchas of Sikkim* (London, 1938); and an outstanding early woman's life-story in Mary F. Smith, *Baba of Karo: A Woman of the Muslim Hausa* (London, 1954).

37. *We Are Our Lives*, pp. ix–x. Somebody was also playing with such ideas in New York: witness the caricature of Professor Sea Gull, with his vast project of 'An Oral History of Our Time', an informal history of 'the shirt-sleeved multitude', incomplete after 26 years

bar-room tippling and flophouse dossing, of Joseph Mitchell's *McSorley's Wonderful Saloon* (New York, 1938), 68–86.

38. Aspasia Camargo, Valentina da Rocha Lima, and Lucia Hippolito, 'The Life History Approach in Latin America', *Life Stories* (1985), 41–54; Georg M. Gugelberger (ed.), *The Real Thing: Testimonial Discourse and Latin America* (Durham, NC, 1996).

39. For a recent collection of Australian oral history, Kate Darian-Smith and Paula Hamilton (eds.), *Memory and History in Twentieth-Century Australia* (Melbourne, 1994). Ian Buruma contrasts German expiation of war guilt with Japanese suppressions in *The Wages of Guilt* (New York, 1995).

40. *Tianjin Daily* (28 Apr. and 20 June 1958); Stephen Thompson and Yang Li-wen, 'Oral History in China', *Oral History*, 15/1 (1987), 17–25.

41. Irina Sherbakova, 'Voices from the Choir: Reflections on the Development of Oral History in Russia', and Daria Khubova, Andrei Ivankiev, and Tonia Sharova, 'After Glasnost: Oral History in the Soviet Union', in Luisa Passerini (ed.), *Memory and Totalitarianism* (Oxford, 1992), 89–116; Robert Perks, 'Ukraine's Forbidden History: Memory and Nationalism', *Oral History* 21/1 (1993), 43–53.

42. Including notably Franco Ferrarotti, *Vite di baracati* (Naples, 1974) and *Vite di periferia* (Milan, 1981); Alessandro Portelli, *Biografia di una città* (Turin, 1985); Luisa Passerini, *Torino operaia e fascismo* (Rome, 1984); Nuto Revelli, *Il mondo dei vinti* (Turin, 1977) and *L'anello forte* (Turin, 1985).

43. Lutz Niethammer, 'Die Jahre weiss man nicht . . .'; Lebensgeschichte und Sozialkultur im Ruhrgebiet 1930–60; 'Hinterher merkt man . . .'; and 'Wir Knegen jetzt andere Zeiten' (Bonn, 1983–5).

44. On antecedents in France, see Philippe Joutard, *Ces voix qui nous viennent du passé* (Paris, 1983). The study of local folklore developed in the early 19th cent., especially in the peripheral regions of Brittany and Provence; the systematic national study of dialect and peasant ethnology was established from the 1870s, and the Musée des Arts et Traditions Populaires in Paris founded in 1937. Popular interest in oral history was awakened by Alain Prévost's *Grenadou: Paysan français* (Paris, 1966), a life-story of family life, farm work, and war in the northern countryside near Chartres, derived from tape recordings but thoroughly rewritten. It was televised, and

inspired a series of popular autobiographies in the 1970s, including the best-selling Pierre Jakez Hélias, *Le Cheval d'orgueil* (Paris, 1975; from Brittany) and Serge Grafteaux, *Mémé Santerre* (Paris, 1975; about a northern miner's daughter). The television showing of the film 'Le Chagrin et le Pitié' in 1971, a documentary of collaboration in a town during the German occupation based on retrospective interviews, was also an important influence in the start of oral history work.

45. E. P. Thompson, *The Making of the English Working Class* (London, 1963), 12–13.

46. Judith Okely and Helen Callaway (eds.), *Anthropology and Autobiography* (London, 1992). Another barometer of change can be found in the changing methodological texts of Norman Denzin, from his positivistic approach in *The Research Act in Sociology* (Chicago, 1970: 'The Life History Method', pp. 219–59), to his most recent views in *Interpretive Ethnography: Ethnographic Practices for the 21st Century* (Thousand Oaks, Calif., 1997: 'Reading Narrative', pp. 231–49).

47. David Butler, *The Electoral System in Britain 1918–51* (London, 1953), 214.

48. *SSRC Newsletter* (31 July 1976), 6.

49. For a more moderate, but still uncomprehending critique of oral history from this standpoint, see Louise Tilly and the ensuing debate on 'People's History and Social Science History', *International Journal of Oral History*, 6/1 (1985), 5–46.

50. Arthur Marwick, *The Nature of History* (London, 1970), 142: he has indeed shifted since, but very grudgingly—1981 edn., p. 141.

Notes to Chapter 3: The Achievement of Oral History

1. George Ewart Evans, *The Days That We Have Seen* (London, 1975), 24.

2. Robert Harms, *River of Wealth, River of Sorrow: The Central Zaïre Basin in the Era of the Slave and Ivory Trade, 1500–1891* (New Haven, 1981); Elizabeth Roberts, 'Working-Class Standards of Living in Barrow and Lancaster, 1890–1914', *Economic History Review*, 30 (1977), 306–21; Christopher Storm-Clark, 'The Miners, 1870–1970: A Test-Case for Oral History', *Victorian Studies*, 15/1 (1971), 49–74; Christopher Storm-Clark, 'The Miners, the Relevance of Oral Evidence', *Oral History*, 1/4 (1973), 74. Other works using oral sources for little-documented pre-colonial economies

include Roy Willis, *A State in the Making* (Bloomington, Ind., 1981); William Beinart, *The Political Economy of Pondoland* (Cambridge, 1982), ch. 5; Elias Mandala, *Work and Control in a Peasant Economy* (Madison, Wis., 1990).

3. Allan Nevins, *Ford* (New York, 1954–62); George Ewart Evans, *Where Beards Wag All* (London, 1970), the foundry, migrant brewery labour, craftsmen; Trevor Lummis, *Occupation and Society: The East Anglian Fishermen 1880–1914* (Cambridge, 1985); Paul Thompson with Tony Wailey and Trevor Lummis, *Living the Fishing* (London, 1983).

4. George Ewart Evans, *The Horse in the Furrow* (London, 1960), *The Farm and the Village* (London, 1969), and *Where Beards Wag All*; David Jenkins, *The Agricultural Community in South West Wales at the Turn of the 20th Century* (Cardiff, 1971).

5. Jan and Ray Pahl, *Managers and their Wives* (London, 1971); Carl B. Klockars, *The Professional Fence* (New York, 1975); Daniel Bertaux and Isabelle Bertaux-Wiame, 'Artisan Bakery in France: How it Lives and Why it Survives', in F. Bechhofer and B. Elliott (eds.), *The Petite Bourgeoisie* (London, 1981), 155–81; Robert Scase and Robert Goffee, *The Real World of the Small Business Owner* (London, 1980); Michael Roper, *Masculinity and the British Organization Man* (Oxford, 1994); Cathy Courtney and Paul Thompson, *City Lives: The Changing Voices of British Finance* (London, 1997); Paul Thompson, 'The Pyrrhic Victory of Gentlemanly Capitalism: The Financial Elite of the City of London, 1945–90', *Journal of Contemporary History*, 32 (1997), 283–304 and 427–40.

6. David Edge, *Astronomy Transformed: The Emergence of Radio Astronomy in Britain* (London, 1977).

7. Saul Benison, *Tom Rivers: Reflections on a Life in Medicine and Science* (Cambridge, Mass., 1967); Joanna Bornat, Robert Perks, Paul Thompson, and Jan Walmsley (eds.), *Oral History, Health and Welfare* (London, 1999); Diana Gittins, *Madness in its Place: Narratives of Severalls Hospital, 1913–1997* (London, 1997).

8. Hugh McLeod, 'Religion: The Oral Evidence', *Oral History*, 14/1 (1986), 31–49; Robert Towler and Audrey Chamberlain,'Common Religion', *Sociological Year Book of Religion in Britain*, 6 (1973), 1–28; Paul Landau, *The Realm of the Word: Language, Gender and Christianity in a Southern African Kingdom* (London, 1995); Henry Munson, *The House of Si Abd Allah* (New Haven, 1984); Robert Moore, *Pit-men, Preachers and Politics* (London, 1974).

9. John Saville and Joyce Bellamy, *Dictionary of Labour Biography* (London, 1972–); John Burnet, *Useful Toil: Autobiographies of Working People from the 1820s to the 1920s* (London, 1974); Alice and Staughton Lynd, *Rank and File: Personal Histories by Working Class Organisers from America* (New York, 1973); Paul Buhle, 'Radicalism, the Oral History Contribution', *International Journal of Oral History*, 2/3 (1981), 205–15; Margaret Powell, *Below Stairs* (London, 1968); and Angela Hewins, *The Dillen* (Oxford, 1981).

10. Peter Friedlander, *The Emergence of a UAW Local 1936–1939* (Pittsburgh, 1975); Alun Howkins, *Poor Labouring Men: Rural Radicalism in Norfolk, 1872–1923* (London, 1989); Joanna Bornat, 'Home and Work: A New Context for Trade Union History', *Oral History*, 5/2 (1977), 101–23; Sidney Pollard and Robert Turner, 'Profit-Sharing and Autocracy: The Case of J. T. and J. Taylor of Batley, Woollen Manufacturers, 1892–1966', *Business History*, 8/1 (Jan. 1976), 4–34; Hywel Francis, *Miners against Fascism: Wales and the Spanish Civil War* (London, 1984); *Oral History*, 11/2 (1983), 'Labour History Issue'.

11. Robert Waller, *The Dukeries Transformed: The Social and Political Development of a Twentieth-Century Coalfield* (Oxford, 1983); Jacquelyn Dowd Hall, James Leloudis, Robert Korstad, Mary Murphy, Lu Ann Jones, and Christopher Daly, *Like a Family: The Making of a Southern Cotton World* (Chapel Hill, NC, 1987); Paul Thompson, *Living the Fishing* (London, 1983); Raphael Samuel, '"Quarry Roughs": Life and Labour in Headington Quarry, 1860–1920', in Samuel (ed.), *Village Life and Labour* (London, 1975), 1–26.

12. Thomas Dublin, *When the Mines Closed: Stories of Struggles in Hard Times* (Ithaca, NY, 1998); Michael Frisch and Milton Rogovin, *Portraits in Steel* (Ithaca, NY, 1993); Studs Terkel, *Hard Times: An Oral History of the Great Depression* (New York, 1970); Barry Broadfoot, *Ten Lost Years* (Toronto, 1973); Wendy Lowenstein, *Weevils in the Flour* (Melbourne, 1978); Dennis Marsden and E. Duff, *Workless* (London, 1973); Elliot Liebow, *Tell Them Who I Am* (New York, 1993).

13. Studs Terkel, *Working* (New York, 1974), pp. xxxii–xxxviii; cf. Trevor Blackwell and Jeremy Seabrook, *Talking Work* (London, 1996).

14. Luisa Passerini, *Fascism in Popular Memory* (Cambridge, 1987); Alessandro Portelli, *Biografia di una città* (Turin, 1985); Tamara

Hareven, *Family Time and Industrial Time* (Cambridge, 1982); Pierrette Pézerat and Danièle Poublan, 'French Telephone Operators', *Oral History*, 13/1 (1985), 28–42, and Cristina Borderias, 'Idendidad femenina y camblo social en Barcelona entre 1920 y 1980', in Mercedes Vilanova *et al.*, *El Poder en la Sociedad* (Barcelona, 1986), 35–52; Giovanni Contini, *Paesaggi del marmo* (Venice, 1994); Bob Gilding, *The Journeymen Coopers of East London* (History Workshop pamphlets; London, 1971); Miriam Glucksmann, *Women Assemble: Women Workers and the New Industries in Inter-war Britain* (London, 1990); Ronald Fraser, *In Search of a Past: The Manor House, Amnersfield, 933–1945* (London, 1984); Daniel Bertaux, 'Stories as Clues to Sociological Understanding: The Bakers of Paris', in Paul Thompson (ed.), *Our Common History* (London, 1982), 93–108; Elizabeth Clark-Lewis, *Living In, Living Out: African American Domestics in Washington D.C., 1910–1940* (Washington, DC, 1994); David Douglass, 'The Durham Pitman', in R. Samuel (ed.), *Miners, Quarrymen and Salt-workers* (London, 1977), 205–96; Paul Thompson, 'Playing at Skilled Men: Factory Culture and Pride in Work Skills among Coventry Car Workers', *Social History*, 13 (1988), 45–69.

15. George Ewart Evans, *From Mouths of Men* (London, 1976).

16. Bernard Donoughue and George Jones, *Herbert Morrison: Portrait of a Politician* (London, 1973); Donoughue, *Oral History*, 2/1 (1974), 83–4.

17. Thomas Harry Williams, *Huey Long* (New York, 1969); Valentina da Rocha Lima, *Getulio: Una historia oral* (Rio de Janeiro, 1986); cf. John Toland, *Adolf Hitler* (New York, 1976); Jung Chang, *Wild Swans: Three Daughters of China* (London, 1991); Rigoberta Menchú, *I, Rigoberta Menchú: An Indian Woman in Guatamala* (London, 1984: for criticism and defence, see *Guardian*, 16 Dec. 1998).

18. Kathleen M. Blee, *Women of the Klan: Racism and Gender in the 1920s* (Berkeley, Calif., 1991; Jeremy Seabrook, *What Went Wrong? Working People and the Ideals of the Labour Movement* (London, 1978); Molly Andrews, *Lifetimes of Commitment* (Cambridge, 1991); Daniel Weinbren, *Generating Socialism* (London, 1997); Terence Ranger, *Peasant Consciousness and Guerrilla War in Zimbabwe* (London, 1985); Steven Feierman, *Peasant Intellectuals: Anthropology and History in Tanzania* (Madison, Wis., 1990).

19. William Manchester, *The Death of a President* (New York, 1967);

William Hinton, *Fanshen: A Documentary of Revolution in a Chinese Village* (London, 1966), and *Shenfan: The Continuing Revolution in a Chinese Village* (London, 1983); cf. James and Ann Tyson, *Chinese Awakenings* (Boulder, Colo., 1995); Kim Lacy Rogers, *Righteous Lives: The New Orleans Civil Rights Movement* (New York, 1993); Oscar Lewis, *Pedro Martinez* (London, 1964); Jerome Mintz, *The Anarchists of Casa Viejas* (Chicago, 1982); Martha Ackelsberg, *Free Women of Spain: Anarchism and the Struggle for the Emancipation of Women* (Bloomington, Ind., 1991).

20. On Fascism and the Resistance: Luisa Passerini (ed.), *Memory and Totalitarianism* (Oxford, 1992: *International Yearbook of Oral History and Life Stories*, 1); H. R. Kedward, *Resistance in Vichy France* (Oxford, 1978); Paul Thompson (ed.), *Our Common History* (London, 1982). On the Holocaust: Martin Gilbert, *The Holocaust: The Jewish Tragedy* (London, 1978); Isabel Wollaston, *War against Memory? The Future of Holocaust Remembrance* (London, 1996); Anna Bravo and Daniele Jalla, *La Vita Offesa* (Milan, 1986); Claudine Vegh, *I Didn't Say Goodbye* (London, 1984); for a very critical view of survivors' testimonies, Lawrence Langer, *Holocaust Testimonies, the Ruins of Memory* (New Haven, 1991). Donald Miller and Lorna Miller, *Survivors: An Oral History of the Armenian Genocide* (Berkeley, Calif., 1993). For Hiroshima survivors: R. J. Lipton, *Death in Life* (New York, 1968). On Spain, Ronald Fraser, *Blood of Spain: The Experience of Civil War, 1936–9* (London, 1979), and *In Hiding: The Life of Manuel Cortes* (London, 1972).

21. Sarah Fishman, *We Will Wait: Wives of French Prisoners of War, 1940–1945* (New York, 1991); Mary P. Motley, *The Invisible Soldier: The Experience of the Black Soldier, World War II* (Detroit, 1975); Lyn Macdonald, *Somme* (London, 1983); Felicity Goodall, *A Question of Conscience: Conscientious Objectors in the Two World Wars* (Stroud, 1997); Alistair Thomson, *Anzac Memories: Living with the Legend* (Oxford, 1994); Alessandro Portelli, *The Battle of Valle Giulia: Oral History and the Art of Dialogue* (Madison, Wis., 1997), pp. vii-viii; see also n. 42 below.

22. Colonial history: Charles Allen, *Plain Tales from the Raj* (London, 1975), and *Tales from the Dark Continent* (London, 1979).

23. Paul Radin, *Crashing Thunder* (1926); Leo Simmons, *Sun Chief* (New Haven, 1942); Nancy O. Lurie, *Mountain Wolf Woman: The*

Autobiography of a Winnebago Indian (Ann Arbor, Mich., 1961); Gregorio Condori Mamani, with Ricardo Valderrama and Carmen Escalante, *Autobiograf'a* (Cuzco, 1992); James Freeman, *Untouchable: An Indian Life* (Stanford, Calif., 1979); A. M. Kiki, *Kiki: 10,000 Years in a Lifetime* (London, 1968); Mary Smith, *Baba of Karo: A Woman of the Muslim Hausa* (London, 1954); Tim Keegan, *Facing the Storm: Portraits of Black Lives in Rural South Africa* (London, 1988); Pat Caplan, *African Voices, African Lives: Personal Narratives from a Swahili Village* (London, 1997).

24. Joseph Miller (ed.), *The African Past Speaks* (Folkestone, 1980); David W. Cohen, *Womunafu's Bonafu* (Princeton, 1970) and *The Historical Tradition of the Busoga* (Oxford, 1972); Andrew Roberts, *A History of Bemba* (Madison, Wis., 1973); Steven Feierman, *The Shambaa Kingdom* (Madison, Wis., 1974); John Lamphear, *The Traditional History of the Jie of Uganda* (Oxford, 1976); Roy Willis, *A State in the Making: Myth, History and Social Transformation in Pre-colonial Ufipa* (Bloomington, Ind., 1981); Paul Irwin, *Liptako Speaks: History from Oral Tradition in Africa* (Princeton, 1981); Terence Ranger, 'Personal Reminiscence and the Experience of the People in East Central Africa', *Oral History*, 6/1 (1978), 45–78; Terence Ranger, *Peasant Consciousness and Guerrilla Resistance in Zimbabwe* (London, 1985).

25. Kai Erikson, *In the Wake of the Flood* (London, 1979); Farley Mowat, *Preserve the Earth: Conversations with the Green Crusaders* (Toronto, 1990); Andrèa Zhouri, 'Trees and People: An Anthropology of British Campaigners for the Amazon Rainforest', Essex Ph.D., 1998; J. E. Dizard, *Going Wild: Hunting, Animal Rights and the Contested Meaning of Nature* (Amherst, Mass., 1994); Michael I. Ninan, *People of the Rainbow: A Nomadic Utopia* (Knoxville, Tenn., 1997). Nigel Cross and Rhiannon Barker, *At the Desert's Edge* (London, 1991); Robert Harms, *Games Against Nature: An Eco-cultural History of the Numi of Equatorial Africa* (Cambridge, 1987); Melissa Leach and James Fairhead, *Misreading the African Landscape: Society and Ecology in the Forest-Savanna Mosaic* (Cambridge, 1996), 1.

26. Paul Thompson, *The Edwardians: The Remaking of British Society* (London, 1975), 4.

27. George Ewart Evans, *Ask the Fellows Who Cut the Hay* (London, 1956), and *Where Beards Wag All* (London, 1975); Ronald Blythe, *Akenfield: Portrait of an English Village* (London, 1969).

28. Nuto Revelli, *Il mondo dei vinti* (Turin, 1977) and *L'anello duro* (Turin, 1985); Pierre Jakez Hélias, *Le Cheval d'orgueil* (Paris, 1975; *The Horse of Pride*, New Haven, 1978); Samuel, 'Quarry Roughs', in *Village Life and Labour*; Mary Chamberlain, *Fenwomen* (London, 1975).

29. C. M. Arensberg and S. T. Kimball, *Family and Community in Ireland* (Cambridge, Mass., 1940) and a critical restudy, Hugh Brody, *Inishkillane: Change and Decline in the West of Ireland* (London, 1973); W. M. Williams, *The Sociology of an English Village: Gosforth* (London, 1956), and *A West Country Village: Ashworthy* (London, 1963); James Littlejohn, *Westrigg* (London, 1963); Ian Carter, *Farm Life in North-East Scotland, 1840–1914* (Edinburgh, 1979); Eric Cregeen, 'Oral Tradition and Agrarian History in the West Highlands' and 'Oral Sources for the Social History of the Scottish Highlands and Islands', *Oral History*, 2/1 (1974), 15–33 and 2/2 (1974), 23–36; David Jenkins, *The Agricultural Community in South West Wales* (Cardiff, 1971).

30. Richard Hoggart, *The Uses of Literacy* (London, 1957); Jeremy Seabrook, *The Unprivileged* (London, 1967), and *City Close-Up* (London, 1971).

31. Paul Thompson, 'Voices from Within', in Michael Wolff and H. J. Dyos (eds.), *The Victorian City* (London, 1973), 59–80; Jerry White, *Rothschild Buildings: Life in an East End Tenement Block 1887–1920* (London, 1980); and *The Worst Street in North London* (London, 1986); Studs Terkel, *Division Street: America* (New York, 1967).

32. Angela Hewins, *The Dillen* (Oxford, 1981); Tamara Hareven and Randolph Langenbach, *Amoskeag: Life and Work in an American Factory City in New England* (New York, 1978); Ruth Finnegan, *Tales of the City: A Study of Narrative and Urban Life* (Cambridge, 1998); Robert and Helen Lynd, *Middletown* (New York, 1929); Margaret Stacey, *Tradition and Change: A Study of Banbury* (London, 1960); Melvyn Bragg, *Speak for England: An Essay on England, 1900–1975, Based on Interviews with Inhabitants of Wigton, Cumberland* (London, 1976).

33. Brian Jackson and Dennis Marsden, *Education and the Working Class* (London, 1962); Iona and Peter Opie, *The Lore and Language of School Children* (Oxford, 1959); John Dillard, *Black English* (New York, 1973); Bruce Rosenberg, *The Art of the American Folk Preacher* (Oxford, 1970); Roger Abrahams, *Deep*

Down in the Jungle (Chicago, 1970); Henry Glassie, *Passing the Time in Ballymenone* (Philadelphia, 1982); George Ewart Evans and George Thomson, *The Leaping Hare* (London, 1972).

34. Edward Ives, *Joe Scott* (Urbana, Ill., 1978); Robin Morton, *Come Day, Go Day, God Send Sunday*, on John Maguire of Fermanagh (London, 1973); David Buchan, *The Ballad and the Folk* (London, 1972); Brian Jackson and Dennis Marsden, *Working Class Community* (London, 1971); William J. Schafer, *Brass Bands and New Orleans Jazz* (Baton Rouge, La., 1977); Sally Alexander, *St Giles Fair 1830–1914* (History Workshop pamphlet 2; Oxford, 1970); Lawrence S. Ritter, *The Glory of their Times: The Story of the Early Days of Baseball* (New York, 1966); Andrew Davies, *Leisure, Gender and Poverty: Working-Class Culture in Salford and Manchester, 1900–1939* (Buckingham, 1992); Pilar Folguera, 'City Space and the Daily Life of Women in Madrid in the 1920s', *Oral History*, 13/2 (1985), 49–56.

35. Oscar Lewis, *The Children of Sanchez* (New York, 1961); Arensberg and Kimball, *Family and Community in Ireland*; Michael Young and Peter Willmott, *Family and Kinship in East London* (London, 1957); Colin Rosser and Christopher Harris, *The Family and Social Change: A Study of Family and Kinship in a South Wales Town* (London, 1965); Lee Rainwater, *And the Poor Get Children* (Chicago, 1960).

36. Emmanuel Le Roy Ladurie, *Montaillou: Cathars and Catholics in a French Village, 1294–1324* (London, 1978); Martine Segalen, *Love and Power in the Peasant Family: Rural France in the Nineteenth Century* (Oxford, 1983); J. A. Banks, *Prosperity and Parenthood: A Study of Family Planning among the Victorian Middle Class* (London, 1954), 127, 144, 201; Diana Gittins, *Fair Sex: Family Size and Structure, 1900–39* (London, 1982).

37. *Oral History*, 3/2 (1975); John R. Gillis, *For Better, For Worse: British Marriages 1600 to the Present* (Oxford, 1985); Stephen Humphries, *Hooligans or Rebels?* (Oxford, 1981); Thea Thompson, *Edwardian Childhoods* (London, 1981); T. C. Smout, 'Aspects of Sexual Behaviour in Nineteenth Century Scotland', in A. A. MacLaren (ed.), *Social Class in Scotland* (Edinburgh, 1976), 55–85; Paul Thompson, *The Edwardians*, 'Childhood', 'Youth', and 'Adulthood and Old Age'; Gill Gorell Barnes, Paul Thompson, Gwyn Daniel, and Natasha Burchardt, *Growing Up in Stepfamilies* (Oxford, 1997).

38. Charles Van Onselen, *The Seed is Mine: The Life of Kas Maine, a South African Sharecropper, 1894–1985* (Oxford, 1996); Tamara Hareven, *Family Time and Industrial Time* (Cambridge, 1982).

39. Peter Townsend, *The Family Life of Old People* (London, 1957); Jane Lewis and Barbara Meredith, *Daughters Who Care* (London, 1988); Paul Thompson, Catherine Itzin, and Michele Abendstern, *I Don't Feel Old: The Experience of Later Life* (Oxford, 1990); Daniel Bertaux and Paul Thompson (eds.), *Between Generations: Family Models, Myths, and Memories* (Oxford, 1993); Elizabeth Roberts, *A Woman's Place: An Oral History of Working-Class Women, 1890–1940* (Oxford, 1984), and *Women and Families: An Oral History, 1940–1970* (Oxford, 1995).

40. Sherna Gluck, *From Parlor to Prison: Five American Suffragettes Talk about Their Lives* (New York, 1976); Chamberlain, *Fenwomen*; Sheila Rowbotham and Jean McCrindle, *Dutiful Daughters* (London, 1977); Daphne Patai, *Brazilian Women Speak: Contemporary Life Stories* (New Brunswick, NJ, 1988); Fatima Mernissi, *Doing Daily Battle: Interviews with Moroccan Women* (London, 1988), 1; Nayra Atiga, *Khul Khaal: Five Egyptian Women Tell their Stories* (London, 1988); Belinda Bozzoli, *Women of Phokeng: Consciousness, Life Strategy, and Migrancy in South Africa, 1900–1983* (London, 1991), 3; Gaby Kupers, *Compañeras: Voices from the Latin American Women's Movement* (London, 1994); Margaret Randall, *Sandino's Daughters Revisited, Feminism in Nicaragua* (New Brunswick, NJ, 1994); Andrew Morton, *Diana: Her True Story—In Her Own Words* (London, 1997).

41. e.g. nn. 10–14 above; Bornat, 'Home and Work'; Hall, *Like a Family;* Glucksmann, *Women Assemble;* Clark-Lewis, *Living In, Living Out; Oral History,* 5/2 (1977), 10/2 (1982), 21/2 (1993), 'Women's History Issues'; Jan Carter, *Nothing to Spare: Recollections of Australian Pioneering Women* (Melbourne, 1981); Leonore Davidoff and Belinda Westover (eds.), *Our Work, Our Lives, Our Words: Women's History and Women's Work* (London, 1986); Anna Bravo, 'Solidarity and Loneliness: Piedmontese Peasant Women at the Turn of the Century', *International Journal of Oral History,* 3/2 (1982), 76–91; Paul Thompson, 'Women in the Fishing: The Roots of Power between the Sexes', *Comparative Studies in Society and History,* 27/1 (1985), 3–32.

42. Sherna B. Gluck, *Rosie the Riveter Revisited: Women, the War and Social Change* (Boston, 1987); Janet Hart, *New Voices in the*

Nation: Women and the Greek Resistance, 1941–1964 (Ithaca, NY, 1996), 6; Paula Schwartz, '"Partisanes" and Gender Politics in Vichy France', *French Historical Studies*, 16 (1989), 126–51; Penny Summerfield, *Reconstructing Women's Wartime Lives: Discourse and Subjectivity in Oral Histories of the Second World War* (Manchester, 1998), 284–5; Ackelsberg, *Free Women of Spain*; Blee, *Women of the Klan*, 3.

43. Penny Summerfield and Nicole Crockett, '"You Weren't Taught That with the Welding": Lessons in Sexuality in the Second World War', *Women's History Review*, 1 (1992), 435–60; Katherine Holden in Leonore Davidoff, Megan Doolittle, Janet Fink, and Katherine Holden, *The Family Story: Blood, Contract and Intimacy, 1830–1960* (London, 1998); Hall Carpenter Archives, *Inventing Ourselves: Lesbian Life Stories* and *Walking After Midnight Gay Men's Life Stories* (London, 1989); Elizabeth Lapovsky Kennedy and Madeline D. Davis, *Boots of Leather, Slippers of Gold: The History of a Lesbian Community* (New York, 1993); Luise White, *The Comforts of Home: Prostitution in Colonial Nairobi* (Chicago, 1990), 51.

44. James Bennett, *Oral History and Delinquency* (Chicago, 1982); Clifford Shaw, *The Jack Roller: a Delinquent Boy's Own Story* (Chicago, 1930); Helen Hughes, *The Fantastic Lodge: The Autobiography of a Girl Drug Addict* (Boston, 1961); Klockars, *The Professional Fence*; Tony Parker and Robert Allerton, *The Courage of His Convictions* (London, 1962); Tony Parker, *The Unknown Citizen* (London, 1963), *The Twisting Lane: Some Sex Offenders* (London, 1969), *Life after Life: Interviews with Twelve Murderers* (London, 1991), *Lighthouse* (London, 1975), *Soldier, Soldier* (London, 1985), and *May the Lord in His Mercy Be Kind to Belfast* (London, 1993); Walter Probyn, *Angel Face: The Making of a Criminal* (London, 1977); Roger Hood and Kate Joyce, 'Three Generations: Oral Testimonies on Crime and Social Change in London's East End', *British Journal of Criminology*, 39 (1999), 136–60; Barbara Weinberger, *The Best Police Force in the World: an Oral History of English Policing from the 1930s to the 1960s* (Aldershot, 1995); Raphael Samuel, *East End Underworld: Chapters in the Life of Arthur Harding* (London, 1981).

45. William I. Thomas and Florian Znaniecki, *The Polish Peasant in Europe and America* (Boston, 1918–20); Wendy Lowenstein, *The Immigrants* (Melbourne, 1978); Joan Morrison and Charlotte

Zabusky, *American Mosaic* (New York, 1980); George R. Mormino and George E. Pozzetta, *The Immigrant World of Ybor City: Italians and their Latin Neighbours in Tampa, 1885–1985* (Urbana, Ill., 1987); Amrit Wilson, *Finding a Voice: Asian Women in Britain* (London, 1978); Isabelle Bertaux-Wiame, 'The Life History Approach to the Study of Internal Migration', in Paul Thompson (ed), *Our Common History* (London, 1982), 186–200, or *Oral History*, 7/1 (1979), 26–32; Gina Harkell, 'The Migration of Mining Families to the Kent Coalfield between the Wars', *Oral History*, 6/1 (1978), 98–113; Bill Williams, 'The Jewish Immigrant in Manchester', *Oral History*, 7/1 (1979), 43–53; Carolyn Adams, 'Across Seven Seas and Thirteen Rivers', *Oral History*, 19/1 (1991), 29–35 (Sylhet); Rina Benmayor and Andor Skotnes (eds.), *Migration and Identity* (Oxford, 1994: *International Yearbook of Oral History and Life Stories*, 3); Mary Chamberlain, *Narratives of Exile and Return* (London, 1997), 53.

46. Paul Bullock, *Watts, the Aftermath* (New York, 1969); Alex Haley, *Autobiography of Malcolm X* (New York, 1965); Bob Blauner, *Black Lives, White Lives: Three Decades of Race Relations in America* (Berkeley, Calif., 1989); Studs Terkel, *Race: How Blacks and Whites Think and Feel about the American Obsession* (New York, 1992); William Montell, *The Saga of Coe Ridge* (Knoxville, Tenn., 1970); George Rawick, *From Sundown to Sunup, The Making of the Black Community and The American Slave–A Composite Biography* (Westport, Conn., 1972); Eugene Genovese, *Roll, Jordan Roll: The World the Slaves Made* (London, 1974); Lawrence Goodwin, 'Populist Dreams and Negro Rights: East Texas as a Case Study', *American Historical Review*, 76/5 (1971), 1435–56.

47. Theodore Rosengarten, *All God's Dangers: The Life of Nate Shaw* (New York, 1974).

Notes to Chapter 4: Evidence

1. *Oral History*, 1/4 (1973), 93.
2. Marwick, *The Nature of History* (London, 1970), 133–7.
3. D. Read, *Documents from Edwardian England* (London, 1973), 305–7; Robert Blake, *The Unknown Prime Minister, the Life and Times of Bonar Law* (London, 1955), 130.
4. 'Populist Dreams and Negro Rights: East Texas as a Case Study', *American Historical Review*, 76/5 (1971), 1435–56.
5. *Oral History*, 1/3 (1973), 35, 46.

6. *Suicide*, trans. (London, 1952), 37; Jack Douglas, *The Social Meanings of Suicide* (Princeton, 1967).

7. *Census of England and Wales for* 1911, vol. xiii, 'Fertility and Marriage', p. xv; Bryan Rodgers, Chris Power, and Steven Hope, 'Parental Divorce and Adult Psychological Distress: Evidence from a National Cohort', *Journal of Child Psychology and Psychiatry*, 38 (1997), 867–72.

8. Frances Widdowson, 'Elementary Teacher Training and the Middle Class Girl', Susan Miller, 'The Happy Coincidence: Rural Poverty and the Labour Migration Scheme of 1835–7', and Eve Hostettler, 'Cottage Economy', University of Essex MA dissertations and Oral History projects, 1976.

9. Gudie Lawaetz, 'History on Film', *History Workshop*, 2 (1976), 124, cf. p.137; Royden Harrison, *Times Higher Education Supplement* (23 July 1976).

10. R. H. S. Crossman, *Listener* (1 Feb. 1973), 148; George Ewart Evans, *From Mouths of Men* (London, 1976), 174–5.

11. See Alessandro Portelli, 'Oral History, the Law and the Making of History', *History Workshop*, 20 (1985), 5–25, on the Aldo Moro trial of the Italian Red Brigades.

12. For a good summary of psychological research, Martin Conway, *Autobiographical Memory* (Milton Keynes, 1990).

13. Steven Rose, *The Making of Memory* (London, 1992).

14. Re-recording, e.g. Calum Johnston, recorded by Alan Lomax of the School of Scottish Studies in 1951, *Tocher*, 13, p. 166, and for our own survey, interview 293, pp. 1–8, 1971.

15. Michael Ross and Diane Holmberg, 'Are Wives' Memories for Events in Relationships More Vivid than their Husbands' Memories?' *Journal of Social and Personal Relationships*, 9 (1992), 585–604; David Jenkins, *The Agricultural Community in South West Wales* (Cardiff, 1971), 5; Ian Hunter, *Memory* (London, 1964), 161.

16. Maurice Halbwachs, *Les Cadres sociaux de la mémoire* (Paris, 1925), and *La Mémoire collective* (Paris, 1950; trans. *Collective Memory*, New York, 1980); see also Paul Connerton, *How Societies Remember* (Cambridge, 1989), and James Fentress and Chris Wickham, *Social Memory* (Oxford, 1992). Alistair Thomson, *Anzac Memories: Living with the Legend* (Oxford, 1994); Raphael Samuel and Paul Thompson (eds.), *The Myths We Live By* (London, 1990).

17. F. C. Bartlett, *Remembering* (1932), 204.

18. Paul S. Appelbaum, Lisa A. Uyehara, and Mark R. Elin, *Trauma*

and Memory: Clinical and Legal Controversies (New York, 1997), notably Elizabeth Loftus.

19. Rider Haggard, *Rural England*, i. 446–7.
20. Hunter, *Memory*, 227; A.T. Welford, *Ageing and Human Skill* (London, 1958), 233.
21. Ken Plummer, *Documents of Life* (London, 1983), 103.
22. Herbert H. Hyman, *Interviewing in Social Research* (Chicago, 1954), 238–42; Jean Peneff, 'The Observers Observed: French Survey Researchers at Work' and subsequent debate, *Social Problems*, 35 (1988), 520–35, and 36 (1989), 310–15.
23. Elliot Mishler, *Research Interviewing: Context and Narrative* (Cambridge, Mass., 1986), 18–19; Hyman, *Interviewing*, 115.
24. Hyman, *Interviewing*, 159–61.
25. Jan Vansina, *Oral Tradition* (London, 1965), 93.
26. Norman Denzin (ed.), *Sociological Methods* (Berkeley, 1970), 199–203.
27. Carol Faiers, 'Persistence and Change in a Suffolk Village', Essex University Sociology BA project, 1976, p.36.
28. *Oral History*, 4/1 (1976), 47.
29. 'Implications of Oracy: An Anthropological View', *Oral History*, 3/1 (1975), 41–9.
30. Denzin, *Sociological Methods*, 324; Hyman, *Interviewing*, 234.
31. P. M. Blau and O. D. Duncan, *The American Occupational Structure* (London, 1967), 459, 467.
32. D. Butler and D. Stokes, *Political Change in Britain* (London, 1969), 273; Charles More, *Skill and the English Working Class 1870–1914* (London, 1980), 58–61, 66–7, 70–1; Alan Baddeley, Diana Gittins, and Cohn Hindley in Louis Moss and Harvey Goldstein (eds.), *The Recall Method in Social Surveys* (London, 1979); Shirley Dex, *The Reliability of Recall Data: A Literature Review*, Working Paper 11, British Household Panel Study, University of Essex, 1991.
33. Vansina, *Oral Tradition*, 190–2.
34. B. L. Neugarten (ed.), *Middle Age and Aging* (Chicago, 1968), 173–7.
35. Herbert Blumer, *Critiques of Research in the Social Sciences*, i. *An Appraisal of Thomas and Znaniecki's The Polish Peasant in Europe and America* (New York. 1939), introduction to revised edn. (New Brunswick, NJ, 1979), p. xxxiv; Yves Lequin and J. Metral, 'Une mémoire collective: Les Metallurgistes retraites de Givors', *Annales*, 35/1 (1980), 149–66.

36. Unpublished interview, Paul Thompson and Thea Vigne, 908, pp. 10–16; cf. *Oral History*, 1/4, p. 31.

37. Dex, *Reliability*, 24.

38. Raphael Samuel, *History Workshop*, 1 (1976), 202 and *Miners, Quarrymen and Saltworkers* (London, 1977), 4; Peter Friedlander, *The Emergence of a UAW Local* (Pittsburgh, 1975), p. xxx.

39. *Oral History*, 1/4 (1973), 116–20; Munson in *Contemporary Review* (1975–6), 107–8.

40. *Oral History*, 1/3 (1973), 39; *Oral History*, 2/1 (1974), 84.

41. Melvyn Bragg, *Speak for England* (London, 1976), 7.

42. Jenkins, *Agricultural Community in South West Wales*, 5.

43. Allan Nevins, *Ford* (New York, 1954–62), i. 67–8, 389–93.

44. Alessandro Portelli, *The Death of Luigi Trastulli and Other Stories* (Albany, NY, 1991), 'The Death of Luigi Trastulli: Memory and the Event', 'What Makes Oral History Different', and '"The Time of My Life": Functions of Time in Oral History'.

45. Roy Hay, 'Use and Abuse of Oral Evidence', unpublished paper.

46. Portelli, *Death of Luigi Trastulli*, 'What Makes Oral History Different'.

47. Portelli, *Death of Luigi Trastulli*, 'Uchronic Dreams: Working-Class Memory and Possible Worlds'.

48. Raphael Samuel and Paul Thompson (eds.), *The Myths We Live By* (London, 1990).

49. Henry Glassie, *Passing the Time in Ballymenone* (Philadephia, 1982), 55; John Berger, *Pig Earth* (London, 1985), 9.

50. Jan Vansina, *Oral Tradition as History* (London, 1985), 21, 68–9; Mary Chamberlain and Paul Thompson (eds.), *Narrative and Genre* (London, 1998).

51. Pierre Gaudin and Claire Reverchon, 'Le Sens du tragique dans la mémoire historique', papers of the International Oral History Conference, Aix-en-Provence, 1982, pp. 89–98; Françoise Zonabend, *La Mémoire longue* (Paris, 1980), 107–11, 299–304.

52. *Oral History*, 5/1 (1977), 23.

53. Vansina, *Oral Tradition as History*, 56, 103; Paul Irwin, *Liptako Speaks* (Princeton, 1981); David Henige, *Oral Historiography* (London, 1982), 72–3; Howard and Frances Morphy, 'The "Myths" of Ngalakan History', *Man*, 19/3 (1984), 459–78.

54. Steven Feierman, *The Shambaa Kingdom* (London, 1974), 15; Anna Bravo and Daniele Jalla, *La vita offesa* (Milan, 1986), 63; Luisa Passerini, 'Work Ideology and Fascism', in Paul Thompson

(ed.), *Our Common History* (London, 1982), 54–78; Kim Lacy Rogers, Selma Leydesdorff, and Graham Dawson, *Trauma and Memory* (London, 1999).

55. Carolyn Steedman, *Landscape for a Good Woman* (London, 1986), 39; Vansina, *Oral History*, 5/1, pp. 22–3; Ronald J. Grele, *Envelopes of Sound* (Chicago, 1975), 57, 61.

56. F. A. Salome, 'The Methodological Significance of the Lying Informant', *Anthropological Quarterly*, 50 (1977), 117–24; Vansina, *Oral Tradition as History*, 8; Frank Coffield, P. Robinson, and J. Sarsby, *A Cycle of Deprivation? A Case Study of Four Families* (London, 1980), 13–14, 33.

57. Jack Goody, *Literacy in Traditional Societies* (Cambridge, 1968), 27–68; Vansina, *Oral Tradition as History*, pp. xii, 92, 94, 120–3, 162–5; Joanne Rappaport, *The Politics of Memory: Native Historical Interpretation in the Colombian Andes* (Cambridge, 1990); Robert Borofsky, *Making History: Pukapukan and Anthropological Constructions of Knowledge* (Cambridge, 1987); Leroy Vail and Landeg White, *Power and the Praise Poem: Southern African Voices in History* (Charlottesville, Va., 1991), p. xii.

58. Jerome Mintz, *The Anarchists of Casa Viejas* (Chicago, 1982), pp. xi, 271; Eric Hobsbawm, *Primitive Rebels* (London, 1959), 90.

59. James W. Wilkie, 'Alternative Views in History: Historical Statistics and Oral History', in Richard E. Greenleaf and Michael C. Meyer (eds.), *Research in Mexican History* (Lincoln, Nebr., 1973), 54; Vansina in Joseph Miller (ed.), *The African Past Speaks* (Folkestone, 1980), 276.

Notes to Chapter 5: Memory and the Self

1. Another example, combining group and individual memory and drawing on a diary as well as oral memories is Luisa Passerini, *Autobiography of a Generation: Italy, 1968* (Hanover, 1996).

2. R. Fraser, *In Search of a Past* (London, 1984), 85, 118.

3. Gill Gorell Barnes, 'Systems Theory and Family Therapy', in M. Rutter and L. Hersov (eds.), *Modern Child Psychiatry* (London, 1985), 216–29; Jeremy Holmes, 'Family and Individual Therapy: Comparisons and Contrasts', *British Journal of Psychiatry*, 47 (1985), 668–76.

4. Timothy Ashplant, 'Psychoanalysis in Historical Writing', *History Workshop*, 26 (1988), 102–19.

5. Juliet Mitchell, *Psychoanalysis and Feminism* (London, 1974);

Nancy Chodorow, *The Reproduction of Mothering* (Berkeley, Calif., 1978).

6. Richard Ely and Allyssa McCabe, 'Gender Differences for Speech', in Selma Lydesdorff, Luisa Passerini, and Paul Thompson (eds.), *Gender and Memory* (Oxford, 1996), 17–30; Isabelle Bertaux-Wiame, 'The Life History Approach to the Study of Internal Migration', in Paul Thompson (ed.), *Our Common History* (London, 1982), 192–3.

7. David Lowenthal, *The Past is a Foreign Country* (London, 1985), 17.

8. Judith L. Herman, *Trauma and Recovery: From Domestic Abuse to Political Terror* (New York, 1992); Linda Hunt, Mary Marshall, and Cherry Rowlings, *Past Trauma in Late Life: Perspectives on Therapeutic Work with Older People* (London, 1997); Gadi Ben-Ezer, 'Trauma and Trauma Signals in the Narratives of the Migration Journey of the Ethiopian Jews to Israel', in Kim Lacy Rogers, Selma Leydesdorff, and Graham Dawson (eds.), *Trauma and Life Stories* (London, 1999).

9. Donald Miller and Lorna Miller, *Survivors: An Oral History of the Armenian Genocide* (Berkeley, Calif., 1993).

10. Anna Bravo and Daniele Jalla, *La vita offesa* (Milan, 1986), 160; Anna Bravo, 'Italian Women in the Nazi Camps', *Oral History*, 13/1 (1985), 20–7; Claudine Vegh, *I Didn't Say Goodbye* (London, 1984), 29, 161.

11. Arthur Ponsonby, *English Diaries* (London, 1923), 8–9; Faraday and Plummer, 'Doing Life Histories', *Sociological Review*, 27 (1979), 773–98.

12. Peter Coleman, 'Issues in the Therapeutic Use of Reminiscence with Elderly People', in Ian Hanley and Mary Gilhooly (eds.), *Psychological Therapies for the Elderly* (London, 1986), 41–64; R. Dobrof, introduction to M. Kaminsky (ed.), *The Uses of Reminiscence: New Ways of Working with Older Adults* (New York, 1984: special double issue, *Journal of Gerontological Social Work*, 7/1–2); Robert Butler, 'The Life Review: An Interpretation of Reminiscence in the Aged', *Psychiatry*, 26 (1963), 65–76, 'The Life Review: An Unrecognized Bonanza', *International Journal on Aging and Human Development*, 12 (1980–1), 35–8, and *Why Survive?* (New York, 1975), 412–14; Arthur Kleinman, *Illness Narratives: Suffering, Healing and the Human Condition* (New York, 1988); Glenn Roberts and Jeremy Holmes (eds.), *Healing Stories: Narrative in Psychiatry and Psychotherapy* (Oxford, 1999).

13. S. Merriam, 'The Concept and Function of Reminiscence: A Review of the Research', *Gerontologist*, 20 (1980), 604–9; V. Molinari and R. E. Reichlin, 'Life Review Reminiscence in the Elderly: A Review of the Literature', *International Journal on Aging and Human Development*, 20 (1984–5), 81–92.

14. Debbie Frost and Kay Taylor, 'Life Story Books: This is My Life', *Community Care* (7 Aug. 1986), 28; Malcolm Johnson, 'That was Your Life: A Biographical Approach to Later Life', in Vida Carver and Penny Liddiard (eds.), *An Ageing Population* (London, 1979), 147–61.

15. John Adams, 'Reminiscence in the Geriatric Ward: An Under-valued Resource', *Oral History*, 12/2 (1984), 54–9; J. Lesser *et al.*, 'Reminiscence Group Therapy with Psychotic Geriatric Patients', *Gerontologist*, 21 (1981), 291–6; Andrew Norris and Mohammed Abu El Eileh, 'Reminiscence Groups: A Therapy for both Elderly Patients and their Staff', *Nursing Times*, 78 (1982), 1368–9. See also *Recall—A Handbook*, (Help the Aged; London, 1986); Andrew Norris, *Reminiscence with Elderly People* (London, 1986); Maureen O'Connor, *Generation to Generation* (London, 1993); Faith Gibson, *Reminiscence and Recall: A Guide to Good Practice* (Age Concern; London, 1994).

16. Peter Coleman, in Hanley and Gilhooly, and 'The Past in the Present: A Study of Elderly People's Attitudes to Reminiscence', *Oral History*, 14/1 (1986), 50–7. See also Peter Coleman, *Elderly People and the Reminiscence Process* (London, 1986); *Oral History*, 17/2 (1989), 'Reminiscence' issue; Joanna Bornat (ed.), *Reminiscence Reviewed: Evaluations, Achievements, Perspectives* (Buckingham, 1994).

17. H. Hazan, *The Limbo People* (London, 1980), 27–8. The true source of this poem, which has been cited in several places, is unclear, but it has a suitably mythical origin in a London old people's centre.

Notes to Chapter 6: Projects

1. Allan Redfern, *Talking in Class: Oral History and the National Curriculum* (Oral History Society; Colchester, 1996); National Curriculum History Working Group, *Final Report* (HMSO; London, 1990), 178; on recent American work in schools, *Oral History Review*, 25/1–2 (1998), special issue, 'Practice and Pedagogy: Oral History in the Classroom'.

2. Sallie Purkis, *Oral History in Schools* (Oral History Society; Colchester, 1980), and *Thanks for the Memory* (London, 1987).

3. Alistair Ross, 'Children as Historians', *Oral History*, 12/2 (1984), reprinted in Robert Perks and Alistair Thomson (eds.), *The Oral History Reader* (London, 1998), 432–47.

4. Liz Cleaver, 'Oral History at Thurston Upper School', *Oral History*, 13/1 (1985), 11–12.

5. Elliot Wigginton, *Foxfire One* (New York, 1972), 141, 221, 363, 375; *Oral History Review*, 1 (1973), 30–6. For other pioneering American educational work, see also John Neuenschwander, *Oral History as a Teaching Approach* (Washington, DC, 1976); and in higher education, James Hoopes, *Oral History: An Introduction for Students* (Chapel Hill, NC, 1979).

6. The poem is reprinted from *Write First Time* (June 1981), by permission of the author. See also Jane Mace, *Working with Words: Literacy beyond School* (London, 1979).

7. Shaun Nethercott and Neil Leighton, 'Out of the Archives and onto the Stage', *Oral History*, 18/1, reprinted in Perks and Thomson, *Oral History Reader*, 457–64; Elyse Dodgson, 'From Oral History to Drama', *Oral History*, 12/2 (1984), 47–53, and Elyse Dodgson, *Motherland* (London, 1984); *Oral History*, 18/2 (1990), 'Oral History, Theatre and Performance' issue.

8. Alastair Thomson, *Undergraduate Life History Research Projects: Approaches, Issues and Outcomes*, Working Report, University of Sussex, Brighton, 1998. Since 1993 the Open University's distance learning course A422, 'The Oral History Project', has been available to students throughout Britain.

9. Janis Wilton, 'Share and Compare: Ideas for Teaching Oral History', *Oral History Association of Australia Journal*, 18 (1996), 17–26; Sue Bruley, 'Women's History, Oral History and Active Learning: An Experience from Southern England', *Women's History Review*, 5/1(1996), 111–27; Ronald J. Grele, 'Values and Methods in the Classroom Transformation of Oral History', *Oral History Review*, 25/1–2 (1998), 57–69.

10. A selection of these projects is published in Leonore Davidoff and Belinda Westover (eds.), *Our Work, Our Lives, Our Words* (London, 1986).

11. On early community projects, see Stephen Humphries, *The Handbook of Oral History* (London, 1984); Richard Gray on Peckham People's History, Graham Smith on the Arbroath MSC History

Project, Robert Perks on Bradford Heritage and Sian Jones on Southampton Museum in 'Oral History and Community History', *Oral History*, 12/2 (1984); and *Oral History*, 14/2 (1986), 'Museums and Oral History' issue.

12. *History Workshop*, 1 (1976), 198-9.
13. *History Workshop*, 1 (1976), 1-2.
14. *My Apprenticeship* (London, 1926), 362.
15. *History Workshop*, 1 (1976), 117-20.

Notes to Chapter 7: The Interview

1. For a range of approaches, see Robert Perks and Alistair Thomson (eds.), *The Oral History Reader* (London, 1998), part II, 'Interviewing'; and Robert Weiss, *Learning from Strangers* (New York, 1994).
2. Roy Hay, unpublished paper, 'Use and Abuse of Oral Evidence', p. 15.
3. *Oral History Review*, 4 (1976), 30.
4. *Oral History*, 3/1 (1975), 21; Beatrice Webb, *My Apprenticeship* (London, 1926), 361-3.
5. e.g. Charles Parker, *Oral History*, 1/4 (1973), 53-4. 'Tradition-bearer' is a common term among folklorists; 'narrator' with American programmes. On feminist approaches, Sherna Gluck and Daphne Patai (eds.), *Women's Words: The Feminist Practice of Oral History* (London, 1991), especially Kristina Minister, 'A Feminist Frame for the Oral History Interview', pp. 27-42, Kathleen Borland, '"That's Not What I Said": Interpretative Conflict in Oral Narrative Research', pp. 63-75, Judith Stacey, 'Can there be a Feminist Ethnography?', pp. 111-20, and Daphne Patai, 'US Academics and Third World Women: Is Ethical Research Possible?', pp. 137-53; Catherine Riessman, 'When Gender is Not Enough: Women Interviewing Women', *Gender and Society*, 1/2 (1989), 172-207; Personal Narratives Group, *Interpreting Women's Lives: Feminist Theory and Personal Narratives* (Bloomington, Ind., 1989); Liz Stanley, *The Auto/biographical I* (Manchester, 1992).
6. Hay, 'Use and Abuse', 13-14.
7. Ken Plummer, *Documents of Life* (London, 1983), 103; Pierre Bourdieu (trans. Bridget Fowler), 'Understanding', *Theory, Culture and Society*, 13 (1996), 17-37.
8. Alessandro Portelli, *The Battle of Valle Giulia: Oral History and the*

Art of Dialogue (Madison, Wis., 1997), 11–13, 72–8; George Ewart Evans, 'Approaches to Interviewing', *Oral History*, 1/4 (1973), 62–3.

9. Janet Askham, 'Telling Stories', *Sociological Review*, 30 (1982), 555–73; Eva McMahan and Kim Lacy Rogers, *Interactive Oral History Interviewing* (Hillsdale, NJ, 1994).

10. Willa Baum, *Oral History for the Local Historical Society* (Berkeley, Calif., 1971), 33.

11. Hence Beatrice Webb's view, *My Apprenticeship*, 362; or Thomas Reeve's experience with liberal intellectuals, *Oral History Review* (1976), 33.

12. *Oral History*, 1/4 (1973), 56.

13. Saville, *Oral History*, 1/4 (1973), 56; Edge, *Oral History*, 4/2 (1976), 10; Webb, *My Apprenticeship*, 363.

14. *Tape Recording of Local Dialect*, Standing Conference for Local History, 1971.

15. Webb, *My Apprenticeship*, 362; Bourdieu, 'Understanding', 24.

16. Ann Oakley, 'Interviewing Women: A Contradiction in Terms', in Helen Roberts (ed.), *Doing Feminist Research* (London, 1981), 30–61. For her own earlier study of housework she had used an elaborate formal interview schedule, but investigating the experience of childbirth through repeated interviews and sometimes presence at the birth itself required a more flexible, intimate, and mutual approach.

17. *My Apprenticeship*, 362.

18. Portelli, *Battle of Valle Giulia*, 37.

19. Peter Oliver, 'Oral History: One Historian's View', *Canadian Oral History Association Journal*, 1 (1975–6), 14. On interviewing politicians and other leaders, see also Anthony Seldon and Joanna Pappworth, *By Word of Mouth: Elite Oral History* (London, 1983); and James Wilkie, 'Alternative Views in History: Historical Statistics and Oral History', in Richard E. Greenleaf and Michael C. Meyer (eds.), *Research in Mexican History* (London, 1973), 49–62.

20. *Oral History*, 1/3 (1973), 35–8; Oliver, 'Oral History', 14; Portelli, *Battle of Valle Giulia*, 12

21. Hugo Slim and Paul Thompson, and Jan Walmsley, in Perks and Thomson, *Oral History Reader*, 114–25 and 126–39.

Notes to Chapter 8: Storing and Sifting

1. David Lance, *An Archive Approach to Oral History* (London, 1978), and Frederick J. Stielow, *The Management of Oral History Sound Archives* (New York, 1986); Paul Thompson, 'Sharing and Reshaping Life Stories', in Mary Chamberlain and Paul Thompson (eds.), *Narrative and Genre* (London, 1998), 167–81.
2. Alan Ward, *Copyright, Ethics and Oral History* (Oral History Society; Colchester, 1995); John Neuenschwander, *Oral History and the Law* (Oral History Association; Albuquerque, NM, 1993).
3. Willa Baum, *Oral History for the Local Historical Society* (Berkeley, Calif., 1971), 41–4.
4. Kathleen M. Blee, *Women of the Klan* (Berkeley, Calif., 1991), 6.
5. Michael Frisch, *A Shared Authority: Essays on the Craft and Meaning of Oral and Public History* (Albany, NY, 1990), 'Preparing Interview Transcripts for Documentary Publication: A Line-by-Line Illustration of the Editing Process'; Dennis Tedlock, *The Spoken Word and the Work of Interpretation* (Philadelphia, 1983); Kate Moore, 'Perversion of the Word: The Role of Transcripts in Oral History', and commentary by Michael Frisch, *Words and Silences: Bulletin of the International Oral History Association*, 1/1 (1997), 26–31.
6. Raphael Samuel, 'Perils of Transcript', *Oral History*, 1/2 (1972).
7. Ronald Blythe, *Akenfield* (London, 1969), 32.
8. George Ewart Evans, *Where Beards Wag All* (London, 1970), 212.
9. Currently the most popular are CAQDAS (Computer-Asssisted Qualitative Data Analysis) programmes such as WinMax, Ethnograph, NUD.IST and Atlas\ti. Specialized information on the latest available programmes is offered by the Institute of Social Research, University of Surrey, Guildford, Surrey.

Notes to Chapter 9: Interpretation: the Making of History

1. Dan Sipe, 'The Future of Oral History and Moving Images', in Robert Perks and Alistair Thomson, *The Oral History Reader* (London, 1998), 379–88; Michael Frisch, *A Shared Authority: Essays on the Craft and Meaning of Oral and Public History* (Albany, NY, 1990), 172.
2. Samuel Schrager, in Perks and Thomson, *Oral History Reader*, 285.
3. *Oral History*, 5/1 (1977), 22; Jan Vansina, 'The Power of Systematic Doubt in Historical Enquiry', *History in Africa*, 1 (1974), 109–27.
4. Ronald Grele, 'Listen to their Voices', *Oral History*, 7/1 (1979), 33–42, and *Envelopes of Sound* (Chicago, 1975).

5. Raphael Samuel and Paul Thompson, *The Myths We Live By* (London, 1990); Vieda Skulkans, 'Remembering Latvian Childhood and the Escape from History', *Auto/Biography*, 6 (1998), 5–13.

6. Mary Chamberlain and Paul Thompson (eds.), *Narrative and Genre* (London, 1993), especially introduction, Alessandro Portelli, Chris Mann, T. G. Ashplant, and José Sergio Leite Lopes and Rosilene Alvim; Ruth Finnegan, *Oral Literature in Africa* (Oxford, 1970); Elizabeth Tonkin, *Narrating Our Pasts* (Cambridge, 1992); Alessandro Portelli, *The Battle of Valle Giulia* (Madison, Wis., 1997), 4.

7. Portelli, *Battle of Valle Giulia* (war stories); Ken Plummer, *Telling Sexual Stories: Power, Change and Social Worlds* (London, 1995); Kathryn Montgomery Hunter, *Doctor's Stories: The Narrative Structure of Medical Knowledge* (Princeton, 1991).

8. Philippe Lejeune, *Je est un autre: L'Autobiographie, de la littérature aux médias* (Paris, 1981).

9. Luisa Passerini, *Fascism in Popular Memory: The Cultural Experience of the Turin Working Class* (Cambridge, 1987).

10. Stefan Bohman, 'The People's Story: On the Collection and Analysis of Autobiographical Materials', paper to conference on Working-Class Culture, Nörrköping, Sept. 1986.

11. William Labov, *Language in the Inner City: Studies in the Black English Vernacular, Philadelphia,* 1972 (Oxford, 1977), chs. 5 and 9; Shirley Bryce Heath, *Ways with Words: Language, Life and Work in Communities and Classrooms* (Cambridge, 1983); Isabelle Bertaux-Wiame, 'The Life Story Approach to the Study of Internal Migration: How Women and Men Came to Paris between the Wars', in Paul Thompson (ed.), *Our Common History* (London, 1982), 186–200.

12. Elliot Mishler, *Research Interviewing: Context and Narrative* (Cambridge, Mass., 1986), pp. vii–viii, 18–19, 53 ff.; E. Culpepper Clark, Michael Hyde, and Eva McMahan, 'Communication in the Oral History Interview', *International Journal of Oral History*, I/I (1980), 28–40; Eva McMahan and Kim Lacy Rogers, *Interactive Oral History Interviewing* (Hillsdale, NJ, 1994); Pat Caplan, *African Voices, African Lives: Personal Narratives from a Swahili Village* (London, 1997), 229.

13. Catherine Riessman, *Divorce Talk: Women and Men Make Sense of Personal Relationships* (New Brunswick, NJ, 1990), and *Narrative Analysis* (Newbury Park, Calif., 1993), pp. vi, 50; William Labov,

'Speech Actions and Reactions in Personal Narrative', in Deborah Tannen (ed.), *Analysing Discourse: Text and Talk* (Washington, DC, 1982), 219–47; David E. Michalski, 'The Uses of Oral History in Poetry', paper to Oral History Association annual conference, Buffalo, 17 Oct. 1998.

14. Fritz Schütze, 'Pressure and Guilt: The Experience of a Young German Soldier in World War II and its Biographical Implication', *International Sociology*, 7/2–3 (1992), 187–208 and 347–467; Gabriele Rosenthal, 'The Biographical Meaning of a Historical Event', *International Journal of Oral History*, 10/3 (1989), 183–93, and 'German War Memories: Narrability and the Biographical Functions of Remembering', *Oral History*, 19/2 (1991), 34–41; Reinhard Sieder, 'A Hitler Youth from a Respectable Family: The Narrative Composition and Deconstruction of a Life Story', in Daniel Bertaux and Paul Thompson (eds.), *Between Generations* (Oxford, 1993), 99–120; Roswitha Breckner, 'The Biographical–Interpretive Method: Principles and Procedures', in *SOSTRIS Working Paper* 2 (Centre for Biography in Social Policy, University of East London; London, 1998), 91–104; Michael Rustin, address on 18 Sept. 1998, and 'From Individual Life Stories to Sociological Understanding', *SOSTRIS Working Paper* 3 (1998), 112–27.

15. Daniel Bertaux, *Les Récits de vie: Perspective ethnosociologique* (Paris, 1997).

16. Trevor Lummis, 'Structure and Validity in Oral Evidence', *International Journal of Oral History*, 2/2 (1981), 109–20; *Listening to History* (London, 1987), 94–106; and *Occupation and Society* (Cambridge, 1985).

17. *Canadian Oral History Association Journal*, 1 (1975–6), 28–9.

18. *Adolf Hitler* (New York, 1976), p. xiv.

19. Course D301, radio programme, 'The Small Household'; Richard Jensen, 'Oral History, Quantification and the New Social History', *Oral History Review* (1981).

20. Annabel Faraday and Ken Plummer, 'Doing Life Histories', *Sociological Review*, 27 (1979), 773–98; cf. Ken Plummer, *Documents of Life* (London, 1983), 119ff.

21. *The Poverty of Theory* (London, 1978), 229–42.

22. P. Friedlander, *TheEmergence of a UAW Local* (Pittsburgh, 1975), pp. ix–xxxiii.

23. Tamara Hareven and Randolph Langenbach, *Amoskeag* (New

York, 1978), 381–8, and Tamara Hareven, *Family Time and Industrial Time* (Cambridge, 1982).

24. Joanna Bornat, 'Home and Work: A New Context for Trade Union History', *Oral History*, 5/2 (1977), 101–23.

25. Paul Thompson, 'Women in the Fishing: The Roots of Power between the Sexes', *Comparative Studies in Society and History*, 27 (1985), 3–32; Paul Thompson, 'Life Histories and the Analysis of Social Change', in Daniel Bertaux (ed.), *Biography and Society* (Beverly Hills, Calif., 1981), 289–306.

26. Daniel Bertaux and Paul Thompson, *Pathways to Social Class: A Qualitative Approach to Social Mobility* (Oxford, 1997); Paul Thompson, 'Family Myth, Models and Denials in the Shaping of Individual Life Paths', in Daniel Bertaux and Paul Thompson (eds.), *Between Generations: Family Models, Myths and Memories* (Oxford, 1993: *International Yearbook of Oral History and Life Stories*, 2), 13–38; Gill Gorell Barnes, Paul Thompson, Gwyn Daniel, and Natasha Burchardt, *Growing up in Stepfamilies* (Oxford, 1997).

27. Theodore Rosengarten, *All God's Dangers* (New York, 1974), 453–4.

Index